Education in Rural America

Westview Special Studies in Education

Education in Rural America:
A Reassessment of Conventional Wisdom
edited by Jonathan P. Sher

Indifference has not always characterized American attitudes toward rural children, nor has neglect always been the cornerstone of state and federal policy toward rural education. Indeed, for nearly a century there was an avid and influential—though ultimately ineffective—rural school reform movement in the United States. But in recent years, rural education has become a "skeleton in the closet" of the education profession. More than 14 million children attend rural schools that receive only minuscule amounts of the nation's financial resources and professional attention.

The authors of this book carefully analyze the beliefs, assumptions, policies, and practices that have shaped and continue to shape education in rural America, concluding that conventional wisdom in rural education has proved to be considerably more conventional than wise. They offer pragmatic suggestions for changes in rural schools, in educational policy, and in programs designed for rural communities. As Robert Coles tells us in his Foreword to the book, they "give us clear, strong, uncluttered prose—a good sign that they are able to offer sensible, honest, unpretentious suggestions and useful ideas. They give us. . . . a social history that enables perspective . . . and [they give us] practical, well-argued suggestions for a public policy both humane and capable of realization for our rural areas."

Dr. Sher is education director of the National Rural Center, Washington, D.C., and a consultant on rural education to the National Institute of Education and the National Conference of State Legislators.

Other Titles in This Series

Beyond Surface Curriculum: An Interview Study of Teachers' Understandings, Anne M. Bussis, Edward A. Chittenden, and Marianne Amarel

Education in Rural America

A REASSESSMENT OF CONVENTIONAL WISDOM

edited by Jonathan P. Sher
Foreword by Robert Coles

CONTRIBUTORS

Faith Dunne
Stuart Rosenfeld
Jonathan P. Sher
Rachel Tompkins
Timothy Weaver

Westview Press
Boulder, Colorado

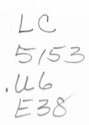
Westview Special Studies in Education

Copyright © 1977 by the Center for Community Change
Published in 1977 in the United States of America by
  Westview Press, Inc.
  1898 Flatiron Court
  Boulder, Colorado 80301
  Frederick A. Praeger, Publisher and Editorial Director

This work was developed under a contract with the U.S. Department of Health, Education, and Welfare, National Institute of Education. However, the opinions and other content do not necessarily reflect the position or policy of the agency, and no official endorsement should be inferred.

Library of Congress Cataloging in Publication Data
Main entry under title:

Education in rural America.
  (Westview special studies in education)
  Bibliography: p.
  1. Education, Rural—United States—Addresses,
  essays, lectures. I. Sher, Jonathan P.
LC5153.U6E38   370.19'346'0973   76-57184
ISBN 0-89158-201-0
ISBN 0-89158-203-7 pbk.

Printed and bound in the United States of America

Contents

Tables

Foreword

This book couldn't come forth at a more appropriate and potentially useful time—just as the nation obtains a new president who is no stranger to rural problems and is committed to furthering the welfare of the poor. Many of our poor are the rural poor—living in the rural South, in Appalachia, in the Rio Grande Valley of Texas, on the reservations of New Mexico and Arizona, or across the Alaskan tundra: black families and white families, Chicanos and Indians and Eskimos. They are tenant farmers or migrant workers or "hollow folks" or so-called "natives" of an Arctic village. They are village people who work small acreage for subsistence or hold one of the few nonagricultural jobs available. They number, still, millions. But their importance is not only numerical. One can say that they are spiritual as well as blood kin of other millions who now live in our cities.

For decades, blacks from Mississippi, Alabama, Georgia, and other southern states, and whites from Kentucky and West Virginia have taken themselves to northern and western cities (and southern ones, too) in search of work, bread, and not least, the promise of a new life—the vote, the dignity of citizenship, release from the fear a sheriff and his deputies, or a lynch mob, constantly have imposed. Yet, once in those vast, impersonal slums or ghettoes those rural people have had occasion, often enough, for second thoughts. If there are jobs, there are also crowded, rat-infested tenements—the cold and alien anonymity of Chicago's South Side, Harlem, industrial Detroit, or Cleveland. And the jobs, those intense magnets of wartime expansionary economies, have all too commonly disappeared, leaving thousands stranded, idle, terribly disappointed, confused, and embittered. The rest is contemporary American social history: crime, violence, drugs, and not least, chronic truancy and other severe educational deficits.

What has all that to do with the educational and social issues taken up in this important book? A good deal. The urban schools are continuing recipients of the children of rural families—rather commonly, still in touch with relatives "back home." Indeed there is a back-and-forth, migratory pattern all over the country: departures for the North, returns to the mountains or the Black Belt. And this is not only the case of migratory farm workers. In the past few years more blacks have left the North for the South than have trekked north from the Delta or the rural counties of states like Alabama and Mississippi. As for Appalachian families, they often don't consider themselves "really" urban residents—they are only in the cities "for a while." The dream is of a happy return to the soil—to a family's roots, traditions, familiar world, to kin and folk ways, and very important, certain cherished values and ideals.

How ironic, then, that in the very bosom of that rural life, those values and ideals are under constant assault—and for no good reason, commonly, other than a mixture of gullibility, faddishness, and social vulnerability. For years I have worked with rural children in the South, Appalachia, the Southwest, and Alaska. I have watched them learning in school, talked with their teachers, tried to gain some sense of how they grow up and come to terms with the world. All too often, these rural children are not so much short-changed by inadequate school facilities, books, and supplies—the physical or technological side of education—as by a more insidious, and arguably, more dangerous assault, described accurately and thoughtfully in the pages that follow. Here is a West Virginia mother doing a bit of describing of her own: "We had a fine little school here. It was small, and the teachers knew how to get on with our kids. We had no trouble sending them off; everyone loved school. Then they 'consolidated.' It was supposed to be the best thing in the world. It was called 'progress.' Well, we were all for that! But what happened? What did we get? We ended up with our kids being lost in that building; and hearing how 'backward' we are here, and how 'forgotten,' and how 'ignorant.' It's no good, when you have your kids coming home and telling you that the teacher is all the time looking down her nose at people like us."

An old, sad story, alas; James Agee describes one version of it in his marvelous chapter "Education" in *Let Us Now Praise Famous Men*. Any number of social observers in recent years—political activists, Vista workers, reformist educators—have more than confirmed the persistence of the problem. A people possessed of its own intelligence and sensibility is given credit for neither, made the subject of all sorts of manipulative schemes, sometimes rather costly, in the name of "modernization" or "progress." In truth, boys and girls all too often learn to think less of themselves, get as lost or dazed or harassed as their older counterparts who walk the streets of cities—also in the name of "progress." Even as rural children who come to the city get overlooked, misinterpreted, and insulted by various "authorities" all too sure of themselves, boys and girls in the rural sections of this country have been outrageously victimized by condescension, aloofness, and yes, the ignorance and callousness of arrogant bureaucracies.

No one is urging that the past be romanticized. The point is not to call for a self-indulgent nostalgia. Many rural communities do indeed have great need of "outside interference"—of sorts: the school lunch program, help with curricula, textbooks, and so on. But those communities also deserve from all of us respect, tact, a willingness to respond to their particular circumstances—and not by any means least, an acknowledgment of how very much they have to offer us, to teach us, even at times to help us out. I think of the Foxfire tradition—so much learned, so much for us to think about. I think of political activists I worked with in the 1960s in Mississippi, or Appalachia. They were college students anxious to help the "culturally deprived," the "culturally disadvantaged," not to mention the terribly segregated or impoverished or both. Yet, over and over again those well-educated youths, now doctors and lawyers and teachers and professors, found themselves, eventually, in awe of the people they were set to help "liberate." No doubt about it, there was every reason for those students to be where they were, to do as they were doing. But they were wise enough, many of them, to see what a number of rural communities *had* as well as lacked. They saw, in fact, what novelists like William Faulkner or Ralph Ellison or N. Scott Momaday have always known various rural people to possess: character, independence, dignity, resourcefulness, a closeness to the land, a certain respect for life's ironies and ambiguities and, inevitably, tragedies.

This book ought to help us as we once again (it is to be hoped) begin to respond to the sometimes severe difficulties that plague many American people, certainly including those who live in our rural areas. The authors give us clear, strong, uncluttered prose—a good sign that they are able to offer sensible, honest, unpretentious suggestions and useful ideas. They give us cause to pause and think; they give us a social history that enables perspective; and they give us practical, well-argued suggestions for a public policy both humane and capable of realization in our rural areas. We are lucky for their efforts—those of us concerned about the subject and ready to buy books and also those millions whose lives, one hopes, will be touched favorably by a considered (and considerate) application of the knowledge that comes across in the pages that follow.

Robert Coles

Editor's Acknowledgments

This book is the product of the efforts, ideas, and commitment of many individuals and institutions. Without their generous support and steadfast faith, it would have been all but impossible to complete this venture.

Credit is due first to the School Finance and Organization Division of the National Institute of Education (particularly Mr. Denis Doyle and Ms. Elissa Feldman) for their sound advice, consistent goodwill, and financial assistance. Appreciation must also be extended to the staff of the Center for Community Change in Washington, D.C., for their wise counsel and institutional support. In addition, I would like to thank the Hazen Foundation (Dr. William Bradley), the Rockefeller Foundation (Dr. Clarence Gray III), the Ford Foundation (Mr. Ralph Bohrson and Mr. Paul Judkins), and the National Rural Center (Mr. Jack Cornman) for their support of various stages of my research and writing for this book. And finally, I would like to thank Dr. Paul Ylvisaker, Mr. Alan Weiss, Dr. A. John Holden, Dr. David Ramage, Dr. Neil Sullivan, and Dr. Emmanuel Lombard for their guidance and encouragement over the years.

It is with special gratitude that I acknowledge all the help given by my wife, Ada, and the patience extended by my children, Matthew and Evelyn. I would also like to applaud both the superb editorial assistance of Mr. Daniel R. Stein and the excellent secretarial assistance of Mrs. Susan Williamson. Dr. Dunne would like to acknowledge the intelligent and indefatigable assistance of Janet Bailey.

Above all, however, I am deeply grateful to my colleagues and collaborators on this book: Dr. Rachel Tompkins, Dr. Stuart Rosenfeld, Dr. Faith Dunne, and Dr. Timothy Weaver. These highly competent and dedicated individuals have sacrificed much of their own time, energy, and resources to produce the work appearing in this volume. Their high professional standards and deep concern for America's rural schools has made working with them a uniquely satisfying and enriching experience.

Jonathan P. Sher

The Authors

FAITH DUNNE, assistant professor of education at Dartmouth College, has been interested in rural education since 1968 when she served as a field consultant and evaluator for the New York/Vermont Cooperative Youth Project. She is now director of both a U.S. Office of Education project on career education for rural high school women and Dartmouth's Rural Internship Program. Dr. Dunne has been a public school teacher and has done research on a longitudinal study of adolescents in Roxbury, Massachusetts. She has master's and doctoral degrees in education from the Harvard Graduate School of Education.

STUART A. ROSENFELD is currently an Educational Policy Fellow with the School Finance and Organization Division of the National Institute of Education. He has served as director of the New School in Plainfield, Vermont, and as a member of the editorial board of the *Harvard Educational Review*. Previously, Dr. Rosenfeld was president of a planning and management information company in Wisconsin. He received his master's degree in education from the University of Wisconsin and his doctorate in administration, planning, and social policy from the Harvard Graduate School of Education.

JONATHAN P. SHER, editor and principal author of *Education in Rural America*, is currently education advisor to the National Rural Center. Work on this volume was completed while Dr. Sher was Education Director at the Center for Community Change. Previously, he has served as a Ford Foundation Leadership Development Fellow in northern New England and as a consultant on rural education to the National Institute of Education and the National Conference of State Legislatures. Dr. Sher received his master's and doctoral degrees in administration, planning, and social policy from the Harvard Graduate School of Education.

RACHEL B. TOMPKINS was born, raised, and educated in rural West Virginia. After completing a master's degree in public administration at Syracuse University, she worked on rural youth and adult education programs through West Virginia University. She has a doctorate in administration, planning, and social policy from the Harvard Graduate School of Education. Dr. Tompkins served as a research analyst in the President's Office of the University of Massachusetts and currently is associate director of the Citizens' Council for Ohio Schools.

W. TIMOTHY WEAVER, associate professor of education at Boston University, combines research interests in forecasting, planning, systems analysis, and school organization. Formerly, Dr. Weaver was a research fellow at the Educational Policy Research Center of Syracuse University, and he has consulted extensively with state departments of education, school systems, hospital associations, and private organizations. He received a master's degree in education from the University of Maryland and a doctorate from Syracuse University.

Education in
Rural America

Pluralism in the Countryside:
A Brief Profile of
Rural America and Its Schools

Jonathan P. Sher

Like the parable of the blind men and the elephant, attempts to describe rural America are confounded by both its nature and its dimensions.

Just as the blind man holding the elephant's trunk thought that the whole animal must be very much like a snake, while the other blind man, feeling its leg, thought elephants closely resembled trees, so too, distorted images of rural America have grown from vivid descriptions of small segments of it. For example, one popular image of rural America is that of an agglomeration of farmers and farm workers. Yet, as of 1975, over 80 percent of America's rural population neither lived nor worked on farms.[1]

The simple fact is that rural people, rural communities, and rural conditions are so diverse that one can find evidence to support nearly any characterization. Someone wishing to describe rural America as a collection of Lilliputs or as bastions of racism, cultural and economic stagnation, reactionary politics, and stifling social environments will not have a difficult time finding rural communities that substantiate this negative analysis. However, another person desirous of portraying rural America as a network of stable, efficient, thriving communities, or as the nation's best example of social egalitarianism, economic independence, cultural continuity, participatory democracy, and institutional accountability will have equal ease in justifying this favorable characterization.

The point is that rural America is far too heterogeneous and complex to be amenable to simplistic definitions or comfortable stereotypes. Remembering that fishing villages in Maine, coal company towns in Appalachia, farm communities in Iowa, Delta counties in Mississippi, recreation communities in Colorado, Indian reservations in South Dakota, small college towns in Minnesota, migrant settlements in Texas, retirement communities in Florida, and Alaskan native villages are all "rural" leaves one feeling less than sanguine about sweeping generalizations.

The traditional heritage of pluralism has had (and will continue to have) three implications of profound importance to the formulation of rural programs and rural policies.

First, rural initiatives must always be based upon the primacy of local circumstance. Policymakers who assume that the success of a particular policy or program in one rural area guarantees its success elsewhere, or who attempt to circumvent local traditions, conditions, and values are destined to eventual failure.

Second, today the term "rural" has little political currency. The great diversity of the rural population has encouraged political organizing in rural areas to emphasize various regional, racial, ethnic, economic, or occupational alliances, while concomitantly inhibiting the creation of a broad-based "rural" constituency. Thus, as a political entity, rural America currently equals far less than the sum of its parts.

Third, definitions of rural America are destined to be both population-based and arbitrary. Although intellectually and emotionally unsatisfying, it is both easier, and more accurate, to define rural America in terms of what it is *not*, rather than what it is. Thus, the Census Bureau carefully defines "urban" and then classifies all that remains as "rural," while statisticians and researchers continue to break out data into two categories: "metropolitan" and "nonmetropolitan." We know in a general way that "rural" implies both small communities and low-population density ratios. But since "rural" is a relative term, all population and density-based definitions are suggestive rather than definitive.

Beyond the problem of distorted popular images, several factors (including geographic isolation, the lack of a unified political identity, and historic migration patterns) have combined to call rural America's very existence into question. All too often, rural America is regarded as an anachronism in our modern cosmopolitan society; a place long gone, though warmly remembered.

Yet, recent statistics yield a substantially different impression. Depending upon the definition used, America's 1970 rural population ranged from 37.5 million to 65.1 million individuals,[2] representing from 18.5 to 32.0 percent of the total United States population in 1970.[3] This is hardly an inconsequential collection of individuals and communities. More important, however, is the fact that since 1970 rural America's population base has experienced a significant resurgence. As one of the nation's leading demographers, Calvin Beale, concluded:

> The vast rural-to-urban migration of people that was the common pattern of U.S. population movement in the decades after World War II has been halted and, on balance, even reversed. During 1970-73, nonmetropolitan areas gained 4.2 percent in population compared to only 2.9 percent for metro areas.[4]

Thus, for the foreseeable future, rural America's existence as both a significant segment of our population and a vital sector of our economy seems assured.

Like rural America as a whole, rural schools and school districts are distinguished by their diversity. Despite increasing standardization, rural schools still tend to reflect the pluralism found among the rural communities they serve.

Rural education encompasses everything from a one-room schoolhouse in an Appalachian hollow to a western school district responsible for education within a several hundred square mile region. It includes both units having lots of students but very little money, and units with lots of money but very few students. The fastest growing school districts in the nation are in rural areas, but so are the ones experiencing the most rapidly declining enrollments. Some rural schools are quite self-sufficient and would be considered excellent by nearly any standard, while others are woefully inadequate and desperately in need of assistance. As a consequence, treating rural schools and school districts as if they were a unified, monolithic entity would be a serious mistake. The "primacy of local circumstance" is as applicable to the formulation of rural educational policy as it is to rural communities in general.

Despite this caveat, it is clear that rural schools have historically shared several common problems. For example, reducing student nonenrollment and absenteeism, recruiting highly competent teachers and administrators, providing special education and other specialized services, securing needed capital and operating funds, and compensating for the inherent isolation and population sparsity of rural areas are all problems that have both persistently plagued rural schools and that remain largely unsolved even today.

Educational attainment has been another major problem within rural schools across the country. Adult attainment statistics reveal the long-term nature of this problem. In 1970, there were 500,000 rural adults who had had no schooling whatsoever.[5] Further, a 1974 Census Bureau survey found that more than 2 million rural adults had had less than five years of school, and thus were considered to be functionally illiterate.[6] As always, these problems were even more pronounced among rural black and hispanic populations. In fact, 24.1 percent of all black adults and 30.7 percent of all hispanic adults in rural areas had dropped out of school by the fifth grade.[7]

Sadly, this trend continues today. A recent research report indicates that at least 5.3 percent of all rural school-aged children are not enrolled in any school.[8] This represents a nonenrollment rate nearly twice that of urban areas.[9]

Even when enrolled and in regular attendance, attainment problems persist. No matter what testing systems or assessment programs are employed, researchers have found that rural schoolchildren consistently rank lower than their metropolitan counterparts.[10] For example, the National Assessment of Educational Progress indicates that rural children score significantly lower than the U.S. average in almost every subject area.[11]

Nevertheless, it is inaccurate to portray rural schools strictly in negative terms. Among the very diverse rural systems are many rural schools that compare favorably in terms of educational quality with their larger and wealthier urban and suburban counterparts. The broad statistics mask these successes and tend to divert researchers away from studying the characteristics of outstanding small schools.

Still, attainment statistics are not particularly helpful in ascertaining the unique qualities of rural education. Since the attainment data for central city schools are similar to that for rural schools, it may only confirm that socioeconomic factors (like parents' income and education) that tend to be markedly lower in both rural communities and central cities are powerful determinants of student achievement everywhere.

Much of what is unique about rural schools and school districts defies quantitative analysis or statistical description. The slower pace and less pressured environment, the spirit of cooperation, the opportunities for leadership development, the less formal interactions among students, staff and parents, and other similar qualities that have long been associated with rural schools are not easily measured by the tools of educational research. This would be of little consequence were it not for the fact that researchers and policymakers have tended to discount that which they cannot measure. Thus, when rural communities opt for these "intangible" qualities (for example, by choosing to keep their community school instead of busing their children to a large consolidated school having a bigger library or more sophisticated equipment), they are labeled as "deficient" rather than merely different.

The fact remains that rural schools are different. And, while the particular manifestations are numerous, these differences tend to spring from two sources: first, the close relationship between rural communities and their schools; and second, the size of rural schools and school districts.

Although professional control of the schools has increased dramatically in recent decades, rural education is still a community enterprise to an extent unknown in most urban school systems.[12] Thus, there is considerable irony in the fact that "citizen participation" and "community control" have come to be seen as urban education issues, for it is in rural America that these forces have been most firmly entrenched and their strengths and weaknesses most readily apparent.

Still, the primary attribute of rural education is its small-scale nature. Even after fifty years of consolidation efforts, rural schools and school districts remain far smaller than their urban and suburban counterparts (see Table 1). For example, nonmetropolitan school districts in Nebraska have an average enrollment that is less than 5 percent of the average enrollment of metropolitan districts in the state (see Table 2).[13]

One more point warrants attention. Occasionally, it is asserted that rural school arguments are just small-school arguments, and that the problems or potentials of rural education have equal applicability in small, community-controlled schools, no matter where they are located. While this statement is not completely false, there are two facts that seriously compromise its validity.

First, rural schools, unlike small schools elsewhere, must contend with unique problems of sparsity and isolation. This implies more

TABLE 1

Size of Public Schools and School Districts in Metropolitan and Non-Metropolitan
Areas of the United States, 1971-72

Area	Total Enrollment (K-12)	Percentage of Total U.S. Enrollment	Number of School Districts	Average School District Enrollment	Number of Schools	Average School Enrollment
All Metropolitan Areas of the U.S.	30,408,000	66%	4,781	6,360	47,849	635
All Non-Metropolitan Areas of the U.S.	15,615,000	34%	11,800	1,323	39,544	395
U.S. Total	46,023,000	--	16,581	2,776	87,393	527

SOURCE: U.S. Bureau of the Census, 1972 Census of Governments: Governmental Organization (Vol. 1) (Washington, D.C.:
U.S. Government Printing Office, July 1973), Table 17; also U.S. Department of Health, Education and Welfare,
Statistics of Local Public School Systems, Pupils, and Staff, Fall 1971, National Center for Educational Statistics
(Washington, D.C.: U.S. Government Printing Office, 1975), Table A.

TABLE 2

Size of Public Schools and School Districts in Selected Areas of Ten States, 1971-72

Area	Total Enrollment (K-12)	Number of School Districts	Average School District Enrollment	Number of Schools	Average School Enrollment
San Francisco	80,796	1	80,796	127	636
California (Metro)	4,536,458	654	6,936	6,110	654
California (Non-Metro)	344,111	411	837	976	352
Denver	94,838	1	94,838	118	803
Colorado (Metro)	402,705	35	11,505	600	671
Colorado (Non-Metro)	163,804	146	1,122	517	317
District of Columbia (All Metropolitan)	140,959	1	140,959	200	705
Hawaii (All Metropolitan)	183,083	1	183,083	211	868
Omaha (Douglas County)	85,112	16	5,320	147	579
Nebraska (Metro)	139,304	45	3,096	262	532
Nebraska (Non-Metro)	192,232	1,329	145	1,592	121
New York City	1,149,068	1	1,149,068	897	1,281
New York (Metro)	2,990,033	439	6,811	3,507	853
New York (Non-Metro)	530,280	341	1,555	940	564
Philadelphia	292,741	1	292,741	275	1,065
Pennsylvania (Metro)	1,828,691	343	5,331	3,103	589
Pennsylvania (Non-Metro)	521,529	176	2,963	1,225	425
Dallas (Dallas County)	299,234	16	18,702	358	836
Texas (Metro)	2,040,497	364	5,606	2,946	693
Texas (Non-Metro)	667,320	772	864	1,973	338
Vermont (All Non-Metro)	103,475	272	380	440	235
Wyoming (All Non-Metro)	85,977	70	1,228	375	229

SOURCE: U.S. Bureau of the Census, 1972 Census of Governments: Governmental Organization (Vol. 1) (Washington, D.C.: U.S. Government Printing Office, July 1973), Tables 17 and 19.

than simply overcoming difficulties caused by geography or distance. It also refers to the fact that rural schools tend to be isolated from the educational, governmental, and economic support systems found in metropolitan areas. It also means that sources of assistance to rural schools (from universities, mental health centers, teacher centers, cultural institutions, and other potential allies) are notably absent in most regions.

Second, small public schools and school districts have become increasingly rare in America's metropolitan centers. Urban schools and districts have always been bigger than rural ones, but this gap is growing even greater as declining enrollments in the cities and suburbs have caused remaining small schools to be shut down. Thus, in the near future, small-school issues (at least in the public domain) will be almost exclusively rural, for that will be the only place in which more than a handful of such schools will continue to exist.

Slowly, over the course of more than a century, a set of assumptions and theories about rural education achieved widespread acceptance throughout America. Today, this body of knowledge and beliefs constitutes the "conventional wisdom" of rural education.

Exploring this conventional wisdom and examining its merits in the light of both accumulated experience and recent research is the express purpose of this volume. Yet, like rural America, this book is perhaps best defined by what it is not.

It is not a blanket condemnation of past policies, programs, and reforms, for such harshness is not warranted by the facts. It is not a report based upon major new data collection efforts, for, while previous research in this field was often incomplete or deficient, there was simply not sufficient time or resources available to conduct extensive primary source research. And, finally, it is not a defense of rural schools as they exist today, for the excellent schools have no need for such a defense and the inferior schools don't deserve it.

At heart, the intent of this volume is to spur policymakers, practitioners, parents, and other interested individuals to rethink rural education's conventional wisdom and to reopen rural educational issues as legitimate topics of discussion and debate. Considerable attention is paid to the potential of small rural community schools, for we are convinced not only that thousands of such institutions will exist well into the future, but also that they can become as excellent, productive, and beneficial as schools anywhere in the nation.

Part One
Panaceas as Policy

1 The Urbanization of Rural Schools, 1840-1970

Stuart A. Rosenfeld and *Jonathan P. Sher*

Introduction

For nearly a century, leading educators and reformers have endeavored to "save" America's rural schools by rearranging or replacing them. Tens of thousands of small rural schools and school districts were either eliminated or required to consolidate during the course of this reform movement.

However, physically eliminating all rural schools and districts was neither possible nor desirable. Therefore, rural school reformers concomitantly adopted a subtler and more pervasive approach. By identifying what became widely known as *The Rural School Problem*, these leaders created a rationale for a widespread "modernization" and "urbanization" of rural schools. At heart, their intent and goal was to reshape rural schools until they became miniature replicas of America's urban (and later, suburban) schools.

This strategy engendered widespread support among state policy-makers, professional administrators, and other progressive forces. By consistently advocating the adoption of urban educational standards, urban innovations, urban architecture, urban textbooks, urban curricula, and urban-trained teachers, these reformers were able to perceive themselves as rescuing rural schools by rejecting their uniquely rural character and heritage.

In a significant number of rural communities at the turn of the century, this trend toward urbanization produced genuine and lasting benefits. Most grossly inadequate and unpleasant schools were shut down; the most rudimentary resources (for example, books and maps) were widely acquired; and teachers endowed with a measure of competence to complement their good intentions were no longer a rarity.

Still, for most rural communities, the urbanization of their schools proved a decidedly mixed blessing. Making rural schools more and more like urban ones often meant that policies and practices developed for city schools were implemented in rural communities far removed from the particular problems, circumstances, and socioeconomic context originally envisioned and addressed. Not surprisingly, this wholesale adoption of urban educational models created long-lasting tensions within rural communities and contributed to a diminished continuity between rural life and rural education.

This chapter will trace the gradual urbanization of rural schools—the events that shaped it and the regional patterns that emerged. Specifically, Chapter 1 will focus on the primary manifestations of urbanization: the consolidation of schools, the centralization of administrative control, the rise of professionalism and specialization among teachers and administrators, and the emphasis on efficiency and business management. Dividing this analysis into five phases, each paralleling a distinctive period in American social history, will make apparent the close relationship between broad national trends and specific rural educational reforms.

1840-1870: The First Stage of Urbanization

Prior to the 1830s, education was primarily the responsibility of the family. Typically, a group of neighboring families who were socially and economically homogeneous would bond together and sponsor such schools and educational activities as they collectively deemed proper. This method of operation was sanctioned in most eastern states by laws such as the District School Law of 1789 in Massachusetts, which allowed each town to divide into many separate and independent school districts.

However, by the mid-1800s, when eastern cities and towns were forced to confront the new political, social, and economic forces unleashed by rapid industrialization and heavy immigration, the traditional methods of school organization came under attack as haphazard, inefficient, and inappropriate. The state, social reformers now contended, must control education.

The leading spokesman for centralization and state control was Horace Mann, then secretary of the Massachusetts Board of Education. Mann, who blamed the highly decentralized district system for most educational deficiencies, including inadequate school support and incompetent teachers, had a talent for making his theories appear not just right, but righteous as well. For example, in proposing his idea of centralized town schools, Mann contended:

> It is an undeniable fact that the schools are best conducted when they are managed by the town and not the district. Under the town system, all the interested as well as all the benevolent tendencies favor improvement.[1]

Understandably, Mann received few accolades for his firm centralist stance from local parents and community leaders. However, among educators and other progressives of the era, Mann and his ideas were warmly embraced.

One of Mann's staunchest supporters was Connecticut's State Superintendent of Schools Henry Barnard. Given the circumstantial similarities between Massachusetts and Connecticut at that time (both were experiencing a significant influx of industry and immigrants), Barnard's support, as well as his own centralist tendencies, made sense. Yet, Mann's other great supporter, surprisingly, was Vermont's State Superintendent Horace Eaton. Eaton was also an avid centralist but, in Vermont, no social or economic realities validated his position. Vermont lacked any urban/industrial centers and thus was far more rural and culturally homogeneous than either Mann's or Barnard's state. Still, Eaton espoused the same arguments, developed the same rationales, and advocated the same solutions originally put forward by his urban counterparts.

Despite the assistance of his colleagues, Mann's centralist positions placed him in political jeopardy at home. Jacksonian Democrats controlled Massachusetts, and one of their leaders, Orestes Brownson (editor of the *Boston Quarterly Review*), spearheaded the fight against the consolidation efforts of Mann, a Whig. While Mann argued that the control of schools had to be transferred to the state's most intelligent and enlightened leaders, the Democrats counterargued for the maintenance of broad-based local control. As one historian noted:

[The Democrats] asserted the authority of the people in place of the authority of the few, not only in government but also in education itself. The district school and the local school committees were intended to maintain popular authority in the one area of community life that was important to every Democrat.[2]

Soon, the Democrats attempted to directly dissipate Mann's influence by trying to legislatively dismantle his power base, the Massachusetts Board of Education. They complained:

The establishment of the Board of Education seems to be the commencement of a system of centralization and of monopoly of power in a few hands, contrary in every respect to the true spirit of our democratic institutions. . . . The right to mould the political, moral, and religious opinions of his children, is a right exclusively and jealously reserved by our laws to every parent.[3]

Although Mann and the Massachusetts Board successfully weathered this attack, the movement toward centralization and standardization was perceptibly slowed in Massachusetts.

Still, Mann's influence persisted. For example, in 1845, Mann and his supporters persuaded Vermont to enact a law designed to break down local autonomy by creating a system of state-controlled supervision.[4] When Vermont succeeded in passing this law, a jubilant Mann exclaimed:

We rejoice with unspeakable joy at the accession of Vermont to the Party of Progress. Rhode Island has already joined it. When will New Hampshire and Maine wheel into the ranks?[5]

The reforms urged by Mann and Barnard were designed to meet the emerging problems besetting city schools—from training productive industrial workers to "Americanizing" recent immigrants. The conditions spawning such policies were less pervasive in rural areas; yet rural schools were continually made the object of these urban-oriented reforms.

The village dweller and the farmer understood the importance of education, but in a much less institutionalized way. Rural New England, where the resistance to centralization was greatest, took pride in its strong tradition of local self-government. Rural New Englanders had already created an extensive system of schools without state assistance or interference. Although these schools did not resemble urban ones, they were generally regarded by local citizens as being satisfactory.

The nation's westward expansion during this era presented still another set of circumstances with which schools and school reformers had to contend. The newly settled areas of the West did not have the same strong traditions and community stability found in New England. Consequently, western school systems tended to organize along county lines. The same pattern of organization was prevalent in the southern states, where all governmental services were delivered on a countywide basis. Thus, it seems clear that the general political organization of a given rural area was one key determinant of how schools were organized, administered, and controlled.

The theories and reforms advanced by Mann and Barnard were quoted widely in state policy and planning documents throughout the nation, without regard to the similarities of the other states to Massachusetts or Connecticut. It made little difference whether they were industrialized or agricultural, urban or rural. These educational statesmen were the salesmen for centralization and bureaucracy, and their efforts set the stage for the creation of a common, standardized system of schools. Most important, they established the notion that the state was responsible for the education of the child, and that the teacher operated *in loco parentis*. This concept, which differed from the colonial notion of schools as an extension of families, was a critical precondition for the evolving state and professional control of schools.

1870-1895: Spreading the Gospel of Urbanization

While the country was being psychologically conditioned to accept a centralized and uniform system of schools, little consolidation actually was taking place. It was still largely professional rhetoric, pursued from the top down, by "segments of the elite classes, for both humanitarian and crassly paternalistic reasons."[6] As with most reforms of the period, it was *not* initiated by the intended beneficiaries. Reforms were difficult to implement for any purpose. The country was not yet effectively organized nationally, and there were no established centers of authority and communication through which to mandate change. America of this period was described as "a society of island communities" with "the heart of American democracy being local autonomy."[7]

Still, the primary goal of educators was to advance the concept of education as a legitimate state function and to make the state's role so authoritative that it could be questioned only in degree, not in substance. Professionalization, specialization, and standardization were the mechanisms by which schools were to be controlled. The organization of the schools began to reflect the new social relationships of industry.[8] However, that model was essentially urban, and it can be argued that the suggested reforms were not consistent with rural living. There were, in fact, significant rural-urban differences that were purposely ignored by the centralization movement, because the reformers considered urbanization to be both a desirable and an irreversible trend.

These differences between urban and rural life went beyond simple variations in scale. The factory system and immigration quickly altered city life, and new values reflecting the task-oriented, time-oriented, hierarchical, authoritarian factory system influenced school reform. Each educational reform mirrored a change perceived in American society. Specialization reproduced the change in economic patterns from integrated family industries to task-oriented, production processes. Standardization reflected the need to assimilate the new immigrants into the then predominant Anglo-Saxon value system. Professionalism reflected the growing complexities of the hierarchical structure of the industrial system.

Rural life was also changing. The farmer was no longer just the self-sufficient yeoman trading the fruits of his labor, but was also a capitalistic land speculator trying to increase his personal profits through mechanization and specialization. As Hofstadter noted, "The characteristic product of American rural society was not a yeoman or villager, but a harassed little country businessman who worked very hard, moved all too often, gambled with his land, and made his way alone."⁹

Yet, certain traits continued to be characteristically rural. The family was still the primary unit of production, schedules were guided more by natural conditions than by time clocks, responsibilities were more dispersed, and the farmer was expected to be a jack-of-all-trades. Technology and capitalism had reached even the remote rural areas, but social relations in remote villages managed to maintain a distinctly rural flavor.

The first school consolidation laws enacted during this period were permissive. Educators hoped that rural communities would accept the wisdom of centralization and voluntarily relinquish control of the schools. In fact, however, rural citizens rarely capitulated to this "soft-sell" approach and, if anything, local resistance to consolidation solidified.

The reasons for such a strong desire to retain local control of schools are difficult to extract from the historical evidence. Most of the available documents were written by educators or politicians having vested interests in further consolidation. Town histories and local reports normally recorded only votes and financial conditions, not the internal community tensions and debates surrounding consolidation. Much of the resistance was due to fear of higher school costs, depreciating land values, and squabbles over school location. There is also evidence, however, that school organization was important because it imparted to rural citizens a sense of power and control over their lives and the lives of their children.

Once again, Massachusetts led the crusade to centralize school authority and control. It was in Massachusetts that the consolidation of schools into town systems was first proposed. In 1852, Sears, Mann's successor as secretary of the Massachusetts Board of Education, polled the towns in an effort to amass data supporting town school systems. However, much to Sears' chagrin, local people still overwhelmingly desired retention of their existing small schools. Sears attributed this outcome to political ignorance:

> The only argument of seeming importance that has been urged in favor of perpetuating the school districts is that they are essential to the highest degree of popular lib-

erty. . . . it is in the present instance misapplied, for, as the American system of free government knows of no political organization above the union of the States, so it knows none below the towns.[10]

In 1860, the new secretary, Boutwell, again polled Massachusetts towns and now suggested that:

as the result of extensive correspondence and interchange of sentiment with the people of the State, their attachment to the district system is not as strong as I formerly supposed.[11]

Yet, Boutwell was not confident enough to push for legal adoption of the town system. He argued:

It may not, however, be wise to legislate upon the subject immediately; but I deem this fit occasion to invite the inhabitants of the towns . . . to take matters into their own hands and reconstruct their school system upon a basis which will admit of economy, efficiency, and progress.[12]

Boutwell's urgings aside, it was not until 1882 that support for the town system in Massachusetts was substantial enough to allow the passage of a legislative act requiring schools to organize along town lines.

Even during this formative stage, the battle lines on school consolidation and administrative centralization were well defined. Professional educators and their progressive allies supported these reforms, while local community leaders, parents, and their conservative allies became the loyal opposition. With minor variations, these dominant issues and adversaries remained the same for the next century.

Neither party in this continuing debate could honestly lay claim to having only the best interests of rural children at heart. Educators were just beginning to assert their professionalism and felt few qualms about advocating any "reform" which resulted in an expansion of their own power, authority, and control. Self-interest often took precedence over more altruistic motives in determining the causes educators chose to champion. A marked paternalism was also common among educators of this era who felt it their moral duty and political right to transfer control of the schools from "unenlightened, backward" parents to "more intelligent and responsible" people such as themselves.

Similarly, nineteenth century rural residents often based their opposition to structural reform on self-interest rather than on educational merit. They worried about depreciating land values, local jealousies, border disputes, the availability of their children for chores, and the added costs of consolidation. Major property owners and their allies usually controlled the rural schools, and thus were the ones most directly affected by any loss of local autonomy. Still, these local leaders were far closer and more responsive to the concerns of rural parents than either the policymakers at the state capitol or the business-oriented urban administrators could ever be.

Despite this closeness, the wishes and the arguments of local rural leaders were largely ignored by state legislatures during the 1880s and 1890s. The increasing pressures of industrialism and immigration, coupled with the eloquent advocacy of reform by state-level progressives, finally convinced legislators to *mandate* educational change.

Massachusetts abolished the district system in 1882; New Hampshire established a town system in 1885 and mandated it in 1892; Vermont did the same in 1892; and Maine followed suit in 1893. Rhode Island and Connecticut continued to have a permissive district system existing side-by-side with the town system because these states were urban enough to enact school consolidation without administrative reorganization. Other eastern and midwestern states followed reorganization patterns similar to the New England states. By the end of the century, New Jersey, Pennsylvania, Ohio, and Indiana had mandated a township system, while Michigan, Wisconsin, and Minnesota passed legislation urging its adoption.

In the West, issues of school reorganization were not yet of major importance. This is attributable, at least in part, to the distinctive socioeconomic patterns in the western states. The community-based, independent, precapitalist farmer was, for the most part, a myth in the newly settled territories.

A competitive, capitalistic spirit encouraged by the railroads, land companies, and skyrocketing land values altered the traditional rural stability represented by the New England farmer. The schools, while important, were not centers of either controversy or community life. It was possible, therefore, for Utah to achieve consolidation without public approval via the decision of county commissioners. Even where dissent did occur, parental objections to centralization in the West were more closely related to issues of cost and distance than issues of governance and control.

By the 1880s, consolidation and centralization were promoted by educators nationwide, without regard or reference to local conditions and concerns. The benefits were accepted a priori, because they reflected the educational preferences and theories of America's most influential urban leaders.

Rural schools generally needed to be improved. The one-room schoolhouses of this era, with only six or eight students, untrained teachers, and atrociously inadequate facilities, were particularly in need of assistance. However, the inordinate emphasis on organizational issues and the growing conflicts over control of the schools tended to preclude critical substantive improvements. Structural reforms during this period tended to further politicize education in rural communities. This primarily served to divide residents into opposing factions rather than uniting them to strive for educational improvements.

By the 1890s, the ethic equating quantity and growth with progress had become deeply imbedded in the American consciousness. Small rural schools were now, by definition, vulnerable to assault on the grounds of economy and efficiency, and reformers lost no time in adding these arguments to their repertoire of complaints. National events, such as the economic depression of 1893, exacerbated the financial difficulties many rural communities had in supporting their schools. In turn, this lent considerable credence to the consolidators' contentions.

State legislators reacted quickly. As noted earlier, Maine, New Hampshire, and Vermont all mandated town systems during the 1890s. During the same decade, Ohio authorized the first union high schools (1892); New York passed legislation enabling the creation of "joint contract" districts (1896); Connecticut passed its first statewide school transportation laws; and California legislated union high school districts (1891).

Although rural life styles continued to be cherished, the values and standards of urban life became dominant throughout America. City schools were the accepted model of educational excellence and, rather than attempting to revise the model to ensure its consistency with rural life, reformers sought to change rural schools so that they would become consistent with the urban model. As one historian noted:

country schools suffered from an unanticipated handicap, for urban standards were used to judge rural educational progress.[13]

In 1895, the National Education Association established the Committee of Twelve on Rural Schools. In its final report, the committee urgently pressed for administrative consolidation, and attributed any opposition to the "power of conservative habit," a "fondness for office-holding," and a "misconception and ignorance of the merits" of consolidation.[14] The report, written by a select group of educational leaders, was widely distributed among educators and politicians across the nation. This report, as much as any other, helped establish the foundation for our present system of schools: centralized, standardized, and professionally administered.

1896-1920: Urbanization Comes of Age

The close of the nineteenth century marked a turning point in educational policy and educational reform. Ideologically, if not in practice, the struggle for control of the schools was over. Education—now compulsory in most states—was accepted as a legitimate state function. Of course, local communities still operated schools, but basic issues of policy were increasingly being resolved at the state level.

Buoyed by these emerging trends, the new generation of educational leaders—men like Ellwood Cubberley, Harold Foght, George Betts, and Leonard Ayers—stepped up their attacks on *The Rural School Problem*. These leaders wanted country schools to embody the kinds of progress and development evidenced in America's cities.

According to the head of the National School of Social Research, the cities were where "practically all the noteworthy developments in government, in sanitation, in association, in recreation, in business, and in education have taken place."[15] Two distinguished education professors of this period, Julius Boraas and George Selke, claimed that "the farmer had become as cosmopolitan as the urbanite" and, as a consequence, rural communities needed "to make the schools more efficient now, to build up their effectiveness until it approximates that of the urban schools."[16] Cubberley argued that the industrial revolution had "changed the entire nature of rural life" and that consolidation and centralization were necessary to ensure that rural schoolchildren could keep pace with their urban counterparts.[17] All of these educational reformers deemed urban education superior, urban children more advantaged, and urban models appropriate for rural implementation. As noted historian David Tyack observed about these leaders:

> With certain modifications dictated by rural conditions, they wished to create in the countryside the one best system that had been slowly developing in the cities.[18]

Unlike Mann, Barnard, and other educational statesmen of the mid-1800s, this new corps of leaders was comprised primarily of pragmatic schoolmen and administrators. Mann and his contemporaries were fundamentally politicians and social philosophers who embraced education late in their careers as a means of forwarding the social and moral priorities they advocated. However, Cubberley and other leaders of the early twentieth century were professionals, immersed in educational affairs throughout their careers and deeply concerned about the inner workings of schools and the intricacies of school management.

Raymond Callahan, in a remarkable book entitled *Education and the Cult of Efficiency*, described the new self-image characteristic of this era's leading educators:

> After 1900, especially after 1910, [educational administrators] tended to identify themselves with the successful business executive. That this business orientation was a prerequisite for success and tenure on the job was clear, and the schoolmen knew it. As early as 1900, for example, the president of the National Education Association prophesied that "the real educational leaders of the age whose influence will be permanent are those who have the business capacity to appreciate and comprehend the business problems which are always a part of the educational problem."[19]

Callahan goes on to document in great detail:

> The material achievements of industrial capitalism in the
> late nineteenth century were responsible for two develop-
> ments which were to have a great effect on American
> society and education after 1900. One of these was the rise
> of business and industry to a position of prestige and
> influence, and America's subsequent saturation with
> business-industrial values and practices. The other was the
> reform movement identified historically with Theodore
> Roosevelt and spearheaded by the muckraking journalists.
> These two developments, and the vulnerability of the
> school administrator, contributed to the conditions in
> American society which explain the tremendous impact of
> Frederick Taylor and his system of "scientific manage-
> ment," and the continuing influence of the business-
> industrial ideology upon American society and education
> after 1911.[20]

Needless to say, the two key developments Callahan identifies
were wholly the products of an urban context. The "industrial
capitalism" becoming dominant in America's cities gained few
footholds in the countryside. And the "muckraking journalists,"
particularly those concerned with education, confined their activities
almost entirely to the urban scene.

Nevertheless, although rural life was far removed from the
conditions and pressures spawning these developments, their influence on rural communities and rural schools was pervasive. Educational leaders of this era continued to urge rural schools to adopt
reforms and programs designed to solve urban-based problems.

Once again, these policymakers turned to the consolidation of
schools and the centralization of administration as their primary
vehicles for reform. Although not a new strategy, these reforms were
now endowed with a new rationale: the quest for economy, efficiency, and sound business management in the schools. The consolidation
movement, stalled because of citizen opposition in recent years,
began to snowball again.

Evidence of this renewed professional enthusiasm for urban-
oriented reforms abounds. President Roosevelt's Commission on

Country Life made rural school consolidation an integral part of its reform agenda. Vermont's superintendent of schools asserted:

> The maintenance of the small school is not in accordance with business principles, the returns are meager in comparison with the time and money invested.[21]

The 1901 Report of the State Superintendent in Wisconsin stated:

> This is an age of consolidation, in business, in industry, and, let us believe, in education. Says Supt. Stryker of Kansas: "Combination and concentration are the order of the day. This concentration, this combination, this division of labor, this increased skill of each laborer, this increase in the product, this crowding out of the smaller by the larger, must continue until it becomes universal in every department of human activity. The rural school will be no exception. It is only a question of time, and a question of how to accomplish the change with the least friction."[22]

State educators in Arkansas lamented that:

> The great economic principle of division of labor, which has multiplied a hundred fold the production capacity of manufacturing industries, finds no application in the rural school district.[23]

And, finally, another state report of this period concluded with characteristic certainty:

> Consolidation is inevitable. The intelligence of the times advocates it and rural conditions demand it. . . . Consolidation is a natural sequence to the evolution of the modern industrial system.[24]

Professional reformers rarely had much tolerance for community opposition to their plans, and their attitudes became increasingly acrimonious during the first years of the twentieth century. For example, a 1904 Bulletin of the University of Texas typified the feelings of many educational reformers:

as might be expected, human ignorance and human selfishness always led people to oppose the consolidation of schools when first proposed. To those local tyrants who are determined to run things their own way, or to those who think that their friend or kinsman must be furnished a little school to teach regardless of the welfare of the children or of the community, nothing can be said.[25]

Beyond the desire to bring rural schools into line with business-industrial values, consolidation advocates advanced a series of additional rationales. They argued that consolidation would result in better supervision, age-graded schools, specialized teachers, broader curricula, increased professionalism, and expanded resources. All of these reforms had already been enacted in urban schools. Reformers simply assumed that they were all appropriate for implementation in rural schools, and that consolidation was the only method by which these benefits could be secured.

The final argument for consolidation and centralization was that it was necessary to keep control of the schools out of the hands of recent immigrants. It was a clever rationale, for, by this time, immigrants were being widely blamed for the growing decay of America's cities. Determined to prevent any "undesirable influence" exerted by immigrants residing in rural areas, this argument gained popular support. Ellwood Cubberley's description of the "immigrant problem" was representative:

As foreign farm tenantry is introduced, the effect on local self-government becomes even more marked. . . . In marked contrast with the farmer he displaces—strong, opinionated, virile, deeply conscious of his personal worth, and deeply interested in political affairs—the newcomer is too often docile, subservient, and without decided opinions on any question. If the new tenant is of south European stock, he is almost devoid of the Anglo-Saxon conceptions of the importance of local self-government, and he is naturally but little interested in our forms of government or our political life. . . . Jose Cardoza, Francesco Bertolini and Petar Petrovich are elected as school directors; Nels Peterson as township clerk; and Alexis Lodowsky as township trustee. The process is of course educative to

these newcomers, though a little hard on local government.[26]

Earlier, in Vermont, Superintendent Stone warned that without
centralization, the diffusion of old New England stock would lead the
administration of schools to "fall into incapable and indifferent hands
and, as an inevitable result, our schools become correspondingly
inefficient."[27] Other leaders of this period also blamed the lack of
educational leadership on the influx of immigrants from the poorer
and less educated classes of southern and eastern Europe.[28]

However, the immigrant issue lacked much factual merit in rural
America. Not only did it embrace the most reprehensible kind of
ethnic prejudice, but it also greatly exaggerated the true extent of
"foreign" migration to rural communities. During the decades in
question, the vast majority of immigrants lived and worked in
America's cities. The trickle of immigrants settling in the countryside represented a statistically insignificant population. In short, the
prediction of hordes of ignorant immigrants descending upon America's rural communities and taking over the schools never came to
pass.

Though unsupported by existing demographic data, the immigrant
argument was an absolutely ingenious political strategy. Rural
residents have always had very mixed, almost contradictory, feelings
about urban life. Now, for the first time, educational reformers had
devised a strategy that could take full advantage of this attrac-
tion/repulsion. For, when consolidation and centralization could not
be successfully promoted as manifestations of urban progress, they
were advocated as a means of preserving rural control. Still, whether
consolidation was adopted out of hope or out of fear, the net effect
was the same: the locus of power over rural schools was transferred
from community leaders to administrators, and from amateurs to
professionals.

Implementing Centralization

As with many of the reform movements of the early twentieth
century, actual accomplishments failed to match the expectations of
the advocates. The educational documents of the period would lead
one to believe that a nationwide consolidation movement was under
way, and schools and districts were rapidly consolidating and

centralizing. But, in fact, by 1920 there were still more than 195,000 rural one-room schools in the country and only 10,000 consolidated rural schools (many of which were only two-room schools). Even in Massachusetts, with consolidation laws in effect for almost half a century, the ratio in 1920 was 801 one-room schools to 333 consolidated schools. Thus, it is clear that consolidation remained more policy than practice up to this point.

To remedy this situation, professional educators and their allies turned, once again, to the legislative process for assistance. A variety of laws encouraging consolidation were passed throughout the nation during this period, but the two key legislative thrusts involved transportation and state aid. Because consolidation of schools meant longer distances for rural children to travel, the state took on the added responsibility of getting the child to and from school each day. The success of consolidation was contingent upon a safe and dependable system of transportation. Massachusetts passed a transportation law as early as 1869. By 1894, all of the New England states and Florida had transportation laws. Every other state in the country passed some form of transportation law between 1894 and 1919. Horse-drawn wagons, barges, sleighs, steam engines, and early motor vehicles were all employed to get students to their central schools.

In many early state policy statements, transportation and consolidation were viewed as separate and distinct issues. However, in neighborhood schools, little formal transportation was required. Most children were able to walk to school. Transportation became an essential element in creating more distant, centralized schools. These laws extended the authority and responsibility the state had over the child by regulating the means and the conditions of his or her travel to and from school.

Despite the benefits of public transportation (such as increased attendance), many parents still objected to the travel involved. They feared for their child's safety, now in the hands of a hired driver; they feared immoral activities and influences while en route; and, they resented keeping the children away from home longer, thus preventing children from carrying out chores. Most of the fears proved unfounded. Public transportation systems, for example, were relatively safe. The lost time, however, was real. Even though most states placed one-hour limits on travel, the total travel time was often far greater.

Transportation was not the only objective barrier to widespread consolidation. One of the most basic impediments to rural school reform was rural poverty. New consolidated schools were expensive; yet, even during good times, rural incomes were markedly lower than the national average. Limited rural educational resources were often caused by a lack of revenue rather than any indifference to schooling.

Therefore, to stimulate educational change, state aid was introduced or (if already in existence) increased. The use of state aid as an incentive for centralization began in the early nineteenth century when Horace Mann required that districts in Massachusetts comply with state requirements to qualify for state funds. As the amount of state aid was increased, the "strings" attached were also increased. Much of the rural school consolidation between 1910 and 1925 was both prompted by and linked with a series of financial incentives.

Oklahoma, Alabama, North Carolina, Wisconsin, and Tennessee offered state aid for school buildings to encourage consolidation and the establishment of schools having distinct grade levels. The Rural School Act in Alabama was amended in 1917 to favor large buildings and grounds. The Oklahoma legislature of 1911 paid one-half the cost of buildings for union, graded, or consolidated schools. In 1913, Wisconsin also passed a building aid law that offered a progressively higher rate of financial assistance to larger, graded schools.

Iowa, Nebraska, South Dakota, West Virginia, Delaware, Tennessee, and Texas are examples of states offering direct assistance to consolidated schools. In 1913, the Iowa General Assembly voted aid to all schools of two rooms or more. As a result, 226 new consolidations took place in Iowa by 1917. In Nebraska, a consolidated school law in 1915 provided state aid in relation to school size and curricular diversity.

Still, despite similar legislative efforts, consolidation proceeded somewhat differently in each geographic region.

The southern states had traditionally extended authority over school affairs to county administrators. Most of the southern states gave county boards the power to divide the county into as many school districts as they deemed advisable (for example, such laws were passed in Florida, 1889; in South Carolina, 1896; in Louisiana, 1902; in Maryland, 1904; in Kentucky, 1908; in Alabama, 1910; and in Georgia, 1911).

Louisiana's experience with consolidation was typical of the region at this time. In Louisiana, the parish (that is, county) school boards

> in general, may do anything they deem needful for the successful conduct of the schools, and legally they were free from either prohibition or direction in the matter of consolidated schools.[29]

Louisiana had its first school consolidation in 1902. Interestingly, the first consolidation was instigated by a natural act rather than educational rhetoric or legislative mandate. A cyclone destroyed a one-room school. Rather than rebuild it, the Lafayette district transported the children by wagon to a nearby school. The idea caught on, and eventually Lafayette Parish (one of the state's most densely populated areas) consolidated all of its schools. The concept of central schools continued to spread in Louisiana, but not with the zeal of Lafayette Parish.[30] In 1912, there were 210 consolidated country schools in Louisiana, but there were also still almost 1,500 one-teacher schools.

In the western states, the consolidation movement focused on the centralization of administration rather than the immediate merger of existing schools. Educators urged the adoption of county school boards and county school systems, not unlike those already found throughout the South.

In Utah, for example, the notion of creating county school systems was first proposed in 1888. Initially, it was opposed by rural leaders fearing that it would give too much control to the county school board. By 1905, this attitude had mellowed and county school systems were made operational by state legislators. Still, the idea's popular appeal remained suspect. As historian Edward Bateman conceded:

> It is probable that leaders in education, government and business were in general in favor of consolidation, but that the proposition to consolidate the schools would probably have been defeated in a popular vote.[31]

It was not until 1915 that the Utah legislature was able to muster the votes needed to pass a mandatory county unit law.

Another western state, New Mexico, established county boards of education in 1917, following a statewide Rural School Survey that pointed out what was referred to as the "deplorable condition of some of the rural school districts."[32] The new boards had four appointed members and one elected member who was also the county superintendent. New Mexico's boards had extensive powers, including the right to consolidate schools, choose school sites, purchase equipment, approve teachers, and apportion funds.

As in Louisiana, the most rapid consolidation occurred in the most densely populated areas such as Bernalillo County. Fifteen consolidated elementary schools and a central high school were erected in Bernalillo County between 1912 and 1918, which were reported to have a "remarkable influence in the improvement of rural life and educational conditions in the county."[33] As a result, the U.S. Bureau of Education reported, "a large number of people of a very desirable class have been attracted to the county and are buying land and building fine homes."[34]

Consolidation in the Midwest occurred more slowly and sporadically. Some states, such as Indiana and Ohio, established policies of consolidation early and achieved some successful implementation. Other states, such as Minnesota and Kansas, established centralist policies but effected little actual consolidation of schools because they could not persuade communities to give up their district schools voluntarily. Wisconsin, however, resisted consolidation even as policy and instead chose to retain the district system.

In Indiana, early state support of school transportation (1889) coupled with the persuasive powers of the state superintendent led to relatively rapid consolidation.[35] Between 1906 and 1920, the number of consolidated schools in the state grew from 361 to 1,040. Not surprisingly, from 1902 to 1920, the number of children transported to school increased from 2,599 to 62,490, while transportation costs grew from less than $100,000 to almost $2,000,000.

A 1923 evaluation of consolidation in Randolph County, Indiana (where 137 schools had been consolidated into 24), was extremely favorable.[36] This report, prepared by the U.S. Bureau of Education, indicated that children went to school more regularly and for a longer time; high school enrollment was rising; and the schools themselves were better equipped and more pleasant. Also highlighted as "conclusive evidence" of the effectiveness of consolidation was the fact that teams from consolidated schools had recently won the district basketball tournament, the baseball championship, and the track championship. Standardized test results were not yet influencing policy as they do today, so basketball scores and trophies had to represent the quantitative benefits of larger units.

Other, less favorable, facts, though downplayed in the report, were also evident. Costs had risen sharply and the number of school-age youths in the county had dropped by 16 percent, indicating that predicted school economies were not achieved and that the consolidation of schools had not stemmed migration to the urban areas.

In contrast to Indiana's steady centralization, Iowa had a history of advances and reversals. Iowa attempted to organize schools at the township level as early as 1858 and managed to reduce the number of school districts from 3,500 to 900. But in 1872, public opposition forced the legislature to permit townships to subdivide again and, by 1889, there were more than 9,000 districts in the state. Little progress was made toward consolidation until 1906 when legislation urging consolidation passed. This legislation provided a framework for centralization, but few districts took advantage of it and only eighteen consolidated districts were formed over the next seven years. In 1913, substantial state aid for consolidation was added as an incentive, and by 1920 there were 430 consolidated districts formed. Then, despite the publicized success of the consolidations that occurred, and the continued campaigning on its behalf, the movement stopped almost entirely.

In the northeast section of the nation, the county was of little importance in educational policy. The town was the primary political unit and therefore was the more acceptable educational unit. Formation of centralized administrative units, high schools, professional supervision, and reorganization of state departments absorbed the energy of educational reformers. Northern New England was considered too sparsely populated and geographically segmented for drastic consolidation. The fact that the schools in the more urbanized, southern part were already consolidating and growing significantly satisfied educators that their policy was successful.

Throughout most of New England, centralization was effected through the creation of supervisory unions from combinations of towns for administrative purposes and to provide professional leadership. Because each town still maintained its own local school directors with policy responsibility, the supervisory union was quite different from the county unit. The county board had more power and autonomy than the supervisory union and was usually larger. In 1919, the average New England union involved 62 square miles and 18 school buildings, while the average county unit covered 1,672 square miles and was responsible for 84 school buildings.[37]

The supervisory union was made optional in New Hampshire in 1897 and in Vermont in 1906. As incentives in both instances, the state offered to reimburse about one-half of the superintendent's salary. In 1907, twenty unions were formed in Vermont, mostly in the more densely populated areas. The supervisory union and union superintendent became mandatory in Vermont in 1915, following the Carnegie Commission survey of Vermont's educational system. Administrative centralization did not induce the expected school consolidation. In rural areas, the schools were still primarily one-teacher. In 1919, Vermont had only 40 consolidated rural schools and more than 1,200 one-room schools.

The state of New York, which developed neither the town system of New England nor the county system of the South and the West, created a larger, intermediate supervisory unit under the Rural School Supervision Act of 1910. It was similar to New England's union of towns, but the towns themselves were not educational entities in New York.

By the end of World War I, centralization was well established among leading administrators and reformers nationwide as the "proper" policy direction, but among voters and many rural educators at the local level there remained considerable doubt.[38] New York State had been trying for forty years to pass a township system bill. Finally, in 1917, the legislature succeeded in making the township an educational entity, but "a tremendous wave of opposition arose, and, as the months passed, increased until it became the greatest shower of protest ever made against a law enacted by the legislature."[39] Still, the legislature did not back down. However, to avoid further confrontations, state level educators in New York and elsewhere solicited research and evaluation studies that would provide a more convincing basis for future centralist educational policies.

One of the means used to provide this research was the comprehensive study of educational conditions. Beginning with the Carnegie Commission investigation of Vermont in 1914, twenty-one states requested full-scale, statewide surveys (see Table 1.1). Most were carried out by prominent educational statesmen and were based on available evidence and observations. Many of the later surveys also incorporated quantitative test results, which, they concluded, dem-

TABLE 1.1

State Surveys of Educational Conditions

Date	State
1914	Ohio, Vermont, Washington, Texas
1916	Maryland, Wyoming
1917	Illinois, Colorado
1918	Arizona, South Dakota
1919	Alabama, Delaware, Massachusetts
1920	Virginia, North Carolina, Hawaii
1921	Kentucky, Arkansas
1922	New York, Oklahoma, Indiana

onstrated the superiority of larger schools. Each survey, of course, recommended further centralization.

The actual implementation of rural school consolidation still fell far short of the goals set by its proponents. In 1920, there were twenty-two one-teacher schools to every rural consolidated school in America. Many of the educators supporting the consolidation movement had commendable intentions. They wanted to upgrade rural education; provide comprehensive high schools to all rural school children; and give rural students the same materials, resources, and curriculum available in city schools. However, good intentions did not lead to equally commendable results.

Paradoxically, the consolidation movement overlapped with the progressive education movement. At the same time that John Dewey was advocating individualization, superintendents were pressing for standardization. As Dewey wrote of lifelong learning, administrators were rapidly classifying and grading students and developing the meritocratic order. Administrators espoused the progressive ideas of Dewey and others when necessary, but their primary efforts were directed toward building an organizational structure that directly contradicted the progressive philosophy.

The explanation for this paradox can, in part, be found in larger societal trends of the period. As education was embracing progressivism, the economy was completing its transition to corporate capitalism. Educational policymakers and administrators found themselves trapped between the humanistic imperatives of their own field's leading theorists and the demands for economy, efficiency, and sound business management voiced by the nation's business and political leaders. Rather than taking the risks inherent in decisively choosing between two such dichotomous sets of demands, these educators attempted to forge an impossible alliance. However, unofficially, and perhaps even unconsciously, the balance was tipped by educational administrators toward the side of business and political demands. Progressive rhetoric was still heard, but whenever conflicts arose, policymakers chose to err on business' behalf. Ultimately, the progressive movement was undermined by this tendency, and its influence gradually waned.

Rural school consolidation, on the other hand, flourished in this period. Since it was designed to conform to urban standards of administrative practice, resistance to it continued to come solely from local rural communities. As corporate capitalism became increasingly dominant, local autonomy and small schools came to be seen as the enemies of "progress." As economists Bowles and Gintis point out:

> The small decentralized common school was manifestly anachronistic, both in its internal social relationships and in the degree to which it could be centrally controlled through enlightened social policy.[40]

Such "enlightenment," of course, was to spring from the nation's urban-oriented industrial and political leaders and be implemented by America's educational administrators.

1920-1944: Urbanization as Conventional Wisdom

During the period following World War I, the reform-oriented activism of Teddy Roosevelt and the muckrakers was replaced by the complacency and conservatism of Warren Harding and Calvin Coolidge. The Immigration Act of 1924 restricted the flow of foreigners into the country; "Americanization" programs were well under way; and the problems of assimilation did not seem as urgent as they had a decade earlier. Urban America was the new norm, and village life was increasingly seen as a relic of the past.

Even the self-image of rural Americans began to change and

become more urban with the advent of large-scale commercial operations in farming and other natural resource-based pursuits. Farming, fishing, and forestry were now seen as "industries" rather than as ways of life in rural America. Agri*culture* was being supplanted by agri*business*, and the yeoman of yesteryear was giving way to the businessman of the future.

As a consequence, there was less pressure, even among rural parents, to preserve traditional rural values through the educational system. Educational administrators took swift advantage of these changing circumstances and in the 1920s inaugurated a concerted effort aimed at obscuring the differences between urban and rural schools and schoolchildren. Standardization was the order of the day. All aspects of the educational enterprise—teacher training, school architecture, textbooks, and state regulations—succumbed to the ideal of creating the "one best system" in urban and rural schools alike.

The National Society for the Study of Education reported in 1931:

> There is now general acceptance of the idea that the aims and objectives of our public schools are the same for the rural as for the urban elements.[41]

To no one's surprise a key objective turned out to be continued consolidation. As rural education analyst Harold Foght wrote:

> It is probably safe to say that the period of experimentation in school consolidation has passed. The movement has now been accepted as good national policy.[42]

Even though there were still many more one-room schools than there were consolidated schools, the consolidated, age-graded schools were growing and enrolling a major proportion of rural students. Massachusetts, for example, had more than twice as many one-room schools as consolidated schools in 1919, yet 96 percent of all pupils in Massachusetts attended consolidated schools.

In actual accomplishments, the rural school consolidation movement produced mixed results throughout these years. Once again, regional differences were apparent.

Implementation of consolidation plans was most pronounced in the southern and western states, where community control was the weakest and county governance the strongest. Between 1919 and 1929, the number of one-room schools in the South decreased by 37 percent, while similar schools in the West decreased by more than 32 percent. By contrast, only 17 percent of the existing one-room schools in the Midwest and 23 percent in the eastern states were consolidated during the same decade.

The economic depression of the 1930s had a marked effect on the consolidation movement. Because of the relatively high costs of building and operating new consolidated schools, leading educational policymakers and administrators tempered their advocacy with the knowledge that the rate of centralization could not begin to meet their aspirations until it became financially feasible.

These leaders were correct in their analysis. In states such as Iowa, declining farm income made it difficult for farmers to pay school taxes, let alone build new consolidated schools. In 1930, there were still about 9,400 one-room schools in the state. Although Iowa gave extra state aid to consolidated schools, it was not nearly enough to compensate for the added costs. Even as late as 1946, 98 percent of Iowa's school revenues were raised through property taxes—a heavy burden indeed for landowning farmers with few liquid assets.

Still, the absence of a major national drive for consolidation during the 1930s did not preclude its occurrence across the nation. This time, however, the impetus was abject poverty rather than progressive rhetoric. The depression hit so hard and lasted so long in some rural areas that it became impossible to support even the meager financial requirements of existing community schools.

In West Virginia, the 1933 state legislature was forced to abolish the 450 existing school districts and create 55 county units in their place. West Virginia's rural communities were unable to maintain their own schools and had little choice but to accept this consolidation plan. Arkansas, also suffering through the depression, drastically reduced all state aid, abolished all county school boards, and vested control over school affairs in the county courts. Finally, in Kansas, adverse economic conditions forced the closing of more than 1,000 schools between 1933 and 1939.

At the close of the 1930s, rural America was beginning to emerge from the deprivations of the past decade. Normally, this economic recovery would have signaled a renewal of the quest for consolidation and centralization by prominent educators. However, another national movement was gaining momentum and one of its side effects was to impede school consolidation efforts. Put simply, American perceptions of events in Germany, Italy, and Japan triggered a strong reaction against any reform having the centralist tendencies associated with fascism. Given this pervasive national mood, educators' hopes for increased consolidation were frustrated.

Ironically, long-time proponents of centralization and urbanization were now voicing sentiments remarkably similar to those of their historic community-based adversaries. For example, in 1939, the American Association of School Administrators (as stalwart a group of consolidators as could be found) suddenly exhorted their colleagues to:

> Keep the schools and the government of the schools close to the people, so that the citizens generally, including the parents and taxpayers, may know what their schools are doing, and may have an effective voice in the school program. . . . the relationship of the school to the natural community and the closeness of the school to the people are of first-rate educational significance and are not to be sacrificed in the interest of "efficiency." If such a sacrifice is made to establish economical districts, we will find in a generation that something of deep significance which money cannot buy has been destroyed.[43]

Though economics and politics had stymied long-term goals for more than a decade, the movement to urbanize rural schools was by no means dead.

1944-1970: Urbanization in the Modern Era

In 1944, toward the end of World War II, the first White House Conference on Rural Education was convened. Officially, the participants were gathered to study the relationship between rural education and rural life. However, the implicit purpose was to resurrect *The Rural School Problem* after more than a decade of relative inaction and inattention. The recurring theme of the conference was centralization; that is, the argument that adaptation to a changing, increasingly urban world required large schools and districts providing greater specialization, professional control, and expert management. As a report growing out of this conference asserted:

> Efficiency, economy and equity in the distribution of the tax burden all require a reorganization of the structure of school district organization and local school administration in a very large part of rural America.[44]

Though the traditional remedy for rural problems—urbanization—remained intact, the rural schools themselves had changed enormously since the early days of the consolidation movement. The ramshackle, ill-equipped, one-room schoolhouse occupied by fewer than ten students and an untrained teacher—the particular object of the early consolidators' ire—was a rarity in the post-World War II era. State requirements for course offerings, teacher certification, building specifications, and financial aid, coupled with the standardization of achievement tests, teacher training programs, and curriculum packages, had created a nearly uniform public educational system throughout America. However, "nearly uniform" schooling could not mollify administrators and policymakers in an age exemplified by the "Organization Man" and in a nation committed to the pursuit of conformity.

For rural educators, the task was now one of deciding how to make rural schools conform. Size was still the primary factor that made rural education distinct and kept it from precisely conforming to the urban norm. Yet, administrators realized that population sparsity and geographic isolation made the creation of urban-size schools all but inconceivable in many sections of rural America. The dilemma was obvious, but educators proved equal to the challenge.

Their solution was district reorganization. The rationale was simple. The logistical problems (population and geography) that precluded exponentially larger rural *schools* were not an impediment to creating urban-size *school districts*. This strategy had two additional features which recommended it to policymakers: (1) it could be presented to rural interests as a way of letting them have their cake (by initially retaining their small community schools) and eat it too (by being part of "modern" urban/suburban model school systems); and (2) the administrators knew that reorganization would, in fact, make eventual school consolidation more feasible by removing control from the local community and placing it in the hands of a more remote, more professionalized bureaucracy which could (and would) consolidate schools as it became technically possible to do so.

Educational policymakers had finally hit upon a strategy which could catapult consolidation from a standard *policy* to a widespread *practice* in rural America. In the ensuing decades, district reorganization was implemented across the country with startling swiftness and effectiveness. Only the most rural states, such as Vermont, Nebraska, and Montana, managed to retain their small districts in the face of this renewed consolidation drive.

The case of Illinois is illustrative. In 1945 (when a piece of semi-permissive consolidation legislation—The Illinois School Survey Act—was passed), Illinois had approximately 11,000 school districts in the state. Yet, by 1955, the number of school districts in Illinois had been slashed to just over 2,000. While the eradication of 9,000 school districts in one state in one decade is amazing, it merely mirrored a burgeoning national trend.

In 1950, there were 83,718 school districts in America. By 1960, a mere ten years later, the number of school districts was *halved* to 40,500. And it was halved again during the following decade, so that by 1970 only 17,995 school districts remained. Finally, after a full century of ardent advocacy, the centralist dreams of the early reformers were being brought to successful fruition.

Nonetheless, drinking from the cup of success only made the consolidators' thirst to purge everything small from the American educational system insatiable. For example, in 1959, after tens of thousands of school districts had already been eliminated, three of the nation's leading educators insisted that:

> At least 85 percent of the school districts found throughout the United States are too small to provide an effective program of education at any cost.[45]

Nor was school consolidation forgotten in the rush toward rural district reorganization. For, as administrators had suspected earlier, reorganizing districts and transferring control to more centralized authorities did indeed make school consolidation easier to achieve. Thus, while there had been approximately 60,000 one-teacher schools operating in 1950, only 2,000 remained by 1970. Similarly, the number of elementary schools in the United States dropped from about 128,000 in 1950 to 66,000 in 1970, even though student enrollments were booming during these decades.

By the 1960s, consolidation, as a political issue, had ceased to be a legitimate subject of debate or policy analysis. Consolidation and other urbanizing practices were no longer perceived as *reforms* championed solely by the progressive elements of society. Rather, they had become accepted educational *standards* supported not only by the full range of the education profession, but also by the mainstream of American society.

Over the course of nearly a century, consolidation had slowly supplanted local control as the cornerstone of the status quo in rural education. Consequently, opponents of consolidation and urbanization were no longer regarded as respectable "conservatives" or "traditionalists" who, though "misguided" or "ill-informed," had a legitimate basis for dissent. Instead, any opposition was now deemed "irrational," while remaining opponents were characterized as "reactionaries" and "extremists."

The genius of this tactic, from the consolidators' perspective, was that it transformed consolidation, centralization, and urbanization from substantive political issues into technical and administrative problems. Since educators had long ago assumed their position as the final arbiters of "technical" and "administrative" concerns, consolidation and urbanization were now rendered virtually impervious to attack. Rural America could now be assured of membership in the "one best system" of education—like it or not.

Conclusion

Official policies about rural schools and school districts have historically been directed toward massive consolidation, centralization, and standardization. The schools have changed, rural conditions have changed, and educational needs have changed. But the policy has not changed.

Clearly, rural school consolidation and district reorganization resulted in some marked educational improvements. These policies helped to establish minimum standards, to make new educational resources accessible to previously neglected rural schools, and to eliminate the most marginal and inadequate rural facilities.

However, it is doubtful that the responsibility for these benefits and improvements can be attributed solely to centralist policies. In communities throughout the nation, investments in education were rising much faster than the gross national product. By the mid-1900s, it was unnecessary to convince people in most rural communities of the economic value of schooling. Education already represented the road to status and money. As a consequence, schools were requiring (and receiving) sophisticated equipment, buses, hot lunch programs, and other extras considered extravagant a few decades earlier. Thus, it is nearly impossible to determine precisely which improvements were caused by centralization and which were the result of an expanding national commitment to educational excellence.

Even though rural schools had grown, improved, and moved toward meeting urban educational standards, leading policymakers and administrators remained dissatisfied. Rural schools considered quite good in both size and program in any given generation became objects of reform in the next generation. The original consolidators would have been pleased to organize rural districts having two hundred pupils. However, their successors in the early twentieth century were demanding districts of two thousand students, while modern consolidators sought districts of twenty thousand or more.[46] As time passed and professional power expanded, the "right" policy was determined primarily by what was *possible* rather than by what was *necessary*.

Even though this chapter has been no more than a cursory review of this historically significant educational movement, the following lessons clearly emerge.

1. *Rural school reform sought to emulate the organizational patterns, curriculum, and standards established in urban and suburban school systems.* Reformers fervently advocated the adoption of these urban models, even though they were rarely consistent with rural conditions, rarely desired by rural parents and community leaders, and rarely appropriate to the social and educational needs of America's rural children.

2. *Rural school reform had significant effects on community life in rural America.* By transferring control from the community to hired professionals, the traditional sense of involvement, intimacy, and identification existing between rural parents and their schools was diminished. By inaugurating a formalized, standardized, and urbanized educational system, the traditional continuity between rural education and rural life was weakened. And, by inculcating rural children with urban values, urban aspirations, and urban skills, the

reformers encouraged out-migration while discouraging the preservation and improvement of traditional rural schools and communities.

3. *Rural school reform relied so heavily on organizational and structural changes that needed substantive improvements were often deferred or forgotten.* Reformers simply assumed that consolidation and centralization would automatically improve the quality of rural education. Alternative improvement strategies which were not tied to any structural reform were usually scorned. Although genuinely needed, a serious examination of the meaning and content of a good *rural* education was routinely set aside. By putting all of their improvement "eggs" into the same organizational "basket," these reformers put themselves into the position of having little to salvage upon discovering that bigger schools and districts are not necessarily better.

Slowly, over the span of more than one hundred years, consolidation, centralization, and standardization ceased to be coherent (if not always correct) responses to the very real and difficult problems confronting rural schools, and became elements of an ideology instead. It was an ideology of growth, efficiency, and conformity designed to support the nation's rising commitment to industrialism, corporate capitalism, and urban life.

It was not an ideology that rural people invented, sought, or supported. In fact, it was largely antithetic to the nature and meaning of rural life. However, this mattered little to urban reformers obsessed with saving rural children from their parents, and rural parents from themselves.

This was truly a reform movement steeped in the American tradition. Just as reformers had "civilized" the Indians, and "Americanized" the immigrants, so too would they "urbanize" rural citizens through the schools. That this particular reform failed to solve the problems besetting rural schools and rural children can hardly be considered surprising. When ideology replaces analysis, and the desire for conformity takes precedence over common sense, the quality of community life and the needs of children are the inevitable victims.

2 Economy, Efficiency, and Equality: The Myths of Rural School and District Consolidation

Jonathan P. Sher and *Rachel B. Tompkins*

Introduction

The most successfully implemented educational policy of the past fifty years has been the consolidation of rural schools and school districts. One-room, multi-graded elementary schools have been eliminated in favor of larger, many-roomed, age-graded schools. Small rural high schools have been closed down, and new, centrally located schools built to which most students are bused. Small school districts have merged with neighboring ones and larger schools have been built within the new district. Table 2.1 shows just how powerful the trend toward consolidation has been.

The slight increase in the absolute number of secondary schools is not at variance with the trend toward consolidation. Rather, it is attributable, first, to the construction of secondary school facilities in communities and neighborhoods never before served by such institutions (a side effect of the movement toward universally available secondary education), and second, to the rise of junior high schools as independent units (a development that added thousands of new institutions to the secondary school category).

Massive consolidation at the secondary level is evidenced by the fact that the number of traditional (four-year) high schools (the one kind of secondary school found throughout rural America) was halved during the same period in which the average secondary school enrollment tripled.[1]

TABLE 2.1

Number of Public Schools and Districts, 1930-1972

Year	Districts	Elementary Schools (Total)	Elementary Schools (1-Teacher)	Secondary Schools
1930	128,000	238,000	149,000	24,000
1940	117,000	185,000	114,000	25,000
1950	84,000	128,000	60,000	24,500
1960	40,000	92,000	20,000	25,700
1970	18,000	66,000	2,000	25,400
1972	16,960	64,945	1,475	25,922

SOURCE: Digest of Educational Statistics (Washington, D.C.: U.S. Office of Education, National Center for Educational Statistics, 1974). Figures prior to 1972 have been rounded.

The policy of rural school and district consolidation was implemented successfully primarily because of a consensus among influential policymakers that it represented a reform of enormous potential for solving most of the problems long considered endemic to rural education.[2] Indeed, this consensus is the hallmark of consolidation research, for while technical issues like optimum size were often debated, the basic premise that "bigger is better" was never seriously challenged in the literature. Many educators (particularly at the state and national level) genuinely saw consolidation as a panacea and, consequently, displayed considerable zeal in developing consolidation plans, marshalling favorable evidence, and lobbying on its behalf with state and local policymaking bodies.

Objections came primarily from rural parents (and occasionally their elected representatives) who either did not want their children going to distant, unfamiliar schools or who feared the effects of such consolidation on the life and vitality of their individual communities. As Tyack noted:

> Country people may have been dissatisfied with their school buildings and with an archaic curriculum, but they wanted to control their own schools. In a major study of rural schools in New York State in 1921, for example, 65 percent of rural patrons wanted to elect their county superintendent; 69 percent opposed consolidation of

schools. Subsequent studies showed that rural people in Ohio, Wisconsin, and Idaho also opposed unification. The impetus to consolidate rural schools almost always came from outside the rural community. It was rare to find a local group that "had sponsored or spearheaded the drive for reorganization."[3]

However, even those individuals and communities with fundamental objections to consolidation were willing to concede that consolidated schools would save money through a combination of scale economies and increased operating efficiency. Similarly, everyone simply assumed that the more highly educated teachers and administrators often found in consolidated schools would inevitably be "better" than their less-credentialed counterparts.

In the final analysis, large new rural schools and school districts were a tangible and effective symbol of the modernization that increasingly permeated all aspects of rural life in America. In education, modernization itself was a proxy for the higher quantity and quality of educational resources (teachers, laboratories, vocational education, and so on) that had been both long desired and long denied. Rural people wanted these resources because they both assumed and had repeatedly been told that such resources would lead directly to increased learning and, thereby, an increased chance of success for their children.

The values of smallness—local control; the close relations possible among professionals, parents, students, and community; and the opportunity for many more students to participate in school activities at a more meaningful level—were discussed but seemed overshadowed by the promise of new buildings, more courses, and sophisticated equipment. All in all, the benefits of consolidation seemed overwhelming and the costs minimal by comparison.

Given the enthusiasm with which consolidation was advocated, one would expect the empirical evidence supporting this policy to be overwhelming. It is not. The evidence on consolidation is incomplete. Most of the research not only fails to document the alleged benefits of consolidation, but also fails to acknowledge potential liabilities or problems. With rare exceptions, this body of research is methodologically unsound, with almost every study open to criticisms severe and significant enough to make the findings extremely suspect. The conclusions are, at best, inconclusive, and, at worst, simply incorrect. In short, there is no strong empirical base to support the assumptions and assertions of school and district consolidation advocates.

We will review and analyze the evidence and discuss consolidation's popularity even in the absence of solid and reliable supporting evidence. The purpose here is not to rewrite history, but rather to make a contribution to contemporary rural education.[4] In numerous rural communities nationwide, school consolidation and reorganization programs proceed unabated; the same old arguments continue to be advanced; and faulty evidence is still presented and accepted without careful examination.

The Myth of Economy

Do large schools in rural areas save money?[5] Supposedly, there are both economies of scale and greater efficiencies through improved management in larger schools. Since economies of scale were being widely touted in much of the private sector (including agriculture), consolidation advocates found it reasonable and convenient to assume that these scale economies would also exist in public sector activities such as education.[6] The actual evidence from education, however, illustrates the drawbacks in being sanguine about such assumptions.

Economy of scale—that is, the reduction of unit costs as size increases—is both a simple and a much abused concept. Consolidation proponents have made this concept the cornerstone of their arguments for the economic advantages of large schools and districts.

However, the primary problem with the research in this area is that it consistently fails to acknowledge the presence of offsetting diseconomies of scale; that is, new or enlarged costs attributable to increased size of operations. Diseconomies of scale in consolidation dramatically weakens the consolidators' arguments.

For example, the bulk of the relevant research ignores the additional capital expenditures, salaries, and operating costs associated with the greatly increased transportation required by consolidation. Children who formerly walked to school now must be bused. Children who used to ride for four or five miles per day now must frequently ride twenty or more miles to reach the "centrally located" school. All of this means more buses, more drivers, higher fuel costs, and faster depreciation than was the case prior to consolidation.

A 1973 article by White and Tweeten illustrates the importance of considering transportation costs. Using data from Oklahoma schools they estimate optimum district size in rural areas to be 800 students, when measuring only educational costs adjusted to a standard quality of program (thirty academic and eight vocational units).[7] However, when transportation costs were included, the optimum district size drops to 675 students.

In fact, the authors indicate that in most rural areas there are no inherent differences in the operational costs of districts anywhere within the range of four hundred to eleven hundred students. They conclude:

> Cost economies in instruction and attendant functions accrue from larger numbers of students, but cost diseconomies from transportation arise as more students must be brought to school.[8]

White and Tweeten also calculate optimum size in areas having varying student density ratios. Average student density in Oklahoma's rural areas is 1.8 transported students per square mile. A positive relationship exists between density and size, so that a district with a density of 0.6 transported students per square mile has an optimum size of 300, while a more densely populated district with 3.0 students per square mile reaches optimum size at 1,075 students.[9] Once again, these calculations are adjusted to the standard quality of program mentioned earlier.

The point of this research is simple. When transportation diseconomies are included in the determination of overall educational costs in rural areas, the economies from consolidation tend to decrease markedly or vanish altogether. As transportation costs increase, small school districts in sparsely settled areas are becoming even more economically advantageous.

Transportation is by no means the only area where important diseconomies occur. Purchasing has been cited throughout the research on consolidation as an area that perfectly illustrates how economies of scale can save rural schools and districts money. In fact, however, it perfectly illustrates the shortsightedness of disregarding offsetting diseconomies of scale.

During the 1960s, many small rural school districts banded together to form joint purchasing units so that these presumed scale economies could be captured. Instead of saving money, they discovered that all the money saved by volume purchasing was lost in one or more of the following ways: in distributing the purchases to participating districts, or by having to hire new personnel to organize and operate the purchasing/distribution operations, or by having to overpurchase supplies to get the volume discounts. As Zymelman concluded:

> Administrators should carefully consider the full costs of central purchasing because savings might not exceed the added costs of distribution. There are also possibilities of delays and loss of flexibility involved in central purchasing. Finally, there is the use of scarce administrative manpower to manage a purchasing and distribution operation that could be handled in the private sector.[10]

Or, as one school superintendent more bluntly put it, "When we realized just how much time and energy we were spending on a cumbersome system that wasn't saving us a dime anyway, we scrapped the whole joint purchasing idea."[11]

The point is not that economies of scale are nonexistent in rural education, but rather that they must be considered in conjunction with existing diseconomies. Doing this not only results in a more accurate method of analyzing economic data, but also reveals that the overall impact of these scale economies is simply far less than intuition would suggest. A more specific examination of some of the economic issues engendered by rural elementary and secondary school consolidation is informative.

While one study by McLure finds some instructional economies in schools up to three hundred pupils,[12] and Greider reports that peak economy in instruction for elementary schools is achieved with four hundred pupils,[13] there is a remarkable paucity of research that systematically examines cost/size relationships in rural elementary schools. For example, of the twenty-five studies on optimal elementary school size (urban and rural) reviewed in a 1974 Educational Research Service Report, none were based solely on cost data, and only seven even explicitly considered economic factors.[14]

Some estimates can be made even in the absence of reliable,

comprehensive research. A 1960 NEA report on one-teacher schools indicates that personnel costs (which compose the bulk of any school's operating budget) were usually considerably lower in one-teacher institutions than in larger, multi-teacher ones.[15] Transportation costs also favored one-teacher schools.

Still, consolidation advocates presumed that there must be some economies in operating only one, as opposed to several, schools in a given community—that, for example, it was cheaper to own and operate one furnace instead of three or four. And indeed, they were correct in assuming that some long-term capital costs favored the consolidated schools.

In the final analysis, though, local circumstance was probably the key determinant of the relative economic merits, not only of one-teacher versus consolidated schools, but also of the consolidation process at all levels of implementation. In communities having four ramshackle one-teacher schools with an average enrollment of less than ten pupils, all located within a ten-square-mile area, school consolidation was probably an economically propitious strategy. However, in communities having four well-maintained, one-teacher schools with an average enrollment of approximately twenty students, all spread out over a fifty-square-mile area, school consolidation was probably devoid of any economic justification.[16]

Occasionally, rural school and district consolidation did produce minor economic benefits for participating communities. However, consolidation advocates have had an unfortunate predilection toward disregarding the primacy of local circumstance in determining the economic implications of consolidation. By virtue of their exclusion from the vast majority of proconsolidation literature, one must assume that key local factors such as student density, local valuation levels, salary schedules, marginal costs, and cost comparisons for renovation versus new construction were not thought to be of major importance.

This disregard for local circumstance carried with it the tendency to advocate consolidation for communities in which it was either inappropriate or simply unnecessary. The advocates argued that if consolidation has been helpful in school system W, then it must also be good for systems X, Y, and Z.[17] However, America's history of educational reform constitutes a powerful argument against the casual replication of reforms. After years of painful trial and error, educators have come to understand that the success of any reform cannot be divorced from the circumstantial considerations that spawned and nurtured it.

Advocating consolidation for communities in which local circumstances do not warrant it is very much like giving cancer treatments to an individual who doesn't have cancer. Used appropriately, both consolidation and cancer treatments can be powerful (though not always successful) forces for improvement. However, used inappropriately, these powerful agents not only won't cure anything, but may also themselves be harmful to the recipient.

In terms of economy, the situation is not radically different at the secondary level. While the consolidation of high schools having less than two hundred pupils does seem to produce some instruction-related economies,[18] a further examination of the research reveals that most, if not all, of these "savings" can be attributed to increasing pupil-teacher ratios and the failure to account for transportation and other related diseconomies. In other words, overall or "net" economies are by no means assured.

In one study by Cohn on Iowa high schools, the actual pupil-teacher ratio in schools with under 200 pupils was 17:1; in schools with between 200 and 700 pupils, it was 20:1; and in schools with more than 700 pupils, it was 24:1.[19] Using these ratios and hypothetical salary figures of $7,000 per teacher and $10,000 per administrator, one can construct a reasonable (albeit simplified) scenario of the costs of rural high school consolidation.

Suppose three rural high schools with 140 pupils each close down and are replaced by one new 420-pupil school. Based on the 17:1 ratio, each of the old high schools would have had eight teachers and one principal. However, given the consolidated school's 20:1 ratio, only twenty-one teachers and one principal would be needed (a net reduction of three teachers and two administrators). In the old, small schools, total professional personnel costs would be $198,000. But in the new, consolidated school, these same personnel costs would amount to $157,000—a "savings" of $41,000. This would appear to justify the claims of economy made on consolidation's behalf.

This illusion of economy, however, can only remain intact by ignoring several critical factors. For example, extensive research shows that large consolidated high schools attract a professional staff that has both higher credentials and higher salary requirements (ranging from several hundred to a few thousand dollars).[20] If we

assume a relatively modest average salary differential for professional staff members of $1,000, at least $22,000 of the $41,000 in "savings"
vanishes. The remaining $19,000 disappears when one remembers to
account for consolidation's transportation diseconomies (new bus
purchases, new bus drivers on the payroll, higher transportation-
related operating and maintenance costs, and so on). Material and
equipment costs tend to be higher in consolidated high schools,
primarily because of the purchase of items not normally found in
small high schools. Once again, short-run building and maintenance
costs are higher in the new school, though consolidation occasionally
produces a comparative advantage in this area over time. Far from
saving money, consolidated high schools must discard professional
staff and raise pupil-teacher ratios to maintain even the approximate
level of operating expenses found in the smaller schools.[21]

Consolidation proponents would doubtless point out that while all
these cost arguments might be true, the important thing is that
consolidation brought better resources, and hence a better quality of
education to rural communities. Questions of quality will be addressed later in this paper. The only point being discussed here is
economy: the least expensive delivery system for rural education. In
light of this discussion, the traditional claim that consolidating rural
schools and districts will, ipso facto, save money, appears to have no
empirical or logical basis. It is simply incorrect to assert that
consolidation is synonymous with economy.

The Myths of Economy, Efficiency, and Equality in District Reorganization

With the important exception of the White and Tweeten study,
the evidence presented thus far has focused primarily on school size
and its relationship to cost and quality. Yet, another voluminous body
of literature considers possible economies and the equalization of
expenditures per pupil that come with district reorganization. Much
of this literature is descriptive and assertive, and strongly advocates
the creation of large districts.[22] The campaign has been effective
because the United States now has fewer than 17,000 school districts,
whereas in 1930 there were 127,000. Administrators call for still more
large districts:

I anticipate that within the next ten-year period we will probably see fewer than a total of 10,000 school districts. And at that time we will still be promoting even further reorganization. Ultimately, it is not impossible to think that the people of this country will reduce the number of basic administrative units to not more than about 5,000— one-third to one-fourth of the present number.[23]

It is not at all clear that this reorganization has brought the economy, efficiency, and equality so desired. Six studies of district economies of scale generally conclude that where they exist at all, they are quite small.[24] For example, Hirsch concludes:

This study is unable to find significant economies of scale and suggests that consolidation is unlikely to solve the fiscal problems of schools in urban America. . . . Certainly some rural school districts, and even a few urban ones, could make minor savings if they were big enough to afford more variety in high school offerings and more specialists.[25]

The savings that occur with scale appear to be in administrative costs. ELSEGIS (Elementary and Secondary General Information Study), a sample survey of 1,800 school districts conducted in 1956, reported percentages of instructional budget allocated to central administration by district size (Table 2.2).[26] These figures show a noticeable trend toward relatively higher expenditures for central administration in smaller districts. The magnitude of savings from 0–300 to 301–2,499 is $2,100 for each $100,000 of budget. That is not enough to cover the likely diseconomies of transportation, nor is it enough to warrant the dislocation of large numbers of students.

This sample does, however, raise some interesting points about the nature of efficiency in educational enterprises. Basically, as Zymelman states, "Efficiency and inefficiency are always relative terms."[27] If a school system is attaining more than it used to or more than another system given the same expenditure level, it may accurately be said to have achieved a degree of efficiency. Similarly, if the school system is attaining the same level of performance as it used to or as another system is, given a lower expenditure level, this too can be considered efficient.

With these definitions in mind, let us return to the above example

TABLE 2.2

Percentage of Budget for Administration,
by District Size

0-300	301-2,499	2,500-4,999	5,000-9,999	10,000-24,999	25,000
8.8	6.7	5.2	4.3	3.8	3.8

of the apparent administrative "economy and efficiency" achieved through district reorganization. First, the reported administrative "savings" do not refer to absolute dollar expenditures, but rather to the proportion of total budget allocated to administration. For example, in a small school district having a total budget of $300,000, administrative costs would be approximately $26,400 (according to the ELSEGIS formula).[28] However, in a larger district with a total budget of $3 million, administrative costs would be approximately $156,000.[29]

Yet, the really important point here has to do with efficiency. Spending less to attain the same level of performance is efficient. However, spending less to attain less is a corruption of this concept leading only to false efficiencies. The notion of false efficiency is applicable to this example in two respects.

First, if the school board in the district having 300 pupils decided to allocate just the administrative budget percentage found in the district having 3,000 pupils (5.2 percent), it would discover that it could only spend $15,600 for administration. While someone might be willing to accept the position at that salary level, he or she would certainly be a more poorly trained, less experienced, and, presumably, less competent administrator than whoever could be hired with the old administrative allocation of $26,400. Thus, while the small district would spend less, the overwhelming likelihood is that it would receive much less in return. There is no efficiency to be found here.

The second instance of false efficiency can be found in the larger district. The ELSEGIS study showed that while the proportion of administrative costs to total budget dropped with reorganization, the proportion of administrators to pupils and teachers also dropped dramatically. In other words, each administrator in a larger district is responsible for a greater number of students and faculty. This means that, of necessity, each student, each teacher, each parent, and each school will receive a much smaller fraction of administrative guidance, assistance, and attention. Compare, for example, the time, attention, and leadership the superintendent in a one-town school district of 300 pupils can devote to each of the individuals and groups he serves with the service a superintendent in charge of 12,456 students spread over 57 towns can provide (these are actual figures for one proposed superintendency under the state's district reorganization plan in Vermont).[30] These large districts may spend proportionately less, but only because they receive lower quality administration in return.

The consolidators' misuse of the concept of efficiency regarding administration has its roots in their attempt to create educational equivalents to the industrial model. Originally, economy of scale was intended to apply only to products and it was assumed that quality was held constant. Applying this argument to people undermines the assumption of consistent quality and, thereby, invalidates the use of this concept in arguing for administrative efficiency.

The search for district economies of scale often overlooks one of the major determinants of expenditure—taxable wealth. Districts that have a large tax base relative to the number of pupils will spend more than districts with a low tax base relative to the number of pupils. A recent review of state and local school finance finds that large districts have lower taxable wealth per pupil than small districts.[31] Unless the large district taxes itself at a higher rate or receives more state aid, it will spend less per pupil than the smaller district. What appears on the surface to be a relationship between expenditures and size may, in fact, be a relationship between expenditures and taxable wealth. Rich districts spend more per pupil than poor districts. If districts are both rich and small, it is not at all appropriate to argue that their higher expenditures are caused by smallness alone.

This is a particularly important point when considering equalization of taxable wealth—a problem that plagues the country today.[32] Despite massive reorganization for four decades, there are still sizable inequities between districts in wealth, tax rate, and expenditure regardless of size, type of district, or pattern of state aid.

Comprehensive recent evidence is provided on the question by the National Education Finance Project, a five-volume study of state and local finance in forty-eight states. Sixteen sample states were chosen for a careful evaluation of school district reorganization and state aid

TABLE 2.3

Assessed Valuation, Tax Rate, and Expenditure for
Unified (K-12) Districts by State, 1968

State	Assessed Valuation	Tax Rate (mills)	Expenditure
California	$3,578-26,054	2.64-6.69	$543-1,134
Colorado	2,031-37,651	20.00-61.18	406-1,351
Iowa	4,718-23,926	31.64-80.32	476-989
Maine	3,697-50,167	11.15-50.92	323-747
Mississippi	1,719-11,971	20.75-42.00	269-591
New York	4,755-161,174	6.04-27.79	693-3,001
Pennsylvania	4,935-60,078	5.54-32.12	471-1,347

distribution systems. Table 2.3 indicates some of the variation found in unified districts (K-12) in seven of these states.[33]

Based on an analysis of evidence from all sixteen states, the report concludes, in part:

1. Analysis of current expenditures indicates substantial variation exists in expenditure. The variation exists at all levels of organization—nonoperating, elementary, secondary, and unified. It is as pronounced for low-mean expenditure states as it is for states with high-mean expenditures. States with fewer districts exhibit as much disparity as those with many districts.
2. States with a small number of districts appear to have as much variation in per-student valuation as states with a large number of districts. The variation is found in states which have adopted a single pattern of unified districts, as well as states which have multiple organization schemes. It should be noted that in states with the multiple organization schemes—nonoperating, elementary, secondary, and unified combinations—the disparity in amount of valuation per student tends to be greater than in states with the single plan of organization.
3. Little evidence was gathered as a result of this study which would indicate that stability or equity have been achieved in tax structures. Wide variation is prevalent within states. . . . The variation in tax rates seems to be less in states with only unified districts; however, substantial variation still exists.[34]

TABLE 2.4

Relationship Among School Size, Assessed Valuation,
and Tax Rate in North Dakota, 1967

School	Assessed Valuation	Tax Rate (mills)
168 One-room rural districts	$13,152	34.2
81 Graded elementary districts	8,890	47.2
67 Non-accredited 12-grade	5,632	41.12
211 Accredited 12-grade	4,341	60.88

The evidence demonstrates that equalization of wealth has not been achieved by reorganization. It also suggests that changing population distributions and alterations in the tax base might be better accommodated through state financing mechanisms than by consolidation into ever larger districts. For example, in Vermont, state planners estimate that to have the wealth per pupil and tax rate combinations that they desire requires a consolidation from 278 to 8 districts.[35] Before contemplating a change in school structure that great and that politically difficult, it would seem reasonable to look seriously at alternative financing mechanisms.

The National Education Finance Project also has interesting information on the nature of redistribution that most frequently occurs in district reorganization. In general, small districts have higher assessed valuation per pupil than large districts, and the large districts have higher tax rates.[36]

As shown in Table 2.4, North Dakota provides excellent statistics on this point.[37] If reorganization occurs in North Dakota, children from one-room rural districts are likely to have less wealth backing them, and their parents are likely to pay higher taxes. The standard image of a very small, very poor, rural school district combining with larger, richer neighbors and receiving the benefits of increased resources, while true in many sections of the country, is not always accurate. Whatever the benefits of district consolidation, rural residents have usually paid for them through higher taxes.

Again, those who support consolidation are no doubt impatient with an analysis that considers only taxes, valuations, and expenditure. To them, the important point is that reorganization brought more resources, more variety, and more choice to students. Well, maybe. But there is more to say.

Krietlow's longitudinal data on school district reorganization shows an interesting trend. Reorganized districts had an advantage in several kinds of resources immediately after they reorganized, but over time, the nonreorganized district tended to obtain the same resources.[38] The general national commitment to education has meant steadily increasing resources for everyone, regardless of organizational pattern. The notion that smaller districts had to spend "exorbitant" amounts to secure needed resources is simply without foundation. There is no compelling evidence that proves the consolidation of rural schools and school districts produced significant net economic advantages. Thus, any effort to legitimize the massive rural consolidation programs implemented since 1930 must find its rationale somewhere other than in the economics of the situation.

The Myth of Improved Quality

It has long been argued that consolidation improves the quality of education. Facilities are newer and better equipped; teachers are better educated and more specialized; there are more choices available for students, such as foreign languages, music, art, and vocational courses. Because of these resources, students learn more and have a better chance in life. This argument has two stages: first, that consolidated schools provide more and better resources; and second, that those resources improve learning and life chances.

Much research has been done to document the claim that larger schools have more of everything. The most widely publicized and highly regarded research supporting this argument was James Bryant Conant's study of the American high school, published in 1959.[39] The timing of publication soon after the launch of the Russian Sputnik and Conant's reputation as the elder statesman of educational policy combined to give his conclusions the weight of tremendous authority. In the study's foreword, John Gardner (then president of the Carnegie Corporation of New York, and shortly thereafter appointed as secretary of Health, Education, and Welfare) asserted:

> It would be difficult to overestimate the importance of
> [Conant's] report at this time. Hundreds of thousands of

Americans all over the country are concerned about their schools, wondering what to do about them, seeking answers, hoping for guidance. Mr. Conant has provided that guidance. It is for this reason that some of us believe that Mr. Conant, after a lifetime of distinguished contributions to the nation, has in thus study made his greatest contribution of all. . . .

If I had to recommend a single piece of reading to all Americans who want to improve their schools, I would ask them to read this report.[40]

The public response to the Conant report was uniformly enthusiastic. For example, the *Louisville Courier-Journal* said, "the Conant report is a bombshell. Its import is likely to determine for a generation the direction in which public secondary education develops."[41] That this assessment was not just naive hyperbole is verified by Callahan's study of the social forces affecting public school organization and administration in America.[42] As Callahan states:

It was also predictable that [school administrators and policymakers] would welcome and quickly adopt James B. Conant's recommendations for change in the high schools, for, with his great stature in the country, his suggestions were made to order for defense. Any superintendent who could say that he was adopting Conant's recommendations, or better yet, that his school system had already been following them for years, was almost impregnable.[43]

The most significant conclusion of the Conant report was that small high schools with fewer than one hundred in the graduating class could not offer a comprehensive curriculum or a comprehensive educational program. Sufficient size was a prerequisite to the other twenty-one recommendations made to improve the high school. As Conant put it, "The number of small high schools must be drastically reduced through district reorganization. Aside from this important change, I believe no radical alteration in the basic pattern of American education is necessary in order to improve our public high schools."[44] In other words, simply making schools bigger would make them better.

Conant began by asking whether the comprehensive high school was a feasible idea. "Can a school at one and the same time provide a good general education for *all* the pupils as future citizens of a democracy, provide elective programs for the majority to develop useful skills, and educate adequately those with a talent for handling advanced academic subjects—particularly foreign languages and advanced mathematics?"[45] The emphasis of the study quickly fell on the last part of the question—the development of the academically talented.

Various sources were consulted to determine which schools outside metropolitan areas were good comprehensive high schools. In twenty-six states, a total of 103 schools were selected. Conant was convinced even before doing this study that "a high school must have a graduating class of at least one hundred to function adequately as a comprehensive school."[46] For that reason, he generally visited schools having graduating classes of considerably more than one hundred. In the book, he reports in depth on twenty-two schools; only three have one hundred or fewer in the graduating class.

If the assumption that small high schools are less comprehensive is correct, one might expect those three schools to be noticeably different. They are not. The summary lists fifteen items that a good, comprehensive school should have, such as "adequate instruction in social studies," "adequate non-academic elective programs," "individualized programs," "guidance services," and "good student morale."[47] None of the twenty-two schools got a perfect score of fifteen. Large schools ranked both best and worst. The mean score for the group was 8.9 The three small schools evaluated (A with ninety-five seniors, O with seventy-three seniors, and P with one hundred seniors) have scores of eleven, eight, and eight, respectively, and thus are near, or above, the mean in each case.[48]

Analyzing the checklist in this manner poses problems (notably that of weighting each item equally), but the point is that the three small schools do not (even on Conant's own criteria) support his strongly held view that small schools are not comprehensive. He lists eight of the twenty-two schools that "satisfactorily fulfill" the objectives of the comprehensive school: schools A and P are on that list.[49]

Even if small schools are comprehensive, perhaps they really short-change the academically talented. Conant asked each school to do an academic inventory on the graduating class of 1957. Eight positive responses for each school were possible on the inventory. No school scored eight. Two schools had seven positive responses—school A (with a graduating class of ninety-five) and school C. The mean response for schools was 3.8. Schools O and P had three positive responses each. School V (with 797 graduates) had no positive responses. On this evidence, small school A does very well indeed; O and P are fair, but by no means the worst.[50]

At another point in the report, Conant announces that he is "convinced [that] small high schools can be satisfactory only at exorbitant expense."[51] He presents no cost figures to support his statement. The earlier analysis in this paper of the economics of consolidation suggests that such a statement is greatly exaggerated, if not entirely false.

Conant was advancing two related arguments. First, he asserted that a critical mass of one hundred graduates was necessary to be comprehensive. Yet, his own research presents two schools (O with seventy-three seniors and A with ninety-five seniors) which are both comprehensive (by Conant's standards) and smaller than his critical mass. These discrepancies within Conant's own data make it difficult to believe that one hundred seniors is really so critical a figure after all.

More importantly, Conant was trying to establish the existence of a linear relationship between school size and comprehensiveness. He wanted to make the case that as schools became bigger, they would concomitantly become more comprehensive. Once again, however, Conant's argument is undermined by his own data. In several instances, the largest schools surveyed (such as school V with 797 seniors) were among the least comprehensive, while small school A ranked among the most comprehensive. Ironically, Conant's data persuasively demonstrate that size is a very poor predictor of comprehensiveness.

Conant began with the assumption that small schools could not be comprehensive and concluded that his study supported that view. It does not. What the study does indicate is great variation among schools, but it does not provide much explanation of why that variation occurs. Given that evidence, the widely acclaimed conclusion of the Conant Report is certainly incomplete and probably incorrect.

Recent evidence also refutes Conant's conclusions. For example, in the nation's most rural state (Vermont)[52] the small high schools appear to be performing every bit as well as their larger counterparts on the one available output measure—percentage of graduates entering college.[53]

In 1973-74, there were fifty-nine public senior high schools in Vermont, ranging in size of graduating class from 14 to 491.[54] Thirty-four high schools had fewer than Conant's required one hundred students in the graduating class, and twenty-five had more than one hundred. In addition, of the ten high schools having the greatest percentage of graduates entering college, six were small schools and only four were large (see Table 2.5).[55]

Nor were these results obtained at the "exorbitant expense" Conant predicted. In 1973-74, the average high school per pupil operating cost in Vermont was $1,210.72. For the six best small Vermont high schools (as determined by this one outcome measure), the average operating cost was $1,170.88, whereas the average operating cost for the four best large ones was $1,395.97.[56]

Conant was concerned about the resources provided in high schools. His assumption, and the assumption of all who shared Conant's emphasis on the quantity of resources, was that in-school achievement and success in later life were both directly related to the possession of certain key resources.[57]

However, recent research by Coleman, Jencks, and others has suggested that most of these key resources (inputs) do not necessarily correlate with school achievement (output).[58] In fact, educational research has failed to identify a single resource or practice that is consistently effective in bolstering achievement. Moreover, the presumed linkage between school success and economic success in later life has been shown to be considerably weaker than common sense would suggest.[59]

Even those whose faith in the ultimate value of better resources remains intact have come to concede that the mere possession of such resources is not sufficient to alter achievement results. Rather, they contend, the critical factor is the manner, purpose, and competence with which whatever resources possessed are utilized.[60] In either case, the implications for rural school and district consolidation (which was largely designed as a strategy for improving education inputs) are clear.

If one believes Coleman et al., then rural consolidation becomes little more than an exercise in futility. Because structural reforms

TABLE 2.5

Comparison of Size/Cost Data for 10 Vermont Public High Schools
Having the Highest Percentage of 1974
Graduates Entering College*

School Name	Entering College	Total Number of Graduates	Operating Costs (per pupil)
Montpelier H.S.	68%	146	$1,613.69
S. Burlington, H.S.	57%	245	1,235.76
Craftsbury Academy**	56%	16	1,300.27
Wilmington H.S.	56%	16	1,619.41
Chelsea H.S.	48%	33	1,031.90
Arlington H.S.	47%	43	1,048.73
Poultney H.S.	47%	60	875.53
Woodstock H.S.	47%	123	1,130.26
Champlain Valley H.S.	47%	224	1,631.19
Wallingford H.S.	45%	29	1,149.46

* According to the National Center for Educational Statistics, approximately 40 percent of all 1974 high school graduates nationwide went on directly to college.

** Despite the title of "academy" this school is, in fact, public.

such as consolidation are unlikely to positively affect either academic achievement or lifetime earnings, the Coleman-Jencks school would conclude that it is much ado about nothing. In this view, consolidation serves mainly to divert attention away from both the need to redistribute income and to make the "internal life" of schools more pleasant for all concerned.

If, on the other hand, one believes that proper utilization of existing resources is the central issue, then rural consolidation is useful precisely to the extent that it actually results in a more effective utilization pattern. Local circumstance once again becomes paramount. In some communities, consolidation could conceivably help effect an improved utilization of resources. However, the belief that consolidation is synonymous with better utilization or that small rural schools cannot attain the highest possible level of resource effectiveness is not documented in the literature. If anything, because small rural schools are less complex and more manageable institutions, it is possible that they would have an inherent advantage in efficiently utilizing the resources they do possess.

Those who pushed for consolidation from 1930 to 1965 did not have the benefit of this research, but they did have access to a large number of studies on achievement in elementary and high schools and success in college.

Many of these studies compared achievement scores of children in small schools with children in large schools.[61] However, only a handful of the studies controlled for variables, such as socio-economic status (SES) or IQ, that also affect achievement.[62] This is critically important in evaluating the empirical evidence on consolidation. Indeed, a detailed examination of this research reveals a classic example of the importance of controlling for IQ and social class.

In most of the early consolidation studies, which did not control for IQ and SES, the results showed varying degrees of positive correlation between school (or district) size and student achievement.[63] Consequently, many researchers such as Feldt (who employed no controls) were quick to conclude, "The pupil who received his elementary education in a rural school and his secondary education in a small high school of one hundred or fewer students suffers a form of educational double jeopardy."[64]

However, in recent years, researchers have begun controlling for IQ and social class. The effect of this development has been nothing less than a complete reversal of the traditional conclusions about the correlation between size and achievement. In fact, of the recent controlled studies, there is not one that records a consistent, positive correlation between size and achievement, independent of IQ and social class.[65]

Examples abound. Coleman et al. found school size to be "a variable not significantly correlated with achievement."[66] He also found that "size of the 12th grade is negatively correlated with verbal achievement . . . each additional 200 students is associated with a decline of one-fifth grade level in achievement."[67] Summers and Wolfe indicate that "higher achievement results correlated with smaller schools at both the elementary and senior high school levels."[68] Alkins concluded that "neither district size nor financial inputs showed any significant relationship to student achievement results."[69] Thrasher and Turner "found no significant differences on Iowa test scores that could be attributed to small school size" and "found no differences in grade point averages of small versus large school graduates in freshman year of college."[70]

In another major survey of the effects of school size on achievement, Herbert J. Kiesling found size of school to be negatively related to achievement.[71] Kiesling found, for example, at the twelfth grade level, achievement improved up to about twelve hundred to sixteen hundred students, but when controlled for background of the child, the child's intelligence, and school expenditures, the relationship was converted from positive to negative. The author explains his findings:

> Thus, many of the gross relationships, especially in grade 12, seem to attain a maximum at some size level in the neighborhood of 1200 to 1600 pupils in ADA and then to decline, while *after the three control variables are introduced, the entire relationship becomes negative and linear.* A possible explanation for this is that medium-sized schools exhibit better performance because they have pupils who are either more intelligent or come from better socioeconomic backgrounds, or both.[72]

Because of its rural focus, Richard Raymond's 1968 report on factors affecting freshman year college success also is relevant.[73] Raymond, a professor at West Virginia University, studied approximately five thousand freshman students at WVU.[74]

Raymond used overall scores on the American Testing Program (ACT) and freshman year grade-point averages as his measures of freshman performance. He then analyzed his data while controlling for a variety of financial, organizational, and social class variables (including a proxy for consolidation).

His finding was that consolidation and all other school-based factors were unrelated to freshman performance. Raymond concludes that educational and organizational differences between West Virginia county school systems (as measured here) do not produce differences in freshman performance. The differences that are significant are those beyond the control of schools. As Raymond says:

> The portion of the quality differences, as they have been measured, which result from differences in population characteristics falls largely outside of the control of the school system. This portion is caused by differences in student ability and home environment.[75]

Some of the most extensive research on school consolidation has been done by Burton Krietlow at the University of Wisconsin.[76] Krietlow began a longitudinal study of Wisconsin communities undergoing reorganization in 1949. He chose five reorganized districts (R districts), and matched them with five districts not reorganized (NR districts). Measures were taken of students in the first grade in all districts and the cohort was followed until five years after high school graduation. Data were collected on the schools, communities, teachers, and parents of the students in the cohort. A replication study following the same pattern began five years after initial data collection in each district.

The Long Term Study suffers from the problems of any longitudinal study—the inability to control very many of the factors that operate over time. Four of the five nonreorganized communities (NR) reorganized over the years and 40 percent of the students moved or dropped out. The world changed a lot in twenty years, and it is extremely difficult to sort out the effects of one variable—reorganization—from others. Despite these difficulties, the data collection has been done carefully and the conclusions contain the proper caveats.

Krietlow's results resemble those found in other similar research.

Significant differences in achievement appear at the sixth-grade level between R and NR districts favoring the R.[77] They persist at the ninth-grade level, and some remain at grade twelve—notably in reading and biological science.[78] However, controlling for SES and IQ at grade six wipes out the observed differences in reading and science achievement at grade twelve.[79] In other words, by going back to the original sixth-grade sample and controlling for IQ and SES, it can be shown that by the time these students reached the twelfth grade, there were no significant achievement differences between R and NR samples.

These results illustrate graphically the importance of separating influences on achievement. Without IQ and SES considered, reorganized schools are better on achievement measures. However, the children in these schools are more affluent and do better on intelligence measures.[80] These factors explain the achievement differences more plausibly than do size of school or district.

The Long Term Study also chose a replication cohort of first graders five years after the study began.[81] Comparing differences in achievement between original and replication cohorts within non-reorganized and reorganized districts partly separates the general trend that would increase achievement from the effects of reorganization. Using a total achievement measure, Krietlow finds significant increases in achievement for the replication cohorts in all districts, regardless of district type. Although the reorganized district scores remain higher than the nonreorganized, Krietlow (though a district consolidation advocate) is unwilling to ascribe that difference to reorganization:

> Besides reorganization, significant differences found in favor of the reorganized sample may not be due entirely to reorganization, *per se*, but to hidden variables such as parents' socioeconomic status, level of education, number of children in the family, rate of teacher turnover, innovations in the curriculum, and a general upturn in the values society places in education. . . . The results of this investigation strongly suggest that the significant differences found in favor of a reorganized sample should not be attributed to reorganization alone.[82]

Another fondly held belief among consolidation proponents is that students who graduate from large high schools do better in college than children from small high schools. The reasoning has face validity. Larger high schools usually offer a greater variety of courses, have more credentialed teachers, and provide the more impersonal social relations characteristic of college life. All of these factors would seem likely to positively influence college success.

Once again, the evidence does not support the consolidation advocates' stance. Besides the Vermont and West Virginia data presented earlier, ten studies on this topic were reviewed. Six indicate that size of high school does not correlate significantly with college success;[83] two found a positive correlation between size and success;[84] and two others show mixed results, finding size related to freshman grades but not to later success.[85] (Literature reviews by other authors show the same inconclusiveness among studies not reviewed in this chapter.[86]) The variability in results makes size extremely suspect as an explanatory variable. On the available evidence, it would be incorrect to assert that consolidation improves a student's chance for either enrollment or success in college.

For those who believe that the benefits of consolidation are more intangible, the evidence offers little solace. Krietlow found differences in post-high school aspirations and differences in what the students actually did after graduation.[87] Generally speaking, students in nonreorganized districts were more likely than students in reorganized districts to choose employment. Students in the reorganized districts were more likely to choose college. The reasons for this are not clear from Krietlow's work, unless one simply accepts that something about reorganization (such as its earlier adoption by high SES communities) increases aspirations.

Sewell and Haller's work with a body of data collected on ten thousand high school seniors in Wisconsin illuminates some factors that may be at work.[88] They asked, What affects educational aspirations? They concluded that a whole list of factors were important: whether a student's friends were going to college, whether a high proportion of the senior class was going on, whether his teachers encouraged him to plan on college, and whether he discussed plans with teachers and counselors. Sewell and Haller then correlated college (or no college) plans with a variety of external demographic variables. Interestingly, they discovered that school size had the weakest correlation to college plans of all the variables considered.[89]

The lesson here would seem to be that educational aspirations are determined, in part, by a pattern of expectations possible in both large and small schools. Those expectations are affected by what teachers and students believe about themselves. If teachers and students expect a consolidated school to prepare students for college, this factor will act to encourage them to go. Sewell and Haller's work suggests that if the same pattern of expectations appears in a small school, the students there will also aspire to college.

Still, there is much more that needs to be said about the relationships among size, consolidation, and a variety of personal, social, and other nonacademic qualities.

Roger G. Barker and Paul V. Gump in their remarkable book, *Big School, Small School*, report several significant and important findings relevant to the question of quality of the school experience in small schools versus larger, consolidated schools.[90] The Kansas schools studied by Barker and Gump range in size from 35 students in grades nine through twelve to 2,287 students. Although the largest school in this study exceeds that of most rural schools, 213 out of the total of 218 schools studied by Barker and Gump fell within the range of 42 to 889 students in grades nine through twelve. Thus, the vast majority of schools and students were comparable to conditions that exist or are being proposed throughout rural America.

The findings in the Barker and Gump book may be summarized as follows. The actual proportion of students who can participate in the essential activities that support the academic program, the quality of that involvement, and the satisfaction with that involvement clearly favor the smaller community school over the larger consolidated school. As an example of their general findings, the authors state:

> The proportion of students who participated in district music festivals, and dramatic, journalistic and student government competitions reach a peak in high schools with enrollments between 61 and 150. The proportion of participants was three to twenty times as great in the small schools as in the largest school. The number of extracurricular activities and kinds of activities engaged in during their four-year high school careers was twice as great in the small as in the large schools.[91]

The frequency of leadership involvements clearly favors the small schools. The authors state, "Furthermore, a much larger proportion of the small school students held positions of importance and responsibility in the behavior settings they entered, and they occupied these positions in more varieties of settings than students of the large school."[92]

As to satisfaction, small schools reported "more satisfactions relating to the development of competence, to being challenged, to engaging in important actions, to being involved in group activities, and to achieving moral and cultural values. Large schools reported more satisfaction with 'gaining points' via participation."[93]

Writing in the same book, W. J. Campbell concludes:

> This study of consolidation's effects suggests that if the small school students were transferred to a county high school they would probably undergo the following changes in experience: an increase in the number of school settings penetrated to the entry level; and a *decrease* in (1) external pressures aimed at increasing their participation in extracurricular activities; (2) sense of personal responsibility associated with extracurricular activities; (3) number of school settings penetrated to the performance level; (4) range of supervisory settings penetrated; (5) number of school settings judged to be most worthwhile; and (6) number of satisfactions associated with physical well-being, acquired knowledge and developing intellectual interests, developing a self-concept and zest for living.[94]

As Weaver notes:

> These differences between big schools and small schools are important because they represent qualities generally acknowledged by educators to be among the major goals of schooling. These qualities are also important because they are directly tied to differences in learning.[95] Self-concept and sense of control (attitudes which Barker and Gump and Campbell report are substantially better developed in the small school) were also found by Coleman in his nationwide study to be important factors in explaining gaps in cognitive achievement of children. As Coleman states, "For example, a pupil attitude factor, which appears to

have a stronger relationship to achievement than do all the 'school' factors together, is the extent to which an individual feels that he has some control over his own destiny."[96] Coleman further concludes that "the direction such an attitude takes may be associated with the pupil's school experience as well as his experience in the larger community."[97]

Barker and Gump found that participation in classes followed the same pattern as extracurricular participation. They state, "Although more school classes and more varieties of classes were available to them, the large school students participated in fewer classes and in fewer varieties than the small school students."[98] It was also discovered that in small schools participation was greater in more non-academic subjects such as music, arts, shop, and physical education, but less in academic specialties.

Consistent with their other findings, Barker and Gump report that not only is the actual proportion of children who participate diminished in larger schools, but the larger school is dominated by a small handful of students. For instance, in the case of music performances, the authors state, "Not only was music participation less widespread among junior students of the large school, there was greater concentration of that which did occur within a small circle of relatively few specialists."[99]

Barker and Gump also argue that the small town is both more dependent on its youth and more richly endowed with behavior settings (proportionally) than larger towns. Adolescents were essential performers for significant percentages of the settings in the small towns, ranging from 18.5 percent of the settings in one town to 27.5 percent in another. The authors state, "These figures can be viewed as measures of the extent to which the four Midwest County communities were dependent for their functioning upon the performances of high school adolescents, or, conversely, of the degree to which the towns would be crippled for want of performers if the adolescents were removed."[100]

Once again, Weaver's words are instructive:

> Behavior settings that were deficient in promoting values important for learning were compensated by others in the small Kansas towns studied by Barker and Gump. Since

participation rates are much greater in small towns than in large, it can be argued that what the small-town high school lacks, the community can compensate for, and vice-versa. The authors conclude that small-town children live in "behavior settings that were relatively rich in people and behavior." Children in such towns are not isolated, nor are their schools isolated, from the community's vital support systems.[101]

The significance of the above in arguing against consolidation lies with the obvious interdependence of the small-town high schools and the communities they serve. In each of the small towns studied in Kansas, the town's high school was tightly integrated into the fabric of the community's social life. The communities and their schools were mutually reinforcing. To remove the school from such a community (and thereby alter the reciprocal balance) would be destructive of community. To warrant the acceptance of these negative social costs, one would have to argue that consolidation is a demonstrably better strategy for achieving desired educational and economic outcomes. As this chapter has indicated, despite decades of advocacy for and experience with consolidation, such benefits have never been persuasively documented.

All in all, consolidation has not been able to live up to the plethora of educational and economic claims made on its behalf. Today, some rural educators have recognized and acknowledged this failure. Significantly, the keynote speaker at the 1974 conference of the National Federation for the Improvement of Rural Education (a mainstream professional association) roused little disagreement when he stated:

At one time, the consolidation of school districts was seen as the way to [secure needed services] for large numbers of students at one time. Not any more, after the sobering experience of more than 20 years of trial leading to the conclusion that *big* is not synonymous with *better*. . . . The symbols of consolidation—impressive-looking glass, steel, and concrete structures—came to mean little to the student who spent hours getting to one of these superconglomerates and home again, often to receive less than a "quality education."[102]

Why Did It Happen?

Why has there been so much consolidation and reorganization when so little is empirically justified? There are several possible explanations. It is true that school officials have had to cope with a great population redistribution from the countryside to towns and cities. Some consolidation was necessary simply because schools and districts once filled with children suddenly had only a handful. Coping with necessity, however, does not explain why such a massive movement developed.

The movement to consolidate schools was merely one part of an urbanizing, modernizing trend that affected everything in America. Industrialization, coupled with scientific advances in agriculture, unleashed a steady flow of migrants from farm to city. Modernization dictated new values and new organizational forms that emphasized large size, specialization, and professionalization. Experts replaced amateurs. Small farms, small businesses, and small schools all gave way before the tide of centralization. Those who wished to retain small farms, small communities, and small schools were considered backward and provincial.

Modernization in government was characterized by a move toward scientific management. Efficiency and economy became the prevailing creeds. School size and class size were increased. Much emphasis was placed on per pupil costs. It become important for principals and superintendents to report trivial savings.[103] The zenith of this business influence on the schools was from 1900 to 1930, but the themes linger, particularly in "good government" arguments to rationalize and centralize administration. As Congressman Reuss argues:

> The number of counties, towns, villages, and special districts could be drastically reduced from its present 81,000 in order to enable local government to obtain adequate geographical powers and revenue sources effectively, to solve local problems, and to eliminate wasteful Lilliputs. Many rural counties too small to be efficient could consolidate with their neighbors for regional cooperation. Archaic township governments—17,000 of them—could be steadily abolished. All told, it could be the greatest

decimation of redundant governments since the consolidation of rural school districts under the pressure of state governments in the 1950s.[104]

The rise of the profession of school administration during the heyday of scientific management contributed further to the movement for centralization. Administrative training in prominent schools of education (Stanford, Columbia, and Chicago) was dominated in the 1920s and 1930s by advocates of consolidation, efficiency, and economy. Their textbooks and their students shaped state university and college administrative training in the 1940s and 1950s.[105] These professionals, many of whom came from one-room elementary schools and small rural high schools, returned home to argue that they had learned better ways.

Still, there was a motivation behind the professionals' zeal about consolidation that ran deeper than a simple belief in its intrinsic value. As Tyack perceptively notes:

> On closer examination rural-school reform becomes not so much a paradox as a transfer of power from laymen to professionals. The rural-school reformers talked about democracy and rural needs, but they believed that they had the answers and should run the schools. . . . And while they justified their program as public service, educators also sought greater power and status for themselves. What they needed was authority: "It is the lack of captains and colonels of larger grasp and insight that is today the greatest single weakness of our rural and village educational army. When matched against the city educational army, with its many captains and colonels, and under generals of large insight and effective personal force, the city army easily out-generals its opponent."[106]

Money proved to be yet another force motivating the adoption of consolidation and reorganization. Many states provided substantial financial incentives and rewards for those local districts willing to accept mergers. At least one state (Vermont) offered increased state revenues to local districts which tried, even unsuccessfully, to bring about consolidation. Many states, such as West Virginia and Indiana, made the availability of state school construction funds contingent upon the acceptance of local consolidation plans. In state after state, the money tail wagged the policy dog.

All of these factors help explain some of the underlying motivations for this movement, but they still do not satisfactorily answer the question of why evidence was accepted when it was frequently so flawed. Educational research was not, and is not, held to very high methodological standards, but that does not seem sufficient to explain why so little research was ever done to determine whether there were advantages to small schools and districts. Why were the assumptions and assertions underlying the consolidation movement so rarely examined?

First, the arguments for consolidation have tremendous face validity. To argue that economies of scale may not exist, or are very small if they do, or are outweighed by diseconomies, is counterintuitive. To suggest that newer and more modern school buildings with more educated teachers do not necessarily mean that children learn more turns the educational world on end. Opponents of consolidation generally have not tried to directly refute the advocates. They have argued that factors other than economy and efficiency had great value. They were concerned about local control, about changes in life style, about the loss of the school in their community, and about bigger, less personal institutions. Since the opponents valued other things, they rarely made any attempt to attack the face validity of the proponents' arguments.

So the arguments stood. Asserted over and over again and left unchallenged, they came to be believed. As Ostrom states, in an article that reveals that law enforcement, like education, has been subject to massive consolidation based upon specious evidence coupled with strident advocacy,

> The assertions have been repeated for so many years, and by such righteous groups, that few questions have been raised about their empirical validity.[107]

Symbols of modernization such as new schools, sophisticated equipment, and more credentialed teachers were believed to be important in and of themselves. They were also thought to lead to certain ends. Those who did not believe needed to be convinced. Evidence was collected to show that the symbols work. The preponderance of research on consolidation was done by people who supported its adoption and wanted to demonstrate to others that it was a good practice. For the most part, this research was done in order to convince others to believe in consolidation, rather than to find some objective truth.

Another reason that the evidence was accepted is that performance results of the schools were (and are) hard to measure and even harder to agree upon. Consolidators thought that children scored higher on achievement tests if they went to multigraded elementary schools. They thought that a broader high school curriculum better prepared students for college. Even if these things were always true (and the evidence indicates they were not), not everyone agrees that they are the most important results. However, if we made a list of other results (ability to relate well to others, creativity, strong self-concept) we would have great difficulty measuring them and comparing them over time. Therefore, most research on consolidation simply focused on the input—buildings, teachers, equipment, curriculum—and did not even try to measure and compare results.

Implications for Educational Policy

What do we do now? Go back to little red schoolhouses and start over? Throw out all the professionals who want to reorganize and consolidate? Fund an enormous research project to measure the results of consolidated schools? Probably none of these.

While the policy of rural school and district consolidation is not totally devoid of worth, its strengths were greatly exaggerated, its weaknesses often ignored, and its overall merits as a strategy for educational reform and improvement grievously overstated and oversold.

Despite the massive human and financial investments made on its behalf, consolidation has not dramatically alleviated the educational problems endemic to rural areas. More importantly, consolidated units have not even been shown to be more successful than existing small schools and small districts—which have had to make do with relatively meager resources and scanty professional attention.

By consolidating, rural communities relinquished the advantages of smallness and received little in return. Thus, while consolidation has become the conventional wisdom in rural education, careful scrutiny of the available evidence makes this particular policy appear to be considerably more conventional than wise.

Three lessons seem important. First, *small schools deserve more attention.* Inordinate emphasis on bigness largely preempted serious discussion and research on methods of maintaining and improving existing small schools and districts. There are values in smallness that are lost with reorganization and consolidation. As noted earlier, Barker and Gump document some of these in one of the few pieces of counter-consolidation research that exist.[108] Barker's conclusion is worth pondering:

> It may be easier to bring specialized and varied behavior settings to small schools than to raise the level of individual participation in large schools. Furthermore, the current method of broadening educational offerings by moving hundreds of bodies to a central spot may be both unnecessary and old-fashioned.[109]

Second, *alternatives to consolidation and reorganization should be seriously considered.* Regionalizing such expensive programs as vocational education is one alternative to consolidating entire schools and districts. A range of helpful services can be provided, and in some cases are being provided, by regional units to schools and districts desirous of remaining small.

However, while there is a wealth of potential benefits in strategies linking substate regional units and individual small schools and districts, there are both actual and potential problems inherent in regionalization which must not be ignored. Foremost is that regionalization done without sensitivity and imagination could become the precursor of yet another round of even larger local units, more centralized decisionmaking processes, and less and less direct accountability to rural parents, students, and taxpayers.

Nevertheless, the basic point is that many alternatives for good small programs are possible now at competitive costs with a variety of widely available telephone, radio, microwave, and tape systems. Schools can choose very simple two-way telephone hookups with distant resources or more complex systems using TV.

Other alternatives include the establishment of a teacher corps system using special subject teachers, paraprofessionals, teaching assistants, and tutors to compensate for educational deficits in rural communities or the establishment of voluntary collaboratives for special interest activities. The underlying premise is that resources can be brought to children rather than forcing children to go to the resources. The benefits of smallness can be coupled with the benefits of specialization.

Third, *research done to demonstrate the value of proposed reforms should be scrutinized carefully.* It is likely that a researcher brings with him certain assumptions that go unquestioned. If he believes, he wants others to do the same. This problem continues to be prevalent in most educational research. Because the research is almost exclusively done for professionals by professionals, it would be useful to ponder Cohen and Garet's recommendations for government or foundation funding of research on behalf of groups other than the state and its constituent school districts.[110] Community groups wishing to advocate the benefits of smallness in schooling could marshal and present evidence to support their claims. The decisions about what to do would be political choices among values (which they always have been) but the professional side would no longer be cloaked in scientific rationality.

People came to believe that the values of consolidation were supported by scientific truth. They got their new buildings and fancy equipment. They got highly credentialed teachers, more specialists, and more professional administrators—some of which they probably would have eventually received anyway. Not surprisingly, their taxes continued to increase, as did per pupil costs.

But even with all their spending and all their new resources, rural people still did not generally receive that which they wanted most dearly—better life chances for their children. Those chances are more surely affected by the education and income of parents, the social and economic character of the community, the investment of time, energy, and love by many adults, and plain luck, than they ever are (or were) by the size, newness, or variety of the local school.

Consolidation was deemed a panacea. However, we now discover that panaceas are every bit as mythical in rural education as elsewhere in society. It's an important lesson.

Part Two

Policy and Paradox

3 Choosing Smallness: An Examination of the Small School Experience in Rural America

Faith Dunne

Let us begin near Red Cloud, Nebraska. In 1970, the Pleasant Prairie Grade School served seven children from three Webster County farm families, as it had served that sparsely populated farming region for ninety years. Mrs. Ardis Yost, the Pleasant Prairie teacher, saw in her small school both advantages and difficulties. She appreciated the strong ties between the school and its community; more than eighty people had come to the school's Christmas program that year to listen to the children carol and present their homemade plays. And she valued the kind of individual attention she could give her students. "How many teachers could take two first-graders and give them this much time each day?" she asked. "With Melanie (her lone kindergartner), I'm practically a private tutor." But at the same time, she felt that Pleasant Prairie was educationally inadequate. "They're happy here," she said of her students, "but they like it because they have never been exposed to anything different." James Richardson, parent and school board member, agreed. "I hate to say it, but I think the time is here when we ought to go to the town school. The kids are missing too much."[1]

What were the kids missing? If Mr. Richardson and Mrs. Yost read a pamphlet produced expressly for people like them by the Great Plains School District Organization Project, they got one clear answer. This pamphlet on education in Nebraska promotes school consolidation with an enthusiasm once reserved for snake oil. In it,

Nebraska voters are asked to choose between "Emotion . . . tradition . . . fear of change . . . fear of higher property taxes" and a "comprehensive" education for their children which would allow them to "live reasonably confident . . . work and prosper . . . be thinking men and women . . . to make democracy work."[2] Consolidation, the pamphlet argues, will reduce taxpayer costs, while encouraging broader and more specialized programs, raising teacher quality, and enhancing the capacity of Nebraska's young people to compete in an increasingly urbanized world.

This argument, which has been advanced by professional educators for 100 years, was reluctantly accepted by the people of Pleasant Prairie, and by many like them, in closing their small schools. Ten years ago, there were 1,400 one-room schoolhouses in Nebraska; 500 remain today. Recently, however, citizen acceptance of consolidation (however reluctant) has begun to change into tentative but heartfelt opposition. As consolidation efforts have become more successful in practice, voters in many of the most rural areas of Nebraska have begun to act in defense of their small, locally controlled country schools.

Nebraska's *New Land Review*, a populist periodical with roots in the back-to-the-land movement, ran a long article on school consolidation in the Summer 1975 issue. The article describes the demise of a one-room school in Wayne County, a school which sounds much like Pleasant Prairie. But Mrs. Gloria Lesberg, the District 34 teacher, does not share Mrs. Yost's sense of the inevitable inadequacy of one-room schools. "I feel my students get a good education here," Mrs. Lesberg says. "I have had many former students on the honor roll at Wayne High School, and one was even valedictorian one year." She cites the virtues of small country schools—individual attention, independent study, student self-reliance—and notes, "My first-grader is already reading at a third-grade level."[3]

Mrs. Lesberg's judgments are supported by the Wayne County Superintendent, Fred Rickers. Rickers says that he has studied how the country-educated children do when they reach high school and are in classes with the town-educated children. He has found no indication that the country pupils have received an inferior elementary education. Ricker says, "About one-half the students on the honor rolls of Wayne County high schools were educated in country schools."[4]

Jerry McCall, director of Field Services for the State Department of Education, strongly disagrees with Mrs. Lesberg and Superintendent Rickers. The *New Land Review* quotes him:

> A school district should have as large a land base as possible to work from. Then the district can afford to purchase modern learning aids and have specialized programs taught by teachers who are specialists in a particular field.[5]

McCall feels that "Many of Nebraska's country schools that have been consolidated with the nearest town school are still too small. Nebraska should have no more than 100 school districts—that averages out to about one per county."[6] Currently, much to the chagrin of the Education Department, there are more than 1,200 districts in Nebraska—the most of any state in the nation.

So far, the voters of District 34 agree more with Mrs. Lesberg than with Mr. McCall. More than 65 percent of the district voters petitioned the State Reorganization Board to allow a move to a three-room country school rather than enforced consolidation with the school in a nearby town. But it is not clear that this expression of local support for small-scale schooling will succeed. The State Board of Education is pushing hard for legislation that will set a minimum assessed valuation for land. These, and other proposed state measures will, if passed, have the effect of ensuring consolidation and ending the tradition of small schools and local control in the state of Nebraska.

The battle over small rural schools is not unique to Nebraska. The issues raised in Wayne County are being fought across rural America. Nebraska is special, perhaps, because it has clung longest to the small school and the local district. Many of these districts will not die as quietly as Pleasant Prairie. The fight between the consolidators and those striving to retain the small rural school is rekindling, and it seems likely to increase in intensity over the next decade.

Consolidators vs. Conservators: Two Views of Rural Education

The contemporary version of the old battle between professional educators and rural citizens has taken some new and interesting turns. The two basic camps are still clear. The consolidators' arguments remain the same: small schools are economically inefficient, intellectually unstimulating, low in options, and poor in resources. To them, the answer is simple. Bring together enough children in one place and thus provide the financial base on which to erect one of the long, low, carpeted, red-brick buildings which the suburbs have been raising since the early 1950s. Efficiency, stimulating options, and suburban-style resources will inexorably follow increased size.

The conservators reject this suburban model for a variety of reasons. Some conservators are the classic antagonists of consolidation—country people who remember their own schooling with fondness, or at least with respect, and who do not want their children removed from their sphere of influence. These traditional conservators are now joined by a group of rural revisionists, general-ly from urban or suburban backgrounds, who see the one-room schoolhouse as a vanished idyll, destroyed by ravaging urbanization. The new conservators, especially among professional educators, find in the small rural school the source of innovative techniques now being adapted for suburban and private schools. Versions of the open classroom, peer-tutoring, cross-age grouping, and individualized instruction, they argue, have long been present in America's small rural schools. The new conservators believe that such creative learning environments must not be abandoned. John Holt, in his introduction to Julia Weber Gordon's book about her two years as a teacher in a one-room country school, effectively voices the new conservator view:

> We do not need enormous centralized schools in order to have quality education. This is the reverse of what we have been told and sold. All over the country, we have destroyed small schools in which it might at least have been possible for teachers to do some of the things Miss Weber did. In their place, we have built giant school factories, which we run for the most part, like armies and prisons because they seem too big to be run like anything else.[7]

At the root of the conflict between consolidators and conservators is a differing conception of what constitutes a "good education." To the consolidator, "good" generally means "most like suburban schools," in such expensive commodities as staff specialists, large and well-equipped buildings, and a wide range of programs to meet the needs of a variety of students. The simplest way to get those expensive things is to consolidate; thus, consolidation becomes the obvious policy.

Consolidators used to argue that larger schools were cheaper as well as more effective. That argument is now being abandoned in the face of increasing evidence that consolidation does not necessarily save money.[8] However, the suburban definition of "good education," which is less amenable to simple proof or disproof, has been sustained. Many studies come to the same conclusions as one sponsored by the Massachusetts State Board of Education:

> While it is clear that it costs more to educate secondary students in regional school districts, it is also obvious that, when compared with programs and services offered in small high schools: (1) a much broader program is available in the regional schools; (2) services of guidance counselors and librarians are more often available; (3) the academic status of teachers is higher; (4) teachers have fewer different preparations; and (5) more qualified teachers are attracted to regional high schools than to small high schools.

> The question which must be answered in communities considering regionalization are whether these benefits to high school children are worth the extra cost.[9]

The "costs" considered by the Massachusetts State Board of Education appear to be purely fiscal. But the rural conservators are generally concerned with more than money. The issue, in the eyes of the citizens of Nebraska's District 34, is not so much cash as control. Rural parents are reluctant to delegate school policy to distant "experts," and often feel that a "good education" is close to home, both physically and academically. To rural parents, a full-time librarian might not be worth a two-hour daily bus ride, and teachers with master's degrees may not be worth the sacrifice of ready contact with every member of the school board.

It is difficult to determine whose definition of "good education" is genuinely best for rural children because the aims of rural education are not clear. In an increasingly vocation-oriented educational system, the suburban school has a clear role: to prepare the student for further education which will, in turn, buy him or her a job with sufficiently high status to permit life in a suburb. Urban schools have, as Joel Spring has ably argued,[10] a similar closed cycle: they train their students in the skills necessary to become laborers or clerks, which, in turn, earn them jobs which allow a continuation of workingclass life in the city.

However, rural schools cannot count on a similar smooth absorption of their graduates into a local job market and a local peer group. Not any more. In 1913, George Herbert Betts could safely write:

> The rural school must therefore be different in many respects from the town and city school. In its organization, its curriculum, and its spirit, it must be adapted to the requirements of the rural community. For, while many pupils from the rural schools ultimately follow other occupations than farming, the primary function of the rural school is to educate for the life of the farm.[11]

Looking back over sixty years, Betts' confidence seems endearingly naive. Except in the minority of rural communities, it would be anachronistic for rural schools today to educate for the life of the farm. In 1970, only 6.8 million (13.8 percent) of 49.4 million rural residents lived on operating farms. And those farms dwindle in number daily; it has been estimated that 2,000 farms go out of business each week.[12] In 1967, Nels Ackerson estimated that only one young man in ten presently living in a rural area will find a career in farm work or farm-related work.[13] Ten years later, that number is undoubtedly smaller still.

The decline in farming and in other traditional rural occupations (mining, fishing, lumbering, and so on) has thrown the question of rural school goals into an open and puzzling arena. Should the school teach young people the skills and values of farm life, thus condemning most of them to marginal employment? Should the schools prepare their students to work in cities where they will have to compete with urban-born workers for the same jobs? Should the school try to do something else? What?

Such occupational questions bring with them social issues. The traditional rural community, often characterized as occupationally, ethnically, and politically homogeneous, did not ask its schools to prepare children to fit comfortably into an increasingly pluralistic and diversified world. But today's rural child must come to terms with that world, since it is now on his doorstep—or, more precisely, blaring abrasively from the corner of the living room. Yet, if the schools focus on exposing children to cosmopolitan diversity, and attempt to make their social and political attitudes as suburban as possible, some unique rural life styles will be threatened—life styles cherished by many country people and chosen by many refugees from the suburban "paradise."

These questions are complex and cannot be answered simply with carpeted classrooms or by a return to the ferule and *McGuffey's Reader*. They might be approached by taking a fresh look at the traditional rural school and by trying to make it a basis for developing a uniquely rural way of coping with uniquely rural problems.

The Nature of the Traditional Small School

The traditional rural school was, above all, an extension of its community. Even in the writings of passionate consolidators like Ellwood Cubberley, we find laudatory descriptions of a traditional country school so intertwined with the community as to be virtually indistinguishable from it:

> When a school had once been decided upon, it became, to a marked degree, a community undertaking. The parents met and helped to build the schoolhouse, and hew out and install the furniture; they determined how long they would maintain the school; they frequently decided whom they desired as teacher, and . . . they all helped to provide the teacher with board and lodging by means of the now obsolete "boarding around" arrangements. . . . Schools were essentially local affairs, directly related to local needs and local conceptions.[14]

Cubberley believed that this kind of school died with the advent of the Industrial Revolution. But Homer H. Seerley, writing in 1912, disagreed. "The country school has . . . a first place in the community," Seerley wrote, "as it is recognized as being one of the greater undertakings of the people as a whole."[15] And Seerley's sense of the school as a collective, if not always peaceable, enterprise of the community as a whole permeates the literature on the nineteenth and early twentieth century rural school.[16]

These early schools provided the community with maximum accountability. The teacher, who lived with each family in turn, had daily contact with parents and other taxpayers. Decisions on upkeep were made personally and informally: a local farmer who liked to tinker would assume responsibility for the schoolroom equipment; the village would raise subscriptions for a needed clock or set of lamps.[17]

If the community as a whole undertook to maintain the small district school, the district school took equal responsibility to serve the community as a whole. Before television, most rural areas had few sources of amusement; writer after writer cites the monotony of rural life as a chief reason for the flight to cities and towns. The church and the school provided community entertainment—and the school was the center for secular festivities. In *The Country School*, Clifton Johnson describes the plays and recitations with which the schoolchildren entertained their parents and neighbors.[18] Many school buildings served as general cultural centers for communities. Homer Seerley, advocating consolidation, says that every school ought to provide a room large enough for "lyceums, farmers' meetings, lecture courses, exhibits of products, and public discussion and tests of all problems that affect their work and their success."[19] Ironically, Seerley's traditional belief that the school should serve the educational needs of the entire community was one of the forces that worked against early consolidation efforts such as the ones he promoted.

For all its efforts at broad-based service, the rural district school was a subsistence operation, depending very little on money. Although the school budget usually constituted the largest town expenditure (a condition true even today), it was far below the per pupil costs of the urban districts. Some of the difference was made up in services provided by the citizens. The teacher's salary was supplemented with room and board; the wood for the stove was cut and stacked by local men; repairs were not a budget item. Those things which had to be bought often had to be skimped. In 1869, the Vermont state superintendent of schools reported that the state's 2,800 schools had among them only 329 maps, 137 clocks, 118 dictionaries, and 206 globes.[20] This situation was characteristic of rural areas of this period.

Limited funds meant limited materials; they also limited the selection of teachers to make use of them. In 1921, the median wage for rural teachers was $861; in city schools it was $1,542.[21] Further, city teaching was generally perceived as easier and more prestigious; cities were, after all, the seat of the "one best system." Naturally, the most highly trained teachers were drawn to higher salaries and better conditions, while the country schools attracted who was left. In 1913, Herbert Betts reported that "the average schooling of the men teaching in rural schools in the entire country is less than two years above the elementary school, and of women, slightly more than two years."[22] This does not mean that there were no good rural teachers, but it does mean that the majority were lightly trained young rural women who taught in schools nearly identical to those they had attended, with little access to methods or even information beyond what they had learned in school themselves.

Rural citizens recognized the limitations of their schools. However, an array of new materials and high levels of teacher preparation were not the primary concern of the traditional rural community. Teachers were respected, and often honored. Johnson reports that so many families waited to butcher the pig until teacher came to stay that teacher was often heartily sick of pork by the end of the winter term.[23]

The choice of occupant for this honorable role was often based upon political considerations rather than credentials or competence. The teaching post, even with its small salary, generally represented most of the town leaders' limited patronage. Thus, the job of school-mistress frequently went to an unmarried daughter of a school committeeman. Rural parents felt that schooling was critically important to the lives of their children and the community, but they also thought that the school had "fulfilled its function when it has supplied the simplest rudiments of reading, writing, and number."[24]

This attitude toward academic learning appears to be based in the realities of traditional rural life. Literacy was considered important, but the skills necessary to earn a living were best learned at home, in the corn field or the woodlot, near the fishing boats or the mine. The need for children to be at home, both for training and for labor, set a limit on the length of the school year in rural areas, and further limited academic achievement. As late as 1936, schoolchildren in rural areas attended school for an average of 132.4 days, while urban children stayed in their classrooms for an average of 156.9 days a year.[25] Rural parents could not afford to do without their children during certain crucial months, and they had the political power, through their local school boards, to make their needs the basis of policy.

To the rural community, moral training was a more important school function than the development of advanced academic skills. Rural parents expected the school to reinforce and extend the moral training of the home. Behavioral expectations were rigid, and punishment was quick and physical; a teacher who could not maintain community standards by force or wit rarely lasted beyond his first contract.[26] These policies were evidently effective. In 1918, Charles Lewis found that children from the small rural schools gained higher teacher ratings than town children on character traits such as "obedience to school authority," "application to study," "purpose in life," and "honesty and truthfulness." While Lewis' study did not employ rigorous methodology or controls, it does indicate how town-based high school teachers perceived their rural and town-reared students.[27]

One reason for the consistently strong development of certain character traits in rural children may have been the remarkable continuity of moral training within the community. Rural communities tended to be culturally homogeneous. This did not mean that all rural citizens were of the same ethnic stock—the makeup of America's rural population was, and is, as diverse as that of the cities. Rather, this meant that rural people generally shared with their neighbors a common set of values and common expectations for what should be taught to their children. The country schoolteacher, having the same background, shared that common set of values. The expectations of teachers, children, and the dominant portion of the community formed a seamless mold which shaped and protected the moral and valuative development of the next generation of rural citizens.

This kind of cultural continuity rarely existed outside the rural community. In the cities, the flood of immigrants and rapid population expansion dictated a certain kind of schooling and determined a special attitude toward education. Teachers were, almost invariably, culturally different from their pupils and felt obliged not to reinforce the values of the parents, but to alter them. The urban school never acted adequately as an instrument of the melting pot, where a variety of cultures would come together to be merged in a unique "American way." However, it was a myth in which many believed and upon which much school policy was based.

Rural and urban schools met different individual needs and fulfilled different community functions. In the cities, schools—like other public services—became increasingly differentiated, specialized, and separated from the personal lives of citizens. Urban schools developed vocational programs and college-preparation tracks, training for the handicapped, and literacy programs for the foreign-born.[28] The "Americanization" process extended to moral training and the establishment of new behavioral expectations. In the countryside, however, communities remained small, homogeneous, and relatively stable. Rural people continued to expect their schools to fulfill one important, but small, role in a relatively unspecialized and undifferentiated manner. The impetus to make the rural school take on more community tasks, to fulfill roles traditionally left to the churches and the family, came from outside the community and was urged by individuals who did not recognize the very basic differences in function between the urban and rural schools.

The Rural School Today—What Remains?

Despite the substantial success of consolidators, many rural schools today have much in common with their turn-of-the-century counterparts. Few of the one-room schools remain, but the unalterable circumstances of rural life and the traditional attitudes of many rural people have maintained some of the unique characteristics of country education within the suburban red-brick walls of newer schools. Rural communities have not gotten richer over the last century, nor have the problems of isolation and low-population density been ameliorated by the steady outflow of people from the countryside to the cities. Television and the interstate highway system have brought the rural resident in closer touch with the world outside his community, but the insularity of country life and the long-standing suspicion of outsiders have limited the impact of cosmopolitan influences.

Rural communities are still basically homogeneous, stable, and traditional, and rural schools remain essentially an expression of community life. According to a national Gallup Poll, 43 percent of the residents of small communities felt that their school board represented their views; only 32 percent of big city dwellers felt the same. Further, fully 91 percent of the small community residents were ready to express an opinion about the quality of their schools.[29] Rural residents continue to feel both a right and an obligation to interest themselves in school policy; Gallup found that 43 percent of the small community respondents could name a recent action of their school board, while only 25 percent of the large city residents could do the same.[30] A recent Utah study by Ivan Muse, Robert Parsons, and Edward Hoppe reports similar levels of interaction; their teacher-respondents say that parents are more cooperative in rural areas, although 56 percent also feel that they are "watched more closely than are teachers elsewhere."[31]

Unlike urban school boards, which must rely on the superintendent's office to make the unending, complex decisions involved in running a multimillion dollar operation, country school boards typically involve themselves in decisions that affect daily life in the school. In smaller districts, the school board routinely interviews candidates for teaching positions, helps to select basic curriculum, and has the final vote on grouping patterns within classrooms. Administrators and teachers influence these decisions to an ever-increasing degree, as workingclass parents feel less and less able to comprehend professional educational jargon. But the rural school board remains very close to the community and to the inner workings of the school.

Teachers in the small rural school remain accountable to the community in ways virtually unimaginable in cities and suburbs, where they tend to be viewed as specialists whose personal lives are separate from those of their students' families. Rural teachers still tend to come from the communities in which they teach (or from communities so like them as to be indistinguishable).[32] Practical considerations of distance and housing availability generally compel them to live near their schools. Thus, the role of teacher remains important to the community outside the classroom as well as in it. As a 1940 editorial in *The County Superintendent of Schools* suggests:

> the sincere and conscientious teacher . . . realizes that even a casual conversation with the grocer has educational significance and that in his classroom are thirty little reporters ready and anxious to carry home the news to a willing audience of adults who will relay that news to every corner of the community.[33]

To find job satisfaction as a rural teacher, it is apparently necessary for a person to fit comfortably into this broadened and comparatively unspecialized role. Muse, Hoppe, and Parsons found that teachers from rural backgrounds were most able to do this. They conclude that "the most dissatisfied rural teachers tend to have been raised in urban areas,"[34] and that those same teachers tend to find "social acceptance more difficult"[35] in the country community.

The Utah evidence seems to suggest that the rural schoolteacher is still typically the rural born-and-reared woman, returning home to teach the next generation. She is far better educated than her turn-of-the-century counterpart and is far more likely to have seen some of the world, but she has remained in touch with the basic concerns and values of the rural community. This kind of teacher will help to maintain cultural continuity between home and school, and she will feel comfortable in pursuing this end.

Teaching and reinforcing community standards continue to be the dominant tasks of the rural school. Schooling is still considered critically important; Muse, Hoppe, and Parsons found more teachers than parents who felt it was more important for children to be home at choretime than to be spending additional time in school. The emphasis is still on basic academics and behavior training. In *Small Town Teacher*, Gertrude McPherson writes a description of the Adams School that could as well have been written in 1850 or 1915 as in the early 1970s:

> The Adams teacher was frequently made aware of one parental expectation for her behavior, the expectation that she should be a strict disciplinarian with little humor or flexibility, but with the capacity to keep order and allow no nonsense. . . . The important subjects . . . seemed to be penmanship, reading, arithmetic drill, and spelling; other subjects drew little comment or interest.[36]

The Muse, Hoppe, and Parsons research found similar attitudes among a somewhat broader group of parents. Their study shows that "a sizable proportion of students (38 percent) and parents (30 percent) tend to support the statement that teachers hold too high expectations of the students."[37] Very few of their parent-respondents, however, agreed with the statement, "The schools are too strict." Obedience, discipline, and fundamental skills are central to contemporary rural education; the broad range of social and scientific studies so dear to the suburban schools are viewed with some suspicion in the rural areas.

It is hardly surprising that rural communities have retained their longstanding attitudes toward schools and schooling. Rural political conservatism and cultural homogeneity both encourage the maintenance of stable traditions. It is surprising that professional educators and policymakers have done so little to use this strong traditional structure as a base for rural school reform. Consolidators have been so enamored with suburban facilities and programs that they have tried to simply eliminate the small country school rather than attempting to build it into a unique and effective educational model.

The Virtues and Limitations of the Traditional Rural School

To create an effective model for a small rural school, it would first be necessary to analyze the strengths and weaknesses of the existing institutions. Here we encounter immediate difficulty. Much has been written—in either a revisionist or a romantic vein—about the glories of the little red schoolhouse. However, more facts and figures have been gathered to promote the economic and academic virtues of consolidation. Rigorous comparisons between large and small rural schools, controlled for social class and other important variables, are few and far between, and relatively unbiased studies of country schools as they operate today are virtually unobtainable. Some statistics are available, on comparative academic achievement in small schools and large, and in rural schools compared to urban and suburban ones, but the existing statistics tend to be so broad and undifferentiated that it is difficult to distinguish effects of social class, student motivation, and other possibly important variables.

Part of the weakness in the research on small rural schools appears to be in the attitudes of many researchers. Money and talent in the education profession have not exactly flocked to the study of small rural schools. As Jonathan Sher points out:

> Though more than fourteen million students are dispersed among over ten thousand independent rural school districts, only the scantiest professional attention is accorded

to solving their problems or fulfilling their potential. There is *no* Bureau or Division of Rural Education in the U.S. Office of Education, the National Institute of Education, or the great majority of State Education Agencies. The National Education Association devotes only one-eighth of one individual's time to rural educational concerns. The National Center for Educational Statistics doesn't issue reports or compile data on the current status of rural education. . . . Needless to say, it is difficult to correct deficiencies or foster improvements in school systems which the education profession seems determined to ignore.[38]

Much of the research that does exist seems to be devoted to proving that small rural schools have defects (which they certainly do), and thus must be abandoned as quickly as possible. These studies emphasize the disadvantages of small schools while ignoring their strengths and their areas of potential growth.[39] In the mind of the professional consolidator, this approach makes sense. There is no point in doing close and differentiated studies of an institution you hope to eliminate. After all, no reasonable contractor would set out to renovate a house over which the wrecker's ball was already swinging.

Despite the negative attitude toward small rural schools among educational policymakers and researchers, it is possible to piece together a partial picture of the strengths and limitations of country schools. Some solid and relevant research that has a bearing on rural school issues has been done in related fields. Insights can be gleaned from the unsystematic and even biased reports of some rural writers. And a few high-quality studies and projects have been completed that add some concrete data to the image. It is from this eclectic array of sources that our picture is drawn.

The strengths of the small rural school have traditionally stemmed partially from its size and partially from its place in the rural community. Small unit size is much prized in educational circles (except when applied to rural community schools). When parents consider spending thousands of dollars on a private school education for a child, school and class size is frequently a critical factor; and when gifted children, handicapped adults, or potential Air Force pilots need special training, the first step is generally to place them in small groups. Mrs. Yost, of the Pleasant Prairie School, may have been more aware of her limitations than her virtues, but she knew that she could devote more time to each of her seven pupils than a teacher of thirty children could ever spend, even if the larger group were matched for everything from reading level to hobbies.

Further, while individualization enhances instruction, small unit size appears to have a good effect on intragroup solidarity and morale. Educational policy advisors as diverse as James Coleman and B. F. Brown recommend a reduction in school size as an answer to student alienation.[40] Susan Abramowitz, reporting on the Alum Rock voucher school experiment, notes that teachers in the small mini-schools have substantially fewer interpersonal and organizational problems than do teachers in the larger units.[41]

Considerable research on small group dynamics supports the contention that small groups function more smoothly than large ones. Small groups are more cohesive and less prone to conflict than larger ones.[42] They are more homogeneous in both behavior and beliefs.[43] Members of small groups fulfill a wider variety of functions within the group while members of larger groups tend to specialize; further, each small group member tends to do more, and on a more equal basis, than do members of larger units.[44]

These research findings would appear to be as valid in the classroom as in the laboratory. Small schools have widely recognized advantages for children as individuals. In the small school, the teacher knows each child as an individual and can make special provisions for special needs and talents. Children interact frequently and informally with the teacher and with each other.[45] According to Kevin Swick, small classes focus more on the "positive capabilities of the child," judging work according to individualized criteria rather than in response to some mass measure.[46]

Small schools, like small groups, are also easier to manage. The administrative policy decisions that absorb endless time and energy in large schools do not exist in smaller settings. Individual problems remain individual and do not require uniform regulations which apply to the whole group. No one worried about lines or lavatory passes at Pleasant Prairie; it would be ludicrous to do so in a school four times that size. In *High School*, Fred Wiseman brilliantly documents the tense struggle for power between a mass of students and a mass of administrators in a large urban high school. This combat need not exist in small school settings.

The group dynamics studies have found that in small groups members participate more than they would in large groups. This seems to be true in small schools as well. Although consolidators argue that the large school can offer a wider variety of courses and extracurricular activities, thus encouraging increased student participation, some of the most respectable research in rural education suggests that the opposite may be true. Barker and Gump's classic study *Big School, Small School* found that more students participated in more activities in small schools than in large ones and that more of them felt critically important to the success of their group activities.[47] Leonard L. Baird adapted that study to test the hypothesis on a larger sample: 3 percent of the 712,000 students who took the American College Testing Program tests. His findings substantially support Barker and Gump's, especially, he says, "the most important prediction of their theory—that the extent and level of student participation would be higher in small high schools."[48]

Participation is an important educative tool in its own right. In the community-involved rural schools, it can become a solid basis for the development of self-esteem. In Pleasant Prairie, ten-year-old David Lovejoy remembered the school Christmas program, which eighty people attended, as "the most fun he has ever had in school. *Everybody was there.*"[49] It is impossible to recreate this sense of total participation in large schools, with their A teams and B teams, and their tryouts for coveted parts in the school play. The most talented may thrive on the competition, but the great majority of students are obviously and inherently left out or left behind.

The virtues of smallness are relatively easy to document. The objective data are sparser when we turn to the advantages brought to small schools by their existence in rural areas. Much of the literature on this subject is highly subjective and based on the writers' personal experiences. However, it is possible to make some tentative statements about the virtues of small schools in rural settings by extrapolating from those data that are generally believed to be true.

The traditional intertwining of rural school and rural community augments some of the more general advantages of smallness. One suburban (Montgomery County, Maryland) study, which ultimately favored consolidation, noted that small schools are able to "provide a 'family atmosphere' in which teachers can know all of the children in the school and many of their parents and develop close, supportive relationships with both groups."[50] In the country, where the teacher is far more likely to be a member of the community than in the suburbs and where the teacher-role is more broadly defined, this effect will be enhanced.

Other benefits that flow naturally from the rural situation are not as obvious. Some observers suggest that the rural community suffers from its isolation and cultural homogeneity; Rogers and Svenning say that rural teachers tend to be "limited cosmopolites," as are their students.[51]

However, rural schools provide a kind of *heterogeneity* rarely found in urban or suburban settings—heterogeneity of *social class*. Most central city schools serve primarily poor, working class, and minority students. If remnants of the white middle class remain in them, they are generally tracked separately and have little contact with their poorer peers. Suburbs are almost universally middle or upper-middle class; their homogeneity is even more monolithic than urban schools. But in the country, low population density compels everyone to go to school together. The middle-class parent who is dissatisfied with the quality of the school rarely has access to a parochial or private school option. The principal faced with a troubled or disruptive child cannot simply send him someplace else. The child of the doctor shares a classroom and a playground with the children of farmers or loggers. Differences in educational aims thus must be worked out in the context of a common school.

This mixing of socioeconomic groups can have an extremely salutary effect. First, it cements the traditional sense that the entire community is involved in the school. Second, it compels the different social groups in the rural community to come to terms with one another at an early age and on a comparatively equal basis. Both these circumstances contribute to the stability of the rural community and to its remarkable internal communications network.

This long list of the virtues of traditional rural schools is not meant to suggest that country schools have been without problems. Most of the ancient, peeling buildings deplored by Cubberley and Betts are gone now, and even the tiniest schools have more materials than the average rural school of earlier decades. Still, there are several tasks that the small rural school has not tended to perform well, and there are some problems with the country setting that the isolated rural school will be hard-pressed ever to overcome.

Ironically, some of the major problems of rural schools are the inverse of their virtues. The close-knit relationship between home and school, so lavishly praised earlier in this chapter, has some built-in liabilities. Some teachers use their familiarity with the community and their own broad role definition to the advantage of their pupils. For example, one teacher might use her influence and information to assist the little Brown boy in making a difficult transition into the first grade. But another teacher might use the same power and knowledge to prejudge a child and to convince everyone (including the child's parents) that "No Brown ever passes the first grade the first time." One writer says that the latter reaction was the most common one in the school she studied. "The teacher . . . did not feel surprised when such a child defied her, 'What can you expect? He is a Wingdale; they are all like that.' "[52]

The problem of prejudgment is not necessarily a problem of poor or insensitive teaching. As the work of Robert Rosenthal and Lenore Jackson suggests, teachers generally tend to develop sets of expectations about their students, and these expectations have powerful effects on academic achievement and self-concept.[53] This is true even in cities, where a child's home life is likely to be entirely separate from his life at school, giving him at least one alternative arena in which to develop a positive self-concept. In the country, where the school, the home, and the community are closely tied, the self-fulfilling prophecy is even more likely to form (or warp) a child's self-concept. For the child who embodies the positive values of the community, teacher expectations are likely to have a positive effect. For the lower-class child, or the child whose family does not conform to the local norms, teacher expectations can cement a negative sense of self.

The close ties between school and community can put unpleasant pressures on teachers as well as children. The Muse, Hoppe, and Parsons survey reports that teachers find "community cliques, gossip, and small-town talk,"[54] one of the chief drawbacks to country teaching. Those little messengers ready to spread the good classroom word from one end of the community to the other can be pernicious as well.

The most frequent and serious rural school problem usually cited in the literature is a lack of creative and innovative teaching. Critics often argue, as do Rogers and Svenning, that:

> Many [rural] school systems are pockets of traditionalism, with norms operating against change and innovation.

> When the innovation decisions lie primarily with the tradition-oriented power structure, individual innovativeness (as well as system innovativeness) can be effectively stifled.[55]

The issue of innovation in rural schools is complex and cannot be simply laid at the feet of rural political conservatism and social tradition. In fact, there is some evidence suggesting that rural communities are far more interested in educational innovation than is commonly assumed. Paul Ford's study of small high schools found students yearning for more intellectual stimulation and greater access to new resources.[56] Similarly, Muse, Hoppe, and Parsons found parents, administrators, teachers, and students in strong agreement that their schools needed "innovative teachers with new methods more than additional 'traditional' teachers."[57]

Clearly, community resistance does not account fully for the slow rate of rural innovation. The professional education establishment and the commercial curriculum designers must share in that responsibility. The educational policymakers have generally been too busy working out the politics and economics of consolidation to attend to the improvement of small rural schools. For example, Paul Ford, whose association with rural education programs in the Northwest might indicate some support for small-scale education, begins his section on "The Potential" of small schools by suggesting that as many as possible be eliminated. He argues:

> Each state must develop its own criteria for assigning a high school to the "remote and necessary" category. Schools which do not meet the criteria should be encouraged with all possible means to effect consolidation. Where necessary, state aid to such schools should be withdrawn.[58]

Teacher training programs have paid equally little attention to the needs of teachers in small rural schools. Although the literature is full of moaning about the poor quality of rural teachers,[59] little systematic effort has been made to recruit the best people for rural schools, and even less effort has been made to train them properly. As Muse, Hoppe, and Parsons point out:

A recent study of university offerings revealed that in 1969,

no more than six universities in the nation offered courses
which might be of any prospective value specifically to the
rural teacher.[60]

The training gap is being gradually closed, as the meager efforts of
universities are supplemented by regional centers and in-service
training programs. However, the amount of professional support
given the rural teacher by state departments of education or colleges
and universities will not compare with that given the urban and
suburban teacher for many years to come.

Most rural teachers, then, enter their classrooms with little or no
special preparation for meeting the needs of country children. And,
unlike the urban or suburban teacher, they cannot call on professionally designed commercial materials to help them. For fifteen years,
curriculum developers have undertaken countless projects for urban
children, ranging from Sesame Street to minority-oriented social
studies curricula for the high schools. For twenty years, carefully
designed suburban curriculum packages have been available. During
the same period, virtually nothing has been done for the rural child.
There is no profit in it for the publishing companies because there are
fewer absolute numbers in rural areas, and there is less similarity
among country regions than there is among cities. Unfortunately,
philanthropic and governmental funding sources have not (with some
notable exceptions) made up for this lack of commercial interest in
rural education. As a result, the teacher looking for innovative
materials for a class of suburban or urban children has a vast array to
choose from; a teacher looking for similar resources for a group of
poor country pupils must generally be resigned to teaching about fire
hydrants, manicured lawns, skyscrapers, and other accoutrements of
life in metropolitan America.

Even if the teacher has the resourcefulness to design rural-oriented
materials alone, there are problems to be faced. The characteristic
poverty of rural areas has traditionally tightened the bond between
community and school. The in-kind contributions that replaced the
outlay of money brought the consumers of education nearer to its
source and added to the sense of accountability and responsibility.
Today, however, the needs of schools are so complex and require so
much money and expertise that community contributions fill less of
the gap. The poor school district cannot afford to hire a science
consultant to design a curriculum around their woodland. Usually,

they cannot even afford to buy teachers the time to do it themselves.

Some extraordinary teachers do it anyway. They take the time out of their personal lives and collect materials from the community and from the natural resources of the countryside. But many teachers do not have this creative energy, and they struggle along with outdated textbooks and inappropriate materials which are all that is available to most rural community schools.

Although there are many barriers to innovation in rural schools, they are not insuperable. The conservative and thrifty rural school board must be convinced that a program or curriculum is both educationally valid and worth the cost before they will commit themselves to it. But, once convinced, "small and rural schools are in a unique position to gain community support for innovative programs," as Rogers and Svenning note.[61]

Other problems inherent in rural schools are less complex to define, if not less difficult to resolve. Programs to assist children with special needs are rarely adequate in the country school. If a child needs extra help with reading, the rural teacher may well have an easier time setting up a cooperative home/school tutoring program. But if the child is blind, or crippled, or retarded, the typical small, rural school cannot readily provide for him. In the Muse, Hoppe, and Parsons study, there are few items on which there is as much agreement as the statement "rural schools are largely unprepared to deal with physical and mental handicaps."[62]

Special services are a problem in small schools everywhere, but they take on heightened significance in rural settings. Parents of handicapped children in metropolitan areas can call on resources beyond the local public school; in the countryside, the parents must make do with the available academic setting unless they have the money and the inclination to send the child away.

Small schools can limit normal children as well as those with special needs. Obviously, there are fewer faculty members in a small school than in a large one. In a one-room schoolhouse, a child risks exposure to only one teacher for an entire elementary education. This is inherently limiting, even if the teacher is gifted and flexible. If the teacher is boring or cruel, school can become a chamber of horrors with no prospect of respite. David Tyack quotes a boy in a nineteenth century one-room school who "wrote in the flyleaf of his textbook,'11 weeks will never go away/never never never never never.'"[63] If eleven weeks were instead eight years, virtually any option would seem inviting. Today, there are few one-room schools left, and in most of them teacher turnover replaces the changing classrooms of larger schools. But even in two- or three-room schools, a poor teacher, or a teacher who has a personality conflict with a child, can greatly reduce satisfactions (if not achievement) over a two- or three-year period.

Teachers who must handle multiple grades are limited as well. Depth of preparation is difficult, especially in a variety of subject areas, for instructors who must teach every period. One study of small high schools in Washington State found that:

> Teachers in small schools studied average between five and six preparations in different subject areas each day. It is unrealistic to suppose that a teacher could be adequately prepared in this number of subjects and, in addition, keep up with curriculum development in all the subjects.[64]

Mrs. Yost, the Pleasant Prairie, Nebraska, teacher, voices the same concern. "If I can at least hit the top of a subject," she says, "they won't be awed by it when they come to it again."[65] But she feels inadequate to the task of teaching all subjects to all grades every day.

Many of the problems discussed above are true of small schools anywhere. However, in small *rural* schools, these problems are exacerbated by isolation and a poor institutional self-image. Students and teachers in small urban schools have a sense of options and access to the myriad resources unique to metropolitan areas. Further, teachers and families who choose a small school in the city have usually made a positive choice. Most small urban schools are private, which means that parents must be sufficiently committed to their principles to pay for them, and teachers must find enough job satisfaction in them to sacrifice the higher pay of the public schools. Ready access to external resources and the sense of voluntary commitment to smallness both reduce the effects of the small school's inherent limitations.

Many rural communities with a small school feel the same sense of voluntary commitment to that educational model. That is, they would opt for small schools even if larger ones were readily available. But, in other rural areas, the teachers, the students, and the community have bought the consolidators' message: small is backward, small is poor, small is decrepit. The nineteenth century little red schoolhouse did not have much to offer in the way of modern amenities, but it often was the pride of the community. Today, after 100 years of authoritative pronouncements from professors and state department of education officials, this traditional pride is threatened, if not entirely dissipated. The barrage of articles and speeches that suggest that all rural school problems are a function of smallness has taken its toll in rural communities.[66] Districts that have maintained their small schools in the face of all this expertise feel at best, defensive, and at worst, ashamed of being out-of-date and out-of-touch with the mainstream of American culture.

Unfortunately, once everyone in the rural community "knows" that small schools are inadequate, it does not take them long to become so. Parents come to believe, like James Richardson of Pleasant Prairie, that "the kids are missing too much," and then communicate that feeling to their children. Bright young teachers, emerging from training programs where they have been taught that larger schools are superior, will seek employment in big schools, leaving those who could not "do better" to staff the smaller schools. And the community in general learns that its school is a professional way station.[67]

Muse, Hoppe, and Parsons found that a high percentage of teachers, parents, and administrators agreed with the statement: "Rural teachers often use their positions to make a living until more attractive positions are available."[68] It becomes apparent that self-fulfilling, negative prophecies are as potent in the community and the profession as they are in the classroom itself.

The negative image of the small, rural school which has been sold to country communities is often debilitating. Small schools, for better or worse, are absolutely necessary in some rural areas. Even the most impassioned consolidators know that small schools, like death and taxes, will always be with us. Most educators would have no reservations about the statement: "There are and will continue to be remote, necessary high schools which cannot be consolidated. Climate, topography, and distance are the main deterrents to effective consolidation."[69] It is difficult to maintain that consolidation is in the "child's best interests" if that child spends five hours a day on a bus. Since these "remote but necessary schools" must continue to exist, something must be done for them other than telling them how inadequate they are.

Yet, even where climate or geography do not ensure smallness, the small school has refused to die. After nearly a century of propaganda, there are still numerous rural communities who want to retain control over their children's education and who feel that the small, local school is the only way to guarantee this end. The recent movements in education toward back-to-basics, flexible scheduling, and accountability have given legitimacy to the strongly held beliefs of rural school boards and their constituencies. In some communities, the influx of suburban refugees, who can cite the currently fashionable reforms and who know the flaws in the suburban model, has given added weight to the arguments of local small school proponents.

Within the local rural communities, the defenders of small schools have different motives. Some are old-line educational traditionalists, some are rural revisionists, and some are fiscal conservatives. Each of these groups has a different definition of what "good education" is in rural areas, but all agree that "good" schooling is based in meeting the specific needs of rural communities and drawing on their specific strengths, rather than attempting to replicate the schools of Beverly Hills and Scarsdale.

Small School Improvement and Reform—
Some Recent Projects

Although the preponderance of research and theorizing during the past century has been in the service of consolidation, rural communities that want to maintain small schools, and those who must maintain them whether they like it or not, have not been totally without assistance from professional educators. Particularly during the last ten years, there has been an increase in the number of projects designed to improve small schools rather than to eliminate them, and the number seems likely to increase as the mobile middle class continues to desert the cities and suburbs for the small towns and open countryside.[70] The tradition in modern social science is for research fashion to follow the interests of the intellectual and academic middle classes. In the 1960s, research followed these interests into the reclaimable neighborhoods of the inner city; in the 1980s, it seems likely that it will follow them into the Sun Belt and other rural reaches.

The small schools projects have followed a number of models, each with its own advantages and defects. One early model, which persists, in part because of its ease in implementation, is the college-based small school improvement project. One of the most widely known of these was the Rural School Improvement Project (RSIP) sponsored by Berea College in eastern Kentucky from 1953 to 1957. This project, financed by the Fund for the Advancement of Education, tackled one of the most problem-ridden rural areas in the country—the central Appalachian region surrounding the Great Smoky Mountains. This area is precisely the kind educators think about when they invent such categories as "remote but necessary schools." The difficulties of transportation through the hills and hollows require the continuation of many small schools. The incredible poverty of the region largely preordains their poor condition. Someone who wanted to see what it was that Cubberley et al. had against nineteenth century small schools in poor communities could find it in what the college calls Berea Territory.

Berea, as a teacher-training college, the majority of whose pupils come from Appalachia, had a healthy self-interest in improving small schools. Many of its graduates would teach in those schools and needed training in the kinds of problems they would encounter in them. In the project's report, Berea's president, Francis S. Hutchings, writes:

> Our college students preparing to be teachers [needed] to understand how to get the fire started on a cold morning, how to protect the children's health against illness caused by mud and water on impassable roads, how to create an atmosphere conducive to learning, and how to teach and promote learning on the part of the child.[71]

The RSIP began with a commitment to community participation in the project and an awareness that improvement in education had to be only one component in a total effort to improve the quality of life in mountain communities. The Berea teaching fellows who participated in the project were required to work in the community as well as in the school, and to shore up, rather than tear down, the traditional school-community cooperative structure.

Communities were chosen to participate in the RSIP by need, proximity to Berea, and the willingness of the superintendent and county school board to participate. Ultimately, thirty-eight different communities and their schools were assigned teams of experienced teachers and inexperienced teaching fellows who worked in the school and community with the guidance of area supervisors.

The teams worked with parent groups to define project goals and to involve community members in school projects. These generally began with the most obvious and pressing needs—usually renovation of tattered school buildings—and moved on into more abstract policy and curricular issues. According to the RSIP report, by 1957:

> Each of the project schools has now had a "face-lifting," which may be new paint inside, or other physical improvements. Nearly all of the work has been done by parents with the help of the students and teachers, with money from the school board or raised by themselves. . . . These cooperative projects have family and community values far beyond the schools themselves.[72]

From the evidence of the evaluation committee, the Berea RSIP was quite successful. It is hardly surprising that the volunteer communities were pleased, since they acquired substantial free and well-trained school aides, teachers, and supervisors. But the evaluators felt that the benefit went well beyond the individual schools involved.

> The Project School has been used as a demonstration center for the county teachers for four years. It has meant a great deal to the teachers directly involved and has helped improve teacher practices in the county as a whole.[73]

The Berea RSIP appears to have avoided the most obvious pitfalls of college-based school improvement projects. The Berea people committed themselves to working with the community values and mountain traditions rather than trying to "elevate" the concerns of the parents and school boards. The area supervisors went to the schools (often over horrendous roads, vividly pictured in the Report book) rather than insisting that all participants travel to them. The RSIP planners concentrated on the school as a part of the community and the culture rather than trying to isolate the purely academic processes.

There are, nevertheless, some questions about all college-based projects, even the most sensitive and successful. The first is the question of permanence. The Berea RSIP brought massive infusions of relatively sophisticated people to isolated mountain villages. Sheer personpower and the impact of the educational establishment were bound to make some changes. How many of them, however, were likely to remain? This was a concern of the RSIP planners, who devoted an entire chapter of their report to permanent contributions. They concluded that the enthusiasm of the retrained teachers and the curricular innovations just *had* to last, because people were so excited about them. But those who have watched college-based innovative programs come and go in urban schools, leaving behind them only a few pieces of battered equipment and some bulging file drawers, cannot comfortably share that confidence. A follow-up study of the RSIP schools twenty years later would be illuminating, but remains, as yet, undone.

A second problem with college-based programs is that they usually depend on theoretical conceptions which come from outside the communities served. Parents and school boards were consulted in the Berea Project, but they depended for ideas, leadership, and supervision on the Berea-trained staff. In a sense, this too is a permanence issue, because it involves balancing local independence with a dependence on outsiders. How long do most teachers retain and use ideas that came initially from the outside? We simply do not know.

Finally, there is a question of who is served. Schools were chosen for the RSIP according to need, but proximity to Berea College was an equally critical factor. There is a tendency for college-based programs to serve the rural area nearest them for obvious reasons of convenience. Unfortunately, the twenty-mile radius around a college or university is likely to be comparatively overprivileged; it has an extra job market, a larger number of middle-income citizens, and it is usually the focus of social concern among students and faculty alike. This is not a problem specific to rural areas. New Haven, Connecticut, and Cambridge, Massachusetts, must be two of the most overstudied and over-volunteer-aided communities in the United States. Still, the fact remains that rural college-based programs rarely touch the communities that are most isolated and that, perhaps, most need such contact with the outside world.

There are problems with college- and other externally based improvement programs, but they have their merits as well. They bring academic expertise to schools unlikely to get consulting help any other way. They make the academics more aware of the real conditions in schools and communities. And some of them provide specific training unavailable elsewhere. The Alaska Rural Schools Project, for example, prepares teachers in schools so remote that they can only be reached by air. The Texas Small Schools Project has developed a program of in-service training for experienced teachers in 140 small rural schools. These, and many other outside-agency projects, fill important needs for specialized teacher-training. As long as it is not believed that they are all that is necessary, they are useful.

A second major model for small school improvement is based on proposals from rural school systems themselves. These have been funded by both government agencies and foundations in an effort to encourage local school districts to conceptualize and implement their own reform projects. One of the most important of these is the Experimental Schools Program (ESP), federally financed and administered by the National Institute of Education. According to the ESP evaluation report:

> the Experimental Schools Program was conceived as a mechanism by which school districts—in this case small school districts, serving rural areas—could, under federal contract, assess their own needs and objectives and plan and implement comprehensive programs to accomplish them.[74]

The emphases in the ESP projects were on diversity and change. The planners believed that each rural small school innovation had to be specifically tailored to the needs of its community—that there was no potential "one best system" for rural schools. At the same time, they believed that most small, rural schools needed to be encouraged to innovate—that productive change would not magically emanate from stable and sometimes stagnant places.

The ESP projects were selected from applications submitted by interested school districts. Projects were chosen by local need and apparent significance of the proposed project. One-year planning grants were awarded to pay for the development of rough ideas into concrete objectives and plans, usually with some technical consultation.

ESP funded a wide variety of projects, ranging from in-service curriculum development for Alaskan teachers to an early childhood program in Mississippi. All were elaborately and separately evaluated in terms of their own goals, although the evaluation format was standardized to allow some cross-site comparisons.

The local-initiative model has several advantages that the college-based programs lack. It allows the community and the school to determine their own most pressing needs, without massive outside interventions. The process of application and project development can give the small, rural school some expertise in grantsmanship—a valuable skill usually restricted to the rich suburban and urban districts. And, the final product belongs to the school and the community in a way that few externally devised or externally implemented projects could legitimately claim.

There are, of course, disadvantages as well. The local-initiative project may suffer from the narrow focus of its proponents. People enmeshed in a situation often become too involved to see major issues clearly and sometimes attack the wrong problem or the right problem at the wrong level. Country people add to this general tendency the special problems of rural insularity and conservatism. But high levels of innovative creativity might well be less important in rural areas at the present time than small-scale, specifically tailored reforms which stem from the school and to which the community is committed. The local-initiative programs would appear to have a productive future.

A third model for small school improvement is the regional educational laboratory. These organizations, funded by the federal government, define their roles very differently. At least two have concerned themselves with issues of small school rural education: the Appalachian Educational Laboratory (AEL) and the Northwest Regional Educational Laboratory (NWREL). The AEL has done some of the most creative and imaginative work in rural education. Their Home-Oriented Preschool Education Program (HOPE) combines a Sesame Street-like television program, called "Around the Bend," with a mobile classroom unit and a home visitor program in a multiphase introduction to letters, numbers, and the world inside Appalachia as well as elsewhere. This program, which was subjected to extensive evaluation and comparison with standard preschool efforts, has been a great success. The television component is now being prepared for marketing, and the preschool program as a whole should serve a large group of children for whom such experiences have been traditionally inaccessible.

Since the success of Project HOPE, the AEL has turned to other carefully designed programs for the Appalachian schools, including a career decision-making package and an employer-based career education program. The career education materials are intended for use in a variety of school settings, but the programs are being tested in West Virginia at the present time.

The Northwest Regional Laboratory has taken another view of its appropriate role. While the AEL has concentrated on program development, the NWREL has committed itself to gathering information on rural innovative programs in a variety of curricular areas and making it available to other small, rural schools. The result has been the *Promising Practices* series, which reports on locally generated innovations in early childhood education, career education, small high schools, and the like. The NWREL series focuses on practical reforms that can be implemented without extensive outside support. As one of the *Promising Practices* booklets notes, the NWREL feels that "small rural high schools need creative and inexpensive ways to provide a wider range of experiences for students."[75]

The regional laboratories serve an important intermediate function in small, rural school reform. While the college-based programs are inevitably limited in scope and in dissemination, the regional laboratories can serve as more general clearinghouses, conveying appropriate information and ideas around their region. Further, regional laboratories have an exclusive commitment to research and development, which no responsible college can maintain. The large government programs, like the major foundation projects, tend to be grand in scope, but are less likely to understand nuances of specific local needs and practices. The work of regional laboratories cannot stand alone, but they can contribute significantly to the small school improvement effort.

Two central themes run through most of the recent small school improvement projects. First, the rural community must be the basis for productive change. Second, good innovations in small, rural schools are rarely transferable directly to other parts of the country; changes must be tailored to the needs of the community and the region. Both of these themes reflect an understanding of both rural reality and the primacy of local circumstance—an understanding deeper than consolidators normally exhibited in urging sweeping national reforms. But this understanding brings with it an inherent danger.

Unquestionably, a reform that is unique to the individual small, rural school and that arises from the needs of its community is likely to be realistic, long-lasting, and effective. But it will not necessarily prepare young people to deal with the thorny questions of a complex and increasingly urbanized world. A central question remains: How can we maximize the benefits of rural cohesion and community feeling while minimizing the effects of sparse population and social insularity? How can we make small, rural schools into facilities that will provide their students with genuine options in their search for the good life—a life that can be flexible, satisfying, and unique?

Maximizing the Potential of Smallness

To begin to answer that question (and it would be foolhardy to try to do more than begin), we must first hammer out a new definition of "good education" for rural areas. "Good" cannot mean "the way it used to be" because the world and the job market prohibit that. And it cannot mean "more suburban" because that is clearly inappropriate for rural schools. "Good education" for rural areas must come to mean the invention and adaptation of ways to capitalize on the natural and traditional resources of the rural school, while clearly recognizing the limitations inherent in country living and attempting to compensate for them.

This definition requires that everyone involved with rural schools recognize two things: first, that there will continue to be problems in rural schools; and second, that it is probably better for rural schools to live with their own inherent problems than with problems artificially created by transplanting a suburban model.

If the potential of small rural schools is to be realized, there must be a reorientation of reform, from the monolithic effort to find a "one best system," which has dominated so much of American educational reform, to a more pluralistic conception of quality schooling. This pluralistic view will have to be shared by education professionals and community people if creative leadership and external funding are to be found because both leadership and outside money will be important to lasting small school improvement. Few nonprofessionals have access to the scattered and sometimes tangled research and curriculum development efforts in rural education. Additionally, it is probably impossible to make substantial improvements in underfinanced rural schools without using outside funding, at least to underwrite crucial and expensive equipment. If the same money and expertise that now goes into the consolidation movement were channeled instead into small school improvement, much could be usefully achieved.

High quality reform presupposes an understanding of some immutable facts of rural life. Certain circumstances and attitudes in rural areas are unlikely to be altered unless the countryside is made into something else. Low population density virtually requires busing. The length and duration of the ride can be manipulated by changing the size and location of schools, but the fact of travel remains and puts inevitable restrictions on extracurricular activities and an obvious burden on the town school budget. Low population density also brings with it substantial isolation of many children before they come to school. Efforts can be made to provide preschool socialization experiences for these children; other programs can ensure that older students come in contact, at least vicariously, with a wider variety of ethnic and cultural influences than they are likely to encounter in their own communities. However, the essential isolation and homogeneity of rural areas will not be fundamentally altered.

Similarly, unless oil is discovered under the pastures and corn fields, few rural communities can escape the pinch of poverty. In most rural areas, everything except labor costs more than it does in the metropolitan areas. Shipping costs of paper and other goods add to their price; buses face higher repair bills because they must travel many miles daily on unimproved roads. Often, smaller schools must swallow high costs for large multipurpose rooms, audio-visual equipment, permanent library collections, and other state-imposed requirements.

Cooperative efforts and plans for sharing resources can help to ease the financial strain on a community supporting a small school, but they cannot erase the fact that the small rural school is likely to remain a shoestring operation. In areas where there are a few large taxpayers, the problem is intensified. In some small, rural communities, five or six farmers pay a large proportion of the tax bill. In such places, the annual school budget becomes a balancing act—it must be high enough to meet minimal needs, but low enough not to drive Farmer Brown out of business and endanger the prospects of next year's budget.

Fiscal conservatism puts a brake on educational innovation in rural areas, and it merges with the social conservatism typical of country communities. As researchers found in the Experimental Schools Project,[76] rural communities tend to be suspicious of foreign intervention, and to view even the people in neighboring townships as foreigners. Rural communities tend to be great believers in the theory of "every tub on its own bottom" and are frequently reluctant to take federal funds to initiate new programs. "The government gives you money to start something—then goes off, leaving you holding the bag," one former school board member announced at a Vermont school board meeting. In communities working from marginal school budgets, that is too great a risk to take.

The unchanging aspects of rural life dictate certain basic thrusts for any successful reform of country schools: first, it must involve and reflect the community served; second, it must minimize the effects of isolation, poverty, and rural insularity; third, it must be rooted in an honest and open assessment of the future of that rural area. Successful country school reform must be adaptable, mobile, and supported by the community—otherwise, it is unlikely to last.

Successful rural school improvement will begin with the community as a resource, not as a barrier to overcome or as a difficult client to be won over. Many of the small school projects incorporated community support—frequently by involving the community in the refurbishment of school buildings. This is a useful place to start. The school plant is the most visible aspect of the rural school, and thus the easiest to focus on. It is also the aspect with which parents feel most comfortable. Many feel that they know a solid and attractive building when they see one, but feel less certain that they would recognize a first-rate curriculum or an appropriate piece of school equipment. The Berea RSIP found that involving the community in improving school buildings was a critical move in gaining more generalized support for its programs. It is a logical step for improvement elsewhere.

It is, however, only the first step. School reformers have tended to be eager for community aid in money-raising and plant improvement. They have been noticeably less enthusiastic about allowing local citizens to work on curriculum reform. Professional educators have a keen sense of "turf" and tend to consider the involvement of lay people in "professional decisions" as unwarranted interference. In many places, especially where the majority of the population are blue-collar workers, this perception has been accepted by the local citizens, who are intimidated by professional jargon and conflicting educational theories and fads. Many community people, therefore, only feel equipped to comment on curricular decisions when they believe that rights and obligations of the family are being violated. When community contributions to educational policy are limited to fights over sex education courses or the study of evolution, a substantial potential resource is cut off from the small rural school.

A community actively involved in shaping and implementing a school's curriculum can contribute to the solution of a major rural school problem: the limited number of teachers and school offerings. The rural school can call upon the traditional interconnection between school and community to provide a kind of variety rarely available in cities or suburbs—and at least as enriching, in different ways, as museum field trips and departmentalized third grades. Within even the small, homogeneous rural community there is a wide variety of skills, experiences, and memories. If the school can tap the traditional sense of community responsibility for the school, that wide range of people can be brought into the school to interact with the children, to teach, and to remember earlier times.

Foxfire-type studies and other oral history projects teach a wide variety of skills to children, while engaging them in work of value to the community and to their perception of themselves as country dwellers. In addition, rural areas are ideal sources of oral history, populated as they are by farmers, who can generally spare some time in the middle of the day; old people who feel alone with their memories; and local businesses whose owners might be convinced that their duty to the town lies in letting their employees contribute time to the schools and in letting the schoolchildren come to "learn the business."

The idea of using the community as an educational resource is hardly new. In Westminister West, Vermont, the public primary school is run by Claire Oglesby, Vermont Teacher of the Year in 1970, who is considered something of a miracle worker today. It is Mrs. Oglesby's theory that "If a person is to understand himself and his place in the world, the learning process must be freed from confining barriers and become integrated with the daily affairs of the people of all ages who are the community." Expending great measures of time and energy—but very little money—Claire Oglesby makes this theory work. Townspeople teach "sewing, baking, cooking, tumbling, art, music, foreign languages, photography, and drawing (the latter by a 78-year-old retired civil engineer, especially adored by the children, who had never thought of teaching until recruited by Mrs. Oglesby).["]77

The result is a greatly enriched small school and a community that feels involved with its school and responsible for it. Parents remodeled the school, hold bake sales and square dances to support it, use it as a public library and summer movie theater. Mrs. Oglesby considers her school to be a community school in the most traditional rural sense, and most of Westminister West seems to agree with that view.

This kind of community school is *only* possible in the small setting. If a school has 500 pupils, there are too many contacts to be made, too many permissions to be sought, too many arrangements to be set up. Many of the people involved with the Westminister West school are there because "Claire came and got me." They would have been unlikely to respond to the impersonal request of a large school's community relations specialist. The consistent, informal, personal interaction that Claire Oglesby maintains with her community could not be easily duplicated, even at great expense, in a city. Yet, the small, rural community school, with its access to the local grapevine and its capacity to serve as a gathering place for all citizens, is the natural setting for this kind of schooling.

If the small, rural school can come to treat the community as a resource, perhaps the community can begin again to treat the school as one. In the days of television, it is perhaps unworldly to think of a resurrection of the "Farmer's lyceums" of the nineteenth century, but the adults of rural communities do remain interested in community events and in continuing education. The success of the national Adult Basic Education movement indicates one area of potential school service to the community. The rise in interest nationally in traditional rural skills and crafts (quilting, gardening, canning) suggests that the school might become a center where the older members of the community could come to teach the younger adults. On a simpler level, the school building could be made available for community groups as a recreation hall, a card club center, and a meeting place for a variety of civic events. None of this necessarily adds directly to the quality of the third grade, but it does aid in the welding together of school and community interests. Such a move is ultimately in the best interests of rural education.

Minimizing the effects of rural isolation is a far easier task today than it would have been at the beginning of the consolidation movement. When Cubberley describes life in the country as "lonely, monotonous, and commonplace,"[78] and the rural child as a victim of cultural deprivation, he spoke in a time when neither mass communication nor easy travel was possible in most rural areas. The advent of television, of sophisticated telephone communication, of improved roads and automobiles may have reduced the cultural differentiation between city and country, but it has also reduced the amount of cultural isolation to which the rural child is subjected. Muse, Hoppe, and Parsons wrote:

> One of the hypotheses [tested in their study] was that rural students were culturally deprived, and that this might impose additional stress on the rural teacher. Several indices of cultural deprivation were studied: amount of television watching, amount of reading, number of vacations, amount of travel away from home. While deprivation may in fact exist in isolated instances, most rural students have more exposure in these areas than was suspected. The hypothesis of cultural deprivation does not seem acceptable for rural students in any significant number.[79]

If mass communications and ready travel have already made rural children relatively less culturally deprived than they used to be, these same tools can also be employed to reduce that margin further. If teachers can be trained to look beyond the limits of the community and the individual school for resources, and if those resources can be imported readily through the mediation of a regional agency, the children in small rural schools can come very close to the sophisticated level of cultural exposure of the best urban schools.

The importation of cultural resources to the rural school has been tried, in a variety of ways, across the country. The mechanisms by which resources are requested and delivered range from the most informal, school-based arrangements to very sophisticated cooperative efforts. Because of funding problems and because of the traditional reluctance of rural school districts to cooperate with one another, the more informal means are most common. But there is both precedent and plenty of room for state departments of education and other official agencies to promote and help develop more complex cooperatives and traveling resources.

Many of the small, school-based importation efforts appear to be quite successful. The report from the Rural School Improvement Project suggests that an informal visit from a group of foreigners provided the children of one Appalachian school with their first experience with people unlike themselves:

> After the departure of the group, the teacher was interested to know how much the pupils had learned about the geography of their visitors' country . . . [but] she was greatly amazed at their remark, repeated almost in unison, "Why didn't you tell us that they were *real people?*"[80]

The program problem in this instance was not one of getting foreign visitors to the Appalachian schools (Appalachia is an area of great interest to a wide variety of people), but of retraining teachers to make them aware of the plausibility and desirability of providing this kind of experience for mountain children who are unlikely to find it elsewhere.

Another evidently successful example of a small-scale program is the Student Exchange Program run by Hoonah High School in Hoonah, Alaska. The problems of cultural isolation for rural children in Alaska is perhaps the most acute in the nation, and the problems are more than intellectual. Many rural young people must go to the city to find work, and according to the Northwest Regional Laboratory's account of the program, "trying to adjust to the different living pace and cultural values often is too overwhelming, and the individual returns to his community without really learning how to cope with modern America."[81] One often-suggested solution to the problem is to ship all of the children from the very isolated native villages to central boarding schools in or near urban areas. But Alaskan communities are as attached to their local schools as are rural people elsewhere, and many parents are very reluctant to send their children away for high school. Hoonah High School tried another means of dealing with the problem of limited exposure; an exchange program with a high school in Juneau, the nearest city, provided two weeks of guided exposure to urban life for its students and two weeks of experience in a rural setting for high school students from Juneau.

The program's initiators feel that "it has proven to be a foolproof introduction to the urban setting and a confidence builder." In addition, they feel, "it has shown that stereotyping people because of their cultural identity is a poor practice."[82]

Both of these programs have involved the actual moving of bodies (student or visitor) from one culture to another. Vicarious experiences, through television and books, can be extremely useful as well. As we move into an era of videotape cassettes and seven-foot television screens, the cultural enrichment of rural schools will no longer need to depend on the proximity of television transmitters. Initial equipment investments will almost inevitably have to come from outside money. But once equipment is purchased, it will be as possible (and in many cases more possible) for the rural child to see Nureyev dance and Olivier act as it would be for the urban youngster. Indeed, if we can contemplate a future where two-way television is commonplace, it will be possible for long-distance instruction to take place in subjects outside the repertoire of small-school teachers.

The economical use of this kind of technology in small schools will require an increase in cooperative effort. Cooperatives, in fact, have as much to offer for small schools in the 1970s and 1980s as they did to farmers in earlier years. Small schools will never have the endowment of rich, private schools, nor the tax base of dense suburbs, so (in the absence of greatly expanded state aid) they will have to create an artificial population base to command the money and the demand for rich resources. Consolidated districts are one way to accomplish this; cooperatives provide another, less disruptive, model.

In Linn County, Oregon, for example, there were more than 30,000 items in the district media center in 1971. This quantity of materials, especially if carefully selected, is easily competitive with the resource centers of most school districts. The problem that arises with a group of small schools, rather than a single large one, is retrieval and delivery. Linn County addressed this problem by establishing a county-level computer-based retrieval system that would process requests and provide teachers with complete descriptions and selections of materials appropriate to a specific subject.[83] Given this kind of system, a teacher is enabled to go far beyond his or her personal areas of expertise and is also able to provide a broad base for individualized instruction.

Regional cooperatives can (and in some states already do) serve as media centers, as central agencies for resource people (consultants, specialists in arcane subject areas, program developers), and as clearinghouses for rural curricula. This last function would be especially useful for rural schools given the longstanding neglect of country-oriented curriculum by commercial publishers and academic curriculum developers. Curriculum cooperatives could save overworked teachers from duplication of effort, while also providing adaptable materials for general use. Further, these regional cooperatives could collect rural curricula from all over the country and train teachers to do their own adaptations to meet local needs.

Regional cooperatives could do for many rural school people what some rural improvement projects have tried to do for a few: train teachers to design experimental programs and to write grant proposals which will get funding for them. An irony of federal and foundation support patterns is that they tend to favor the richer school districts which can afford to purchase the services of professional proposal writers. Cooperative effort could provide equal expertise in this area for all small rural districts.

Cooperatives could also be the base for traveling resource centers. Like cooperatives, traveling centers have been tried in a variety of rural areas, to meet a variety of needs. Preschools, laboratories, lending libraries of books, toys, musical instruments all have been fitted into vans which make a circuit through thinly settled areas.[84] The possibilities of the "traveling road show" approach have been barely tapped, partly because much effort has gone instead into promoting consolidation, and partly because the technology has only recently been available to fully exploit this resource. But the idea carries with it the possibility of a remarkable support system for the small, rural school.

Imaginative use of external resources is badly needed if small, rural schools are to realize their full potential. However, imaginative restructuring of the school itself is equally important. Over the past decade, the classroom structures of the best urban and suburban schools have undergone significant changes. Some changes (cross-age teaching, continuous progress instruction, and so-called "family grouping" in the primary grades) stem from practices common to the one-room schoolhouses of the late nineteenth century. Ironically, these same practices have been almost uniformly pruned from the teaching methodology of the small, rural schools during the last twenty years. Many small, rural schools have made an enormous effort to be as much like the larger schools of the 1950s as possible. Teachers systematically attempt to separate children into "graded" groups, and urban or suburban materials (usually somewhat out-of-date) are forced on children who cannot relate fully to the experiences described. Shrag describes the children of the incredibly poor

Appalachian schools reading with bewilderment a book in which "all the children go with their parents in the big, blue family car to pick up the white and green cabin cruiser."[85]

New Models for Rural Education

The attention of rural school reformers needs to be turned to new models for the education of country children. There are many places to look—to the experience of small, private schools, to the history of successful rural practices, to the innovative methods outlined in the Northwest Lab's *Promising Practices* series. The critical precondition for devising successful models is a deep-seated belief that it is possible to have excellent small, rural schools. Then, the trick is to figure out how to make such excellence a reality. Rural educators who search for ways in which small schools fail their pupils are unlikely to discern the pieces which, if put together, would make a fine model (or series of models) for achieving excellence.

In 1970, a group of educational consultants—including a school superintendent, an architect, and two educational consultants—set out to define one such school. Their reason for turning to smallness was not necessity, nor even the tradition of local interaction and control which is inherent in rural areas, but the practical consideration that large schools are not necessarily good, no matter where you put them. Leggett's group quotes a principal who said, "There is something about largeness that attracts more problems. But we continue to build larger and larger schools."[86] The group then set themselves to designing a small school that would enhance intimacy and personal attention while maintaining the variety of offerings that generally characterize larger schools.

Their design, called Smallways, is for high schools ranging in size from 50 to 250 students, with a pupil-staff ratio between 17:1 and 20:1. It is not a difficult or complex model. It builds on the traditional rural approaches of nongraded classes, independent study, and varied scheduling which Julia Weber Gordon employed in her one-room school in the 1930s. Leggett and his co-authors add the currently fashionable notions of short-term mini-courses and recommend a phased scheduling of required courses, but there is nothing in the Smallways plan that requires either exotic technology or a method of operations that would offend the most conservative rural school board.

The flexibility of the Smallways model is one of its most attractive features. Leggett and co-authors project a staff of eleven "generalists" who will cover the "domains" of social studies, humanities and language arts, science, foreign language, math, business skills, industrial arts, home economics, art, music, and physical education. Assisted by technical help recruited from the community, these eleven staff members are intended to provide, within their domains, a very wide variety of courses, ranging from full-semester classes to three-week mini-courses.

Under this system, a college-bound student could pursue simultaneous studies in U.S. history, physical science, French, math, the modern novel, good design, plus physical education and also have substantial blocks of time for independent study. Non-college-oriented students could devote much of their time to home economics, business practices, and industrial programs.

There are problems with the Smallways model—largely in staffing. The teachers would have to enjoy continuous shifts in classroom content and to see guiding independent study as a challenge rather than a nuisance. Still, it remains an attractive and plausible possibility.

The point to make about the Smallways model is not its perfection, but its comparative simplicity. It is cheap, it is readily adaptable to the needs of a locality, and it does not depend (as does effective open classroom instruction, for example) on possession of unusual teaching skills. There are other models for small school improvement that have been generated and could be introduced, if the creative energy of school reform were to be turned in that direction. Already, a number of school districts in rural regions are showing an interest in reintroducing the traditional methodological strengths of rural schools in their classrooms. This is done, not with a nostalgic bent, but as a way to join old strengths with new understandings.

In Sugar City, Utah, a phased program of teaching English skills has been introduced to the high school with considerable success. Like Smallways, it draws on the ability and willingness of small-school teachers to teach a variety of preparations and on the willingness of the community to accept an ungraded approach to this teaching. According to the *Promising Practices* booklet, it has succeeded:

Students who have been low achievers in other programs have done well here because independent instruction and study are available. The high achieving student can start at a level above his peers, and is challenged to complete senior English at a level much higher than he could in a conventional program.[87]

Other examples abound. Rural schools are increasingly interested in forming a hybrid between traditional methods and modern ones. Now they need information, encouragement, and funding to make such reforms work.

Part of this encouragement may be coming from an unexpected source—the suburban schools that, for nearly thirty years, have been in the vanguard of educational reform. As the suburbs have grown, their schools have generally grown with them—into more competitive, more diverse, and often more impersonal institutions. Now, the cycle seems to be coming around again.

In 1976, Lexington, Massachusetts, an exemplary suburb, became embroiled in a raging controversy which could have come straight out of the Nebraska plains. The school committee wants to cut costs. To do so, they planned to close down the four smallest and oldest elementary schools and to bus those children to newer, bigger schools in the outlying neighborhoods. Parents are outraged; they have set up a committee to defend the value of their small schools. The committee, led by a Massachusetts Institute of Technology professor rather than a group of "old-fashioned" farmers, concludes that to close the small schools would be "educational folly." The committee argues that "the smallest and oldest of the local schools provides the best educational value in town. Its test scores are good and its cohesive, intimate atmosphere somehow is reflected in the learning, and attitude toward learning, of its pupils."[88]

The kind of schooling the Lexington parents' committee defends is, if anything, more plausible in the country than in metropolitan areas. Tradition supports it; the nature of the terrain and population sparsity makes it desirable; and it fits well with the small-scale and localized nature of rural politics. But, if small rural schools are ever to fulfill their potential, the views of those in positions of power and influence within the education profession will have to change.

Permanent, widespread improvement of rural schools will require changes in teacher education, in-service training, and ancillary support systems (such as the traveling resource centers described earlier). More basically, it will require a hard-headed assessment of the prospects and options for young people growing up in rural areas today, rather than either nostalgia for nineteenth century farm life or the conclusion that all rural youth must prepare for life in metropolitan America. Rural communities must be involved in this enterprise; these are their children, and they are most concerned about them. But they must, generally, be assisted by people with access to statistical projections and information about the future of rural areas and by people with some perspective on the traditions that are dearly held in rural areas.

There is a tendency, which Schrag points out in his description of Jessup, Iowa, for rural schoolpeople to try to control the contemporary world with "the ideas and techniques of an older America," an America that they feel belonged to them.[89] However, the answer to this stifling tendency is not a willy-nilly push for suburban models of schooling. Instead, professionals and citizens need to weld unique models for schooling rural children, models that take into account the problematic job market and the possibilities of a more diversified economy, the traditional advantages of rural life styles, and the kind of cultural enrichment newly available through improved communications.

The country school can be used as one means of creating a range of rural life styles, each of which could offer personal fulfillment equal to anything found in the cities or suburbs. However, to achieve this goal, there must be people committed to the *improvement* of rural life rather than its *replacement*.

4   Coping with Sparsity:
A Review of Rural School Finance

Rachel B. Tompkins

Money problems have long plagued America's rural schools. And, while rural communities run the gamut from abject poverty to affluence, they tend to be relatively poor in both property wealth and income compared to urban and suburban areas. As a consequence, trying to finance rural schools solely from local sources has proved a fruitless endeavor.

The emergence of state aid programs across the nation indicates that this marked lack of wealth has not gone unrecognized. However, to date, state outlays have not come even close to ensuring that all children, regardless of place of residence or parental wealth, can attend schools endowed with the resources necessary to meet their educational needs. In fact, state aid has served mainly to maintain rural schools and school districts at a subsistence level.

Since few new local sources of revenue exist (or are likely to be found), it is imperative that state funding of rural schools be dramatically increased. Longstanding problems of underfinancing and inequality can only be solved by a new infusion of state resources. Yet, there is considerable resistance to an expanded state role in rural education, not only by urban-oriented state policymakers, but also by rural citizens fearing that increased state funding inevitably leads to increased state control of the schools.

Linking state funding and state control is by no means evidence of rural paranoia, but rather an entirely rational interpretation of recent history. Rural citizens have observed both the growth of state education resources and the even more rapid expansion of state involvement in, and control over, key components of the educational enterprise (from curriculum to certification and from graduation standards to district organization) and have concluded that something beyond happenstance is at work. Rural people are aware that the state initiatives most adamantly advocated (such as consolidation and the imposition of urban standards and education models) have not had a particularly beneficent effect on rural schools and schoolchildren. They are, therefore, reluctant to defer to the alleged wisdom of state-level educators. Thus, in many rural communities, the notion of more state funding triggers reactions ranging from outright opposition to grudging acceptance of a necessary evil. Yet, it is readily apparent that such reluctance and resistance are not directed at state money, per se, but rather at the strings attached to the acquisition of these additional resources.

Therefore, the thesis of this chapter is that substantial benefits can accrue to rural communities by centralizing the collection and distribution of educational revenues while concomitantly decentralizing control over educational programs and expenditures. Making this assertion neither entails an abandonment of minimum state standards nor an abdication of state involvement in substantive educational issues. It is instead a plea to establish a state role in education that focuses on the creation of broad, general goals and standards that can be reached by diverse and flexible strategies at the local level. There are three assumptions underlying this assertion.

1. The linkage between state funding and state control is contrived, not immutable. No economic or natural law created this linkage. Rather, it is the intended effect of deliberate policy initiatives. As such, it is also amenable to change.
2. The cherished rural ideal of local control is seriously compromised by the absence of sufficient resources to allow both real diversity and real choices.
3. The state is the only viable supplier of the kinds and level of educational resources needed to make local control in rural communities more than a battle over crumbs or an exercise in futility.

To provide a basis for analyzing rural school finance problems and discussing means for solving them, this chapter will review briefly the history of school finance, discuss in some detail recent reforms in school finance systems in several states, analyze their effect on the special problems of rural areas, and suggest additional measures to benefit rural schools in the future.

School Finance—History

Reformers have been tinkering with the way schools are financed since the turn of the century. At that time, the battle was for a local property tax to support education rather than simply taxing parents having children in school.[1] Since an educated citizenry benefited the whole community, reformers argued that all should invest some money in running the schools. By the early 1900s, that argument had prevailed in all but a few isolated areas of the country.

As state-imposed compulsory education became the rule and the costs of education rose, local towns and school districts had difficulty raising enough money from the local tax base to operate schools. Increasing industrialization gave some school districts a bonanza of property wealth to tax while others had only farms and residences. The disparity between rich and poor districts was enormous but the initial focus of most state legislation on school finance was not equalization. It was to provide districts that had nothing with a little bit. Again, the reformers argued that educated citizens benefited the whole state, as well as the community, and therefore the state should contribute to the operation of schools.[2] Initial state aid programs were simple flat grants designed to assure that every school district had some money. Property-rich districts got as much per unit as property-poor districts.

In the 1920s and 1930s, concern grew over the inequalities perpetuated by a system based on the local property tax. Districts with valuable property (for example, an industry or a mine) could assess a low tax rate (make little tax effort) and raise more money than districts with not so valuable property and a high tax rate. The education program varied from district to district and was based in large part on the available budget. Little valuable property meant little money for schools and a low quality education program.

Reformers recommended a plan based both on the value of property in a district and the tax rate people chose to levy. Local citizens had to make a specified tax effort to be eligible for state money. Foundation plans, as they were called, guaranteed a minimum level of basic aid to all districts that taxed at a required rate.[3] If the guaranteed minimum were $500 per pupil and the required rate 20 mills, a district with property value per pupil of $10,000 could raise $200 per pupil from its 20-mill rate (20/1,000 x $10,000) and would be given $300 in state aid to reach the guarantee. Districts had to tax at least 20 mills to be eligible for state money, but they could tax more than the minimum and raise more dollars; no ceilings were placed in the plan. Districts were free to spend as much as they wished, which gave an advantage to districts with valuable property. A district with a $25,000 per pupil valuation could raise the whole $500 guarantee from local funds at the 20-mill tax rate. Many states had a combination of flat grants and categorical aid so that all districts received some state funds.

Between 1930 and 1960, reams were written about school finance, consisting mostly of schemes for even more arcane tinkering with existing foundation plans. No one but the school finance experts understood the schemes. The principle of combined state and local support for schools was well established. The principle of equalization was touted as a goal of state efforts through the foundation plans. In fact, the disparities between wealthy and poor districts grew even larger.

Foundation plans did not, in fact, equalize expenditures between poor and rich districts, but it was not until the 1960s that Charles Benson, an economist at the University of California at Berkeley, carefully analyzed why this happened.[4] The size of the state guarantee never kept pace with anyone's idea of adequate spending for education. Almost all districts supplemented the state minimum with additional local tax levies. At every rate level above the minimum, property-rich districts could raise much more money than property-poor districts. Districts with very little wealth sometimes spent only one-tenth the amount rich districts spent.

Benson's analysis showed the disparity in expenditures existing between districts in all states, regardless of the fine tuning done on the foundation plans or the amount of money expended on education. From California to Maine to Florida, the so-called equalization plans did not equalize.[5] If one goal of state school finance plans was to lessen the disparity in resources per child among districts, foundation plans could not possibly be used to achieve it.

While Benson and others analyzed the problems in the existing state finance system, three lawyers at Northwestern—John Coons, William Clune, and Stephen Sugarman—built the legal arguments to challenge the constitutionality of the system.[6] The Fourteenth Amendment to the United States Constitution requires that states guarantee to all citizens the equal protection of the laws. Coons, Clune, and Sugarman argued that a school finance system that allows expenditures per child to vary with the property wealth in a district rather than the wealth of the state as a whole denies equal protection of the laws to children in poor districts. Several federal district courts and state supreme courts agreed with this reasoning and ordered new finance systems created in California, Minnesota, Texas, New Jersey, Kansas, and Arizona.[7] The type of finance system required was not specified, but it had to assure that expenditure per pupil was not simply a reflection of the wealth of the individual school district.

The United States Supreme Court reviewed the Texas school finance system in *San Antonio vs. Rodriguez* and found in a 5-4 decision that while the financing system did, in fact, have inequalities, it did not violate the Fourteenth Amendment of the United States Constitution.[8] Justice Powell concluded for the majority:

> The need is apparent for reform in tax systems which may well have relied too long and too heavily on the local property tax. And certainly, innovative new thinking as to public education, its methods and its funding, is necessary.[9]

Despite the decision turning back the constitutional basis for reform, twenty-two states have acted since 1970 to alter their system of financing schools. Another eighteen have had study commissions look at their system of school finance, but have not yet taken legislative action. The reforms vary, but all focus to some degree on lessening the link between local property wealth and school expenditures.

Equity

School finance plans from past to present raise troublesome issues of equity and local control. Reformers frequently said they wanted equality of educational opportunity for all children or that they wanted to assure an equal chance. But equity has meant varying things and it is important to sort out the definitions and describe how they will be used in this chapter.

Flat grants and foundation plans guaranteed a minimum level of educational expenditure for each child. Historically, that has constituted equality of educational opportunity in school finance. However, that definition no longer is satisfactory because it leaves too many children in too many poor school districts with extremely scanty resources while their neighbors in rich districts have abundance.

A second definition of equity, equality of inputs, requires exactly equal dollars to be spent on each child. This has been proposed fairly recently in several states, but has not received much acceptance. Research and practice argue against it. Secondary education costs more per pupil than elementary education. The same is true for vocational and occupational programs compared to college preparatory ones. Certain children—the physically handicapped or the very poor—require more resources than other children to learn minimal skills such as reading and computation. Equity does not require equal dollars per pupil; indeed, it requires differing amounts based on some measure of need.

Supplying different levels of resources based on educational need suggests a goal of equalizing outputs. This is the third definition of equity: equalizing educational achievement for all children regardless of ability or interest. Embracing this single definition for equity may be an impossible dream because the differences among children are great. Despite years of study, the state of knowledge is slim about appropriate styles of teaching for those very different children. No one can guarantee that the application of a particular amount of teaching in a certain style over a given period of time will produce the same results over and over. What is more, no one agrees on exactly what should be achieved or how much is enough. Even if agreement could be reached, appropriate tests do not exist to measure the skills. Finally, and perhaps most important, homogeneity of achievement (even if it could be attained) is not really what most people want. Most recent finance reforms do include part of this definition by allocating more resources to children with greater needs.

Equalization of tax-paying ability is a fourth definition of equity. In this view, the ability of school districts to raise revenue should be equal even if expenditures are not. If taxpayers in District A levy 20 mills and taxpayers in District B levy the same, taxpayer equity would have the state guarantee that the equal effort raise equal dollars. This principle is referred to as fiscal neutrality, power equalizing, or guaranteed yield.

For purposes of this chapter, equalization and equity include parts of two definitions. First, the resources available for a child's education should not be a function of his place of residence. Second, resources available should reflect the educational needs of the child. Therefore, state school finance policy should include a combination of taxpayer equity, by lessening the link between property wealth and educational expenditure, and student equity, by providing disadvantaged children with additional resources.

A final note on matters of equity. Many critics of school equalization attack the notion of providing additional dollars to low-spending districts on the grounds that research has not demonstrated that dollars make a difference in learning outcomes. In a literal sense they are correct, for just spending more money is not the answer to all educational woes. It is clearly important to target the money toward those resources that do benefit the child's learning. Research and practice will continue to better define those resources that are most valuable. At the same time, it is not at all unreasonable to urge that the total pool of resources available for education be more equitably distributed among districts and children.

Local Control

Definitions of equity are complicated enough, but they frequently have come in conflict over the years with proponents of local control. Realistically, equity requires large infusions of state aid and some equalization of resources among districts. Many people believe that as long as school support taxes are approved locally, local citizens have the best opportunity to control both the level and kind of expenditures for schools. In the tradition of "he who pays the piper calls the tune," people argue that if state money pays for schools, then the state will be able to make the rules about what is taught and how it is taught.

The fact is that the relationship between centralization of finance and centralization of other decisions is not so clear. A recent study of this issue by a team of researchers at the Urban Institute concluded:

1. State statutes and regulations sharply limit the degree of local

board autonomy in the majority of states examined.

2. There is little direct relationship between the percentage of state aid provided and the degree of state restrictions on the operation of school boards.[10]

In other words, local control is limited whether states invest a lot or a little in school support.

The study outlined five categories in which states tend to regulate schools: curriculum, budget and taxing, federal programs, personnel, and district boundaries. Ten states were studied that represent different levels of state funding. State funds in North Carolina, Delaware, and Washington provide between 62 percent and 79 percent of total state and local funding; New York, Michigan, and California provide between 35 percent and 50 percent of total state and local funds; and Kansas, Colorado, South Dakota, and New Hampshire provide between 3 percent and 28 percent of total state and local funds.

Textbook requirements are most restrictive in North Carolina, a high-aid state, and Kansas, a low-aid state. New York, a moderate-aid state, has the most extensive curriculum and course requirements. Washington and Delaware, both high-aid states, have relatively few mandatory courses.

Budgetary and tax controls are more frequently related to source of funding than are other dimensions. However, even this relationship is not consistent. Kansas and California have a relatively high degree of control and provide less than 50 percent of total local district expenditures.

Personnel practices are not affected by the financial pattern, with the possible exception of salary schedules. Two high-aid states have statewide salary schedules, while no low-aid states do. In collective bargaining, however, three of the four low-aid states require that school boards bargain with employees. Only one of the high-aid states has such a requirement. All states exercise substantial control over teacher certification.

With the exception of New Hampshire, states impose great control over consolidation and reorganization regardless of their financial contribution. Local participation in decision making about reorganization is severely restricted in nine of the ten states.

This research strongly suggests that the source of aid to schools and the level of state restrictions on program and expenditure decisions are not directly related. Education is extensively regulated by states, regardless of the level of funding provided. In fact, many poor school districts probably need additional state dollars to implement all the regulations imposed. Ironically, historians may well discover that state regulation (or control) preceded the provision of state dollars.

Two major groups have been most adamant about local control—one suburban and one rural. The suburban interests have argued that local control is important because it allows them to spend a great amount on their schools while other districts who value education less will not spend as much.

Suburban districts also assert that they are the leaders in developing innovative programs that depend upon their ability to spend much more per pupil than other districts. However, the Urban Institute found that high- and moderate-aid states innovated more than low-aid states.[11] Centralization of finance does not appear to stifle innovation. Additional resources, from any source, seem to encourage innovation whether in urban, suburban, or rural districts.

Some rural interests have consistently argued that the state finance schemes are always designed to make them pay more taxes and to encourage larger districts and larger schools with the same educational program as the suburbs and cities. All foundation plans required a minimum tax rate that frequently was higher than the levy in rural districts. To qualify for state dollars, rural districts had to pay more local taxes. At the same time that state foundation plans were developing, states were also requiring consolidation and reorganization. Indeed, state dollars were sometimes linked to specific regulations about the size of school or district.

Minimum standards often resulted in the elimination of very small schools, and financial incentives were promised to districts to reorganize. In Texas, extra dollars were given when districts reached 1,000 Average Daily Attendance (ADA). In South Dakota, no secondary school with fewer than thirty-five pupils could exist within twenty miles of another secondary school.[12]

Construction and transportation funds often greatly favored districts willing to reorganize. In Washington, state assistance in construction is available only to reorganized districts, and Ohio provides state construction dollars only to high schools enrolling 500 or more students.[13] Connecticut pays 80 percent of the cost of school construction in regional districts and 50 percent for town districts.[14] Sometimes funds are available for new construction, but not for renovation and remodeling. The devices differ, but the intent is the same.

For vastly different reasons, rural and suburban districts have fought against greater state regulation. That, however, does not make them allies today on matters of state school finance. In the past, suburban and rural legislators shared interests because urban districts had the largest concentration of wealth. Now, urban and rural interests may have more in common. Suburban districts benefit from state aid plans that do not equalize, while rural districts tend to benefit most from equalization. Because they are relatively rich both in property and income, suburban districts want to raise and spend all the dollars they can locally. Because they are relatively poor both in property and income, rural districts need state dollars, but want to avoid various state requirements. Urban districts are still relatively rich in property but poor in income and need the infusions of state aid targeted on children with special needs.

The general trend has been for educators to characterize suburban selfishness as progressive and good while branding rural reluctance as old-fashioned and bad. Both, however, fight to retain what is important to their locality. Suburban districts have been largely successful in retaining their financial advantages. However, both suburban and rural districts have been largely unsuccessful in avoiding state regulation.

School Finance—Current Reforms

Many changes have been made in school finance systems since 1970. The general nature of the reforms that have been made or are in process provides the setting within which the specific problems and possibilities for rural areas must be considered.

One major outcome of the reforms enacted in eighteen states through 1975 has been to increase the proportion of aid to schools from state sources.[15] Regardless of the method of distribution, more state money and less local money tends to equalize school districts. The equalization is limited in most states by the necessity to maintain or to "hold harmless" property-rich districts at existing levels of support (often by using state education monies that otherwise could have been redistributed).[16] Table 4.1 shows that the state share of expenditures increased substantially in all states enacting reform

TABLE 4.1

State Share of Total State-Local
Expenditures

State	Date of Reform	Last Year Before Reform	First Year After Reform
Arizona	1974	42.0%	54.6%
California	1972	36.7%	45.3%
Colorado	1973	28.9%	39.9%
Connecticut	1975	24.2%	N.A.
Florida	1973	61.3%	62.5%
Illinois	1973	39.3%	44.3%
Indiana	1975	36.2%	N.A.
Iowa	1971	32.5%	36.3%
Kansas	1973	29.8%	47.7%
Maine	1973	38.6%	38.5%
Michigan	1973	49.4%	52.9%
Minnesota	1971	50.7%	60.9%
Montana	1973	27.5%	43.8%
New Mexico	1974	74-5%	77.8%
North Dakota	1973	32.3%	46.1%
Texas	1975	46.1%	N.A.
Utah	1973	58.4%	61.9%
Wisconsin	1973	31.8%	39.0%
18-state average		39.0%	51.0% (est.)

SOURCE: John J. Callahan and William H. Wilkin, eds., School
Finance Reform: A Legislators' Handbook (Washington,
D.C.: National Conference of State Legislatures, 1976),
p. 8.

legislation.

Another major outcome of current reforms has been property tax relief and equalization. Absolute decreases in local property tax rates have been possible in some states where dramatic increases in the proportion of state aid were passed; for example, Colorado, Kansas, Minnesota, North Dakota, and Wisconsin.[17] Only Arizona, Florida, and Minnesota have raised state taxes to pay for the new system.[18]

Property tax equalization has come about as states have guaranteed that each mill levied will raise the same dollars in property-rich and property-poor districts. For example, Ohio passed a law in 1975 guaranteeing that every mill up to 20 mills will provide $48 per pupil.[19] A district with a property base of $10,000 per pupil will raise $10 per pupil per mill from local sources, and the state will provide $38 per pupil per mill up to 20 mills. A district with a $30,000 per pupil valuation would raise $30 per pupil per mill from local sources and

$18 from state sources. While the plan does not completely equalize expenditures, it does assure that a local community's effort to tax itself up to 20 mills will generate the same dollars whether it is rich or poor. Property-rich districts taxing more than 20 mills will still raise more dollars than property-poor ones taxing above the state guarantee.

Various reforms in the administration of property taxes have also come about, in part as a result of school finance reform legislation and in part as a result of lawsuits against local assessment practices. If state finance laws are to be based on local valuation and effort, then the scale by which valuation is calculated must be the same in all districts. Most states, either by design or accumulated practice, were underassessing residential and agricultural property. Therefore, uniform assessment practices require sizable percentage increases in the taxes on farmlands and homes.

New school finance plans have also recognized the special needs of some children and the particular problems of some districts.[20] Special needs such as handicaps and poverty have been addressed either by categorical grants to districts for those students or by weighting systems that count a hard-to-educate child as more than one pupil. For example, certain types of handicapped children are counted as three pupils, so that for each $100 per pupil given, the school district gets $300 per handicapped child. The weights are based on either state or national average costs of educating particular categories of children.

The special problems of urban districts have been recognized in some reform laws through categorical and municipal overburden aid.[21] Central cities generally have relatively high property values (although they are declining), but must spend a greater percentage of their tax dollars on public services other than education. Cities also tend to have high proportions of costly-to-educate children. Some states provide additional aid to districts with high nonschool taxes; others provide more dollars to districts with high concentrations of poor children.

Problems of equalization other than disparities in local property wealth have come to light as legislatures have considered these reforms. One is the distribution of income across school districts which is not always the same as the distribution of property wealth. Level of income is a rough measure of ability to pay taxes as well as other bills. Districts with large concentrations of poor people may have special difficulties in paying for schools and other public services.

A recent study done for the Education Review Committee of the General Assembly of Ohio demonstrates the relationships between median family income and various school finance variables.[22] The research found large variations in median family income among Ohio's 617 school districts. The state median income was $10,313, but the range was $4,574 to $29,048. The distribution pattern of income was very different from the distribution of property wealth and vice versa.

Median family income in a school district had a strong effect on operating millage. Generally speaking, the higher the income, the higher the millage. Median family income, together with property wealth, explains almost all the variation among districts in current operating expenses. Greater property wealth and high income lead to high expenditures.

The study concludes:

> Median family income has such a powerful effect on both operating millage and expenditures per pupil that if all districts had similar incomes, their operating millage and expenditures per pupil could be expected to be similar also.[23]

The implications of this research are that guaranteed yield formulas that help all districts to raise the same number of dollars for each mill levied will only partially diminish the expenditure disparities found among districts. Districts with high family incomes will continue to levy much higher millage than districts with low family incomes. A guaranteed yield plan equalizes revenue per mill but does nothing about a district's ability to levy those mills. The result is that rich children will have better financed schools than poor children.

Five states have incorporated some form of income adjustment into state aid calculations so that low-income districts get proportionately more aid.[24] In all cases, the formulas benefit rural areas. Rhode Island, Maryland, and Connecticut also have designed adjustments that benefit cities.

A second problem that has arisen as school finance reforms have been considered is differences in the cost of living. Metropolitan areas have argued that it costs more to do business in cities than in rural areas, and that differences in school expenditures between urban and rural school districts are to be expected. Indeed, they argue that metropolitan areas should get proportionately more state dollars because the purchasing power of each dollar is less in the city.[25]

The biggest item in all school budgets is personnel salaries (normally at least 70 percent of total expenditures). Pay scales for everyone, including teachers, principals, janitors, and plumbers, are higher in cities. Not only are all personnel costs higher, but such things as supplies and equipment cost more. Cost-of-living studies indicate generally higher prices for all goods in urban areas. The question is whether the *quality* of the goods is the same in all regions and whether these variations in prices of nonschool items have much effect on school costs.

Opponents of cost-of-living adjustments for cities argue that the general standard of living is simply higher in urban areas. The same services do not cost more, rather the services provided in urban schools are of higher quality. For example, urban teachers have more experience, are better educated, and have more credentials than rural teachers. Thus, while it is reasonable for states to help defray higher costs for the same quality of services, materials, and personnel, states should not be expected to pay for higher quality resources in urban school districts.

Evidence from Florida, the only state to enact a cost-of-living adjustment, tends to support the rural opponents of this formula.[26] Florida developed a cost of living index ranging between 90 and 110 percent. The basic aid allotment for highest-cost counties was multiplied by an index of 110 and for lowest-cost counties by an index of 90. The effect of the index is to provide many additional dollars per pupil in Dade, Brevard, and Palm Beach counties, the most urban Florida counties, while providing fewer dollars to twenty-five counties which contain all of Florida's rural areas.[27]

The correlation between the cost-of-living index and median family income for Florida counties is .86.[28] In other words, districts with high incomes get more state dollars, while districts with low incomes get proportionately less. Thus, Florida's cost-of-living adjustment is substantially disequalizing in relation to income. Analysis of the Florida plan suggests that this particular cost-of-living adjustment is supporting a higher standard of living rather than higher costs for the same standard. Much more complex formulas will have to be designed if higher metropolitan costs are to be measured accurately and included in state formulas.[29]

Most of these recent school finance reforms have aimed for greater equity—of expenditure, of tax burden, of ability to pay. In some states, the disparity in expenditure between high- and low-property-wealth districts has been substantially reduced. In others, the reduction is more modest. The specific, severe problems of urban areas have been partially addressed by some states. The problems raised by income disparities and cost-of-living differentials have only begun to be addressed. Twenty-two states have acted; twenty-eight have not. Those who have not continue to operate on some type of foundation or flat grant plan.

Major School Finance Issues in Rural America

Recently enacted school finance systems have benefited rural America in many ways. Some of the reforms have had a direct relationship to specifically rural problems; others have had only indirect or peripheral impacts in rural areas.

Rural school districts are a varied lot. A few have relatively high property wealth, with fertile farm land, a large mine, or a public utility providing a stable and lucrative source of revenue. Others are dismally poor, with limited property value and high unemployment. Some rural districts are largely Caucasian; others have high populations of Black, Chicano, Native American, or Puerto Rican children. Some districts have large seasonal influxes of migrant children.

Rural districts may be in farming areas (where 2,937,074 school-children lived in 1970) or they may be in nonfarm areas with mining, fishing, or forestry as major employers or in small towns with a mixed economy.[30] In 1970, there were 11,421,366 schoolchildren in such districts.[31] While rural Americans are clearly a minority, some 14 million schoolchildren depend upon education systems in rural areas for their schooling.

The major school finance problem in rural America remains the uneven geographic distribution of wealth measured both by property and income. A second large issue is the relative sparsity of population, which leads to high expenditures for services like transportation and higher per pupil expenditures for some educational programs. A smaller, yet nagging, issue in rural areas is paying for capital expenditures, some of which were necessitated by requirements to

TABLE 4.2

Ten Local Districts with Lowest Property Value in Ohio, 1974-1975

District	Enrollment	Property Value (per pupil)	Expenditures			Millage		
			State	Local	Total	Operating	Debt Service	Total
Western Local (Pike Co.)	916	$3,458	$609	$ 71	$680	20.6	7.5	28.1
Huntington Local (Ross Co.)	1,266	3,722	595	85	681	23.0	1.9	24.9
Trimble Local (Athens Co.)	1,216	5,354	577	146	723	27.3	9.5	36.8
Washington Local (Scioto Co.)	2,411	5,376	574	107	681	20.0	4.0	24.0
Dawson-Bryant Local (Lawrence Co.)	1,700	5,756	619	102	721	17.8	2.1	19.9
Eastern Local (Pike Co.)	1,093	5,757	581	118	700	20.6	5.5	26.1
Southern Local (Perry Co.)	1,356	5,986	529	160	690	26.8	4.3	31.1
Symmes Valley Local (Lawrence Co.)	1,079	5,991	598	106	705	17.8	1.1	18.9
Northwest Local (Scioto Co.)	1,965	6,104	570	122	692	20.0	9.0	29.0
Fairland (Lawrence Co.)	1,998	6,126	552	109	661	17.8	1.1	18.9
State Average	2,080	$20,023				28.6	4.3	34.5

SOURCE: Basic Financial Data of Ohio School Districts, 1975 (Columbus, Ohio: Ohio Education Association, February 1975).

NOTE: Joint vocational operating expenditures are not included in the table. All figures are for the year prior to implementation of the Guaranteed Yield Formula.

consolidate or reorganize. Laced throughout all the money problems is the issue of who controls school expenditures.

Wealth

Measured by property wealth, the poorest school districts in any state are rural districts. Table 4.2 shows the ten poorest districts in Ohio in per pupil property value. All are rural districts and have per pupil tax valuations that range from one-third to one-sixth of the state average of $20,023 per pupil. All of the districts levy less than the state average for operating millage, but four levy more than average for capital expenditures and debt service. Even if the districts doubled their operating millage to 40 mills, they could not raise as much per pupil from local sources as the average district with $20,023 valuation and a 20-mill tax levy.

This is not a phenomenon peculiar to Ohio or a few other states. A study of thirteen states in all regions of the country done by the Syracuse University Research Corporation indicates the extreme fiscal disadvantage of rural areas.[32] In all thirteen states, rural areas had the lowest amount of per pupil expenditures proportionate to their state and local revenue effort. Joel S. Berke concludes:

> The rural disadvantage in school finance most probably stems from the absolute shortage of taxable property in many rural areas, the only modest equalizing power of many state aid systems and the fact that many rural districts are too poor to take advantage of the full effect of equalizing aid systems in many states because their tax effort does not enable them to receive the full level of foundation aid that most state aid systems provide.[33]

As earlier evidence indicates, the millage level in a district is largely determined by median family income in the school district. Rural districts suffer a double whammy because they are not only the poorest in property, they are also the poorest in income. Median family income in urban areas in 1970 was $7,974; in rural nonfarm areas, it was $7,036; while in rural farm areas, it was $6,565.[34]

To indicate even more clearly the income disparity in rural areas as compared to urban and suburban areas, Table 4.3 shows the percentage of households earning under $3,000 and the percentage earning

TABLE 4.3

Household Income in Selected Areas, 1970

Area	Percentage of Households with Income Under $3,000	Percentage of Households with Income Over $10,000
Boston	19	28
Suburbs	5	49
Massachusetts rural	24	28
Newark	10	28
Suburbs	5	58
New Jersey rural	13	32
New York City	14	39
Suburbs	7	60
New York rural	13	40
Indianapolis	13	41
Suburbs	12	39
Indiana rural	19	30
Minneapolis-St. Paul	15	38
Suburbs	6	57
Minnesota rural	24	23
Cleveland	17	30
Suburbs	7	56
Ohio rural	23	25
Milwaukee	13	36
Suburbs	7	55
Wisconsin rural	23	23
Atlanta	18	34
Suburbs	10	48
Georgia rural	28	22
Louisville	20	28
Suburbs	10	43
Kentucky rural	32	20
San Francisco-Oakland	19	34
Suburbs	14	49
California rural	21	29
Denver	18	32
Suburbs	10	40
Colorado rural	23	21
Seattle	18	36
Suburbs	10	31
Washington rural	19	31

SOURCE: Joel S. Berke, Answers to Inequity (Berkeley, Calif.: McCutchan
Publishing Corp., 1974), p. 81

over $10,000 by city, suburban, and rural categories in twelve regions of the country. In all states but New York, the highest concentration of families earning under $3,000 is in rural areas. With the exceptions of New Jersey, New York, and Massachusetts, the lowest concentration of families earning over $10,000 is in rural areas. More poor people and fewer rich people means the ability to pay school taxes or other taxes is extremely limited.

Sparsity

Population sparsity is a fact of life in all rural areas. For some states it is a particularly vexing problem because students must be transported many miles a day to and from school; parents and citizens cannot easily be involved in school activities; and interschool events, whether athletics or teacher training, are hard to organize. Additional costs are associated with population sparsity, particularly high costs of transportation, and high per pupil costs of some educational programs. For example, Alaska has both the lowest population density and the highest per pupil transportation expenditures of any state in the nation.

Approximately $2 billion is spent nationally on transportation costs and nearly one-half of all schoolchildren are transported to and from school. The proportion of children transported is higher in rural than in most urban and suburban areas. Costs per pupil mile are also relatively high, in part because large buses operate below capacity and small buses result in high per pupil costs for salaries and equipment.

Many sparsely settled rural areas have a high ratio of professionals to pupils. At the secondary level, some schools attempt to maintain a very broad curriculum and hire a variety of specialists who teach very few pupils. Special education costs, a high expense per pupil item anywhere, can be even greater in rural areas because of the low incidence of students. In some cases, these high costs could be eliminated by organizational changes—sharing teachers among schools, regionalizing support services for staff and special programs, and perhaps consolidating some schools. In most instances, however, consolidation is not desirable, and despite staff sharing and other techniques, per pupil costs will remain high.

Capital Outlay

The total cost of school construction has ranged around $4 to $5 billion annually in recent years.[35] Much of this is financed by the sale of bonds paid for out of funds raised specifically for that purpose. Total expenditures for debt service on construction in earlier years is $1.5 to $2.0 billion annually.[36] Only twenty-five states provided state-collected revenues to aid local districts in financing capital facilities.[37] As a result, many rural districts have had to either defer or cancel much needed school renovation and construction programs.

Capital costs pose particular problems for rural districts. First, they are very large expenditures in proportion to resources available for operating costs. This means that available property wealth and ability to levy higher tax millage are significant factors in paying for capital needs. In Iowa, for example, the poorest school districts needed to make seven times the effort required of the richest district to fund the average debt service of $52 per pupil.[38]

The Arizona Supreme Court, in its decision in that state's school finance case, concluded:

> However, funds for capital improvements in school districts are even more closely tied to district wealth than are funds for operating expenses. The county and state make no contribution whatever to the costs of capital improvements. The capability of a school district to raise money by bond issues is a function of its total assessed valuation.[39]

The second reason that capital costs are a problem in rural districts is that funds must basically be raised by the sale of bonds. Bond ratings for rural districts are frequently lower than those for the state as a whole. Oregon planners estimated that using the state's higher credit rating would ultimately save the state's schools $3.5 million annually on interest costs.[40]

Third, rural districts that have built new schools, some required by state regulations on reorganization and consolidation, carry very large debt service in relation to wealth and to other operating expenses.

Effects of School Finance Policy on Rural Problems

Historically, state school finance policies have affected rural areas in two ways. First, districts benefited to some degree from the state policy that guaranteed a minimum level of funding for all schoolchildren. Since rural districts were property poor, they raised a smaller portion of the guarantee than suburban and urban districts. State dollars thus provided a greater portion of rural school support than did local dollars. For example, Table 4.4 (the ten poorest Ohio districts) shows that state aid in the districts ranges from $552 to $619 while local revenue ranges from $71 to $160. State dollars are clearly the most significant part of the local district budget. Yet total expenditures in these districts are about $400 below the average state expenditure in Ohio.

The second prong of state policy has been to encourage larger districts to expand and equalize the local tax base. Reorganization was also urged to improve efficiency. Usually states have encouraged or prescribed some optimum size for districts or some optimum property valuation per pupil. As the years have gone by and costs of education have increased, the optimum size has simply grown larger and the property valuation required has become higher. The policy for larger size districts is thus partly grounded in a finance system based on local property tax wealth. In Vermont, for example, a recent state department of education proposal found it would be necessary to break the entire state into eight school districts to achieve a property valuation of $15,000 per pupil.[41] Vermont currently has 278 districts.

Rural legislators were justifiably proud of the foundation plans that provided a great percentage of their local district budget. The minimum guarantee in state aid, however, required a certain local tax effort. In general, the philosophy was that local districts should tax at the maximum they are capable of before state dollars are used. "Maximum capable" is always a political decision about what the traffic will bear. It is the school finance counterpart to a welfare philosophy that requires all able-bodied persons to work and subtracts what they earn from their welfare check. Not a bad policy, perhaps, but it does not really address the main problem, because

TABLE 4.4

Property Tax Valuation Per Pupil in Six Ohio Counties
Containing the Ten Poorest Districts
in the State, 1974-1975

County	Tax Valuation (per pupil)
Athens	$17,136
Lawrence	9,865
Perry	8,672
Pike	8,778
Ross	14,111
Scioto	13,924

SOURCE: Basic Financial Data of Ohio School Districts, 1975
(Columbus, Ohio: Ohio Education Association, February
1975).

many people on welfare are not able-bodied and there are not enough jobs for everyone in our society. The school finance policy of encouraging local effort is also perhaps not a bad policy, but it does not solve the basic problem because some districts are so poor in property that the minimum makes little difference in additional state dollars and yet makes a great deal of difference to the families with low incomes that must pay the tax.

For example, the ten poorest Ohio districts tax about 20 mills on the average, with a per pupil property value of about $5,000, thus raising about $100 per pupil locally. With 15,000 pupils in those districts, local revenues come to $1.5 million. State aid averages about $575 per pupil for a total of $8.6 million. If the local minimum were 10 mills and each district chose to tax only the minimum, with the state guarantee remaining the same, local revenue would be $750,000, a 50 percent decrease, and state revenue would increase to $9.3 million, an 8 percent increase. The point is not that the minimum *should* be lowered, but rather that the value of the minimum is not fiscal but political.

Reorganization and consolidation have had very limited success in solving rural fiscal problems. Reorganization into larger districts aided in solving the wealth problem only when one of the districts to be joined was property rich. Unfortunately, in most states, wealthy rural districts are extremely scarce. The poorest Ohio districts again exemplify the problem. Reorganization into county districts is often proposed in Ohio. Four of the poorest districts would benefit from this reorganization: Huntington, Trimble, Washington, and Northwest. The remaining six districts improve their position slightly but remain among the poorest in the state because the entire county is poor. Table 4.4 shows the countywide tax valuations per pupil, all of which remain below the statewide average of $20,023.

Traditional state school finance policies have only partially solved the problem of limited wealth in rural America and have further exacerbated the problem of population sparsity. Centralization of schools, which ordinarily follows reorganization, incurs capital and debt service costs and increases transportation costs. The results are a partial remedy for wealth and worsening problems in sparsity and capital expenditures. That is not much progress.

Recent Reforms

The more recent school finance reforms have substantially benefited rural districts with problems of low property wealth. In some states, such as New Mexico, sparsity problems have been addressed with specific corrections, as have the high costs of special-needs children. A few states have built-in adjustments benefiting low-income districts; others are considering such measures.

Rural districts also benefited from altered patterns of aid distribution that concentrate even greater proportions of state money on poor districts. Some states went so far as to completely eliminate aid to rich districts. Michigan allocates no general aid to sixty-one districts, and Wisconsin has cut off sixteen districts.[42] Such redistribution aids rural areas in most cases.

Four states have placed provisions into law that recapture some aid from very wealthy districts and redistribute it. Maine had already redistributed $7 million; Wisconsin will reallocate about $3.4 million in 1977; and Montana and Utah have yet to implement provisions requiring mining districts with enormous tax duplicates to contribute to state coffers for redistribution to other districts.[43]

Regardless of the type of financial reform, whether power-equalizing of weighted-pupil formulas, or simply greater state assumption of costs, the districts most frequently benefiting are rural.

The "hold harmless" provisions for suburban and urban districts limit the benefits. In practice, the one reform measure that clearly benefits urban and suburban areas at the expense of rural districts is a cost-of-living plan.

Some of the pressure generated in earlier years to reorganize districts and to form larger schools remains, particularly in categorical aid provided for capital costs and for transportation. State capital dollars tend to go for new construction rather than for remodeling and renovation. State laws on transportation provide assistance if the student lives more than a certain distance (usually two miles) from school. Thus, to take advantage of these provisions, rural districts tended to build new buildings at some distance from children's homes.

Rural Finance in the Future

The aim of this section will be to sketch an agenda for those who are interested in the financing of rural education. Some parts of the agenda are speculative and need further research to demonstrate their precise value. Parts of the agenda are undoubtedly more applicable in some states than in others because demographic, economic, and political variables have great importance in designing school finance plans. Attention has been paid to the needs and wishes of urban and suburban schools in developing these recommendations. Since school finance reforms must be passed by state legislatures, there is little political sense in devising plans that cannot be supported by some urban and suburban school officials and legislators.

The general policy framework for state school finance should be governed by goals of adequacy, stability, equity, and flexibility. Each child should be provided with adequate resources to learn, regardless of the child's place of residence. The finance system should provide school districts with predictable and stable levels of resources. Equity requires that differences in the level of dollars per pupil among districts should be based on differences in the educational needs of children and not on the accidents of property wealth and income level. Finally, finance plans should allow local districts the flexibility to develop educational programs most suited to community needs.

Those are value statements not easily measured, but they do act as guideposts against which specific policies can be judged. For example, exact dollar equalization among districts does not fit well with those goals. Proposals for full state assumption of finance, coupled with provisions for the same dollars per pupil everywhere in the state, can be discarded quickly. Proposals for teacher salary determination through statewide collective bargaining clash with the goal of flexibility. All proposals for reform can be tested against these goals.

The agenda for rural school finance within these broad goals should include the following items.

1. States should assume an increased proportion of total educational costs. This furthers the goals of adequacy, stability, and equity.
2. Distribution of aid should provide proportionately greater assistance to districts with low property wealth and low income. A variety of mechanisms can be used to distribute the money.
3. Flat grants to districts should be eliminated entirely. Some rich districts will probably get no state aid.
4. States should consider assuming the full cost of transportation and capital expenditures.
5. School district reorganization will not solve rural financing difficulties. Financial aid should not be tied to incentives for larger districts.
6. Expenditure and budget decisions (within the constraints of broad state laws) should be decentralized to the school level.
7. A review of state standards in all areas should be made to determine whether the rules are really necessary to quality education. Flexibility should be allowed for local district decisions within broad guidelines.

Centralization and Redistribution

The analysis of available property wealth and income in rural areas makes it clear that an even higher proportion of state dollars is needed to adequately finance rural schools. This lack of wealth has been repeatedly identified as a problem, yet only halfway measures have been applied. States probably must supply about 70 percent (the exact figure will vary from state to state) or more of total state and local school expenditures through a distribution system that provides proportionately greater assistance to poor districts for the wealth liabilities of rural districts to be ameliorated. Since the average state contribution in the United States is less than 50 percent, most states have a major task ahead in increasing the proportion of state outlays.

Simply increasing state dollars, however, is not enough. The demands of equity require that allocations redistribute the wealth. That is politically the most difficult task. Since states are responsible for educating all children within their borders, it is a reasonable tenet of state policy to require that all children share equitably in the resources available to the state. Variations in expenditure will continue to exist among districts even under an optimal system. Different districts have different mixes of children with varying needs. However, the range of expenditure per child from high district to low district probably should vary less than 1.5 to 1. Since many states still have a range of 5 or 10 to 1 in expenditure per child, the job to be done here is also large.

Another clear item to attack in state finance systems is flat grants of general aid that go to all districts. They are highly disequalizing. Power-equalizing finance plans, weighted-pupil plans, and many variations on each are all possible alternatives for states to consider. Weighted-pupil plans probably focus more precisely on the needs of special groups of children; however, it is possible with a combination of power-equalizing basic aid and categorical grants to target dollars to children and to districts that most need them.

Centralization of school finance can help alleviate two other problems, one longstanding and the other emerging. The longstanding issue is the phenomenon of company towns where the major tax contributor to schools is a single industry or agribusiness enterprise. The tendency is for great influence to be exerted on school policy by the one large contributor. That can become an unhealthy situation and is ameliorated to some degree if the state contribution to the schools is increased. The emergent problem has occurred in some southern districts as whites have fled desegregated public schools for private white academies. The white population then becomes reluctant to support public school tax issues at the local level. Large state contributions to local finance help maintain adequate levels of support for the public schools in these areas.

Centralization and distribution of aid raises the question of the federal role in education finance. If it is proper for states to foot the bill, why not centralize to the federal level? At least two major reasons exist for arguing against that.

First, education is a function of state government and always has been. State constitutions call for the state to be responsible for the public education of children. The federal government role has always been to provide aid for specialized programs—training, libraries, disadvantaged children, handicapped children. If states did not have sufficient tax bases to provide general aid for the schools, then perhaps federal aid would make some sense. However, most states have ample untapped resources at their disposal.

Second, school enrollment is declining and will do so for at least another ten years. The relatively stable and declining birth rate suggests that after a slight increase in the 1980s, school enrollment in the 1990s may also be stable. That greatly lessens the pressure for federal aid and may over time lead to lower costs. The current major cost pressure is teacher salaries, and the major lobbyist for federal general support is the NEA.

The general policy framework established in this paper does not require large new doses of federal aid for implementation. The federal role should probably continue to be that of providing substantial aid for "unlucky children"—the handicapped, the very poor, the child with special learning problems.[44] Evidence suggests that distribution patterns for certain federal categorical programs favor metropolitan areas.[45] Current federal categorical aid and all future allotments need better coordination with state and local dollars to assure that the policy goals of equity and flexibility are achieved. Those concerned with rural schools can accomplish much by continuing to focus attention on state capitols rather than on Washington.

Capital and Transportation Costs

Two categories of costs that fall heavily on rural areas are capital outlay and transportation. It would be extremely beneficial to rural districts if those costs could be assumed by state funds. Substantial benefits would also accrue to urban districts; therefore, state assumption may be politically possible.

As earlier analysis indicates, the ability to pay for capital expenditures is linked to property wealth in the same way as operating expenditures. Taxpayer equity can generally be achieved only when the ability to build new buildings and remodel old ones are related to need and not to the accidents of location. It is patently absurd for a district like Northwest Local, in Scioto County, Ohio, to levy 9 mills for capital outlay and debt service while they can levy only 20 mills for educational programs. Those 20 mills generate a combined total of $692 per pupil, some $400 less than the state's average expenditure. Rural districts have a particular claim on state resources for capital outlay and debt service since state-mandated consolidation and reorganization have saddled rural areas with substantial debt obligations.

Capital outlay costs also drastically affect urban districts. Site acquisition costs are dear in densely populated cities. Construction costs are higher in urban areas than in rural areas. In addition, the stock of buildings in many cities has been allowed to deteriorate badly as maintenance was foregone for other pressing needs. Remodeling and rebuilding the schools of urban America will take greater investment than local sources can provide.

Florida and Maryland have fully assumed the costs of construction. Careful analysis of the outcomes of full state funding there should provide guidance to other states. Even if paying total capital bills is politically impossible, other more limited reforms of capital expenditure would benefit rural areas. First, information systems should be developed at the state level that describe the existing stock of school buildings. Only a few states have such systems. Second, the twenty-five states that contribute little or nothing toward capital costs should provide some assistance. Third, states should allow their higher credit ratings to be used by local districts when borrowing for capital expenditures. These three short-range steps would benefit children in rural districts and do not foreclose possible full assumption of capital costs in the future.[46]

Transportation costs vary with geography. Rural districts are saddled with higher proportional costs because children are scattered over a large territory. There seems to be little sense in limiting instructional dollars in poor rural districts by requiring local districts to pay for transportation.

Some states have general aid formula corrections for small schools and small districts or for population sparsity. These are always politically controversial because of the longstanding belief that big schools and large districts are "better." Full assumption of transportation costs may be more palatable in those states where other sparsity factors are not already included in state formulas.

Transportation costs in urban areas are increasing, partly because of constitutional requirements to desegregate, which sometimes involve transportation of additional pupils. Current emotional political rhetoric probably makes full assumption of transportation costs impossible in those states where court orders for desegregation are pending. In those states where desegregation plans involving transportation are a reality, however, urban districts may well join with rural ones to urge state legislative support for greater transportation subsidies.

Local Control

The final three items on the proposed agenda deal with state and local governance relationships or local control. As earlier analysis suggests, the political slogan of local control is largely overrated. In school finance, the major tenet of local control is that local districts should determine the level of spending for education by voting for operating millage. But analysis indicates that operating millage is a function of income, which means that local control guarantees that rich children have better-financed schools than poor children. Local control of educational programs is also greatly attenuated by state regulations and by decisions made by textbook companies, test publishers, and organizations of professional educators.

Maintenance of existing patterns of "local control" largely benefits the suburbs and the education professionals. Suburbs are rich and have well-financed schools. They want to keep it that way. Education professionals have major influence on state legislatures through organizations that lobby in state capitols. They argue that only educators should decide about educational matters and use the ideology of maintaining local control to obscure their dominant influence in state capitols and on local school boards.

America's schools desperately need to redefine "local control" and to develop a new order of relations between citizens and professional educators. It is beyond the scope of this chapter to outline in detail that new relationship. The important point is that providing ample resources from state sources need not restrict a decentralization of decisions about program, budget, and school organization. In fact, it may be possible to increase citizen involvement in rural schools (as well as urban ones) through school finance reform.

Several school finance reforms have included new assessment and accountability requirements in response to the argument that dollars do not make a difference in what children learn. Other states have instituted, or have under study as part of financial reform, decentralized budgeting systems that allow for greater principal, teacher, and citizen involvement from the school level up.

For rural districts, three issues in local-state relations are especially important. First, it is long overdue for educators and financial experts to stop pretending that school district reorganization alone will solve rural school finance problems. It will not. And the resulting distant, alien achool administration does nothing to enhance parent, citizen, and student involvement in education. State finance policy should recognize that small schools and small districts have value and are worth continuing. If further tax base equalization is deemed desirable, there are many proposals to develop regional tax collection areas while maintaining the administration and operation of schools in existing districts.

Second, because many rural school districts are already fairly large, they will benefit from the decentralization of budget and expenditure decisions to the school level. In simple terms, each principal would be given an annual allocation of money for a school. The budget for the year would be developed in cooperation with teachers, noncertified staff, and an advisory council of parents, citizens, and students. Decisions about program, staffing patterns, and special programs can be made as budgets are developed. Such a process allows for maximum community flexibility in the use of resources.

Florida has mandated school site budgeting statewide; many districts in other states are experimenting with various parts of it. The process has enormous problems: principals must be retrained; collective bargaining agreements must be carefully interpreted; and computer budget management is needed. No one argues that decentralization of budgeting is easy, but it does seem a sensible first step in reordering citizen-professional relations about school expenditures.

Third, and finally, a reordering of those relationships will not come about until state standards affecting all areas of public education are reviewed and revised. Many of the regulations were written at a time when professional educators were trying to gain control over the school enterprise. They badly need review in the light of collective bargaining, special problems in rural and urban areas, new priorities in secondary education, and the need for greater diversity throughout the system. Education professionals will fight to control this process of review and revision. State legislators, citizen organizations, and parents will need to participate actively if such revisions are to benefit parents and children.

Conclusion

Money has always been scarce for rural schools. That problem continues. There are, however, ways to ameliorate this scarcity by building on existing school finance reform efforts. Those concerned about providing adequate educational resources for rural children should continue the pressure for further centralization of school finance. In addition, full assumption of costs for capital outlay and transportation will greatly benefit rural school districts.

Centralization of school finance does not have to result in a further erosion of local control. In fact, local control is not very useful if resources are not plentiful enough to provide real choices. Those in rural areas who are concerned about local control should focus on reshaping the balance between education professionals and citizens in their schools and districts. They will find many allies on that issue in urban and suburban districts.

Further, centralization of school finance should not make citizen involvement in educational decision making more difficult to attain. It may, in fact, make it easier, as education professionals and citizens alike stop spending so much time arguing about taxes and finance problems and spend more time focusing on children and educational programs. Such a redirection of emphasis and attention can only serve to benefit America's rural schools and schoolchildren.

Part Three
The Real World

5 Class Conflict in Rural Education: A Case Study of Preston County, West Virginia

Timothy Weaver

Editor's Prologue

Few things make Americans as uncomfortable as arguments and analyses based upon class distinctions. The very existence of explicit social and economic classes has long been either ignored or denied by the mainstream of American public opinion and political rhetoric. Thus, to assert that class interests often lie at the very heart of the formulation and implementation of public policy in America is a direct affront to our self-portrait of egalitarianism, participatory democracy, and an unbiased meritocracy.

While this image of classlessness (or at least of class having no discernible influence on our conduct of public affairs) is accepted throughout America, it has always been particularly cherished and championed by America's small towns. Rural sociologists have consistently noted the discrepancy between the fact of social and economic stratification in rural communities and its acknowledgment by rural citizens.

James West, for example, in his study *Plainville, U.S.A.* observed, "Many, if not most, Plainvillers completely deny the existence of class in their community."[1] Similarly, Vidich and Bensman, in their classic work *Small Town in Mass Society* argue:

> The public ideology of equality has its economic correlates. One must not suppose that inequalities in income and wealth go unnoticed; rather, they are quite closely watched and known in Springdale. However, such differ-

ences, as in the image of the frontier community, are not publicly weighed and evaluated as the measure of the man. In everyday social intercourse, it is a *faux pas* to act as if economic inequalities make a difference.[2]

In part, this occurs because the public pretense of egalitarianism allows such small, closely knit communities to operate with a minimum of friction and dissension. Yet, the fact remains that this illusion of classlessness serves primarily the middle and upper classes by preserving the status quo. In other words, a public ideology that espouses equality and purports to seek the "common good" actually masks underlying class conflicts and discourages the explicit recognition of class discrimination.

No facet of rural life, including education, has escaped the ramifications of this contradiction. For example, in the continuing struggle over school and district consolidation in rural America, the combatants have been described in a variety of ways over the years. Originally, consolidation was viewed as pitting "enlightened and progressive" citizens against their "ignorant and provincial" counterparts. Most often, the characterization is one of professional educators versus parents and local taxpayers, or, more simply, experts versus amateurs. And, because consolidation usually implied that *all* children in a given geographic area would attend the same school, it was occasionally seen in the southern states as a conflict between segregationists and integrationists. Other labels included liberals versus conservatives, urbanites versus ruralites, and consolidators versus conservators. Still, the single formulation in the consolidation controversy that remained largely unidentified is that of opposing class interests.

Identifying elements of class conflict is not a rejection of the validity of other explanations for the continuing animosity and controversy engendered by consolidation. Rather, it is a supplemental explanation that can fill in some of the gaps left by more traditional analyses. Specifically, an examination of the politics of consolidation which directly confronts class interests can shed considerable light on three key questions.

First, why have the opposing factions been so monolithic throughout the nation and over time? Tyack and other historians have observed that consolidation was rarely, if ever, initiated or actively supported by rural (predominantly lower- and workingclass) communities.[3] However, even more remarkable is the astounding consensus about the value and importance of consolidation found among education professionals and other middle-class interests, a group normally prone to widespread dissension on even the most trivial issues and policies.

Second, why has so little valid and unbiased research been conducted on consolidation-related issues? Sher and Tompkins have provided some of the answers. Their observation that educational research has never been subject to rigorous standards is particularly apt.[4] Still, few other educational "reforms" have been promoted with the zeal accorded to consolidation. More important, few other bodies of professional literature and research have been as blatantly propagandist (indeed evangelical) as that developed in support of consolidation.

Third, why does consolidation continue to be advocated not only in the face of staunch opposition by the alleged beneficiaries, but also despite evidence and experience that refutes the "rational" arguments for it? Consolidation is no longer a new and untested reform strategy. Actual experience has weakened and undermined its rationality. The theorized economies and efficiencies have not, in fact, materialized, and the academic performance and life chances of students in consolidated schools have not demonstrably surpassed those of small community school pupils (exclusive, of course, of IQ and family background).

The thesis of this chapter is that an undercurrent of conflicting class interests has permeated the consolidation debate. The contention is that the desire to further (or at least maintain) distinct class interests is a strong explanatory variable of the "irrational" behavior patterns that typify this controversy. For members of the middle class (including professional educators), consolidation is an effective way to strengthen influence and control within the community, while furthering their aspirations for their children. Yet, to the rural poor and working classes, consolidation represents an attempt to destroy what is often their only sphere of public influence and their last vestige of control over their children's education and socialization.

The implications of this underlying class struggle are both simple and profound. Above all else, it reveals that consolidation is, at heart, a political rather than an educational issue. Proponents have continually manipulated the rituals and symbols of education by trying, for example, to link consolidation with improved educational inputs and increased academic achievement. But, as this chapter will document, disproving these linkages and presenting viable nonconsolidation alternatives for improvement do nothing to dissuade their advocacy or diminish their fervor. In fact, this investigation suggests that the consolidation debate would persist, even if ironclad, airtight, indisputably conclusive evidence were found about consolidation's effect upon educational costs, student aspirations and achievement, and operating efficiency. This remains a moot point, however, because such evidence is a long way off. Unfortunately, what we don't know about achieving desired educational outcomes is exceeded only by our current inability to accurately measure that which we do understand.

There are two further implications. First, more research on the economic and educational merits of consolidation, while interesting and useful, is not likely to bring this debate to a lasting resolution. Second, this controversy is unlikely to be quelled at all in the absence of either outright capitulation by one side or an explicit acknowledgment of the political underpinnings of the issue coupled with an attempt at political compromise.

This chapter is devoted to examining consolidation's underlying class conflicts within one rural school district: Preston County, West Virginia.[5]

Section One: Case History

Overview

On May 11, 1976, a school bond election was held in Preston County, West Virginia, the fourth since September 18, 1973. All four bond issues were defeated by the voters. However, the last bond election differed from the previous three in one very important respect. It presented a community school plan to the voters, whereas the other three bonds presented school consolidation plans.

By prearrangement, the school board moved ahead on May 12, 1976, to begin implementing a consolidation plan using *state* funds under the Better Schools Amendment Act. The school board's consolidation plan has been approved by the local board and the state board. This plan neither required nor received endorsement by the voters. The plan is similar in many respects to the three consolidation plans that were defeated. In effect, the school board in Preston County is now able to accomplish by default what it could not accomplish through the ballot.

This chapter examines the policy arguments and ideas that emerge in the Preston County controversy. These arguments are examined against the social class interests that underlie much of the policy debate in American education and in the light of recent educational research on school size and achievement. That research has begun to raise important questions about the relative effects of resource differences on achievement, once family background and aptitude are controlled. If we modify the input side of the school equation but find that output is little changed, then the dominant arguments for consolidation are called immediately into question. If more subjects, bigger schools, new buildings, or more specialists make little difference in achievement, independent of the effects of family and aptitude, why then disrupt families and communities by closing small schools?

Our analysis of Preston County shows that none of the arguments presented in favor of consolidation deal with likely outcomes for children. Rather, the arguments advanced by the county school board and other consolidators focused on administrative and economic efficiency and on variety in the curriculum. For example, one element of the board's consolidation plan is an arrangement for five-year-olds to be in school all day for ten weeks and then at home all day for ten weeks. The rationale presented is that this arrangement will save money on transportation to offset the costs of consolidation.

Because the research data contradict some longstanding assumptions about the benefits of consolidation, one would have expected at least some re-examination of those assumptions by the proponents of consolidation. Instead, the research was rejected as obviously incorrect or simply unbelievable because it failed to agree with preconceived notions. It was argued that a community school plan simply *could not* promise as much as consolidation because it would not reduce the number of schools or significantly enlarge their size. Therefore, a community school plan was rejected by some voters because of its perceived curricular deficiencies, even though the small school plan in question actually proposed the same courses as the board's final consolidation plan.

The arguments most frequently presented for consolidation in Preston County are those of classic liberal progressivism. It was contended that professionals know best, that small schools cannot prepare rural youth for participation in a complex world, and that children benefit from newer buildings, broader and more varied curriculum, more specialized staff, and differentiation of function. These are only possible through consolidation because it is the only *feasible economic* way to provide these benefits. Those who opposed consolidation not only opposed progress, but opposed reason.

The irony of this situation is that the basic issue of consolidation was never tested in the election process. Consolidation simply did not mean to the average voter what it meant to the education professionals. Consolidation, as we will show, has practically no acceptance among voters in Preston County when it means to any given community that its school will be closed or its children transported a farther distance.

Because neither the economic argument nor the improved quality argument are valid in Preston County, although they were frequently used, other explanations were sought. One is social class. For instance, during a presentation of the board's consolidation plan before the state superintendent, a consolidation supporter characterized the opposition as "barefoot and pregnant" and suggested that such persons would be the prime beneficiaries of bigger and better schools.

This chapter presents a description of Preston County; an analysis of the results of the four board elections in which various school plans were presented; a brief examination of the educational research relevant to Preston County; an analysis of the school board's consolidation plans and the community school plan; and, finally, an examination of the key underlying issues, especially social class.

Demographic Background

Preston County (population 25,455) is a sparsely settled, relatively poor, rural county in West Virginia. As Table 5.1 indicates, Preston County lags behind both West Virginia and the United States as a whole on most economic and educational indices. However, Preston County citizens spend proportionately more local funds on education and health than either their state or the United States as a whole. The county is currently taxed to 100 percent of capacity under a 1973 Special Levy for operational support of the schools. Therefore, it

TABLE 5.1

Social and Economic Indicators for Preston County,
West Virginia, and the United States, 1972

Indicators	Preston County	W. Va.	U.S.
Median years of schooling completed by persons 25 and over	9.6	10.6	12.1
Percentage of persons 25 and over who have completed 4 years of college or more	4.3	6.8	10.7
Percentage of workers classified as professionals-managerial or sales-clerical	27.7	40.5	48.3
Percentage of residents who work outside of county	27.6	17.3	17.8
Median family income	$5,626	$ 7,414	$ 9,586
Percent of families earning $15,000 or more	4.8	8.6	20.6
Average value of owner-occupied single family homes	$7,353	$11,601	$17,130
Percentage of low-income families	26.9	18.1	10.7
Property tax per capita	$ 48	$ 59	$ 129
Percentage of direct local expenditures on education	73.1	68.7	48.0
Percentage of direct local expenditures on health	8.0	3.8	2.3
Percentage of manufacturers with 100 or more employees	4.9	11.7	11.2
Average value of farms per acre	$ 105	$ 136	$ 194
Percentage of farms with sales over $40,000 annually	5.2	20.0	12.8

SOURCE: U.S. Department of Commerce, City and County Data Book   (Washington, D.C.:   U.S. Government Printing Office, 1972).

cannot reasonably be argued that the county's citizens are apathetic in their support of basic human services.

Preston County, like many rural counties, tends to be organized economically and politically around the courthouse. Business, professional, and governmental activities are concentrated in the county seat. A review of the county's listings for business, governmental, professional, and other nonresidential phones reveals that just under 50 percent of all such listings are located in Kingwood, the county

TABLE 5.2

Business, Professional, Governmental, and Other
Non-Residential Telephone Listings for
Preston County, West Virginia

Community	Number of Listings	Percentage of Total Listings	Population	Percentage of Total Population
Kingwood	283	46.7	2,550	10.0
Masontown-Reedsville	85	14.0	1,247	4.8
Terra Alta	81	13.4	1,474	5.7
Brucetown, Brandonville, Valley Point	53	8.7	291	1.1
Aurora (including Eglon, Horse Shoe Run, and remainder of Union District)	34	5.6	1,846	7.3
Rowlesburg	28	4.6	829	3.2
Newburg-Fellowsville	24	4.0	457	1.7
Tunnelton	18	3.0	369	1.4

SOURCE: All listings were derived from the 1975-1976 telephone directory published by the five telephone companies serving Preston County, West Virginia.

seat and largest town; yet Kingwood contains only about 10 percent of the county's total population. Kingwood, Terra Alta, and Masontown-Reedsville (the three largest communities) contain approximately 75 percent of all business, professional, governmental, and nonresidential listings; yet these communities combined have only about 20 percent of the county's population. Table 5.2 presents the listings and population for all major communities in Preston County.

Education is at present far more widely distributed than are business, professional, or other governmental services in Preston County. However, the school board's plan is to remove high schools from Aurora, Rowlesburg, Newburg, Tunnelton, and Bruceton— towns that already have the fewest services. Children from these communities will attend school in the three towns that now dominate the county's business, professional, and other governmental activities.

TABLE 5.3

Social and Economic Indicators for
Communities within Preston County, 1970

	Average Family Income	Percentage of Families Under Poverty Level	Percentage of Prof., Tech., & Managerial Residents	Percentage of Population over 25 Completing High School
Dominant communities[a]	$8,224	19.0	22.2	49.8
Other communities[b]	$5,649	28.9	12.8	37.6

SOURCE: Figures from 1970 Census of Population and Housing, Fifth Count
Information (Ithaca, N.Y.: National Planning Data Corporation,
1976).

[a]Kingwood, Albright, Masontown, Reedsville, and Terra Alta

[b]Rowlesburg, Bruceton, Tunnelton, Newburg, and Union District (Aurora,
Eglon, and Horse Shoe Run)

Socioeconomic Status

The distribution of family income, level of schooling, occupational status, and percentage of impoverished families is consistent with the analysis of phone listings in Table 5.2.[6] The dominant communities (Kingwood, Masontown-Reedsville, and Terra Alta) differ significantly from the remainder of the county, not only in available services, but also in socioeconomic status. For instance, family income among the dominant communities totals $12.8 million as compared to $6.0 million for the other five communities. Yet, the dominant communities contain only slightly over one-half of the families. The data on socioeconomic status are presented in Table 5.3.

Table 5.4 shows more detailed data on income and level of education for the thirteen magisterial districts that make up the two sets of communities. With one exception, all of the communities that retain schools under the school board's proposed consolidation plan rank in the *top* one-half of the communities, both in income above $10,000 and percentage of population over age twenty-five who have

TABLE 5.4

Social and Economic Indicators in Preston County by Magisterial District, 1970

Magesterial District	Population	Family Income		Families and Unrelated Individuals Earning $10,000 or More		Families Below Poverty Level		Population Over 25 with 12 Years or More Schooling	
		Average	Rank	Percentage	Rank	Percentage	Rank	Percentage	Rank
Tunnelton	358	$ 4,857	13	0	12	43.1	1	32.4	13
Union District	1,846	5,119	12	7.6	9	28.0	4	32.8	9
Terra Alta II*	750	5,306	11	4.3	11	39.8	3	33.0	8
Rowlesburg I	118	5,646	10	0	13	41.4	2	31.4	12
Bruceton	221	5,696	9	5.6	10	22.6	8	36.8	7
Newburg	523	6,598	8	14.4	8	20.1	9	32.1	11
Rowlesburg II	715	6,759	7	17.5	5	26.8	7	46.9	4
Terra Alta I*	859	7,176	6	15.8	6	27.1	6	42.4	4
Albright*	427	6,460	5	20.3	4	28.0	5	25.6	10
Masontown*	815	8,108	4	15.2	7	17.0	11	40.9	5
Reedsville*	425	8,254	3	24.8	2	9.5	12	39.1	6
Kingwood II*	1,410	9,073	2	24.1	3	17.0	10	53.6	2
Kingwood I*	1,140	10,170	1	45.1	1	3.3	13	77.9	1

SOURCE: Figures from 1970 Census of Population and Planning, Fifth County Information (Ithaca, N.Y.: National Planning Data Corporation, 1976).

*Children in these voting districts would remain at their current high schools under the proposed consolidation. All unasterisked voting districts would lose their high schools and have to bus their children to the wealthier towns.

completed at least four years of high school. With one exception, all communities scheduled to lose their schools rank in the *lower* one-half of the communities, as measured by education and income.

The pattern is obvious. Towns now generally characterized by higher socioeconomic status and the greatest concentration of business activities will keep or expand their high schools under the board's final consolidation plan. The less fortunate communities lose their schools.

The Schools

In West Virginia, all school districts are coterminous with county boundaries. Preston County has one Board of Education with five members elected at large (with no more than two from any single magisterial district). The administration of the school system is centralized under a superintendent, assistant superintendent, and administrative staff.

The current enrollment in all schools, grades 1-12, is 6,264, representing a net loss of 529 students over the past 10 years. Enrollment projections show a continued net decline, leveling off at approximately 5,363 students in 1984-85.[7] There are currently 8 high schools in the county, ranging in size from 24 seniors to 108 seniors (see Table 5.5). In addition, there are 25 elementary programs organized in a variety of ways (for example, 1-8, K-6, and so on). These elementary programs currently range in size from 22 to 141 pupils. Several of the school buildings are antiquated and 2 elementary school buildings are acknowledged to be structurally unsafe. The generally poor physical condition of the county's schools is uncontested by all parties in the consolidation debate.

Consolidation Plans

The push for consolidation is not new in Preston County. However, the intensity of the debate and the level of consolidation-related efforts have increased in the past decade.

For example, in 1965, the Preston County Board of Education hired two consultants to study education in the county. Their report urged the elimination of all existing high schools in the county and the construction of one consolidated school to which all county high school students would be bused.[8] This new high school, with a

TABLE 5.5

Enrollment and Location, Preston County High Schools,
1974-1975

School	Enrollment	Location
Aurora High School	146	Aurora
Bruceton High School	174	Bruceton Mills
Newburg High School	223	Newburg
Kingwood High School	467	Kingwood
Rowlesburg High School	145	Rowlesburg
Terra Alta High School	234	Terra Alta
Tunnelton High School	187	Tunnelton
Valley High School	365	Masontown

SOURCE: Figures from <u>Comprehensive Facilities Plan</u> (Kingwood,
W. Va.: <u>Preston County Board of Education</u>, 1975), pp.
B18-B26.

projected enrollment of 1,300 to 1,400 students, would have been
built in Kingwood, the county seat and wealthiest town, with a
"branch" offering academic instruction in Terra Alta. Students using
the Terra Alta branch were to be divided into "platoons" that would
be alternately transported to Kingwood mornings and afternoons.
This plan presented no alternatives for high school organization and
improvement other than consolidation. No action was taken by the
board to implement the recommendations.

The board commissioned another consultant report in 1968.[9] Once
again, the consultants called for the construction of a central
vocational-academic high school near Kingwood which would
eventually house all county students in grades 9-12. The plan called
for an environmentally oriented curriculum for the high school,
referred to by the planners as a "living and learning laboratory." All
other high schools would be closed. In addition, this plan recommended consolidation of the elementary school programs, then in 21
different locations, into 11 elementary school centers. All told, the
consultants recommended the closing of 34 school buildings in the
county and the major renovation of 2 buildings. The plan presented
no alternatives for reform other than consolidation. Again, no action
was taken by the board to implement the plan.

The board sought still another study in 1971—this time by an Ohio
State University consultant team. However, noting past resistance to

consolidation, the Ohio State consultants' strategy was more explicitly political. As their own report states:

> The purpose of this study is to plan an intermediate step to improve the educational facilities which exist in this county, and, at the same time, provide a step toward the realization of the longrange plan. The need for this intermediate step became known when the plan proposing one high school met some resistance in the county. Assessment of public opinion indicated that moving to the one high school plan immediately is a more drastic step than will be accepted by the local constituency. For this reason, an intermediate step [of consolidating into four high schools] is suggested.[10]

Though no immediate action was taken by the board, this strategy was later incorporated into their Comprehensive Facilities Plan.

Bond Elections and the Better Schools Amendment

In 1973, the West Virginia legislature passed the Better Schools Amendment Act, which was to provide approximately $250 million to rehabilitate or replace unsafe school buildings. Funds were to be divided pro rata among the 55 counties in the state. Under the provisions of the Better Schools Amendment, Preston County would receive approximately $3.4 million for renovations and new construction. The Better Schools Amendment requires a local plan for the use of these funds. Matching funds are encouraged, but it is unclear whether the counties are supposed to pass a bond issue for the matching funds prior to, or after, receipt of state funds.[11]

The Preston County Board of Education seized the Better Schools Amendment as a way to finally bring a consolidation plan to successful fruition. Beginning in September 1973, the board presented the first of three bond referendums designed to raise the matching funds for a full-blown consolidation effort.

The events between September 18, 1973, and the present show two phases. During the first phase, September 1973-March 1976, the Board of Education attempted, unsuccessfully, to develop a political consensus and majority approval for some form of school consolida-

TABLE 5.6

First Bond Issue Results:
Kingwood-Valley High Precincts

Precinct	Miles (est.)	Travel Time (est.)	Percentage Voting for the Bond Issue
Albright	12	44 min.*	20
Kingwood District (precincts 4, 5, 6, 7)	9	18 min.	22.48-22.86
Valley District (Masontown, all precincts)	3	7 min.	56.47

*Includes transfer point.

tion. No effort was made to compromise with the organized opposition and no alternative to consolidation was ever seriously considered. The second phase, March 1976-May 11, 1976, might be called reluctant compromise. It began with organized citizen protests and ended with a fourth bond in May 1976, which failed to pass. Failure of the last bond meant the board could proceed to consolidate the schools with its share of state funds.

First Bond

On September 18, 1973, a special election was held in Preston County to vote on two issues. One was a special levy to produce approximately $3.6 million over five years for various renovations and for operational and maintenance expenses for the schools. The special levy was passed by a 5 to 1 margin. The other was a bond issue that sought to raise an additional $4.9 million for school consolidation. The bond failed.

The consolidation bond was to be used for new construction, site acquisition, and improvements. It would have combined eight high schools into four: (1) Kingwood-Masontown Valley; (2) Tunnelton-Newburg-Fellowsville; (3) Terra Alta-Aurora-Rowlesburg; and (4) Bruceton. The locations are important because distance from proposed site is strongly reflected in the voting pattern.

    1. The Kingwood-Valley High School was to be located in the Valley District. Voting results from affected precincts in order

TABLE 5.7

First Bond Issue Results:
Tunnelton-Newburg-Fellowsville Precincts

Precinct	Miles (est.)	Travel Time (est.)	Percentage Voting for the Bond Issue
Independence	6	15 min.	24.07
Gladesville (Valley)	6	15 min.	47.62
Newburg (North)	4	12 min.	48.65
Newburg (South)	4	12 min.	59.14
Tunnelton	4	20 min.*	65.12
Fellowsville	4	10 min.	66.79

*Includes transfer point.

of distance from the proposed high school location are shown in Table 5.6.

2. Tunnelton-Newburg-Fellowsville High School was to be located between Tunnelton and Fellowsville on Route 26. Voting results from affected precincts in order of distance from proposed high school location are shown in Table 5.7.

3. The Terra Alta-Aurora-Rowlesburg High School was to be located in Terra Alta. Results from affected precincts in order of distance from the proposed new high school location are shown in Table 5.8.

The first bond issue failed to attract the necessary 60 percent required for passage. The total results were: in favor of the bond—2,674 (46.63 percent); against the bond—3,060 (53.37 percent). The bond issue had been widely publicized by the Board of Education and the local newspapers. Numerous meetings were held around the county to explain this plan to the voters. The board, by its own account, held nine meetings with groups from the major communities in the county. These data show that distance from a proposed high school location was an important factor in explaining the vote—perhaps the *key* factor. With few exceptions, the votes from all seventy-two precincts can be plotted in a nearly perfect rank order by distance from a proposed high school site. In addition, as Tables 5.2, 5.3, and 5.4 indicate, distance is a reasonable proxy for class; that

TABLE 5.8

First Bond Issue Results:
Terra Alta-Aurora-Rowlesburg Precincts

Precinct	Miles (est.)	Travel Time (est.)	Percentage Voting for the Bond Issue
Etam	22	65 min.*	10.77
Horse Shoe Run	18	51 min.*	6.61
Eglon	16	50 min.	15.83
Rowlesburg (North)	12	35 min.	8.20
Rowlesburg (South)	12	35 min.	13.20
Aurora	11	25 min.	10.87
Tanner	6	17 min.	45.45
Terra Alta (precincts 49, 50, 51, 52)	1	under 10 min.	65.35-88.24

*Includes transfer point.

is, there is an apparent correlation between distance from a proposed high school site and several socioeconomic indicators. In general, as distance increases, these class indicators (by community) decrease. Thus, the poorest communities tend to be the ones farthest away from the high school sites proposed under the board's consolidation plan.

Second Bond

On October 8, 1974, a second bond issue to raise $5.3 million for school consolidation was presented to the voters. This time, the board proposed a different combination of schools. There were notable changes in the plan: (1) Kingwood students were to be returned to Kingwood to a new facility instead of being bused to Valley High; (2) Rowlesburg students were to be combined with Kingwood instead of Terra Alta (Aurora remains combined with Terra Alta); and (3) the Tunnelton-Newburg-Fellowsville High School plan was abandoned.

This bond issue also failed to receive the requisite 60 percent favorable vote. A total of 6,014 votes were cast, 3,445 in favor of the bond (57.28 percent) and 2,569 against (42.72 percent). A reversal in the Kingwood District vote accounts for the overall increase in the percentage of votes cast for the bond. Below is a breakdown of the votes for the bond by distance from the high school location.

TABLE 5.9

Second Bond Issue: Kingwood, Rowlesburg Precincts

Precinct	Miles (est.)	Travel Time (est.)	Percentage Voting for the Bond Issue
Etam	22	65 min.*	17.54
Rowlesburg (South)	12	25 min.	18.82
Rowlesburg (North)	12	25 min.	15.13
Albright	3	10 min.	47.62
Kingwood (precincts 4, 5, 6, 7)	1	under 10 min.	68.59-72.22

*Includes transfer point.

TABLE 5.10

Second Bond Issue: Terra Alta-Aurora Precincts

Precincts	Miles (est.)	Travel Time (est.)	Percentage Voting for the Bond Issue
Horse Shoe Run	18	51 min.*	4.80
Eglon	16	50 min.*	14.81
Aurora	11	23 min.	21.09
Terra Alta (precincts 49, 50, 51, 52)	1	under 10 min.	65.35-80.00

*Includes transfer point.

1. Kingwood-Rowlesburg High School was to be located in Kingwood. Voting results from affected precincts by order of distance from proposed location of the new school are given in Table 5.9.
2. Terra Alta-Aurora High School was to be located in Terra Alta. Voting results from affected precincts by order of distance from proposed location of the new school are given in Table 5.10.

Third Bond

On November 23, 1974, a third bond was presented to the voters of Preston County. Only one major change was made in the plan. The

TABLE 5.11

Results of Three Bond Issues, Preston County

	Registered Voters	Ballots Cast	Percentage Voting	Vote For	Vote Against	Total Votes	Percentage For
First Bond Issue	13,701	5,783	42.21	2,674	3,060	5,734	46.63
Second Bond Issue	13,809	6,014	43.55	3,445	2,569	6,014	57.28
Third Bond Issue	14,190	6,983	49.21	3,437	3,546	6,933	49.22

location of the proposed new elementary school for Tunnelton, Newburg, and Fellowsville was shifted from a site between Fellowsville and Tunnelton to a site to be either in Fellowsville or no more than four miles west.

The third bond was also defeated. The totals were: 3,437 votes for (49.22 percent); 3,546 votes against (50.78 percent). The three bond issues all called for approximatèly the same amount of money ($4.9, $5.3, and $5.3 million respectively). The vote totals for the three bond issues are given in Table 5.11. Table 5.12 presents a breakdown of the vote in the three elections.

Analysis

The Preston County Board of Education presented no alternatives to consolidation in the three bond elections. The only questions were *how many* schools would be consolidated and exactly *where* they would be located. The first bond would have resulted in four high schools. The second and third bonds would have resulted in six high schools. The vote on the bonds solidified around distance. Those precincts voting most consistently against the bonds were located most distant from the proposed high school locations. However, in several cases, communities voting most heavily against consolidation themselves had no high schools and were already some distance from existing high schools.[12]

A group of Preston County citizens had organized an active campaign against the third bond issue, calling themselves Equality for All Prestonians (EAP). The group formally opposed the efforts of the Board of Education to consolidate the high schools, but was not opposed either to rehabilitation or to the Special Levy passed earlier to improve the schools. Their reasons for opposing consolidation ranged from educational, financial, and political issues to safety

TABLE 5.12

Results of Three Bond Issues, by District

	Kingwood	Valley	Lyon	Reno	Union	Portland	Pleasant	Grant
First Bond Issue (September 18, 1973)								
Percentage Voting for Bond	32.74	56.47	47.21	44.32	12.43	65.40	37.96	79.71
Total Votes, For-Against	463-951	554-427	144-161	382-480	67-472	584-309	95-162	385-98
Second Bond Issue (October 8, 1974)								
Percentage Voting for Bond	70.28[a]	53.41	35.00[b]	40.75	16.31	66.46	68.10[c]	87.37
Total Votes, For-Against	1071-453	493-430	133-247	339-493	91-467	630-318	190-89	498-72
Third Bond Issue (November 23, 1974)								
Percentage Voting for Bond	65.20	51.00	33.47	27.53[d]	7.44[e]	58.55	65.85	84.15
Total Votes, For-Against	1122-539	518-499	160-318	230-737	55-739	565-400	191-151	547-103

[a] Effect of switching Kingwood High School back to Kingwood.

[b] Probably the result of withdrawing the proposal to renovate vacated Newburg High School for elementary use as planned in the September 18, 1973 bond issue, which would have allowed at that time the closing of the old Newburg Elementary School--widely acknowledged to be unsafe.

[c] The critical factor was the switch of the high school back to Kingwood, reducing travel time for Pleasant District students who attend Kingwood High School.

[d] Two factors probably influenced this change. One was the switch of Rowlesburg High School students from Terra Alta to Kingwood. The other is organized opposition by Equality for All Prestonians (voter turnout rose from 45.17% to 53.53% between the October and November elections).

[e] Since no change in plan was presented for Union District between October and November, this size erosion was due largely to organized opposition by Equality for All Prestonians (turnout rose from 49.25% to 68.83%).

concerns (this last stemming from the increased travel in a county long famous for its poor roads and severe winters). EAP was recognized by the board as a representative of local citizens' concerns and played a key role throughout the remainder of this controversy.[13]

Section Two: An Analysis of the School Board's Comprehensive Facilities Plan

In February 1975, the Preston County Board of Education publicly presented its plan to qualify for funds under the West Virginia Better Schools Amendment, despite the defeat of the three bonds. This proposal, known as the Comprehensive Facilities Plan, was seen as a way to secure the funds needed to consolidate without having to immediately tap local revenue sources or confront local opposition. The Better Schools Amendment contained no language that authorized or encouraged consolidation, but neither did it prohibit the use of funds for such purposes.

The plan itself is divided into three phases, the first of which will be funded solely with state money. The remaining two phases are supposed to be funded with local funds raised through a new bond issue within five years. However, because funds for the last two phases of the plan are highly uncertain, our focus is on Phase I of the plan.

In essence, the plan will eventually reduce the number of high schools from eight to three. The Terra Alta-Aurora attendance area will be reorganized and all senior high school students will attend the present Terra Alta high school buildings (with a new gymnasium and vocational-agriculture center). Kingwood-Tunnelton-Fellowsville attendance areas will be reorganized. All senior high students will be located in the present Kingwood high school buildings. Masontown, Valley, and Newburg high schools will be combined and located in the present Masontown-Valley High and elementary school buildings, with the elementary students transferred to a new Valley elementary school. Rowlesburg high school will remain open temporarily, as will Bruceton Mills high schools. Both will later be combined with one of the three above schools.

Facilities

An examination of how the $3.4 million in state funds is to be spent shows that while the plan will add approximately 20,000 net square feet of space to the school system, most of the net gain is found in two buildings. This net gain is attributable to the replacement of a small high school gymnasium and shop area with a larger gymnasium and shop, and the replacement of a small elementary school with a larger elementary school. The plan enlarges the overall elementary space available, but proportionately reduces space available to high school students in the three reorganized high schools.[14] Although a stated priority of the Board of Education, only 3,400 square feet out of a total of 83,500 square feet of new construction is devoted to special education and speech therapy. No language laboratories, testing facilities, diagnostic teaching centers, or other special needs facilities are proposed.

The number of students in proportion to space available in school libraries, home economics centers, guidance facilities, special education facilities, gymnasium and other athletic facilities, restrooms, student work areas, teacher work areas, science laboratories, and vocational facilities will rise substantially in the reorganized high schools. Thus, space shortages in almost all areas needed to support the instructional program will result from the consolidation at the high school level. In brief, the plan is a patchwork approach, expanding space in some places and taking it away in others. The plan's net effect is a proportionate reduction of access to all facilities other than classrooms. The negative results of this kind of tradeoff for children attending consolidated schools is documented by Barker and Gump in *Big School, Small School*.

Safety of the Buildings

The Comprehensive Facilities Plan (in Phase I) fails to meet even the most minimal objective of the West Virginia Better Schools Amendment—to safeguard the health and welfare of the children using public school buildings in the state. The Preston County plan, by the local board's own admission, fails to correct most infractions of the fire code. As the plan states:

Two hundred twenty-three infractions of the fire code
were cited in an inspection during the 1973-74 school term
by the state fire marshall's office. Fifty-nine of these
infractions would be eliminated with the construction in
Phase I.[15]

The remainder are left in doubt by the plan.

It is difficult to estimate the total cost of eliminating the
remaining infractions in Phase II, Part A, as it would most
likely take five to ten years to complete this program.
Therefore, future costs would be uncertain for this reason
as well as the fact that the fire code would probably be
revised several times within that correction period.[16]

In a revised addendum to the original plan, the board once again
affirms that it will not correct the fire code violations:

Four hundred and five infractions of the fire code were
cited in an inspection during the 1974-75 school term by the
state fire marshall's office. Eighty-eight of these infractions will be eliminated with the construction in Phase I.
. . . Estimated costs for correcting all infractions of the
state fire code is $850,000.00, as indicated in Section E. It
will take approximately ten years to correct all infractions.[17]

Transportation

The sharply increased numbers of students riding buses for longer
distances under the provisions of this plan clearly pose a serious
liability, not only for learning opportunities, but also for the physical
health and welfare of children in Preston County.

Phase I of the plan would *double* the percentage of students in grades
7-8 riding buses one way for 45 minutes or longer (from 11.74 percent
to 22.43 percent); and *more than double* the percentage of students in
grades 9-12 riding one way for 60 minutes or longer (from 14.98
percent to 32.07 percent).[18] In Phase III of the plan, the percentage
riding 60 or more minutes one way in grades 9-12 nearly *triples* (by

rising to 39.39 percent).[19]

The reader should be aware of the unusual circumstance created by the rugged mountain roads in Preston County, the sparse population, and severe winters. These will have a serious impact on the learning opportunities of children in outlying areas and will produce substantially higher safety risks than are now necessary.

Distances of no more than 30 miles can require more than 1½ hours travel time for a child. Using figures prepared for the Preston County Board of Education by Allen and Baldwin,[20] children from the southernmost point in the Aurora-Terra Alta attendance area traveling to the vocational center in Kingwood would spend a minimum of 88 minutes between home and school in good weather. Other travel times from outlying areas range from 75 minutes in the most distant Fellowsville-Tunnelton-Kingwood area to 63 minutes in the Bruceton-Mills area. These estimates did not account for either the winter weather conditions in Preston County or the frequently closed roads in the areas mentioned.

Oklahoma Study on Busing and Achievement

Recent research, conducted at the University of Oklahoma by Yao-Chi Lu and Luther Tweeten, shows that busing has an adverse impact on achievement, even when IQ and socioeconomic status are controlled.[21] These negative effects are particularly significant at the eighth-grade level. Lu and Tweeten state, "If all other factors were held constant, each hour per day spent bus-riding would be predicted to reduce achievement test scores by . . . 4.0 points for eighth-grade students."[22] Considering the distances and times involved in Preston County, this finding takes on considerable significance.

In Preston County, the children bused the greatest distances are from lower socioeconomic backgrounds. Once again, the burden of longest travel will be placed on the county's most disadvantaged families—those already living farthest from libraries and other community-based learning centers. These families, the most marginal economically, are also the people least able to make up with supplementary resources for any loss of opportunity in school. These already disadvantaged children will be unable to compete effectively in the academic program when in attendance (and even attendance will suffer as roads become impassable during the winter). Of equal importance, these low-income children will be unable in many cases to participate in any extracurricular activities (such as dramatics, school clubs, journalism, and athletics) that require after-school time.

Organization

The plan proposes, without rationale or comment, a baffling set of school organization patterns. For grades K-8, the school feeder patterns and administrative arrangements show nearly as many variations as there are schools. In the three attendance areas to be reorganized under Phase I, there will be sixteen different configurations for grades K-8, representing no known educational theory or accepted practice of school management. The plan seems totally lacking in consistency or rationale leading one to conclude that the decision making here rested solely on expediency in consolidating the schools.

The plan not only does not make administrative sense, but it also ignores such research as the Summers and Wolfe study, which presents convincing evidence of the importance of incorporating grades seven and eight into the total elementary school program. These authors state, "It seems, however, much more beneficial to be in an eighth grade that is part of an elementary school than in one that is not."[23] Further, in the Valley attendance area of the county, children would experience four different physical locations and organizational patterns prior to completion of grade eight.

Worse yet, under the plan, five-year-olds attending early childhood classes throughout the county will attend classes all day for ten weeks and then be home all day for ten weeks. This arrangement appears on the surface damaging to learning and developmental processes as well as disruptive of family life. The expressed purpose of this arrangement is to offset busing costs of the entire consolidation effort. As stated in the plan, "However, plans have already been made to place the early childhood education program on a full-day basis beginning with the 1975-76 school term, which will save an estimated $52,409.60. Thus, the estimated additional transportation cost for the Phase I program is only $665.40 per year more than the cost of the present program."[24]

Misdirected Priorities

The Preston County plan has misdirected its priorities by focusing its attention on expanding curricular specialties at the secondary level, by arguing that such an expansion is not possible without consolidation, and by spending a large proportion of its available funds on a new gymnasium while leaving unattended more than 300 violations of the fire code for up to five years. In stark contrast to the board's priorities is the overwhelming evidence of need in West Virginia to correct deficiencies in reading, writing, mathematics, speech, and general health among children at the earliest possible time in their school experience.

Numerous studies show that southern rural areas, including West Virginia, are below average in basic skills. The state department of education's own study in 1970 shows cognitive skill development in West Virginia to be significantly below national norms.[25] The NAEP data for southeastern states (including West Virginia) show the region to be behind national average in all subject matters surveyed, including basic skills in reading and writing.[26] A study conducted for the Preston County Board of Education by Masters Enterprises states, "children begin school with lower IQ scores, especially in verbal ability, and then fall further behind because they cannot master the subject."[27]

A comprehensive study of the needs of children in Appalachian schools was conducted by the Appalachian Educational Laboratory in 1971.[28] The study asked specific questions about the learning, social, emotional, and physical problems children exhibited in school as perceived by teachers and principals. In West Virginia, a random sample of 212 teachers and 17 principals was asked to estimate the severity of 66 specific problems. The top 4 in rank order for West Virginia schools are "written expression," "reading comprehension," "work habits," and "spelling." Reviewing several sources, the authors of the Appalachian Educational Laboratory study conclude that basic skills are the predominant educational need in the region's schools.

The Preston County Board of Education could have turned its attention to basic needs, but it did not. The plan does little to alter any of the county's elementary school problems. Offering courses like

German I-IV may aid middle-class children in the college preparatory track, but it does little to aid the disadvantaged child struggling to master basic skills. In programmatic terms, this consolidation plan advances the interests of most middle-class parents, but ignores the needs of disadvantaged children.

Distribution of Funds

Comparing the distribution of funds with a breakdown of voting results for each of the three defeated bonds and with the Comprehensive Facilities Plan is informative. Although none of these proposals argued that educational needs changed significantly between September 18, 1973, and February 1975, each of the four plans called for a different distribution of funds and projects. None of the plans veered from the goal of consolidation, but the plans all would have resulted in different resource allocations among the various communities in the county. Table 5.13 breaks down the distribution of capital resources by community for the four plans.

Three examples are instructive. First, with the exception of the Denver elementary addition, no funds will be spent under the Comprehensive Facilities Plan in any communities that did not support the previous three bonds.

Second, the initial bond issue provided for $250,000 for renovation and new construction to convert the Aurora and Rowlesburg high schools to elementary use. The high school students were to be combined with Terra Alta. In the October 8, 1974, and November 23, 1974, bonds the funds were withdrawn. For Aurora, $50,000 was withdrawn even though the Aurora high school students were to be consolidated with Terra Alta in all three bonds and the old high school at Aurora converted to elementary and kindergarten use. For Rowlesburg, $200,000 was allocated for renovation in the September 18, 1973, bond to convert the high school for elementary use. The high school students were to be consolidated with Terra Alta. In the October 8, 1974, and November 23, 1974, bonds, the $200,000 was withdrawn even though the high school was still to be converted to elementary use. In both cases, funds were withdrawn after heavy opposition at the polls, even though the educational plans for the communities in question remained the same. No educational rationale was ever given for these actions. (Some renovations were made

TABLE 5.13

Proposed Distribution of Construction Funds and Results of
Three Bond Issue Elections, by Community

Community	First Bond Issue (September 18, 1973)		Second Bond Issue (October 8, 1974)		Third Bond Issue (November 23, 1974)		Comprehensive Facilities Plan (February 1975)
	Vote For Bond	Proposed Expenditure	Vote For Bond	Proposed Expenditure	Vote For Bond	Proposed Expenditure	Proposed Expenditure
Kingwood	22-28%	$400,000(E)	68.75%[b]	$ 2.5M(S)	70-75%[d]	$ 2.5M(S)	$962,928(E)
Tunnelton	65%	2.1M(S)[c]	60%	172,500(E)	22%[d]	172,500(E)	0
Masontown	45-69%[e]	2.8M(S)	45-50%	0	43-45%	0	0
Arthurdale	60-71%	0	56-67%	1.8M(E)	51-65%[d]	1.8M(E)	586,720(E)
Newburg	48-59%	25,000(E)[c]	36-36%	0	28-28%[d]	0	0
Rowlesburg	8-13%	200,000(E)	15-18%	0	9-10%[d]	0	0
Aurora	10%	50,000(E)	21%[b]	0	10%	0	0
Albright	20%	0	47%[b]	0	44%	0	0
Terra Alta	84-89%	1.5M(S)	71-80%	1.5M(S)	59-72%	1.5M(S)	1.3M(S)
Bruceton	83%	1.02M(S)[c]	90%	1.2M(S)	88%	1.2M(S)	100,000(S)
Fellowsville	66%	100,000(E)[c]	41%	1.3M(E)[g]	57%[d]	1.3M(E)[h]	228,168(E)
Denver	74%	0	74%	0	18%[d]	0	187,200(E)

NOTE: E=elementary school; S=secondary school; M-millions of dollars.

[a] This column contains no percentages because there was no election.

[b] Change in vote from September 18, 1973 due to switching high school back to Kingwood; the plan in the September 8, 1973 bond was to build a new consolidated high school in the Arthurdale-Masontown area for Kingwood, Masontown, and Arthurdale.

[c] New high school to be shared by Fellowsville, Newburg, and Tunnelton to be located near Tunnelton.

[d] Appears to be the result of organized opposition by EAP in the Tunnelton-Newburg-Rowlesburg-Aurora areas.

[e] New high school in the Arthurdale-Masontown area to serve Kingwood, Masontown, and Arthurdale.

[f] Appears to be the result of abandoning the idea of a new high school to be shared by Fellowsville, Newburg, and Tunnelton.

[g] New Elementary school to be located between Tunnelton and Fellowsville to be shared by Tunnelton, Fellowsville, and Newburg.

[h] The new shared elementary school to be shared by Tunnelton, Fellowsville, and Newburg relocated in or very near Fellowsville.

later in Rowlesburg, using Special Levy funds.)

Third, the erosion of support in the Newburg-Tunnelton area, following the withdrawal of the plan proposed in the first bond to build a new high school to be shared by these communities and Fellowsville, shows the Board of Education ignoring an opportunity to work with communities willing to cooperate. The board's support eroded. Subsequently, all funds for renovation were withdrawn from Newburg and Tunnelton in the February 1975 plan. No educational rationale is given for these actions, which, in the final plan, also included the closing of the high schools in both communities and consolidating them with Valley and Kingwood.

Analysis

The Comprehensive Facilities Plan exacerbates unequal opportunities by closing schools in those areas of the county where the educational needs are greatest. The communities adversely affected by this plan are also plagued by the county's highest unemployment, greatest job loss, lowest income, and lowest levels of education attained by parents. By action of the Board of Education, children from the poorest areas of the county will have to shoulder the greatest loss of educational opportunities while assuming the highest risk to personal safety and welfare riding on school buses up to three hours per day. The plan in this sense is clearly discriminatory and inequitable.

The Preston County Board of Education apparently proposed its plan not to enhance the education of all of the county's children, but rather to obtain funds for a consolidation effort that had been frustrated for more than a decade. The board did not weigh the strengths or weaknesses of any alternative plans, nor did it ever appear ready to seriously consider an improvement plan that did not include consolidation.

Events Following the Release of the Comprehensive Facilities Plan

Following is the sequence of events after the introduction of the Preston County Comprehensive Facilities Plan in February 1975.

1. On April 1, 1975, the attorney representing Equality for All Prestonians (EAP) wrote to the superintendent of schools in Preston County expressing EAP's opposition to the Comprehensive Facilities Plan and requesting an opportunity to discuss alternatives to consolidation. The superintendent replied in a letter dated April 30, 1975, and expressed some confusion as to whether EAP wanted to present its alternatives to the local or state board. EAP was informed that it could present its own plan at the next meeting of the Preston County Board of Education on May 12, 1975. However, EAP would have to request time formally by May 7, 1975. The EAP attorney was also informed that he could request a special meeting of the local board to discuss EAP's plan. The attorney replied in a letter dated May 12, 1975, that his organization had learned of the public hearing of the "State Board" too late to present an alternative plan. However, EAP did present the State Board with a petition seeking withdrawal of the Preston County Board of Education plan. The EAP attorney requested on May 12, 1975, an executive meeting of the Preston County Board of Education to discuss alternatives to consolidation. The request was not acted upon.

2. On May 23, 1975, an anticonsolidation petition was presented by EAP at an open hearing held by the West Virginia State Department of Education (not the Board of Education) to discuss the Preston County Comprehensive Facilities Plan.

3. On May 30, 1975, a formal request was made by members of EAP in attendance at a Preston County Board of Education meeting to have a consultant to EAP recognized and given time to present arguments against the Comprehensive Facilities Plan. The request was granted and a presentation was made. The board did not act upon any of the recommendations presented.

4. On June 6, 1975, State Superintendent Taylor informed EAP that it would not be able to make a public presentation at the State Board of Education meeting on June 13, 1975, when the State Board was to take up the matter of the Preston County plan. No public presentation has ever been made to the State Board on this issue.

5. On June 13, 1975, the State Board of Education approved the Preston County plan with one vote against.

6. On June 23, 1975, an order to show cause brought by EAP was refused by the West Virginia State Supreme Court of Appeals. On July 17, 1975, the order was refused in Circuit Court, Kanawha County.

7. On January 16, 1976, an injunction was sought in Preston County Circuit Court against the Preston County Board of Education seeking to stop implementation of the Comprehensive Facilities Plan. The grounds for the injunction included the alleged diversionary use of Special Levy funds to consolidate the schools in lieu of the purposes set forth in the Special Levy. The case was subsequently transferred to Barbour County Circuit Court and dismissed in March 1976.

8. On February 27, 1976, approximately 130 students gathered in front of the Preston County Board of Education building in Kingwood to protest the school consolidation plan. School buses were blocked in some communities and students boycotted schools in Newburg, Tunnelton, Fellowsville, and Rowlesburg.

9. On March 4, 1976, all Preston County schools were closed because of a countywide gathering of protesters in Kingwood. A Board of Education meeting was disrupted by 100 protesters and forced to end without considering bids on the new buildings to be constructed under the Comprehensive Facilities Plan. Mines, businesses, and manufacturing plants were closed by pickets. A protest march of 500 persons was held in Kingwood. The Board of Education agreed to a special meeting on March 10, 1976, to hear the EAP's plan.

10. On March 10, 1976, an alternative to consolidation was presented by EAP to the Board of Education at a special meeting. The plan called for seven high schools, shared resources, and a curriculum identical to the board's own plan. The basic difference between the plans was number and size of schools to be retained. At that meeting, it was agreed to drop the planned appeal of the injunction decision against EAP.

11. On March 15, 1976, the Board of Education voted 4-0 to present a bond proposal to the voters on May 11, 1976, as part of the West Virginia primary election ballot. The bond was to incorporate the EAP community school plan.

12. On April 29, 1976, the superintendent announced his resignation effective June 30, 1976. The board immediately voted 4-1 to accept his resignation and to appoint the assistant superintendent to fill the vacancy.

Section Three: The Community School Plan and the Fourth Bond Issue

As noted above, a community school plan was presented to the Preston County Board of Education in April 1976. This plan, which was to be the basis of a fourth bond referendum in May 1976, received little distribution in Preston County until the week preceding the actual election. The development of this plan was spearheaded by local citizens under the coordination of Equality for All Prestonians, and thus came to be known as the EAP plan.

The physical plant needs were ascertained with the help of the central staff of the school system. However, the initial determination of what each community wanted was made by the membership of EAP, working first at the community level and then as a policy body to determine necessary trade-offs and priorities. The plan differs from the board plan not only in what it proposes, but also in how it was developed.

The EAP plan intentionally reflects the interests and hopes of those citizens and communities whose schools were to be closed. It was initiated by "ordinary" people, working without benefit of a paid staff or the organizational resources of the local and state school boards.

This plan was shaped largely by what parents and taxpayers wanted for their schools. As a result, the EAP plan reflects a firm commitment to the principle that all citizens of Preston County, not just professional educators and their middle-class supporters, have an equal voice in shaping the lives and education of the county's children. In addition, the plan incorporates three key EAP assumptions: first, that the vote to defeat the three previous consolidation bond issues was neither capricious nor based on a refusal to pay for educational improvements; second, that the effort to defeat consolidation reflected reasonable concerns for the education, safety, and welfare of the county's children; and third, that an informed citizenry has a right to be deeply and significantly involved in shaping the organization and content of their children's education.

The United States Supreme Court has recently affirmed the

position that local citizens should be full partners in the educational enterprise. Mr. Justice Powell, in the *Rodriguez* decision, argued:

> The persistence of attachment to government at the lowest level where education is concerned reflects the depth of commitment of its supporters. In part, local control means, as Professor Coleman suggests, the freedom to devote more money to the education of one's children. *Equally important, however, is the opportunity it offers for participation in the decision-making process that determines how those local taxes will be spent* [emphasis added]. Each locality is free to tailor programs to local needs. Pluralism also affords some opportunity for experimentation, innovation, and a healthy competition for educational excellence. An analogy to the nation-state relationship in our federal system seems appropriate. Mr. Justice Brandeis identified as one of the peculiar strengths of our form of government each state's freedom to "serve as a laboratory . . . and try novel social and economic experiments." No area of social concern stands to profit more from a multiplicity of viewpoints and from a diversity of approaches than does public education.[29]

The EAP Plan

The community school plan, otherwise known as the EAP plan, includes the following key elements:

1. Seven high schools, instead of three, would remain in Preston County (ranging in size from approximately 145 to 455 students in grades 9-12).

2. One hundred seven new courses would be offered at the high school level, exactly duplicating the curriculum proposed in the Comprehensive Facilities Plan. The objective was to ensure that no opportunity to take a course under the consolidation plan would be denied under the community school plan.

3. There would be new construction and renovation in the amount of $6.14 million in addition to the $3.4 million coming to Preston County through the Better Schools Amendment. Those communities slated to receive state funds for new facilities under the Comprehensive Facilities Plan would receive those same funds under the

community school plan.

4. Deliberate equity in distribution of capital funds and instructional resources to the various towns in the county was proposed. The $9.54 million expenditure, including both local and state funds, basically conformed to population distributions in the county.

5. The basic difference between the community plan and the board's consolidation plan was sharing a few teachers among several small schools as opposed to transporting a lot of children to big schools. The community school plan required a total of twenty-one new teachers (thirteen to be shared between two schools) while the consolidation plan required approximately sixteen new teachers; the difference in the number of teachers needed was accounted for in travel time, duplicate classes, and smaller classes.[30]

6. High schools would be retained at Aurora, Rowlesburg, and Bruceton; the board's proposal would have removed them. High schools at Tunnelton and Newburg were to be combined as a new cooperative community school rather than with Kingwood and Valley High Schools. Kingwood, Valley, and Terra Alta would remain as they were—community schools serving their respective towns. Kingwood and Valley were not only to receive state funds as planned, but also receive an *additional* $1.6 million in local funds for further improvements.

The local citizens based their plan on more than just intuition. The plan rests on a substantial amount of research on school size and school consolidation. None among twenty-eight recent studies reviewed showed any significant positive relationships between the size of school and how much children learn, independent of home and family background.[31] When significant relationships exist at all, they were shown to be negative.

The studies of midwestern schools and communities of size and quality of experience in school lead to similar conclusions. If larger schools have such negative consequences for attitudes and feelings of satisfaction among children, it would be unreasonable to assume learning would be unaffected. Furthermore, in those instances where data were available, not one study that controlled for family background showed any positive relationships between college success and school size.[32] This finding is emphasized because many proponents of school consolidation point to the advantages presumed to follow for college performance. The facts do not support this notion, as will be further discussed below. These findings were presented to both the local and state school officials in West Virginia. The fact that they contradict longstanding assumptions about the desirability of consolidation has to our knowledge led to no discernible reexamination of those assumptions.

The Supreme Court has recognized that no clearly demonstrated link exists between school resources and educational quality. In *San Antonio vs. Rodriguez*, Mr. Justice Powell states:

> On even the most basic questions in this area the scholars and educational experts are divided. Indeed, one of the hottest sources of controversy concerns the extent to which there is a demonstrable correlation between educational expenditures and the quality of education. . . . The ultimate wisdom as to these and related problems of education is not likely to be divined for all time even by the scholars who now so earnestly debate the issues. In such circumstances the judiciary is well advised to refrain from interposing on the States inflexible constitutional restraints that could circumscribe or handicap the continued research and experimentation so vital to finding even partial solutions to educational problems and to keeping abreast of every changing condition.[33]

EAP's purpose was to show that voters in Preston County who ejected similar consolidation plans in the past and now voiced opposition to the Comprehensive Facilities Plan were exercising reasonable judgments about the purported educational benefits of the various plans. A vote against the bond issue was not necessarily a vote against improved education. Indeed, research accumulated over two and a half decades consistently suggests that to err on the side of preserving the local smaller high school is wiser than buying the promises of greater variety and efficiency of the larger consolidated school. No reliable evidence can be found to show that consolidation improved achievement results, attitudes, or college performance independent of family background. What the courts won't buy from educational experts, one cannot expect the citizens in Preston County to buy.

Roger G. Barker and Paul V. Gump in *Big School, Small School* report several significant findings relevant to the quality of the school experience in small community schools versus larger consolidated schools.[34] Because the school sizes in the Barker and Gump study approximate those existing and proposed in Preston County, the findings are particularly interesting. The Kansas schools studied by Barker and Gump range in size from a low of 35 students in grades 9-12 to a high of 2,287 students. Although the largest school in this study exceeds any school proposed in Preston County, 213 out of the total of 218 schools studied by Barker and Gump fell within the range 42 to 889 average enrollments in grades 9-12. Thus, the vast majority of schools and students were comparable to conditions that exist or are being proposed in Preston County.

Barker and Gump found that the actual proportion of students who can participate in the essential activities that support the academic program, the quality of that involvement, and the satisfaction with that involvement clearly favor the smaller local school over the larger consolidated school. The significance of this finding in arguing against the consolidation of Preston County schools is the obvious interdependency of the small-town high schools and their places in the community social setting. In each of the small towns studied in Kansas, the high school was tightly integrated into the fragile fabric of the community's social life. The communities and their schools were mutually reinforcing. To remove the school from such a community and thereby alter the reciprocal balance would be destructive of community. To achieve some goal at such a great cost would have to mean that such a goal is extremely important and also is attainable. No such case was made for school consolidation in Preston County.

The Lund, Nevada, Case

These arguments and research findings are affirmed by the Supreme Court of the State of Nevada in *Robert Bartlett et al., Appellants, vs. The Board of Trustees of the White Pine County School District, Respondents,* No. 8434, June 1976. In this landmark case, the State Supreme Court reversed a lower court decision and ordered Lund high school (with an enrollment of thirty students) reopened. The school had been closed by the county school board, and the children were being bused forty miles away to a consolidated school (White Pine high school in Ely, Nevada). The Court's opinion, written by Justice Thompson, acknowledges that per-pupil costs at Lund are higher because of smaller class sizes, but argues:

This, however, inevitably is true whenever a per-pupil cost comparison is made between a rural and an urban school. Consequently, we do not, as did the majority of the trustees and the District Court, attribute persuasive force to this statistic. To do so would place the continued existence of rural high schools in extreme jeopardy. We, therefore, do not consider that finding supportive of closure.[35]

The court also acknowledged that the curriculum at the consolidated school is broader in scope than that offered at Lund, but held that this also may be an inevitable difference between rural and urban schools. Justice Thompson writes:

However, it does not necessarily follow from this alone that the quality of education is superior at White Pine when other relevant factors are considered. On this point, the Court relied on expert testimony. It was pointed out that busing students for two hours or more per day, in this case over eighty miles, reduces the quality of their education, and reduces their participation in school activities.[36]

Especially important to the Court was that Lund students would be adversely affected by transferring from a small class size situation to a larger class situation. The Court's opinion includes a direct quote from expert testimony provided by Dr. Trione of the University of Nevada:

It is my opinion that the students and community of Lund will lose a great deal by the closure of its high school. While the school may not have the latest of equipment and the finest of facilities, the community setting, the community's respect and involvement in school activities, and the students' opportunity to attend small classes cannot be ignored. The community of Lund has something very precious to American education which has been deteriorating in larger communities, and that is the close relationship of the home and the school. These are two very powerful influences which shape the lives of future citizens. The positive result when these two influences work hand-in-hand is obvious. That situation presently exists in the Lund community and the Lund high school.[37]

These factors were deemed by both the Court and the residents of Lund to be the central issues in this case. The similarity to Preston County seems clear.

The Raymond Report

Of all the studies done in recent years that have attempted to link increased school size with increased academic performance, only one has been based on West Virginia student data: Richard Raymond's research report, "Determinants of the Quality of Primary and Secondary Public Education in West Virginia."[38] Raymond, a professor at West Virginia University, studied 5,000 freshmen students at WVU between 1963 and 1966, controlling for obvious differences in aptitude by equalizing grade-point averages in selected senior high school subjects.

Given the enormous variations in school size within West Virginia's fifty-five countywide school districts, and considering the variance in curricular offerings among high schools, the expectation would be that measures of freshman year performance would yield significant differences between West Virginia's school systems. Raymond felt that way when he began his study. The two measures of freshman performance he employed were overall scores in the American Testing Program (ACT) and freshman year grade-point averages.

Raymond examined the effects of "consolidation" separately by using a proxy—that is, the degree of urbanization in each West Virginia county. His finding was that *the degree of consolidation and most of the other school factors were unrelated to performance.*[39] These other factors included: percent of teachers teaching in two or more fields; number of library volumes in excess of standards; and current expenditures per pupil. Consolidation, the key variable in Raymond's study for our argument, becomes a *negative* influence on learning in the freshman year when family and other community variables are controlled. As the degree of consolidation increases, the performance of freshmen declines. Raymond was obviously disappointed with his findings, as the following statement suggests:

the contention was made that, within our sample, high levels of urbanization represent economies in the operation of school systems. Therefore, urbanization, *ceteris paribus*, should be associated with high quality. It is difficult to muster support for the urbanization hypothesis.[40]

Raymond concludes that educational difference among county school districts, as measured in this research effort, do not produce differences in freshman performance. The differences that are significant in Raymond's opinion are beyond the control of schools. He states:

The portion of the quality differences, as they have been measured, which result from difference in population characteristics falls largely outside the control of the school system. This portion is caused by differences in student ability and home environment.[41]

Fourth Bond Election Results

The community school bond was defeated by a vote of 5,473 (against) to 5,035 (for) on May 11, 1976. This bond, like its predecessors, required 60 percent of the votes for passage. However, it received only 47.9 percent of the vote. The 10,508 votes tallied represented 67.4 percent of the eligible voters—a significantly higher voter turnout than for any of the previous bond elections.

The vote totals from the May 11, 1976, bond election (together with the last consolidation bond of November 23, 1974) are given in Table 5.14. The voting pattern of the May 1976 bond election differs in one essential respect from the pattern of the November 1974 bond. Those communities that strongly opposed the November 1974 bond, as well as the two previous consolidation bonds, strongly supported the May 1976 bond. Conversely, those communities that strongly supported the November 1974 bond, and thus endorsed consolidation, voted strongly against the May 1976 bond. For instance, the Kingwood and Terra Alta communities, which both voted heavily for the November 1974 bond, cast fewer than 20 percent of their votes for the May 1976 bond. The voting results by communities are given in Table 5.15.

TABLE 5.14

Results of Third and Fourth Bond Issues

	Registered Voters	Ballots Cast	Percentage Voting	Vote For	Vote Against	Total Votes	Percentage For
Third Bond Issue	14,190	6,983	49.21	3,347	3,546	6,933	49.22
Fourth Bond Issue	15,569	N.A.	67.40	5,035	5,472	10,507	47.92

TABLE 5.15

Results of Third and Fourth Bond Issues, by Community

Community	Third Bond Issue (November 23, 1974) Percentage For	Fourth Bond Issue (May 11, 1976) Percentage For
Kingwood	70-75	10-17
Tunnelton	22	90
Masontown	43-45	14-22
Arthurdale	51-65	19-23
Reedsville	48	28
Newburg	28	88-95
Rowlesburg	9-10	75-82
Aurora	10	83
Albright	44	24
Terra Alta	59-72	5-10
Bruceton	88	73
Fellowsville	57	92
Denver	18	94

Analysis

The election results show that the three communities (Kingwood, Terra Alta, and Masontown) scheduled to retain their schools, whether this fourth bond passed or not, voted most heavily against the bond. A local newspaper, the *Preston County News*, argued editorially that Terra Alta voters (already set to receive $1.5 million in state funds) had nothing more to gain from the bond, and therefore, were urged to vote against it. The Terra Alta vote reflects that view. The Kingwood and Valley voters could have gained more capital resources had the bond passed, but the vote in those areas was also against, although not so overwhelmingly as in Terra Alta. On the other hand, those communities (Rowlesburg, Newburg, Tunnelton, and Aurora) scheduled to lose high schools if the bond failed voted heavily for the bond.

The fourth and most recent election is not to be confused with an actual choice between consolidation and community schools. The voter was only choosing in the sense that by voting against the bond, the school board would (by default) implement its own plan; a plan that neither required local endorsement, nor received it.

The argument was set forth that defeat of the latest bond thus gave the school board a mandate to proceed with its own plan to consolidate. That would be true, of course, if the voter were choosing between plan A (community schools) and plan B (consolidated schools). That was not the case, and therefore, a majority vote against plan A does not constitute an endorsement of plan B. People vote against school bonds for many reasons, but it does not follow that a vote *against* can be interpreted by default as support *for* something else. Reasons for supporting bonds are often quite different than reasons for opposing them. Indeed, it is likely in Preston County that some people voted against *all four* bonds for reasons that have nothing to do with education or schools.

The basic idea of consolidation has practically no support in any community in Preston County. Its endorsement by the majority in a community vanishes anytime it means closing a school in that community or increasing the distance that a community's students must travel. Consolidation is only supported by the majority in any given community in Preston County when it means, "You send your kids to our school."

An example is the behavior of the majority of voters in Kingwood in the September 1973 bond election, which would have closed the high school and moved it nine miles away to another district. The vote was heavily against that bond proposal in Kingwood (more than 70 percent opposed). But the next bond, one year later, returned the high school and proposed transporting children from another town to Kingwood. That bond was just as strongly endorsed in Kingwood as the previous one was defeated (more than 70 percent in favor).

It seems absurd under these circumstances to conclude that a vote against any school plan in Preston County is an endorsement for consolidation. It might more aptly be thought of as an endorsement of a policy that allows the middle class to strengthen their interests through the schools, but clearly that does not imply any faith in the basic idea of consolidation.

Section Four: Conclusion

Education historian, David Tyack, once noted:

In their diagnosis and prescription, the rural school reformers blended economic realism with nostalgia, and efficient professionalism with evangelical righteousness.[42]

Such evangelism was readily apparent during the consolidation debate in Preston County. For example, in formulating the county's consolidation plan, the superintendent of schools claimed that he knew he was right because he had God's help. Similarly, one consolidation advocate (after invoking divine endorsement of the board's plan) got down on her knees and prayed that God would forgive the one board member who was opposed to consolidation.

The drive for consolidation represented a shift in control of the schools from people in local communities to professionals who presumably seek to act in the interests of all they serve. The preceding analysis of Preston County shows this faith in the egalitarian instincts of professional educators to be groundless in the rural West Virginia hills. The primary interests served by these educators are those of the middle class.

The Preston County School Board's plan would have spent 90 percent of the $3.4 million in state funds in only three towns. Not surprisingly, these same three communities (with 20 percent of the county's population) have 75 percent of the professional, business, and governmental entities in the county and most of the county's middle-class residents. They, incidentally, are also represented by four of the five members of the Preston County Board of Education.

There are five other towns in Preston County with high schools. These communities lost their high schools under the board's plan and receive few other benefits at the elementary school level.

The belief in the superiority of professional ideas over the ideas of laymen is well-entrenched in Preston County. Thus, the editor of a local newspaper could argue in his effort to defeat the community school plan:

The Preston County schools' central staff has an *infinite understanding* of what is politically possible and educationally sound for the children of Preston County, having been personally involved with the needs as well as the demands of every section of the County. The *Comprehensive Facilities Plan*, under the direction of the Board, was designed by the County's experienced staff and is therefore sound and correct.[43]

A letter to the same newspaper from a resident of an adjacent county is a classic presentation of the consolidator's perspective. In support of building one consolidated high school for the entire county, he asserts:

Consolidation has always been the smartest move in any school system. . . . You would have one efficient teaching staff directly responsible to one highly-qualified administrative staff. New courses and programs could be instituted for the students' benefit. . . . I attended such a school in Pittsburgh. In one school, we very efficiently educated more junior high school and senior high school students in one school than Preston has in grades 1 through 12. . . . So, quit arguing, Prestonians, and move toward *progress*.[44]

The conflict is obvious for those who oppose consolidation. No one wants to oppose progress. Rural people who oppose consolidation may also be dissatisfied with their school buildings and with an archaic instructional program, but those things do not supersede their instinctive interest in maintaining control of their schools.

James West, Roger Barker, Paul Gump, David Tyack, and others argue that rural schools are essential, cohesive forces in communities otherwise lacking the numerous and elaborate organizations and resources of large towns and cities. Preston County clearly shows that view is not deeply held by the middle class (including educators). For example, the assistant superintendent of schools in Preston County (later promoted to superintendent) stated in a newspaper article:

I think a person will have to weigh the social attributes of the EAP plan with the academic aspects of the Comprehensive Plan. From my standpoint, I am more interested in what can be done, from the educational point of view . . . this is my concern for my children. This varies with people throughout the County. Some are more interested in whether they'll have the opportunity to play basketball . . . whether they'll have the opportunity to be in the band. For my children this is important too, but when it comes to choosing, I probably weigh my values a little different.[45]

To some in small rural communities, schools are valued as much for their benefits and contributions to the ongoing life of the community as for their performance in teaching academic skills. To others, such community interests can be sacrificed to promote the academic advancement of their own children. The teacher and parent whose letter appears below takes the position that she will seek cognitive advantages for her children at almost any cost. Her letter said:

I want [my children] to have new building facilities— elementary *and* high school; increased opportunities in a wider cross section of learning from the money I'll be putting into the schools. I want this for them whether it takes consolidation, non-consolidation, 1 school, 2 schools, 3 or more schools, if it takes busing or not, if it takes relocating my family, or if it takes as a last resort—private schooling.[46]

Presumably, it is worth any sacrifice to ensure that one's own children enter into the Kingdom of Heaven—or, in this case, middle-class status.

The point made by West, Tyack, Barker, and Gump is crucial. The small-town school has a different kind of symbolic meaning. Schools came to be valued in themselves, quite apart from the goal of teaching cognitive skills and the specific knowledge required to enter professional and managerial careers. David Tyack suggests, "the town high schools gave local people the feeling that they had access to a mass society while they still enlisted local loyalties and integrated rural people in social networks."[47]

In both instances (community schools and consolidated schools), schooling functions as a kind of social club. To be educated is to gain entry to a club in which certain values, beliefs, and definitions of reality are shared. The structural features, functions, and mechanics of that club are embedded with those values and beliefs. These structural elements are designed to reinforce and perpetuate those values. The community school concept manifests the values of social cohesion, while consolidation embraces the ideology of individual achievement.[48] These value systems and ideologies primarily reflect different class interests.

This does not entirely explain the reasons behind the middle-class push for consolidation in Preston County. The question remains: Why not just let the foolish small-town folks keep their schools? The answer is not simple. The lower class has long been challenged to become "cultured" too, if they seek to achieve the American dream. The lower-class response has always been ambivalent, but education professionals (themselves often beckoned up from the lower class) feel a missionary zeal to do the same for others. They want others to become educated persons, believe it is important, and argue that being educated is to everyone's advantage. Their purposes differ from those of their middle-class followers as the priesthood's purposes differ from those of their parishioners.

There are other factors as well. The claim has to be made that the schools can serve *all* needs better—otherwise, the rationale for public support diminishes. The "moneysworth" argument, nevertheless, means middle-class parents (who incorrectly believe that they are paying all of the bills) will not deny their children any possible educational resource just to humor the "provincial" and "back-wards" desires of their poorer, more rural neighboring communities.[49] The thesis espoused repeatedly by Preston County School Board members was that the wealthy, populous sections of the county would not, under any circumstances, have to support costly small schools for poorer, less populous areas within the county. Since the wealthy communities won't be "robbed" to pay for the luxury of the poor attending small schools, and since the professional staff promises that big schools will "do it all for you," the consolidation argument combined the force of economic and political realism with evangelical righteousness to save the children of these poor, mis-guided, rural folks.

There is yet another compelling force, more hidden than the above, which pressed consolidation on those who wish to preserve small schools. Simply put, they are needed by the middle class. The differentiation of function works to the advantage of the middle class. However, it works well only if there are large numbers to be differentiated and if there is a lower group—much as a pecking order works only when there is someone lower to peck.

Specialized academic subjects (such as German III) will be dominated by the middle class, but the few lower-class children who bubble up provide by their numbers a necessary justification for variety and a demonstration that all can make it. Those left behind, the large majority of poor and otherwise disadvantaged, serve another purpose. Their failure is a necessary condition for teaching the lessons that some succeed while others fail and that the system is fair. Those who fail are themselves at fault. This is an absolutely fundamental lesson in a capitalist society. Having a class that fails provides the necessary precondition to developing a class identity among those who succeed.

Thus, the very identity of the middle class, possible only because *there is a lower class*, is strengthened by consolidating small, rural schools into bigger, town schools. When there are sixty high school courses offered instead of thirty, the possibilities exist for greater differentiation and separation among students by subjects taken, skills learned, and knowledge possessed. Academically, there just is not very much difference among kids, regardless of social class, when a school offers only the basics. The people from small towns and big towns both sense this instinctively. Their interests in preserving or changing it will usually follow class lines.

The proposed community schools plan failed to do two things. Its curriculum was not attractive to the middle class (although it provided the same course offerings as the consolidation plan) because it did not provide a set of conditions in which class differences could be magnified by failure. Furthermore, it failed to address the "moneysworth" argument which, in Preston County, came to mean that "We only get our money's worth if the school which remains is located in our town."

The consequences, under these circumstances, are predictable. The powerful take what they can and the weak suffer what they must. Schools will be removed from the communities that can least afford to lose them and will be placed in communities already doing relatively well—a procedure reminiscent of the battlefield concept of triage. The meek may inherit the earth, but, at least in Preston County, they will have to forego inheriting the schools.

6 Centralization versus Decentralization: A Case Study of Rural Education in Vermont

Stuart Rosenfeld

Introduction

In May 1975, the Vermont State Department of Education concluded a sixteen-month study of school district organization by urging the "orderly and systematic consolidation of all public school districts in Vermont."[1] This report advocated a sweeping reorganization and centralization program that would eliminate all of the existing 274 local public school districts and the 56 supervisory unions in Vermont and replace them with a very small number of new regional units.

At the same time that the Department of Education was preparing its report, some school districts were planning their own counterstrategies. These rural districts were seeking further decentralization, greater local autonomy, and a closer working relationship with their superintendents. Consequently, they initiated an effort to secede from their present supervisory unions and become independent units.

These two divergent and opposing forces are archetypes of a tension that has existed in Vermont for over a century. State administrators and state-level professional educators have been striving for better education through standardization and tighter state control, while local communities have been fighting for the right to determine the type of education their children will receive. Emotions have often precluded the development of rational policy by either side, and the arguments continue to be more political and economic than purely educational. Few in Vermont have seriously attempted to accumulate any authoritative evidence on either the effects of organization or the social and psychological implications of rural consolidation. As a result, the arguments have changed little over the years.

The pro-consolidation report issued in 1975 by the Vermont Department of Education was, therefore, by no means new or unexpected. Studies of school consolidation and district reorganization have been conducted regularly for the past sixty years, and centralization has been expounded as long as Vermont has had a state superintendent of education. Within the past fifteen years, the Governor's Panel on State Aid to Education recommended consolidation to eighteen regional districts;[2] a National Education Association-sponsored report on Vermont advised enlarging school districts;[3] a report to the Vermont General Assembly suggested consolidation into thirty-two districts;[4] a report conducted for the state by the national consulting firm of Arthur D. Little, Inc., recommended thirty-two districts;[5] a Tri-Partite Committee suggested twenty-five districts;[6] and a Governor's Task Force suggested twelve districts.[7]

It has frequently been assumed that this overwhelming mass of documents with such unanimity of opinion is sufficient to dictate a direction for educational policy in Vermont. However, history has repeatedly shown that it is often incorrect to equate unanimity with validity (witness Christopher Columbus).

In Section One of this chapter, the legitimacy of these studies, assumptions, and arguments will be evaluated by examining the evidence presented, the conditions under which they were undertaken, the motives of the sponsors, the recommendations offered, and the public reaction.

Section Two will investigate the relationship between district reorganization and selected educational and social outcomes in Vermont, including analyses of

1. cost of schools
2. effectiveness of the educational process
3. equality of opportunity among students
4. social, economic, and psychological well-being of the community.

To evaluate the association between size and effects, a comparative study of four Vermont high schools—a large, town high school in a large district; a small, village school in a small district; and two mid-sized schools in medium-sized districts—is presented.

Three basic elements distinguish this study and make its findings relevant, not only to Vermonters, but also to all those concerned with the direction and future of rural education. These elements are: (1) the existence of a classic educational policy dilemma pitting local control against state regulation and individual participation against a hierarchical decision-making structure; (2) the fact that the relationship between organizational structure and educational outcomes (at least in Vermont) is largely a counterintuitive one; and (3) the opportunity to analyze the value and appropriateness of employing urban values, practices, and assumptions in the formulation of rural educational policies.

To provide a context for this study, a brief overview of Vermont and its educational system will be presented.

Section One: The Context of Centralization

Vermont 1976: A Sketch of America's Most Rural State

To most Americans, reference to Vermont evokes an image of rural America: dairy farms, hills and pastures, covered bridges, maple trees and quiet villages. The 1970 United States Census denoted Vermont as the most rural state in the nation, as measured by the proportion of its citizens residing in rural communities. The state does not have the primitive uninhabited appearance of many western states, with plains or mountains interrupted by large, urban concentrations of people and industry. Vermont is uniformly rural, dotted with small farms and villages that are separated by hills and gentle mountains and connected only by narrow dirt roads, which are often impassable throughout the long, white winter and the mud season. This ruralness is intrinsic in the geography and location of the state. Consequently, Vermont has remained aloof from many of the factors that altered its neighboring states over the past century—population growth, immigration, and industrialization.

The state is by no means isolated from or unexposed to urbanization. It is bounded by industrial centers: Albany-Schenectady on the west; Manchester, New Hampshire, on the east; Massachusetts on the south; and Montreal on the north. Surrounded by urban dominance, Vermont has worked hard to maintain its own identity and its own character.

Vermonters take their tradition of self-government seriously. As their economic independence has slipped away, they have held on even more strongly to their political independence. Having lost the backbone of their economy—the hill farms, the dairy and sheep industries, and the resort businesses—to out-of-staters, it seems even more important to keep what is left. The most visible symbols of this independence are local schools and town government. Both are still highly decentralized and both are understood and cherished by most Vermont citizens. Any infringement on these institutions or attempts to remove them further from the people have always been vigorously challenged. The ruralness of the state, the high degree of representation in the legislature, the open town meetings, and the small rural schools all contribute to giving the Vermont citizen a sense of participation and control over his life seldom felt in urban or suburban communities.

The structure of the educational system in Vermont reflects this small-scale community orientation. There are 274 school districts of seven distinct types in the state: town, city, incorporated, joint contract, union, unified, and interstate. These districts range from village-based systems, such as Rochester, to large, consolidated systems, such as North County Union (which serves eleven widely dispersed communities). The entire system of 73 public secondary schools and 346 public elementary schools served over 109,000 students in 1975. Of the approximately 7,500 graduates in 1974, 39 percent went on to some form of higher education.

The average class size in Vermont is small. The ratio of 16 pupils in average daily attendance to every teacher is the lowest in the nation. About two-thirds of all students are bused to school. The state's rule of thumb is that no student is supposed to spend more than one hour on the bus. However, many spend considerably longer in transit when the time of travel to the pickup point, waiting time, and bus delays are taken into account.

The cost of education has grown faster in Vermont than in the rest

TABLE 6.1

Educational Statistics: Vermont and the U.S.

Statistic	Year	Vermont	U.S.	Vermont's Rank in U.S.
Current expenditures, per pupil	1973-74	$1,109	$ 1,116	22
Current expenditures, as percentage of personal income	1973-74	5.95	4.44	3
Pupil-teacher ratio	1973-74	16.1	19.8	50
Salaries of inst. staff	1974-75	$9,862	$11,950	38
Percentage state aid	1975-76	28.8	42.9	43
Percentage federal aid	1975-76	7.0	8.6	38
Average district size	1973-74	387	2,720	48
Percentage of children bused	1973-74	65.5	46.1	5

of the country. Once far behind in educational spending, Vermont has now surpassed most other states. Rapidly rising teacher salaries, transportation costs associated with consolidation, and the building boom of the 1950s and 1960s favoring large, modern, urban-style structures have put a financial strain on the taxpayer that is just beginning to take effect. Vermont residents spend a greater proportion of their personal income on education than do residents of forty-seven of the forty-nine other states.

Both tax effort and actual spending vary greatly from town to town and from district to district in Vermont. In 1973-74, eleven towns spent less than $600 on each elementary school student while ten others spent more than $1,200 per pupil. Nine towns were able to support their schools on a tax rate of less than .5 mills, while eighteen others had to pay over 2 (see Table 6.1). Unfortunately, it is the wealthy, not the poor, who are able to make the least effort for equivalent or greater resources.

Vermont has a distinctive rural character that many Vermonters, both old and new, are fighting to retain. Growth is not a popular term when applied to population or to anything else that might adversely affect the environment. General rural-urban differences are both real and appreciated by policymakers, yet educational problems are still treated as if Vermont were no different than Massachusetts, Illinois, or California. Indeed, many of the difficulties besetting Vermont's schools appear to be the result of utilizing urban models and standards within the context of very rural districts and communities.

Review of Vermont Centralization Studies

Since the beginning of public education in Vermont, state school administrators have applied every means of persuasion at their disposal to convince communities to accept centralized, professional supervision. For the first half century they, for the most part, failed. With the exception of the 1892 legislation replacing the district system with the town system, school organization changed little. Schools were still nearly as small and as numerous in the early 1900s as decades earlier. Schools had improved, teachers were better trained, resources were improved, and educational opportunities were expanded. Communities, however, were still in control of their schools.

Despite the reforms, state educators were very aware of the changes in education—such as age-graded elementary schools, comprehensive high schools, and vocational education—occurring in Massachusetts, Connecticut, and other more urbanized states. Fearing that Vermont schools were not keeping pace, they urged legislators to modernize Vermont's educational system. Early in the twentieth century, aided by the growing application of business principles in education and the rising cult of efficiency, these reformers found a new strategy to convince the public of the need for educational change. The strategy was to hire experts to undertake authoritative "objective" studies of Vermont's schools.

Carnegie Investigation: 1912-15

In 1912, the Vermont Legislature requested a study of education in Vermont from the Carnegie Foundation for the Advancement of Teaching.[8] It was the first investigation of its kind in the country. As a result of this comprehensive study, a number of specific changes were proposed, all directed toward one overall policy objective: centralization. The problems of Vermont education, the report predictably stated, were largely caused by the evils of local control and the lack of skilled supervision.[9]

The Vermont Legislature accepted many of the recommendations of the Carnegie experts. The most prominent of these was the establishment of an appointive State Board of Education with the power to select the state commissioner of education (previously elected by the legislature). The study also recommended junior high schools, regional high schools, and mandatory supervisory unions with professional superintendents selected by the state. After the report was completed and the reforms initiated, Commissioner of Education Mason Stone resigned, warning the public that "centralization leads to bureaucracy and bureaucracy leads to paternalism."[10]

As a result of the Carnegie Report, the State Board of Education in 1915 divided the state into sixty-six rural supervisory unions and appointed a superintendent to each. These superintendents were paid in full by the state. This organizational change created a bond between superintendents and the state, destroying the historical allegiance of superintendents to their community. In 1919, reacting to public concern about this loss of local control, the legislature finally rescinded the power of the state board to appoint superintendents (while Mason Stone was lieutenant governor of Vermont), and, in 1923, also rescinded the mandated system of union superintendents. The districts were given the option of employing a town superintendent, a union superintendent, or a supervising principal. This law established the general structure of Vermont's educational system for the next three decades.

Commission on Country Life: 1931

The next major study of education in Vermont, begun in 1928, was part of a statewide survey conducted by the Vermont Commission on Country Life.[11] The three-year study was conducted by Vermonters—200 prominent Vermont citizens—rather than by outside experts, and covered a broad range of state problems.

A major focus of this comprehensive study was to discover ways to improve the quality of life in the state, while, at the same time, preserving the uniqueness of Vermont's culture and traditions. Still, this committee recommended consolidation for reasons that sound quite similar to the current rationale: uniformity, better articulation of elementary schools with high schools, and the equalization of opportunities and tax burdens. Rather than urging mandated reform, the commission organized a publicity campaign which they hoped would convince the public of the need for and desirability of larger educational units. The strategy was one of persuasion rather than imposition. The campaign, however, never fully materialized and centralization was not yet accepted by rural communities.

Vermont State Education Commission: 1934

In 1933, while the country was in the throes of the Great Depression, the legislature requested another study of education in Vermont. Many schools across the country were in financial trouble, and by April 1934, 20,000 schools in the United States had already closed for lack of funds. International events in Germany, Italy, and Japan were also changing the mood of the nation, and the period of emphasis on education for assimilation and economic goals gave way to a new accent on protecting democracy.

The commission exposed inefficiency and inequities within Vermont's system of education, which they claimed were caused by structural defects in finance, administration, and supervision. Their recommendations, therefore, included state aid reform, minimum standards, and an enlarged role for the State Department of Education. This particular group of Vermont educators, however, was unique among previous and subsequent study commissions and committees. They alone pointed out the relationship of district organization to Vermont's culture and were aware of the association between the social relations in the school and the social relations in society. Their report stated:

> The direct and personal contact of the district school has perhaps the greatest possibility for individual uplift and for fortifying the youth for the years ahead than any other form of educational preparation. The rural elements still constitute the heart of our renowned Commonwealth. . . . But they will perish with the passing of the district school.[12]

Centralization may have been determined to be more efficient, but the commission questioned the price to be paid. As they said:

> In the country there are 423,000 school board members, or one member to every two teachers in the country. Absurd, say some. No doubt many could be dispensed with. But national or state autocracy would perhaps be more fatal to our national well-being than 423,000 members of school boards.[13]

the influence of European fascism may have created irrational fears of centralization, yet this group also indicated a strong appreciation of Vermont's heritage.

Reports of the Forties and Fifties

Little change in school organization occurred during the next two decades. Commissioners Noble and Holden both believed in further centralization, yet cherished the state's community-based traditions and valued smallness and involvement. Commissioner Holden, for example, wanted "young people schooled fairly near home and in small enough groups so that they will not be lost in an educational factory."[14] The policies of the forties and fifties were informative and participatory rather than directive. Educators attempted to work with communities toward consolidation instead of trying to impose a centralist policy.

The formal studies, such as the Report of the Committee to Study Supervision of Schools[15] and the Harvard dissertation entitled "Adequacy of the Socio-Economic Unit as a School District,"[16] recommended consolidation. But the conservative politics of the state kept the educators from pushing too hard for centralization, then considered a "liberal" policy. The conservatives were the strongest proponents of home rule and local control. Ironically, the conservatism of the fifties has become, in many ways, the radicalism of the seventies.

Educational Task Force: 1963

During the period between 1962 and 1964, there was a series of studies concerned with centralization. One such study was conducted by an Educational Task Force, appointed by Governor Hoff in 1963. In October, a report was submitted to the governor. The proposal was similar to the most recent state plan: a state school system composed of twelve regional districts, each administered by one school board and one regional superintendent employed by the state. The 1963 report went even further, suggesting consolidation of high schools so that no graduating class had fewer than 100 students.

The argument for this reorganization was based more on philosophical principles than on empirical evidence. There was little discussion of economy or efficiency—the justification was the protection of freedom and democracy. Students were repeatedly compared to soldiers and education to the military:

> The rifle is not for the soldier to use for the purpose of protecting his own life from the enemy. It is for his use in the protection of all of us and our democratic way of life. For this reason we see to it that the soldier gets the best rifle available, regardless of cost. Similarly, the education we give our children is for their use for the benefit of all of us and the decisions that they make as a result of this education will affect all of us. Their education, therefore, like the solider's gun, must be the best available.[17]

Patriotism was exploited to obtain support for educational change. Most of the evidence used to substantiate the proposal was drawn from experiences in other, more urban states. A bill to put the recommendation into effect was introduced by a legislator, and a public hearing was held. But, as a result of obvious community resistance, the bill never reached the floor for debate.

Tri-partite Study: 1966

One other study of the mid-1960s was the Tri-partite Study. The Tri-partite Committee was made up of members from each of the three major professional educational organizations in the state: the Vermont Education Association; the Vermont State School Directors Association; and the Vermont Superintendents' Association. This committee attempted to define quality education and suggest structures in which it could best be attained. The initial recommendation was for twenty-five unified K through 12 districts. The district, governed by a single board and administered by a single superintendent, would be responsible for most policy decisions of the member schools. Attempts, both in 1966 and 1968, to implement this form of consolidation through legislative action failed.

Arthur D. Little: 1967

In 1967, Arthur D. Little, Inc., contracted to do a management study of Vermont's educational system. Their highly polished report argues that structural change in education will automatically lead to improved outcomes, just as it had allegedly done in business.

Using previous Vermont studies of consolidation to justify the advantages of centralization and specialization, the bulk of the report is an organizational study, complete with hierarchical flow charts, position descriptions, and pay scales. The proposal was distinctly a top-down, decision-making structure, with no sensitivity to the possible effects it would have on communities or how the educational benefits projected would be derived. The style of the report was professional. Arthur D. Little was, and still is, one of the nation's leading management consulting firms. However, the content was superficial and demonstrated little awareness of the differences between public schools and private businesses.

Unification Study: 1968

In 1968, a study of school district reorganization, sponsored by the Vermont Department of Education, was conducted by a leading Vermont professor who was also a state senator. The title, *Unified School Districts in Vermont: Advantages and Disadvantages*, implies a degree of objectivity and an attempt to take both sides of the issue into account. The research cited and the evidence used, however, clearly represents the views of professional administrators already committed to centralization as a policy. The rationale this time was modernization. One of the primary sources cited was a national committee of business leaders, urging an 80 percent reduction in the number of all local governmental units.

Thirteen advantages of consolidation were meticulously presented in the report, while three disadvantages were mentioned casually in an attempt to avoid the appearance of bias. No direct action resulted in the aftermath of this study's release. It did, however, add another link in the chain of professional consensus on centralization.

Temporary Advisory Commission: 1968

In 1968, the Temporary Advisory Commission on Reorganization of School Districts issued their final report to the state legislature. The commission was created in 1966 to perform a feasibility study of both unification and consolidation of schools. Thirty-two study regions were defined, and committees in each were given the responsibility for evaluating the recommendation of the commission. Two years later, the commission's report assessed the work that had been done and offered its recommendations for a mandated unification into K through 12 districts, each governed by a single board with a set of financial incentives. Among the thirty-two study groups, twenty-two firmly rejected unification, seven desired it at some later date, and three groups abstained.

Using local study teams gave the appearance of being democratic and participatory. In theory, it was. Unfortunately, when the results of the independent group studies conflicted with the accepted policy, their work was largely ignored.

VEA/NEA Study: 1973

The next major study of Vermont education, entitled *Alternatives to Strengthen Vermont's Schools*, was conducted by a consultant from Virginia and released in September 1973. The accent was on increased spending. This emphasis was understandable and predictable, since the report was the product of state and national teacher organizations. Consolidation was expected to result in improved bargaining conditions.

The analysis contains an overwhelming mass of descriptive statistics, mostly used in comparisons with data from other states to accentuate the lack of support for education in Vermont. Some of the statistics were misleading; virtually none were documented.

The consultants offered no proof that increased spending would actually strengthen schools other than to raise teacher salaries. Granted that higher salaries are a worthy goal, it still is not evident that they would result in improved education. The primary benefits of the suggested changes would go to the same professional educators who sponsored this study. They correctly believed that higher salaries were more likely to be attained in a centralized system controlled by their educational brethren than in a system run by local communities.

Governor's Panel on State Aid: 1975

In 1974, the governor appointed yet another special commission to study the problems of school finance. The panel was chaired by a University of Vermont professor and included the individual heading the 1975 State Department of Education study group on consolidation. Consolidation was only incidental to the objective of the panel (which was school finance reform), but was made a critical ingredient in the final report. Recommendation 7 dealt with school district reorganization. The language urging consolidation was strong. For example:

> The public school systems of Vermont are organized into units which are too small, administered by personnel of which there are too many in number but too few with backgrounds and abilities appropriate to the task, and run at a cost which is excessive.[18]

The central thrust of this study was school finance reform. The conclusions, however, were more comprehensive, based on a general centralization of control that was, in many ways, more extensive than anything proposed by the Vermont Department of Education. The recommendations for consolidation bore no direct relationship to the purpose of the report other than to offer the unsubstantiated assertion that consolidation would lead to a more economical system by reducing overall costs and eliminating waste.

Implications of Centralization Studies

Policies about educational organization in Vermont have been remarkably consistent over the years. The centralization studies supporting these policies all incorporate a liberal, intellectual bias and reflect the opinion that professionals are better able to interpret and implement the desires of the people than are the people themselves.

Beyond having similar views, these studies also share similar weaknesses. First, they contain little evidence, either in "hard" research or in empirical findings from other rural states, to support their recommendations. Second, much of the rationale for consolidation is based on accepted industrial/business practices and the American ideals of growth and efficiency rather than specific successful educational practices. Third, there is a lack of recognition of the noncognitive effects of consolidation on students and communities. Fourth, much of the recent advocacy of consolidation reiterates historical arguments that may once have been valid, but no longer have the same relevance.

These reports were not, nor were they meant to be, objective. All were commissioned and carried out by professional administrators, educators, and politicians, who, naturally, wanted to expand and protect their self-interests.

No research, including this study, can be completely objective, but Vermont's research in this area was burdened by the bias of having always been carried out by those with a vested interest in urging consolidation. In 1975, a State Department of Education spokesman admitted to the press that "every previous major reorganization study started from the premise that reorganization was automatically necessary."[19]

The following section is an attempt to look at the rationality of current centralization arguments to see if there is any substantive basis for the grass roots resistance to consolidation, or whether such opposition is as irrational and emotional as the professionals charge.

Vermont School District Organization: 1975-76

Given the history of tensions over control of the schools in Vermont, neither the results of, nor the reaction to, the state's current centralization plan were surprising. When released, the most recent report received wide press coverage. Therefore, when the State Board of Education requested a special workshop to discuss the issue on the day preceding their December 1975 meeting, the arguments had already been rehashed repeatedly by most of the participants.

The state board listened, as many previous state boards and state legislatures have listened, to professional educators recommending consolidation of school administration. There was little new evidence presented. As one member of the state board described the department's report:

> It was a compilation of assumptions that have been made over and over again and there was no effort to relate them to new facts or to gather any new information.

Although the arguments had not changed over the years, the political climate had. The new State Board of Education was much more skeptical about the effects of centralization and was more sensitive to the potential loss of local control. In Vermont, as elsewhere, size and growth were being de-emphasized in all aspects of life, including education.

The State Department of Education officially began the current study of school district organization near the end of the summer of 1974. When the proposed study of district reorganization was presented to the public, it was publicized by a department spokesman as a new and different approach. He said:

> It's theoretically possible under the approach we're using that we would come up with more school districts, not fewer ones.[20]

Unfortunately, it is difficult to have faith in the veracity of this statement given the centralist orientation of the individuals involved. The person chosen to head this study team (composed of thirteen members of the State Department of Education) had frequently reiterated his position in favor of school reorganization. Just three months earlier, in a talk before a panel of school directors,[21] he had approvingly predicted that within four years the state legislature would *mandate* school district consolidation.

It seemed highly unlikely that the people chosen for this task were going to come up with a plan calling for more school districts. One of the members of the group admitted that consolidation was a "given" and that only the degree was to be decided. As a member of the State Board of Education verified, "The conclusions were made before the report was written."

The final report was a concise reiteration of all the historical and conventional arguments for consolidation. It revealed no new economic or educational evidence to justify its enthusiastic advocacy of reorganization. Rather, the report's authors opted for the time-tested formula of citing the recommendations of past Vermont consolidation studies, which were notably devoid of objective evidence in their own right.

However, it must be remembered that the dispassionate collection and analysis of consolidation-related evidence was not the perceived mission of this report. Instead, the apparent intent was to "pyramid" enough past recommendations, selective research findings, and professional opinions to create an aura of inevitability deemed necessary to establish policy.

Even beyond excluding all unfavorable evidence, such as that found in the massive Coleman Report and subsequent reanalyses of Coleman's data, the authors of this report did not even present the favorable evidence accurately. The best example can be found in the presentation of the findings of past scholarly research efforts. For instance, the following is the full discussion in this report of Burton Krietlow's work:

> Krietlow studied ten communities on the basis of non-consolidated and newly consolidated districts over a period of thirteen (13) years. Tests were administered to some of the students in the sixth, ninth and twelfth grades.

> In the first grade the students from the non-consolidated schools obtained slightly higher scores, but their comparative standings changed as they progressed through school. Final results indicated that boys' and girls' academic achievement was superior in the reorganized situations.[22]

Any reader not personally familiar with Krietlow's work would quite naturally come away from this description believing that on the basis of thirteen years of research, it had been conclusively proved that "boys' and girls' academic achievement was superior in the reorganized situations." If this were true, it would indeed constitute important evidence favoring consolidation. However, a closer examination of the evidence dispels any tendency to be sanguine about Krietlow's findings. Sher and Tompkins indicate:

> [Krietlow's] Long-Term Study suffers from the problems of any longitudinal study—the inability to control very many of the factors that operate over time. Four of the five non-reorganized communities reorganized over the years and 40 percent of the students moved or dropped out. The world changed a lot in twenty years, and it is extremely difficult to sort out the effects of one variable—reorganization—from other changes that occurred over time.[23]

On the findings themselves, Sher and Tompkins note:

Significant differences in achievement appear at the 6th grade level . . . favoring the reorganized districts. They persist at the 9th grade level, and some remain at grade 12—notably reading and biological science. . . . *However, controlling for SES and IQ at grade 6 wipes out the observed differences in reading and science achievement at grade 12.* . . . Without IQ and SES considered, reorganized schools are better on achievement measures. But the children in these schools are more affluent and do better on intelligence measures. These other factors are certainly plausible explainers of achievement differences, no doubt even more so than size of school or district.

Krietlow himself conceded:

Besides reorganization, significant differences found in favor of the reorganized sample may not be due entirely to reorganization, *per se,* but to hidden variables such as parents' socio-economic status, level of education, number of children in the family, rate of teacher turnover, innovations in the curriculum, and a general upturn in the values society places in education. . . . The results of this investigation strongly suggest that the significant differences found in favor of a reorganized sample should not be attributed to reorganization alone.[24]

The research cited on economic factors was also scant. Most of the statistical analyses related to district size (for example, those mentioned in the Nebraska study) could have easily been duplicated in Vermont, but they were not. In fact, further analysis presented later in this chapter denies any relationship between district size and cost per pupil. This was subsequently verified in a state-sponsored study of school finance in Vermont in which the analysts concluded that "a district's size does not affect the magnitude of its operating budget."[25]

Dollars and cents were related to the desire for consolidation in another way. For those most interested in promoting efficiency and centralized administrative control—the superintendents, principals, and some members of the Department of Education—dollars become the carrot to induce reorganization. They spoke of school finance reform as a means of "selling" consolidation, rather than consolidation as a means of achieving financial reform. As one superintendent said, "the way to fight the local control argument is with dollars and cents." The chairman of the group declared that Vermont is overgoverned and that there are not enough competent people to fill the offices. Therefore, he concluded, people have to be taken care of. He emphatically stated, "people forget that education is a state function, not a local option."

The state tried to make it clear that the issue was only administrative consolidation, not the consolidation of actual schools. People would not have to give up their neighborhood schools, only their school boards. Many of the superintendents who would control these regions, however, were inclined toward the eventual consolidation of schools as well. Superintendents represented at the meeting commented that "the problem is worse than ever. . . . What we have is a neighborhood high school concept. It's ridiculous . . . five high schools within a fifteen mile radius." The chairman of the study was part of a recent state-sponsored reorganization study of Rutland County in which he publicly deplored the small high school as "high in cost and low in efficiency." He also claimed to have "conclusive" personal evidence (which he refused to make public) that children achieved higher test scores in large classes than in small classes.

Educational policy issues in Vermont receive wide press coverage, and the reaction to the 1975 education department report echoed across the state. Consolidation is not a popular cause at the community level. The extent of the consolidation recommended, as reported by the papers, was the most extreme yet—from 274 districts to 8. The state claimed that this was presented only as an example and was misinterpreted by the press as a recommendation, but the fact remains that the report concluded with a map of the state divided into 8 regions, with financial data for those regions to be compared to the current situation. The recommended parameters of reorganization were: (1) at least 5,000 pupils per district; (2) at least $400 in property wealth per pupil; (3) at least $11,000 in income per pupil; and (4) minimal disruption to existing social and economic relationships. These parameters inherently dictate an extremely small number of districts and the elimination of well over 90 percent of all existing units.[26]

The following editorial from the *White River Valley Herald* (Randolph, Vermont) typifies local reaction:

Those who favor school district consolidation do so for the best of reasons; but make no mistake about it, this is a terrible idea. Commissioner Withey told the State Board that consolidation wouldn't mean the loss of local control, but by this he apparently means that control wouldn't pass directly into the hands of the state. Rather, it would pass into the hands of the regional district. . . . We think that the worst inequalities between school districts should be corrected by state aid to the poorest districts. This is the theory of the present system, but it is thwarted by the inequities of the Miller Formula for aid to education. The formula should certainly be changed so that state aid can better equalize unfair differences between rich and poor towns. But we must not expect school districts to provide equal educational opportunities in any strict sense. We must recognize that what may be reasonable and economic for urban areas may be impossible for rural areas to provide. Rural schooling, meanwhile, may retain its particular advantages.[27]

As it turned out, public resistance to centralization was more than rhetorical. For, while the state plan was being discussed, towns dissatisfied with the current level of centralization were attempting to decentralize by seceding from their supervisory unions.

Weathersfield was the first test case for decentralization. On March 16, 1976, by a vote of 3-2, the state board rejected Weathersfield's request for autonomy. Even though the issues behind these requests were often more complicated than just the battle for local control (personality clashes were also involved), it certainly brought to the surface the mood of the communities in Vermont. Indeed, the issue was not closed by the negative decision. Other towns were already formulating strategies for decentralization and more local control. Castleton, Benson, and others had expressed similar desires for smaller, more manageable units.

At the April meeting of the State Board of Education, another district, Unified District 21, requested permission to secede from the Caledonia Central Supervisory Union. This time, partly because of a stronger community endorsement of the move, partly because of more persuasive evidence of the need for autonomy, and partly because they were already organized on a unified K-12 basis, the

State Department of Education recommended approval and the state board concurred. The three towns—Groton, Ryegate, and Wells River—will form a new supervisory union in 1977.

The current status of the most recent State Department of Education proposal is still uncertain, but the chances for any significant consolidation seem very slight. At present, there is little incentive to change. According to the commissioner:

> Nothing will be implemented, except on a volunteer basis until there is some reason to cause people to say "this will benefit us."

That may require an extreme shift in economic conditions: either conditions will have to improve so that major financial incentives can be offered or conditions will have to deteriorate so that schools cannot afford to stay open without state support and reorganization. The latter assumes that reorganization could, in fact, save money—a notion which remains unproved.

There will probably be more studies of school reorganization and there will be similar recommendations made for similar reasons. The same time-worn arguments will be presented and there will be little new evidence—only a larger file of studies. The question of whether centralization truly means more effective education, more for the taxpayer's dollar, and more equality of opportunity has remained unanswered and largely unaddressed.

Section Two: Centralization in Theory and Practice

The Arguments—Economy, Effectiveness, Equality of Opportunity, and Control

Through the history of centralization in Vermont run a number of recurrent themes—threads of reform that attempt to weave a solid case for centralization of schools and school districts. They are the arguments for lower costs, increased effectiveness, and equality of opportunity.

The second section of this chapter attempts to shed some light on these arguments. By studying four Vermont high schools and their respective supervisory unions, and by looking at available state educational statistics, we will offer evidence related to the legitimacy of the claims made by educators for centralization.

The arguments have most often been based on theory and artificial assumptions that largely ignore the role of the individual and the community in the process. Thus, when the predicted economies, efficiencies, and equities are not attained, consolidation proponents are always able to rationalize their failures. By studying the actual conditions under which organizational change occurs and the attitudes and opinions of those most directly affected by it, we will draw conclusions about the most likely results of centralization in Vermont school systems.

Although much of the testimony used in this study is subjective, it is based on experience rather than theoretical suppositions. Those interviewed are not, nor do they pretend to be, objective.[28] However, attitudes toward centralization are factors that affect eventual outcomes as much as, or more than, stated policies and plans. Therefore, the use of empirical data as well as statistical data seems not only appropriate but essential.

The Schools and the Supervisory Unions

To understand the attitudes and opinions of those interviewed, it is necessary to know something about the school systems and the communities they serve. To choose representative schools, Vermont's public high schools were stratified into three subpopulations: the ten largest schools; the ten smallest schools; and the ten schools closest to the state average in size. Nine measurable characteristics of schools and communities were selected and weighted according to hypothesized relative importance. The characteristics were: enrollment; expenditures per pupil; number of towns served; income index; district multiplier (from the state aid formula); population of the towns served; dropout rate; pupil-teacher ratio; and the percentage of graduates going on to higher education. From these three subpopulations, four schools were chosen as most nearly representing their respective subpopulations: one large school; one small school; and two average schools. The four high schools studied and the towns that make up their supervisory unions will be briefly described. The

TABLE 6.2

Statistics of Four High Schools in Vermont

Statistic	Ethan Allen	Maple	Dewey	Village	Average
School enrollment (7-12)	1,475	800	735	162	720
Total supervisory union enrollment, K-12	3,618	1,708	1,776	890	1,903
Expenditures, per pupil	$ 1,438	$1,053	$1,346	$1,118	$1,236
Number of towns in union schools	5	6	5	1	3.8
Population served by school	17,400	5,901	5,758	884	6,660
Supervisory union population	17,400	5,901	5,759	3,407	
Teaching staff	105	58	44	13	
State aid multiplier	1.32	0.86	0.83	1.21	
Income index (base 100)	116	106	107	106	100
Percent going to college	41	27	43	41	37
Administrative costs, per pupil	$47	$34	$71	$38	$47
Transportation costs, per pupil	$91	$73	$119	$90	$75
Average teacher's salary	$10,750	$8,580	$9,040	$9,110	$9,110
Average pupils per teacher	14.1	13.8	16.7	12.5	14.7
Dropout rate, percentage	6.0	5.7	5.3	1.7	4.3
Average teacher's experience, years	11.4	6.9	5.3	9.9	
Percentage of teachers with 30 credits beyond B.A.	52.0	13.0	34.0	27.0	

names of the schools have been changed, but the essential characteristics are reported accurately. (See Table 6.2.)

Ethan Allen Union High School: Supervisory Union #10

This high school opened in 1951 and was reorganized as a union high school in 1956. It serves five southern Vermont towns with a total population of about 17,000. The high school enrollment is about 1,500. It also serves as a regional vocational center. Ethan Allen High is located in one of the larger towns in Vermont, but with fewer than 20,000 residents, it is still quite small by national standards. The main industries of the area are tourism, agriculture, and some small manufacturing. Each town has its own school board directing its elementary schools, and each elects representatives to the union high school board.

The high school facility is a large, factory-like brick building, similar to classic 1940s and 1950s school designs. Inside it is a network of hallways, traditionally styled classrooms, and vocational workrooms. The curriculum is diverse and specialized, with over 200 courses from which students can choose, scheduled in twenty-minute modules. There are also many extracurricular activities, but individual participation is limited by the dispersion of communities and transportation between school and home.

The general impression one gets from observing the school in operation is of precision, motion, and remoteness—large numbers of students moving from class to class in unison, tightly scheduled activities, and impersonality. The students eat in shifts in large, open dining areas supervised by teams of teacher-monitors.

The school is administered by a multilevel organization with a headmaster; principals for the senior high, the junior high, and the vocational school; and department heads. A large, complete guidance department is directed by a head guidance counselor who functions solely as a consultant and administrator. The organizational structure is quite rigid and formal and, according to those in the system, has little vertical integration or communication. Ethan Allen High School was the largest school studied.

Maple Union High School: Supervisory Union #20

In 1967, six towns in northern Vermont voted to consolidate their local high schools into one union school, Maple Union High. The towns that unionized are socially and economically diverse, representing both wealthy ski areas and poor agricultural communities. One small industry and a state college contribute to the local economy. The supervisory union serves a predominantly conservative population of over 5,800, including about 1,700 public school children, with 800 of the students attending the union high school. The school also serves as one of the state's sixteen regional vocational centers. Each town has its own school board directing the activities of the elementary schools, and each elects representatives to the union high school board.

The school, housed in a modern, rectangular, brick structure, is colorless and antiseptic-looking inside. The halls and restrooms are clean and devoid of the graffiti or damage that mars city schools. There was little observable commotion or noise, even between classes. Everything seemed to move with military precision. The front halls and office, in fact, were filled with posters and literature on the various military services. According to the guidance counselor, about 30 percent of the class explores military service and about 15 percent actually enlist.

The school offers seventy basic courses in addition to its vocational program and extracurricular activities. Maple High is too small to participate in the more costly team sports such as football or hockey, but it does have basketball, baseball, and other athletic activities. Because the member communities are so dispersed, transportation limits after-school activities. Most students spend long periods on the bus each day.

The general atmosphere is formal, but personal. Students and staff seem to know one another on a much more intimate basis than at Ethan Allen. The principal grew up in the area, and the superintendent has been there for many years. The author's reception was cordial, yet highly structured, with tightly scheduled interviews set up by the administration.

Dewey Union High School: Supervisory Union #30

This new union high school, located in north-central Vermont, serves five communities, with a total population of about 5,800. The population is more heterogenous than much of Vermont, and includes hill farmers, professionals, and intellectual and artisan urban expatriates. Many of the residents are employed in a nearby large town. The supervisory union administers the education of about 1,760 students—740 in the high school and 1,020 in the elementary schools. Each town elects its own school board plus representatives to the union high school board. When the school opened in 1971-72, it was part of a larger supervisory union, consisting of eight towns with three high schools. In 1973, the towns agreed that the unit was too large to serve the individual needs of the schools and they voted to divide into two supervisory unions, each with its own superintendent.

The union high school has had a stormy history, opening as a progressive, experimental school in a politically mixed area and in a time of highly polarized politics. Local reaction has sometimes been intense and, in response, the school has shifted closer to center, philosophically. It still offers an environment markedly in contrast with the more traditional structure of Maple Union High or Ethan Allen Union High. The curriculum is broad and diverse, with mini-courses, quarter courses, and semester courses from which the student can choose. In 1975-76, there were 181 courses listed on the student selection sheet. The atmosphere within the school is informal to the point of sometimes appearing chaotic. Students have the freedom to use resources at will during the free periods, and movement is restricted only minimally.

The teacher-student relationships are relaxed. Each student has a teacher-advisor for academic or personal counseling. The cafeteria activities demonstrate the atmosphere best. Students and staff eat together on a flexible schedule. More important than sharing the same facilities, the lunch area seems to exemplify the kind of genuine student-teacher interaction that characterizes progressive education.

Village High School: Supervisory Union #40

Village High School, with about 160 students, was chosen to represent the smaller high schools in the state. It is located in a rural village of fewer than 1,000 people in central Vermont.

Until the start of the 1975-76 school year, the high school had been operating without a central facility. The town served as the campus for the students, and the Elks Club, the GAR Hall, and the town library were all part of the school system. The school was totally integrated into the community. The State Department of Education had designated the school "substandard" and attempted to close the school just a few years earlier. However, after a closer investigation of the school and its relation to the community, they completely reversed themselves and it began to be presented as an example of how problems of scale can be overcome.

In 1975, the students moved into a new, modern, bright building containing many of the accoutrements of larger, city schools: cement block walls, hall lockers, laboratories, classrooms, an auditorium, a library, and the accompanying new rules and regulations to protect the facilities. As a result, much of the flexibility and freedom of movement of the old system is gone. Even in this new, more conventional building, the atmosphere is quite casual. Students, staff, and administration seemed to know each other. While there, the superintendent (and former principal of the high school) chatted with students and staff. The new principal (from the town, but new to the school) was on a field trip with a group of students. Although professing a traditional view of education, the administration's philosophy of education seemed quite progressive.

Guidance was much less a specialized function than in most larger schools, and counseling was everyone's responsibility. The personal warmth and sense of community was evident from the relationships observed in the teacher's lounge, the dining area, and the offices.

The course offering is large, considering the size of the staff and student body. By alternating courses from year to year, individualizing studies, and using community resources, the school is able to offer a relatively wide curriculum.

Economics of Centralization

Consolidation has often been equated with economy. Potential savings have frequently been claimed to induce local support for reorganization. Today, however, people have become skeptical of economic arguments in relation to consolidation. Even the State Department of Education no longer claims that consolidation will reduce costs. Instead, they argue that taxpayers will get more for their money. The superintendent of Maple Union summed up his attitude on this topic as follows:

> Nobody's sold me on any real savings. We didn't sell our Union High School on savings. Our costs are now $1300 (per pupil per year). Nine years ago it was $360 and we said the maximum it would get to is $550 with our efficiency. . . . Don't sell it on things that history has proven you can't deliver.

This section will analyze the various cost factors and try to determine whether economy does, in fact, exist. The factors considered are: materials and supplies; administrative costs; teacher salaries; transportation; and resources and special services.

Materials and Supplies

An integral part of most arguments for administrative centralization is the cost savings associated with bulk purchasing. It was used as a major potential advantage of reorganization in the state's presentation to the State Board of Education in December 1975. Most distributors of supplies do allow lower unit prices with large orders. And there are other alleged savings in bulk purchasing which result from reduced paperwork and simplified accounting procedures (for example, the need to place only one order). In theory, these savings seem obvious: buy more and pay less. Yet, in practice, it rarely ends up working so smoothly and simply. A combination of indirect costs and human factors actually *increase* costs with bulk purchasing, sometimes more than offsetting the savings. Unit prices and order costs naturally decrease with large quantities. However, inventory and storage costs, coupled with the risk of purchasing errors, all increase with bigger orders.

On the surface, only the savings are apparent. The hidden costs and related diseconomies are considerably more obtuse. For example, the idea of cutting costs by reducing the necessary paperwork is attainable only if a job, or part of a job, can be eliminated. But this rarely happens. According to the superintendent of Maple Union, bulk purchasing

> wouldn't eliminate a secretary or a clerk in the process. It takes some of the frustration out of the job, but the cost isn't high. A secretary or a clerk gets $3 per hour. In an hour they can handle a lot of paperwork. If you cut the paperwork in half, you'd still end up with the same number of people.

The superintendent of the other medium-sized school agreed. When asked if unification would cut purchasing costs, he replied:

> No. It's an illusion. It requires administration, an office, and secretary to cut costs and now the principal and teachers and board members are doing it after hours. As soon as the structure is set up, you may get paper cheaper, but there are other costs: overhead, warehouse costs, etc.

The business manager of Dewey Union put the problem concrete-ly. In his estimation, about 60 percent of the materials needed by the school could be ordered through a centralized system to obtain quantity price breaks. One half-time person working under opti-mum conditions could fill the position. Since the average material ex-pense per pupil in the district is $24 per year, $14 per pupil would be eligible for savings through bulk purchasing. Assuming an average quantity discount of 20 percent, the potential savings would be $2.86 per pupil. Given Dewey Union's total enrollment of 1,760 students, the maximum potential savings total just $5,000 per year. From this total, one must deduct one half-time salary plus administrative and distribution costs. If Dewey Union had to pay more than $5,000 in added expenses, or if the average savings were less than 20 percent, the result would be a net loss. Thus, net savings are by no means assured.

Another argument for centralization is that a specialized purchas-ing agent might also be more knowledgeable about the sources of supplies and be in a better position to take advantage of competitive prices and bargains. This, too, is true. But the cost of improper ordering and loss of flexibility is also significant and difficult to gauge in dollars. The headmaster of Ethan Allen offered an example of the problems when the process of ordering is too far removed from the classroom:

> Six years ago we went to centralized buying for the whole supervisory union for supply items—paper, pencils, etc. We sent in a list of stuff to the central office. When it was delivered we got a good buy on pencils. Nobody bothered to check on differences in needs between age groups or school groups. Someone got a whale of a deal on grade books. Except they were all six week grade books and we're on eight and nine week quarters. You do that with eighteen districts, with different kinds of schools and it would be horrendous. You'd end up with a bureaucratic setup that would cost more than it was worth. You'd lose flexibility in handling your budget and you wouldn't have equipment when you needed it.

If standard supplies are ordered through a central stockroom and drawn by the individual units, there are additional costs to be considered. Central storage of supplies and administration of the supply area increase costs, and users are less careful and tend to overdraw to ensure receiving their fair share. One principal attempted to measure the effect of centralized purchasing on a standard item—light bulbs. The result was a prime example of the human factor in bulk purchasing. Nine towns decided to consolidate the purchase of light bulbs. The administrator found that

> When each town was responsible for the purchase of their own light bulbs, they used 63 percent less bulbs than when we went into central purchasing. They were all good people but since the bulbs were coming out of a central pot they were less thrifty, feeling that they had to draw their share, to make sure that they weren't cheated. People weren't wasteful, but there are few quantity discounts as high as 63 percent. The custodian in one school had developed his own stock room, systematized. When we went into centralized light bulb purchasing, we fouled up his system, he became antagonistic and he no longer cared what happened to his stock. We had taken away part of his autonomy. He took pride in his stock, his inventory. When we removed that, it fell apart.

Services such as insurance and utilities can also be purchased centrally with potential savings. But conversely, as orders become larger it becomes increasingly probable that bids will go to larger, nonlocal vendors. The schools' economic gain could very well be captured at the expense of local business interests. In many rural communities, schools are the single largest consumer of material goods, so the adverse economic impact caused by the schools' avoidance of local business is far more severe than in urban or suburban school districts. Even beyond the direct economic issues, the schools' decision to use outside vendors often results in a legacy of animosity and diminished support which the local school can ill afford.

The evidence indicates that there are potential savings in centralized buying, but that there are also offsetting intangible costs associated with inefficiency, standardization, and loss of control. In addition, it is not even clear why consolidation is necessary to obtain the savings that are valid. Ethan Allen Union is already buying centrally without unification or further consolidation, as is Dewey Union. Centralized purchasing is not dependent on consolidation, only on cooperation.

Administrative Costs

Consolidation advocates have also argued for larger schools, as well as larger school districts. Larger schools are supposed to decrease administrative costs per pupil. For example, the argument goes, if a principal and staff now handling 200 students can just as efficiently administer 250 students, then the unit cost should be reduced by 20 percent. To test this hypothesis within Vermont schools, the percentage of current expenditures attributed to administration can be correlated with school size. This was done within a random sample of six Vermont supervisory unions, using a rank order correlation coefficient. To prevent differing supervisory union costs from confounding the internal school costs, the supervisory unions were not combined. There are still problems because schools do not have a uniform method for assigning administrative costs. The results are presented in Table 6.3. None of the unions even came near to a significant correlation between school size and the proportion of school expenditures allocated to administration.

A factor more important than size in determining administrative expenditures appears to be the organizational style and educational philosophy of individual schools and districts. For 1973-74, Dewey Union High, for example, had a per pupil administrative cost nearly twice that of the other three schools analyzed (see Table 6.2). By choice, Dewey operates a complex system in which the staff performs administrative functions, and consequently, portions of their salaries are allocated to the administrative budget. Conversely, some Vermont districts have more rigid, hierarchical divisions of duties, while still others expect teachers and school directors to perform administrative functions as part of their unwritten (and often unpaid) responsibilities. Ethan Allen (the large school studied) shows a higher per pupil cost for administration than Village High (the small school studied). Though the school is almost ten times as large, the pyramided organizational structure at Ethan Allen, with a headmaster, principals, guidance staff, and department heads, adds many more costs than consolidation has saved.

TABLE 6.3

Correlation Between School Size and
Percent Administrative Expense in Vermont

District	Number of Towns in Supervisory Union	Correlation Coefficient
1	6	0.04
2	5	0.07
3	7	0.15
4	4	Negative
5	5	Negative
6	11	Negative

Teacher Salaries

There is presently a wide disparity among teacher salaries in Vermont. Districts negotiate independently with the VEA and VFT on teacher contracts. Enlarging the bargaining base through centralization is bound to improve the position of the teachers' unions and expedite negotiations.

It seems unlikely that, where variations in pay exist, those at the upper end of the scale will be forced to reduce their salaries to be in line with statewide averages. Far more likely is a general increase in salaries, bringing all to the level of the higher paying districts. This, added to the fact that (as the professionals argue) consolidated schools and districts attract more experienced and higher credentialed teachers, will raise the costs of instruction significantly.

The assumption of consolidation's attractiveness, however, is highly suspect. If size, in and of itself, were a major factor in attracting qualified, experienced teachers, it would be reasonable to expect them to be clustered in large, central city schools, instead of smaller, suburban schools. But they are not, indicating that the community itself plays as large a role, if not larger, in the relative attractiveness of schools. The external conditions that make a school more or less attractive to teachers will not change through consolidation. Structural changes in the school system cannot make Cabot, or Rochester, or Pomfret into metropolitan communities with all the associated amenities.

Conversely, some teachers prefer rural areas simply because they prefer the slower, rural life style and institutions that reflect that style. According to an administrator in the University of Vermont's educational research division, a majority of today's graduating teachers favor rural environments and smaller scale institutions. Size and fancy resources do not have the same appeal today that they are reputed to have had in past years.

Transportation

Busing is an educational cost that could be reduced with administrative (as opposed to actual school) consolidation. In 1974-75, two-thirds of the public school students in the state were bused, and transportation accounted for 4.2 percent of current school expenditures. It seems probable that if buses were controlled through a central office, scheduling algorithms could be used to more fully utilize available vehicles, replacement models could be developed to determine the optimum vehicle life, and centralized garage and repair facilities could reduce overhead costs. These potential savings will probably not occur, however, because all Vermont children are not now adequately served. Thus, if a legitimate state goal is to equalize transportation services, a more extensive system would be required. The added costs of equitable service are likely to offset any dollar savings.

There is one other factor likely to raise transportation costs with consolidation—salaries. For example, within Dewey Union's Supervisory District, the drivers at various schools are paid according to different wage scales. The drivers of the high school buses are paid more for equivalent time and effort. According to Dewey's business manager, any consolidation would probably result in a standardized pay scale at the higher level. Admittedly, this increase could, and possibly should, occur with or without consolidation.

Resources and Special Services

According to the department's district reorganization study, consolidation means that "specialized educational services would be more efficiently and economically provided." Just how this would happen through district reorganization is left to the imagination of the individual. It is true that some resources are now underutilized, but it has more to do with individual school policies and practices than administrative organization. Districts within supervisory unions do share to some extent, but each really wants the flexibility to schedule the resources as needed.

The superintendent of Maple Union was asked about the economics of having the state coordinate special services:

> When the state takes over any service it costs more. They should provide dollars instead and let us buy services. If they contract and negotiate, it will cost more, plus the costs of supervision. I've never been shown that the state can do anything cheaper than the individual districts.

An example of how removing control over funding from the local community affects cost was offered by one Vermont superintendent. He described what happened when driver's education was mandated and funded by the state.

> It became mandated by the state and the state was going to pay for it totally. All the local boards said "fine" and agreed, because the state was going to pay. Look at what happened? [Small school X] runs a program for about twenty students per year, on a shoestring. They get their $60 per pupil from the state and the program about breaks even. But look at the big towns. They went out and bought expensive driving simulators. They hired football coaches as drivers ed teachers and they said it's state money, it doesn't matter any more. Let's get all we can of it and they bilked it. Now they're down to $40 per student here and the legislature is considering dropping the program because they estimated $400,000 and it cost almost a million.

This is not to say that the state should not provide services. This program may have allowed small schools to offer a service they may have not initiated without support. The lesson is that Vermont communities have shown a marked tendency to operate more efficiently and economically when they perceive themselves as spending their own, rather than the state's (or any other outside), money. Local control of education has always been a popular political position in Vermont. Now, however, it may well prove to be economically propitious as well.

From the preceding analysis, it is obvious that there are divergent views on the economics of consolidation. The only thing that can reasonably be concluded is that any argument for or against consolidation cannot legitimately be based solely on economic considerations. The real issue regarding educational dollars is who controls them and how they are spent. People generally are more thrifty with money for which they are directly accountable. Any reorganization that centralizes responsibility runs the risk of reducing responsibilities and efficiency at the local school level.

Cost-effectiveness of Consolidation

As it became obvious to proponents of centralization that economy (that is, the ability to lower costs) was not going to be realized, the strategy moved toward cost-effectiveness as the justification for reform. For example, the Vermont Department of Education stated:

> The present organization of public education in Vermont produced extravagant inefficiency in the use of school tax dollars and people. . . . Experience has repeatedly shown that adequate access to effective educational programs and services is directly related to the size of the school districts and the attendance units which serve students. . . . Vermont needs a system of school organization which will allow more effective utilization of our human and financial resources if our schools are to retain the confidence of Vermont citizens.[29]

The assumption here is that district reorganization will increase the effectiveness of administration, teaching, and resource utilization. The issue to be analyzed is whether centralization does, in fact, achieve these predicted results, or whether there are other, more direct routes to increased effectiveness.

Administrative Effectiveness

One of the strongest motives of administrators in favoring reorganization is that it will eliminate the responsibility for dealing with
multiple school boards. Multiple constituencies, they argue, frag-
ment their attention and the schools suffer. Superintendents unquestionably do spend much time and energy on local boards, and there is
bound to be some duplication of effort. Superintendents favoring
reorganization tend to view schools as distinct and separate from the
community and to see the process of education as something that
takes place exclusively within the classroom. This belief, as opposed
to one explicitly linking the school and the community, becomes an
important distinction when formulating educational policy.

The superintendents of the four unions studied here offered
divergent opinions about unification; their opinions naturally reflect
their own backgrounds and biases as much as the educational needs of
their districts. The superintendent of the supervisory union serving
Village High School treasured the smallness and the intimacy of his
units. He said:

> I serve six towns and if you had one board to serve the
> whole district, it would certainly simplify my life. But, I
> have come to the conclusion that simplifying *my* life isn't
> the objective of the educational process. . . . Sure, it's not
> efficient, but democracy isn't efficient. . . . I think people
> want to maintain close relationships. I sit down at a school
> board meeting with the directors, teachers, and whatever
> parents want to come and together we make decisions. It
> may be new textbooks, or trouble on the bus, or a lot of
> little things. As far as I'm concerned when they leave that
> meeting, they know that they have some control over their
> children's education.

The superintendent of Maple Union, a veteran of over twenty
years in Vermont's educational system, also felt strongly about
retaining individual school boards. His experience had been that it
was easier to work with the decentralized town boards than with the
consolidated union boards because of heightened parental interest
and community involvement. He felt strongly that this local involve-

ment in and support for the schools outweighed any disadvantages that duplication of effort might cause.

The other two district superintendents favored some form of unification aimed at reducing the number of school boards. The superintendent of Dewey Union reports:

> It took a while to get on to dealing with that many boards, that many treasurers, that many clerks, that many deadlines, that many budgets. It seems to me that you can't operate at a very effective level.

The two superintendents who favored the status quo were long-time residents of their areas with strong ties to both the schools and the towns. The two who favored consolidation were both relatively new to Vermont and from more urban school districts.

From the diversity of opinion found among these superintendents, it seems reasonable to believe that administrative "efficiency" is determined more by philosophy and personality than by the actual structure of the organization. Some administrators can more effectively provide leadership through close personal contacts. Creating a theoretically efficient centralized organization may end up nullifying working relationships developed over many years.

The principal of Ethan Allen was asked whether unification would free the superintendent to provide more effective leadership. He responded:

> Never! No more than a principal gets freed up by having an assistant principal.

The chairman of the union school board confirmed this. Conceding that the time a superintendent spends with school boards is a problem, he still felt there was little more that a superintendent in a reorganized situation does to improve the quality of education. As he indicated:

> Superintendents who aren't working with a lot of school boards let other kinds of administrative work fill up their time.

One way in which superintendents and school boards could

increase efficiency without reorganization would be to allow more administrative responsibility to accrue to principals and other school staff members. Much of the discussion at local board meetings revolves around issues and problems with which the principal is more familiar and knowledgeable than the superintendent. If principals were given a fuller measure of administrative responsibility, it is likely that increased efficiency could be achieved without any loss of local control. A structure that allows a genuine delegation of authority rather than simply centralizing power may have the twin benefits of heightened effectiveness and greater compatibility with Vermont's independent political traditions. Though less dramatic a reform than reorganization, this decentralization of responsibility and authority could well prove to be a more sensible solution for Vermont's schools.

Teacher Effectiveness

One principle upon which all agree is the importance of the teacher. According to one superintendent:

> If you measure students, the one thing that will make a difference—excluding parents—is the teacher.

The four schools studied were different enough in scale and organization to provide some clues about the consequences of size and consolidation on teacher effectiveness. Ethan Allen Union High School was the largest, the most thoroughly departmentalized, and also had the most credentialed and experienced teachers. One of the results of increased specialization was diminished contact with the students. According to one teacher with over twenty years of experience:

> When I first started here, there seemed to be a closer and friendlier relationship between student and teacher. We sometimes had kids for two years in a row and got very well acquainted with them. Now we just have them for a semester and that's the last we see of them.

This particular teacher does not experience the school's growth as facilitating staff interaction. She complained of less cohesion among the faculty, especially since the inception of department heads. We don't meet with them and talk with them the same as when they were teachers with us. We don't talk on the same level. . . . It's more of a bureaucracy. The department heads get together and they're part of the administrative council. . . . There was a time when we could walk into the principal's office and talk with him. . . . I don't think that happens anymore.

The headmaster of the school corroborated this teacher's thoughts by confessing that the school (though average by national standards) was too big for effective communication among the staff. He asserted that

if you have a hundred teachers, there's no way you can deal with them on a personal basis, no way you can sit down with them and talk to them and have them understand what you propose on paper. . . . It's misunderstood. In meetings, you don't get questions answered. With thirty teachers, we could talk about it over a cup of coffee and come to an understanding. With this size you lose a lot of personal contact. The same thing happens to kids.

Village High School, with its much smaller faculty, presents a distinctly different picture. Because of the practice of offering alternating courses from year to year, the staff was, of necessity, more flexible and multitalented than the rigidly specialized staffs at the larger schools. The relationships among students, staff, and parents extended beyond the school into the village life. Most of the teachers appreciated this condition, but also were aware of the difficulties it presented. One teacher felt it was

a tremendous advantage to know the kids and know their home environment. Then you know how to react to problems.

Yet, when the contact is personal and people

know each other so well through other contacts—church and community—personality problems are magnified.

Another faculty member, professing to know every student in the school, agreed that

> It is an advantage to know students better. . . . Yet in small classes, if there is a personality clash between student and teacher, there's no way of getting around it.

A teacher who had recently transferred from a large, urban school also knew most of the students in the school and was pleased with the size of the staff. She was grateful for a framework that made it possible to discuss problems immediately with others equally knowledgeable about the situation.

The importance of resources to the teachers varied with subject area and the availability of community and state resources. Teachers at Ethan Allen minimized the significance of resources, possibly because they seemed to have all that they needed. An English teacher there declared that resources were not as important to academic classes as they were to the vocational or business classes. An Ethan Allen science teacher stated that he had all he could effectively use and could see no advantage to further consolidation or growth.

However, the guidance counselor at Village High, with prior experience in a somewhat larger school, felt restricted by the lack of resources. Another teacher in the same school was satisfied that he was able to obtain all that was essential—library books, films, ETV, videotapes, and the like. Most of the faculty at Village High were confident that they could obtain what was essential, regardless of size or organization, and were unwilling to compromise the structure for additional resources. One teacher summed up many of the opinions presented:

> I'll take a small school any day, even without all the ancillary services. I would like more services and materials, but I prefer to be my own person, and I now have the experience and self-confidence to do it effectively.

For teachers, optimum size and organization connotes a situation in which they have access to needed resources, yet remain individually and uniquely important within the school community. Achieving the optimum is dependent on regional traditions as well as more objective criteria. Teachers often choose Vermont's schools at least in part for their rural environment and small scale communities. Thus, they tend to resent the imposition of bureaucratic structures. From the evidence gathered, it can safely be concluded that Ethan Allen is so large that its staff feels uncomfortable and alienated, while Village High School is too small and the town too isolated to prevent personality problems from interfering with teacher effectiveness. In Vermont, the quality of teaching does not discernibly improve with size, nor is there any absolute point of diminishing returns. Rather, individual schools and districts here appear to have their own critical level of organizational complexity and size beyond which they suffer adverse effects.

Utilization of Resources

One fundamental concern of efficiency experts involves the underutilization of available resources. Rarely is inefficiency so obvious as when a school bus or a videotape machine or an expensive science lab sits idle. If a district is small, yet needs expensive, specialized equipment that cannot be totally justified by usage alone, the school has three options: it can purchase the equipment anyway and use it as needed; it can attempt to share the resources with other schools or districts; or it can do without it. Yet, small schools, by themselves, often cannot afford to match the equipment and related resources possessed by larger, urban schools. If they value the resource, their only recourse is some form of sharing.

All of the superintendents interviewed professed to be effectively sharing resources among their member districts. Reading specialists, art and music teachers, school nurses, and psychologists are already shared among elementary schools within most supervisory unions. There is a tendency for some school boards to be jealous of others, believing that they may not be getting their fair share. Still, real dissatisfaction appears minimal.

Administrative reorganization in Vermont could expedite the sharing of resources simply by centralizing decision making (thus eliminating the need for community consensus), but the other logistical problems remain.

A young art teacher is a "shared resource" in a supervisory union adjacent to Maple and Dewey. She works three hours per week in each of two small schools and eight hours per week in a large school, and she is paid in proportion to her time by each of the school districts. It is commonly presumed that working for multiple "bosses" creates undue tensions and inefficiencies and that resource people would prefer to report to a central authority. When unification was suggested to this person as a means of simplifying her job, she offered her opinion of consolidation, as follows:

> I haven't had any dealing with the larger school board, but I have met with the smaller board and I find them very receptive to what I have to say. It's a small group—three directors and the superintendent—and I feel good when I go there because I know I'm speaking to someone very close to the problem. I wonder how it would work if it were a larger group and represented by fewer of the members of the community with which I am working. I don't know how effective I would be in describing the smaller school's problems to a group that had maybe one representative from the town and the rest from the other towns. Those places are really far away. I kind of like it small.

Another type of shared resource involves special materials and equipment. Sharing of such items as films and books is now accomplished through the state library. The heavy scheduling load—especially for films—requires schools to place their order weeks, and sometimes months, in advance, with little room for schedule changes. As utilization approaches 100 percent, efficiency and flexibility have declined rapidly.

Schools do share equipment and resources to some degree now. For example, the schools of the supervisory union in which the art teacher works also share a Title I reading specialist and a nurse, and they are considering sharing a music teacher. Even more could be shared, but to significantly improve the utilization and availability of resources requires not reorganization, but rather increased population density and more funds. These obviously cannot be attained simply through an administrative reorganization.

Consolidation and Efficiency

Efficiency in education is a nebulous and elusive quality. Unit output cannot be related to unit input as clearly as it can be in industry. Yet, it is continually offered as a rationale for centralization in Vermont.

Those areas within the educational system that are most easily controlled (and thereby have the most potential for change) include administration, teaching, and resource utilization. This investigation identified inefficiencies in each component. Administrators are exhausted by the frequency of school board meetings. Teachers often do not work in the most effective environments. Resources are often either underutilized or overscheduled, both of which reduce their usefulness. The issue is not whether it is possible to be more efficient in these areas. Obviously, it is possible. Rather, the important question is whether reorganization/centralization is the best available methodology for realizing needed improvements.

The evidence gathered showed few discernible differences in administrative efficiency between either large and small schools or unified and separate school boards. The duties of the superintendent were similar, the number of meetings attended were similar (administrators with fewer boards attended more subcommittee meetings), and the perceived responsibilities were similar. There were no more in-service training or other leadership activities assumed by superintendents in the larger, more centralized districts. There was, however, a pervasive isolation of administrators from both the community and the educational process in these larger districts. In theory, consolidation and reorganization should facilitate efficiency and effectiveness. But, at least in Vermont, there are frequent slips 'twixt the cup of theory and the lip of practice.

Equality of Opportunity

The most commanding argument for consolidation has been the egalitarian one. Put simply, the argument is that consolidation will equalize educational resources among all of the children in the state. It is persuasive because of the democratic ideal that schools would become the "balance wheel of the social machinery." It is difficult for any American—especially a Vermont Yankee—to take any stance that appears to impede equal opportunity. Thus, the strongest emotional appeal of consolidation lies in its purported egalitarian benefits.

Centralization might well reduce certain inequalities, but only if educational equality is narrowly conceived as a homogenization of educational inputs. Policies, like consolidation, that enhance uniformity and standardization will tend to equalize the resources available to each student. In the commissioner's 1975 presentation to the state board, he affirmed this premise by stating that "equalization of expenditures would be translated to mean equalization of educational opportunity." And, as the state's final report pointed out:

> States which have made significant strides in reducing the number of school districts have found that wide differences among districts in available fiscal resources generally decrease as districts decrease in number.[30]

However, recent research data on educational finance tend to refute this assertion. For example, Hooker and Mueller, after completing a large, sixteen state study in 1970, concluded that

> states with fewer districts exhibit as much [expenditure, valuation, and tax] disparity as those with many districts.[31]

This general concern about equality of resources found among consolidation advocates stems from the following three hypotheses: (1) that children in small rural elementary schools are inherently handicapped and at a comparative disadvantage with children educated in larger schools having greater resources; (2) that educational offerings vary dramatically from school to school, with large, consolidated schools consistently offering a broader curriculum; and (3) that the aspirations of students, as well as their chances for success in the "real world," are significantly influenced by the educational resources offered by the public schools.

The remainder of this section will focus on the validity of these three hypotheses as perceived by a variety of Vermont educators and citizens. An analysis of recent Vermont survey data will also be used in considering the merits of these hypotheses.

Equality among Elementary Schools

Educational administrators in Vermont have voiced two major complaints about small rural elementary schools. First, they argue that there is a lack of "articulation" between these elementary schools and the union high schools they supply. Second, they assert that many of these small schools are not providing even the minimum essential educational program to their students.

The point about "articulation" has achieved the status of a conventional wisdom among the state's professional educators. The notion that differences in program content at the elementary level handicaps children when they reach high school is regarded as a truism in Vermont.

Yet, interestingly enough, the individuals interviewed did not feel this phenomenon had much relevance to their own situations. Neither superintendents serving many elementary schools nor teachers working in the recipient union high schools were willing to attribute differences in high school student performance to elementary program content. Differences in student performance were, of course, observed, but the influence of elementary curricula ranked far below that of native intelligence, teacher characteristics, and socioeconomic background in the opinion of those interviewed. In other words, the judgment and experience of these individuals paralleled recent research findings about the marginal impact of divergent school resources. For example, the principal of Maple Union High felt that the characteristics and classroom styles of teachers, rather than expenditure levels, were the key to student success. He stated:

> Most all towns are fairly comparable in their ability to finance education and their ideas about what they want from schools. The differences [in student achievement] are more attributable to teachers than schools. We receive students from one- and two-teacher schools who reflect the specific strengths and weaknesses of that teacher. If everything were controlled by one school board, I don't think I'd see any differences. After all, they'd still probably have the same teachers.

The guidance counselor at Dewey Union High School attributed student differences to family background:

> I know a lot of the differences people would like to attribute to schools. But I know that it's family—the background from which they came. I can't buy the concept that students from [School A] are better prepared or less prepared than [School B] students.

The guidance counselor at Ethan Allen High School saw few observable differences at all. He insisted:

> Kids that come to us at the seventh or ninth grade are prepared in virtually the same manner. Educationally, academically, they are equally well prepared. Some years ago, when there was less communication, there may have been differences.

This particular counselor—a veteran of more than twenty years in Vermont's schools as a teacher and principal—felt that so much standardization had already occurred that historic differences have virtually been eradicated.

It may be possible to attain better articulation and consistency between elementary and secondary level programs. However, a convincing case for bothering to secure such uniformity has still not been made in Vermont. No current evidence has been found that indicates that any child's education would be discernibly enhanced by the imposition of a more standardized curriculum.

At heart, the quest for articulation is a throwback to the days when educators believed that schools existed primarily to funnel a predetermined package of information into every student's mind rather than to meet the actual educational needs of the individuals involved. In Vermont, as elsewhere, individualized education has gained widespread popularity in recent years. Yet, articulation, which implies standardization, and individualization remain incompatible, for they are predicated upon diametrically opposed sets of assumptions about the meaning and purpose of education.

The issue of articulation aside, small school opponents have consistently argued that such schools are unable to provide the minimum essential education for their students. Once again, this argument is developed in terms of resources offered rather than results achieved. Indeed, it would be difficult to dispute the statement of state education officials that "educational course offerings and services are related to the size of the school district and the attendance unit which serves students."

Still, the real differences between the educational programs found in large and small Vermont schools are far less significant than one would assume from reviewing course offerings and faculty rosters. In fact, these differences often boil down to the fact that larger schools have more specialists and specialized offerings than small schools. However, it does *not* mean that students in small schools are deprived of needed instruction. The lack of an art teacher or a music teacher does not mean that the child is not exposed to art or music; it means only that there is no specialist involved. The teachers, in most cases, still integrate art and music into the school program, either personally or with community help.

Evidence that big schools possess advantages is nonexistent in Vermont. There is, in fact, counterevidence that indicates that there are advantages in smallness for the development of the child.

One teacher who shares her services between a small school and a large school related her impressions on this topic:

> The kids who are in the bigger school—even though those teachers care about them and are really a devoted group—don't get the kind of attention they need. What they're missing is not so much the skills as the confidence. . . . In the smaller school they go at it themselves. They make mistakes, but then they remedy the situation. At the larger school, they make mistakes then try to avoid responsibility.

A teacher in another small school agreed:

> We have all the good things they build a large school for, but we also have autonomy—an identity of our own. The kids feel this too.

Differences among elementary schools are most evident in the area of per pupil expenditures. For example, within Rutland County

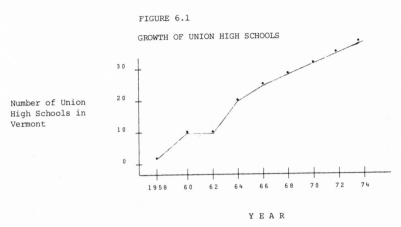

FIGURE 6.1

GROWTH OF UNION HIGH SCHOOLS

Number of Union
High Schools in
Vermont

Y E A R

alone, elementary school costs range from under $600 per pupil in Clarendon, Mt. Holly, and Tinmouth to over $1,100 per pupil in Proctor and Shelburne. It is assumed, by finance reformers and by the courts, that a child in Proctor must, ipso facto, receive a better education than a child in Clarendon or Mt. Holly.

Similar discrepancies occur within Dewey Union, and the superintendent was questioned about their effects. He responded:

> Kids at the $600 school don't receive all the extras. Yet, they do well when they get to high school, even without having had an extensive library, music, or physical education program. They got no add-ons, just good teaching. The school that spends $1,200 has it all, yet their kids still have problems.

The implication here is that dollars are not the sole answer to the educational needs and problems of Vermont's children. State aid still needs reform, both to equalize the burden on communities and to provide equally "pleasant" surroundings for all children. However, the belief that equal resources will, in and of themselves, result in equal achievement seems to be an idea without any basis in fact.

Equality among High Schools

During the past two decades, consolidation has been most widespread at the high school level. In fact, consolidated high schools virtually blanket the state today (see Figure 6.1).

In analyzing the effects of size on high school offerings, large schools have generally been shown to offer a more sophisticated program than small schools. In 1973, the State Department of Education issued a "Survey of Selected Practices in Vermont Secondary Schools." The practices (such as remedial reading, advanced placement, team teaching, and outdoor education) that each school listed as operating moderately or extensively were totaled and correlated with school size. The rank order correlation coefficient for a sample of thirty-four of the state's seventy-three high schools was 0.56, significant at 0.01.

The four representative high schools examined for this study also yielded curricular differences. Ethan Allen had many more courses available than Village High School. In science alone, Ethan Allen listed courses like Bioenergetics, Soil and Water Analysis, and Aristotle, Shakespeare and DNA. Village High, on paper, could show only more traditional courses like Earth Science and Physical Science. Even assuming that titles can be misleading and that Village High might actually cover some of the same breadth of material, the students at Ethan Allen clearly have a more specialized selection of courses.

However, size is by no means an absolute indicator of curricular breadth. Dewey Union, while only half the size of Ethan Allen, is able to offer an equally broad range of courses through innovative and imaginative planning. For example, in the 1975-76 school year, Dewey Union offered eighteen different senior high courses in science alone.

As among the state's elementary schools, there are also significant per pupil expenditure differences among Vermont's high schools. However, these expenditure variations are neither correlated with, nor attributable to, school size differences. For example, in 1973-74, the range of per pupil expenditures for high schools having 1,000 or more students was from $848 to $1,631; for high schools having 500 to 700 students, the range was from $938 to $1,614; and for high schools having 200 to 300 students, the range was from $899 to $1,619. In that same year, five high schools ranging in size from 198 to 1,149 students spent less than $900 per pupil, while six other high schools ranging in size from 200 to 1,026 students spent over $1,500 per pupil. Thus, it is obvious that arguments equating school size and expenditure levels in Vermont are without any foundation in fact.

The traditional concern about teachers rejecting the value of small schools was not borne out by the investigation. Few individuals questioned noted any significant differences in achievement or cognitive development between large and small schools in Vermont. However, almost without exception, teachers and administrators acknowledged the beneficial environment for affective development and personal growth found in small, rural schools. As the former president of Goddard College (in Plainfield, Vermont) stated:

> Goddard student teachers invariably thought school X (a school of under one hundred students) was the best school to work in, although it was the smallest. They particularly liked the intimate relationships between teachers, students, and the community. And, it probably was the best educational institution. It didn't have the variety of courses or the equipment found in big schools, but, if you talk about the development of kids, I'd have to say that the small school was the best.

Even the headmaster of Ethan Allen corroborated this point:

> Small schools gain a lot because you get personal relationships going that you can't get going in a school like this. . . . There's no way you can buy personalness. You just lose it with growth.

A teacher at Village High claimed to like small schools and smaller classes better because "it is easier to work with the kid" and "you can spend more time with each individual student."

The superintendent responsible for Village High and the principal of Maple Union High both remarked upon the effect of smallness on student responsibility. The superintendent told of a student who came to him and asked for the keys to the school:

> I can trust him because he knows that when I give him the key I'm depending on him and he's not going to let me down. . . . One night the kids were in there at eleven o'clock at night working on a school project. This is education. And I think we formalize it and we kill it. When you get too big, you really do have to formalize the thing.

At Maple Union High, the principal spoke nostalgically of his high school days in Vermont:

> I went to a small school where kids took over all the
> services. Students helped the younger students. Schedules
> were informal—you ate when you were hungry and went
> to recess when you were tired. . . . The school was
> eventually closed due to a lack of resources, but there was a
> great sense of responsibility. . . . In small schools, students
> tend to take on a little bit more responsibility for their own
> actions—because it's a very immediate thing. If one
> student fouls up, everyone knows it.

The informal atmosphere of small schools and the amount of responsibility students are willing to accept there are "educational" in ways that are not easily quantified. And they remain as important aspects of the students' social and emotional development. The observations of those interviewed seem to confirm the research conclusions of Barker and Gump.[32] Students in Vermont's small schools *do* indeed appear to participate more directly and meaningfully in school activities and to feel more personally involved and important in the life of their schools than do students in large, consolidated institutions.

School Size and the Chance for Success

The final hypothesis advanced by consolidation advocates is that large, consolidated high schools have a beneficial effect on student aspirations and chances for success in the "real" world. The assumption is that the kinds of programs, resources, and environment found in large schools will better prepare students for life beyond high school.

Even though detailed and sophisticated evidence remains unavailable, there are two recent data sources that can yield modest conclusions about the relationships existing among size, resources, and student success in Vermont. These two data sources are: (1) published Vermont Department of Education reports on the percentage of high school graduates going to higher education; and (2) a 1973 survey of Vermont high school seniors exploring the relationship of various input measures to post-secondary aspirations and accomplishments.

Vermont state data. The State Department of Education publishes an annual statistical report on the educational plans of students after graduation. The 1974 report showed that 39 percent of the 1973-74 graduates entered college. A correlation coefficient was calculated between high school size and percent going to college for 1974-75. The coefficient was 0.15, showing no significance at 0.05 for the simple regression of percent college-bound on school size. In addition, the tails of the size distribution were examined. Two subsamples were compared: the state's ten largest schools and the state's ten smallest schools. In the largest schools, 42 percent were going to college, and in the smallest schools, 41 percent were going to college; there was no significant difference.

These preliminary results are surprising considering that (1) colleges are more accessible to students in larger towns; (2) the socioeconomic status of those in Vermont's larger cities is higher, on the average, than of those in rural communities; and (3) student aspirations are often presumed to be higher in areas of higher business concentration and wealth. In some specific instances, this was borne out by the data. Burlington, for example, has three large colleges and a state university within commuting distance. As might be expected, a large number of graduates from the large Burlington high schools, especially the suburban schools, went on to college. But over half the graduates of Wilmington, a quite small school in southern Vermont, also went to college. And surprisingly, 40 percent of the graduates of Canaan High School (isolated in the remote corner of Vermont's northeast kingdom) went to college last year.

The next section is a further attempt to investigate the effects of size on post-secondary plans, independent of a few of the variables that presumably influence students' chances for success.

Post-Secondary Access Study. The other, more complete set of data, is described in the 1974 Vermont Post-Secondary Access Study.[33] Though intended to be a sample using every tenth high school senior, the completed questionnaires actually represented only about 7 percent of the state's seniors. This study's basic mission was to determine why many students interested in, and aspiring to, post-secondary schooling do not, in fact, continue their education. One part of this effort entailed an examination of the effect various high school experiences had on these noncontinuers.

Part of the coded survey data was retrieved by this investigator to carry the analysis further than it was in the original study. The re-analysis attempted to measure the effect that school size and per pupil expenditures have on student aspirations (as determined by the student's senior year occupational goals). Since information was originally collected on each student's family background, residence, school, and program, a path model was employed to isolate the independent effects of school size and resources on aspirations. After an elimination of incomplete responses, the sample size was 237 and represented 54 Vermont high schools.

The original study also used a path model to determine which variables affected student aspirations. One of their findings was that

> Enrollment in an academic track in high school is the single most important building block experience contributing to aspirations for post-secondary education and actual enroll-ment.[34]

Further, they found that

> Academic ability and family background determine which program a student will take in high school. . . . [Students with high educational and occupational aspirations] also come from more advantaged homes than do other students. The educational and occupational level of their parents is high, and they are no doubt reinforced at home toward academic success and aspirations for further education.[35]

The conclusions drawn from this re-analysis are more modest than those reported in the original study because (1) all of the sample could not be retrieved; and (2) the manner in which some of the questions were worded made their validity suspect. Most of the information was obtained directly and exclusively from students and, as a consequence, data about sensitive information (such as family income) have an inherently high potential for inaccuracy.

The path model employed here assumes specific causal relation-ships among the relevant variables. The variables used in the model were: (1) father's education; (2) father's occupational status, merged into a 6-point scale from the Blau-Duncan 96-point scale; (3) place of residence; (4) enrollment of high school, 1974; (5) expenditures per pupil, 1974; (6) high school program in which the student is tracked; and (7) the preferred occupational goals of the student, using the same scale as for father's occupation.

The results are shown in the path diagrams (Figures 6.2 and 6.3) and in the table of path coefficients (Table 6.4). The relationship of most interest is between school size and aspirations. The path coefficient between the two was −0.125, indicating that students in smaller schools tend to have higher occupational goals. For every increase of one standard deviation in school size, holding all other variables constant, goals would decrease by one-eighth of a standard deviation. In crude, quantitative terms, this means that a school of 300 students would, on the average, encourage students with similar backgrounds and from similar homes to pursue occupations about one-half a point higher on the 6-point scale than would a school with 1,200 students. The path coefficient is not large, but it is significant.

The clear implications of this re-analysis are that size and resources certainly do not create high aspirations nor do they explain much of the variance among students' occupational goals. What little effect increased school size shows tended to be negative (that is, the bigger the school, the lower the aspirations of students). The factor in the model that most strongly affected goals was father's occupational status. Reinforcing the results of national studies, the analysis showed that fathers with high-status positions are more likely to have children who also end up in high-status jobs. Thus, given the available evidence, there is no logical or empirical basis for believing the consolidation advocates' hypotheses regarding student aspirations and life chances.

The Value of Equality

Vermonters pride themselves on their traditional efforts to achieve "just" policies and equality for all. In Vermont, schools are seen as one of the primary instruments for attaining equality of opportunity. All children are supposed to have the same educational advantages, but, as the advocates of consolidation quickly point out, all do not. The traditional premise is that this is because of the structure of our schools. The more radical position is that it is because of the structure of society. In either case, the fact remains that equality does not exist.

Yet, it appears to be unfair and unrealistic to place the full burden of inequality and its resolution upon the schools. Differences in our

FIGURE 6.2

PATH MODELS

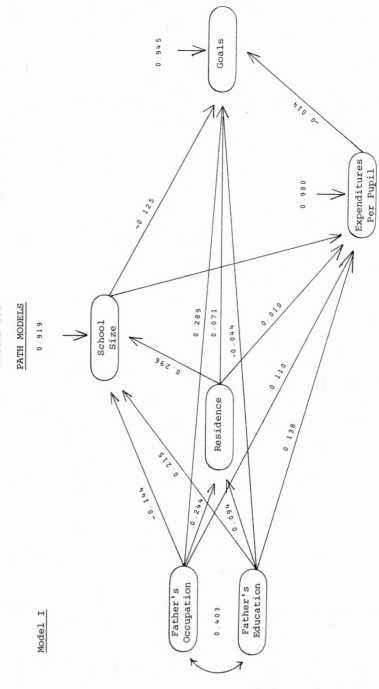

Model I

FIGURE 6.3

PATH MODELS

Model II

FIGURE 6.3 PATH MODELS — Model II

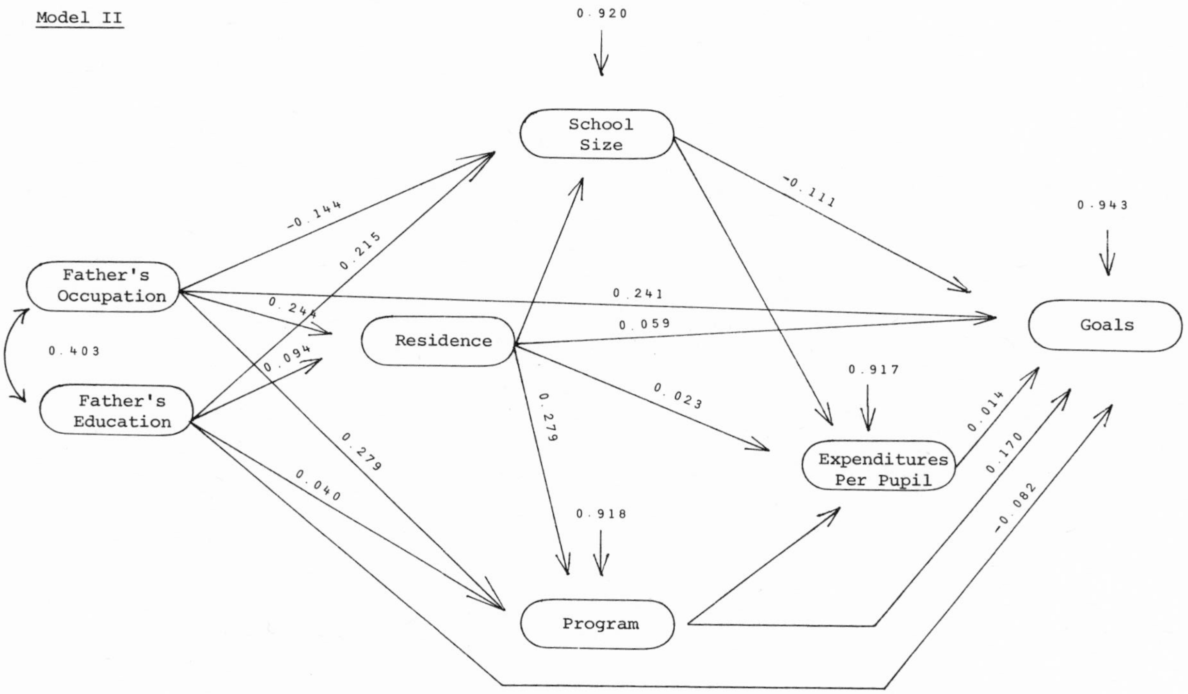

TABLE 6.4

Path Models for Reanalysis of 1974 Vermont
Post-Secondary Access Study Data

Variable		Average	Standard Deviation
X1	Father's Occupation	2.96	1.63
X2	Father's Education	2.15	1.08
X3	Place of Residence	2.66	1.10
X4	School Enrollment	710	434
X5	Expenditures Per Pupil	1254	274
X6	Occupational Goals	3.8	1.81
X7	High School Program	1.49	0.70

Path Coefficients--Model I

	X1	X2	X3	X4	X5	X6
X1	--	0.403	0.244	-0.144	0.110	0.289
X2		--	0.094	0.215	0.138	0.044
X3			--	0.296	0.010	0.071
X4				--	0.087	-0.125
X5					--	-0.014
Unexplained Variance				0.02	0.93	0.94

Path Coefficients--Model II

	X1	X2	X3	X4	X7	X5	X6
X1	--	0.403	0.244	-0.144	0.279	0.159	0.241
X2		--	0.094	0.215	0.040	0.175	-0.082
X3			--	0.296	0.279	0.023	0.059
X4				--	--	0.069	-0.011
X7					--	-0.184	0.170
X5						--	0.014
Unexplained Variance				0.92	0.92	0.92	0.94

society as a whole (whether measured by income, social class, or occupation) have not been shown to be attributable to differences among schools. Poor teachers can harm a child. Insensitive administrators can harm a child. But it appears unlikely, from the evidence gathered, that given competent people in the system, the lack of an art class or a gymnasium or a comprehensive library will harm a child's chances, either in school or in life.

Children should have access to as rich an educational environment as possible, but most of the resource deficiencies attributed to smallness can be made up through imaginative and creative instruction. There is at this point in our history no evidence or reason to believe that small schools or small districts have inferior or less creative teachers. On the contrary, the small school, with its more personal environment, often allows teachers to be more sensitive to and supportive of the needs of their students than is the case in larger, more bureaucratic institutions.

Community and Control

Vermont does have a unique history, a unique spirit, and a unique tradition—unique partly because it is so characteristically rural. No true Vermonter is actually against local control today. It is as much a part of Vermont tradition as maple syrup or covered bridges. Some may want to bend it a little, or modernize it, or redefine it, but never give it up. Therefore, any movement toward centralization must be tempered and camouflaged so that it gives the appearance of at least equivalent control. Thus, in the same statement recommending wholesale standardization and enormous centralization, the state had the temerity to assert that "school district reorganization will not result in a loss of local control."

Local Control

The heart of the opposition to consolidation, since the early days of the district schools, has been concern over loss of local control. The once self-sufficient Vermont rural villages are no longer economically independent. Yet, this loss of economic independence has had the primary effect of reinforcing and expanding the importance of an independent, locally controlled school system. The schools, along with the town meeting, represent the last vestige of localism and self-governance in much of rural Vermont.

A recurrent charge is that local control is only a myth and does not really exist. To some degree this is true. Schools in Vermont are similar to each other and to schools anywhere else in the country. Our perception of how schools ought to operate and what they ought to look like are effectively internalized. They have been formed and molded by the national testing services, multinational textbook and curriculum distributors, standardized teacher training programs, college entrance requirements, professional educational organizations, labor needs, and our own educational experiences. However, these sources of uniformity and apparent barriers to change come from the local community rather than the state or federal government. The actual magnitude of a school's individuality and uniqueness is not the main issue or the major concern. What *is* important is the need of people to feel that they have power over the system and over the development of their children, even if that power is illusory and the possibility for radical variance among schools is slight.

There are substantial differences between rural school boards in Vermont and their urban counterparts. City school boards are usually dominated by professionals, while rural school boards are mainly nonprofessional and more representative of the community as a whole. For example, the twelve-person board of Maple Union is composed of three farmers, three salesmen or merchants, two housewives, a plumber, a retired teacher, a doctor, and a miner. The Dewey Union Board has seven members: a farmer, an analyst, two teachers, a secretary, a realtor, and a business manager.

City boards are often susceptible to political pressures, but because of the size and composition of rural communities, rural boards are more likely to be susceptible to social pressures. To the extent that rural villages are homogeneous, the boards are truly representative. Unlike city boards, most rural school directors know many of the students and their parents personally, and thus the education and socialization of the child have a more direct and more personal bearing on the community and on board policy. The school does not just educate a group of youngsters, but rather teaches the children of friends and relatives. This is an important factor in community life and in the organization of schools. Local control does exist after consolidation, but at a different level and with a different meaning. As social, psychological, and physical distance increases, and as people are further separated from the decision-making process, they become less involved and exhibit a diminished concern for their schools. According to the director of the Vermont State School Directors Association:

> The further they have moved union schools away from individual towns, the less people have been interested in what's going on in the schools, going to meetings, voting on budgets, and so on.

Localism was mentioned repeatedly during the interviews in reaction to consolidation. Dewey Union had been under a state directive to evaluate a K-12 unification plan with one board controlling the entire union. The districts unanimously rejected the plan, holding that

> The "local control" of each town board is felt to be an asset and a less costly means of governing the operation of a school.

A member of the state board also reacted to the potential faults of a centralized system, as follows:

> There's a real fear on the part of so many that we'll lose something that's very dear. We may not be able to offer as much in terms of subjects, but we'll give them [the children] something more.

A principal of one of the state's smallest high schools was asked why his community had repeatedly rejected unionization, even when it was believed that there might be cost savings; he replied:

> It's a very independent community, as you probably know. They want to keep control over their schools.

To many Vermonters, it is as simple as that. Regardless of costs or the effort required, they want to keep control.

Vermont, possibly more than any other rural area, has managed to keep government at a personal and manageable level. For some time now, resistance to government regulation has been seen as conservative and regressive, but with the current wave of interest in participatory democracy and self-government, the libertarians who support decentralized government have an ally in the new left. People in Vermont still look to the government for environmental and economic policies, but there is a renewed interest in establishing community-based institutions. The climate in Vermont for continued decentralized school administration—whether rational or irrational —appears stronger than ever.

Consolidation has other, less tangible, effects on community life and on the students. Small, rural villages identify strongly with their schools. Election of school directors is often the most emotional and hotly contested part of the annual town meeting. For the average rural citizen to take an active interest in the school, he or she must feel comfortable among the staff and directors. Growth of districts and growth of schools inhibit participation. They are, in fact, often antithetical. No proof is necessary to state that people are more comfortable working with (or complaining to) teachers and school directors who are friends, neighbors, and relatives than with a board on which their community has only fractional representation. Generally, in Vermont, town school board meetings create more interest than the union high school board meetings. A member of the Maple Union School Board explained that "people feel that with unionization, they'll have less to say in the school," and, she added, consequently "people don't feel the way about the high school that they do about their elementary schools."

A state-level educator, though favoring consolidation, conceded that with unionization,

> people have felt alienated and they can't address them-
> selves to the problems. In Shelburne, none of the five towns
> feel the school is really theirs.

A State Board of Education member, addressing the issue, said:

> We've lost a certain kind of educational quality that comes
> through personal contact. I don't know how important that
> is, but you can feel the difference.

Differences in personal relationships, participation, and sense of community that are related to size were obvious among the four schools studied. A student at Village High described his education as a "community event," where "everybody is into what everybody else is doing." At the larger school he attended previously, he described himself as a "card in a file." Students and teachers alike all comment-ed on the personal qualities of their schools. The administration and the school directors knew most of the students, and the students felt more rapport with the staff.

The contrast was most noticeable at Ethan Allen Union High, where size largely prohibited personal contact. Even the staff had little communication with the administration, while the students had virtually none. The guidance counselor, though a proponent of consolidation, is worried about the alienation it can cause:

> The anonymity of a large school is obvious. The bigger you get, the less the youngster has any identity. . . . It's the great middle that suffers the most. The bright kids and the problem kids get help.

The chairman of the union school board agreed:

> Our school is too big. . . . I would oppose it getting any bigger. I know now that kids are getting lost there.

It requires little research to realize the importance of schools to Vermont citizens. School issues fill the newspapers each week and school board meetings are major news items in most Vermont towns. All of the interest does not always benefit the student directly. There is resistance to change in Vermont, and it is often difficult to attempt new and innovative educational programs. When the students in the social psychology class at Dewey (one of the state's more innovative schools) were asked whether they would prefer to have their parents or professional educators setting school policy, they almost unanimously chose the educators. They knew that many parents were skeptical of the school's programs and preferred more traditional education. The students were quite aware of the tensions this had invoked throughout the school's short history. But it was taken for granted that their parents would be involved and did care, and that the schools are important in their lives, the lives of their parents, and in the affairs of the community.

Implications

School organization is not a neutral, structural aspect of education, but rather is an integral part of the educational and social process. Social relations in rural Vermont are dissimilar to social relations in America's cities. Rural values and rural economics are distinctive. They are much less dominated by specialization, time-orientation, external motivation, competitiveness, and other values associated with hierarchical organizational patterns. Rural life, even today, is controlled more by the seasons and the weather than time clocks, and the rural hill farmer still prides himself on being a jack-of-all-trades rather than a specialist. The differences are less intense today, but exist nevertheless and are still treasured.

The organization of schools has an effect on rural traditions and rural life styles that transcends the pros and cons of efficiency, economy, and equality. Since these values and the rural way of life are deemed to be important and worth retaining by most Vermonters, it seems natural and correct to have an educational system that will reflect and reinforce them.

Conclusion

The analysis of recent studies of Vermont school district organization reveals an inherent bias among Vermont educational policymakers favoring consolidation—a bias recognized and even accepted as part of the conventional wisdom of administrative policy. There has been little substantive evidence introduced in the studies to support the claims made for centralization. Hypothesized results have been used instead to rationalize a degree of uniformity, standardization, and control deemed necessary to equalize educational opportunities within the state.

The main arguments put forth in support of centralization are that consolidation will

1. allow for economies of scale
2. provide a structure in which teachers and administrators can operate more effectively
3. equalize the educational advantages for all children

The counterarguments are that

1. local communities closer to the situation can more efficiently control costs
2. those closest to the students and their environment know better what their needs are and can provide a higher quality education
3. schools are an integral part of community life and decisions affecting the school affect the entire community and should be made at the community level

Emotional involvement often overshadows the rationality of the arguments. The evidence obtained through interviews, observations, and statistics is by no means conclusive. It did, however, raise many questions about the effects of consolidation and the reasonableness of the claims made on its behalf.

This study shows, above all, the skepticism existing even among members of the Vermont educational community concerning consolidation. Whether this skepticism is born of experience, emotion, or an innate Vermont resistance to change is irrelevant, because it is these people who will be responsible for the success or failure of centralization. Most of those interviewed who were raised in Vermont valued smallness. Indeed, much of the attractiveness of the state today, even to outsiders, is the vision of small community life in which each individual is an essential component of a small-scale system rather than a redundant part of a large system.

The economies of scale that, theoretically, could be obtained under ideal conditions are usually offset by the reality of added administrative costs found in larger, more bureaucratic organizations. The efficiency of the educational system may be increased by additional resources and professional business management, but ultimately it is reduced by the impersonality and alienation associated with larger size. Equality of access to educational resources may be improved through standardization, but true equality of opportunity is still a function of class background and environmental factors. Most research has shown that equal access to resources does very little to equalize outcomes. Removing the parents and the community from the process ignores the evidence that shows the importance of family and peer groups to achievement.

In many ways, attempts to reorganize Vermont's schools are yet another attempt to impose urban standards and industrial management methods on rural schools. The students, under any system, will still be predominantly rural. They come from rural homes, were raised on rural traditions and values, and experience all the strengths and weaknesses of rural life. Making the schools bigger by reorganizing or building a modern factory-like structure cannot change this rural inheritance; besides, that inheritance is viewed with great pride in Vermont.

No evidence was found, nor has it been suggested, that Vermont's schools are inferior to schools in more urban or centralized states.

Thus, it must be asked why rural educators continue to extol the virtues of urban models of organization and curriculum. It seems clear from the interviews that Vermont is no nearer to accepting a centralized decision-making and policy-setting structure in education today than half a century ago; yet the state persists in seeking it.

Ironically, as cities are becoming bogged down in bureaucracy and facing financial crises equal to anything found in the countryside, metropolitan reformers are turning to decentralized models of educational management and control. For once, Vermont has a chance to be a leader, rather than a follower, in the development of equitable and efficient community schools. Vermonters need only capitalize and build upon their long traditions of local control and citizen participation to assume this leadership.

Part Four

Beyond Conventional Wisdom

7 What's Next?
A Research and Action Agenda
for Rural Education

Jonathan P. Sher

Introduction

In recent years, rural education has become the poor country cousin of education leaders unconcerned about rural issues and rural leaders unconcerned about education issues.

Whether from ignorance, disinterest, prejudice, or simple neglect, this wholesale abdication of responsibility by leaders in both education and rural development has relegated rural schools and schoolchildren to the farthest recesses of the nation's consciousness. As a result, only minuscule amounts of time, attention, and resources have been devoted to solving the problems and fulfilling the potential inherent within America's rural schools. Such neglect (benign or otherwise) has certainly not proved a propitious strategy for the improvement of rural education. Rather, it has served primarily to ensure that existing deficiencies continue unabated.

Yet, indifference has not always characterized American attitudes toward rural children, nor has neglect always been the cornerstone of state and federal policy toward rural education. Indeed, for the better part of a century, leading educators, rural advocates, and other reformers displayed considerable zeal in identifying and attacking the *Rural School Problem*. To their credit, these reformers did alleviate some of the most flagrant abuses and eliminate the most inadequate institutions found in rural areas. Still, in retrospect, the overall impact of these reforms upon the bulk of rural individuals and communities was less than beneficent. The incorrect assumptions, major misjudgments, and inappropriate efforts that permeated the rural school reform movement left a legacy of problems that persist today.

Although these results were unintentional, the policies and practices that spawned them were quite deliberate. At heart, these leaders thought they were rescuing rural schools by eliminating their uniquely rural character and heritage. As a result, their policies were directed not toward creating better *rural* schools, but rather toward a wholesale urbanization of such schools.

All too often, "rural" connoted a lack of culture rather than a viable alternative to the urban-industrial culture. Urban (and later suburban) schools were continually held up to "backward" rural people as models to be envied and emulated. Urbanization was synonymous with progress, while attempts to retain or improve uniquely rural institutions, beliefs, and practices were denounced as examples of a lamentable provincialism.

Given the negative attitude toward rural education and rural life embodied by this reform movement and the policies it engendered, the fact that negative results occurred can hardly be considered surprising. Indeed, one of the great ironies of American rural education is that problems resulting from policies of neglect seem to be exceeded only by the damage wrought by policies of active reform.

Resolving this dilemma while rejuvenating rural schools is not an easy assignment. However, it is not the impossible (or worthless) endeavor some policymakers would have us believe. Most important, though, it is an assignment which must be accepted if we, as a nation, are serious about our commitment to provide equal opportunity and educational excellence for all children, whatever their family background or place of residence.

The purpose of this chapter is to outline the elements of a research and action agenda for rural education which is both theoretically sound and operationally feasible. After presenting a set of general guidelines for improving rural education, this chapter will focus on the following two critical components: (1) changes in the organization, financing, and administration of educational services in rural communities (structural reforms); and (2) changes in the kind, level, and quality of educational services that are delivered in rural communities (substantive reforms).

Lessons and Guidelines

As previous chapters have shown, the individuals shaping educational policies for rural communities were burdened both by erroneous assumptions and by an ideology that equated urbanization with progress. That these policies did not produce the kinds of significant and lasting improvements their creators sought has also been documented.

Such a failure, in and of itself, is not unusual in the education world. Indeed, most major education leaders and critics have asserted that American educational reform is littered with the remains of good ideas gone sour. This "good idea-poor implementation-eventual failure" syndrome is now so deeply embedded in the profession's consciousness that cynicism about the viability and utility of *any* education reform effort has become the prevailing attitude. Consequently, the conventional wisdom in education has been expanded to include the oft-heard notion: "What education needs is not more good ideas, but rather better implementation of existing ideas."

In policy terms, it has meant that ever-increasing attention, research, and resources are being expended on developing greater institutional capabilities and productivity. In other words, a major movement in education today is essentially a thrust toward doing the same old things in the most effective manner possible. Such an effort is reasonable and helpful if, and only if, the underlying "good idea-bad implementation" analysis is both correct and appropriate to local circumstance.

Unfortunately, this bit of conventional wisdom has gained increasing prominence among rural educators and community leaders, even though the analysis behind it has little relevance to the experience of most rural school systems. Urbanizing reforms, such as consolidation and standardization, have not produced poor results because they were good ideas badly implemented, but rather because they were bad ideas successfully implemented.

Urban education critics can persuasively argue that team teaching, open education, career education, and similar ideas were (and are) valid and beneficial reforms, which were botched by insensitive or incompetent school personnel. Any rural corollary of this argument, however, would be difficult to substantiate because the major structural reforms (consolidation and centralization) and the major substantive reforms (specialization and standardization) proposed for rural education have, in fact, been adopted all across the country. Yet, while the rural reform experience has been almost the exact opposite of that found in urban and suburban districts, analyses and policies based upon the urban-suburban model continue to be accepted in rural communities.

The policy implications of accepting this urban critique are profound. Fundamentally, it has meant that individuals concerned about the future of rural education have often been drawn into the search for increased system effectiveness while simultaneously being diverted away from the most critical rural need: the development of new and creative "good ideas" for rural education.

This is not to say, of course, that rural schools have little potential for increased effectiveness. It is instead a matter of priorities. Rural districts have already shown themselves to be adept at implementing both substantive and structural reforms even in the face of community resistance. Therefore, the emphasis in rural education should not be on implementing reform, but rather on developing reforms worth implementing.

Preceding chapters have revealed several other examples of the pitfalls of rural education's conventional wisdom. Fortunately, in addition to demonstrating the limitations of such conventional wisdom, some key lessons about implementing reform and improving education in rural America have emerged. These emergent lessons can serve not only as a warning against repeating mistakes of the past, but also as a set of policy guidelines for the future. Yet, perhaps the primary value of these lessons lies in their ability to be used as standards against which any prospective rural education reform can be measured and evaluated.

No set of policy standards (including these) are absolute and unvarying. Still, it seems safe to assume that proposed reforms that run directly counter to these guidelines are unlikely to produce lasting and significant improvements in rural schools, whereas reforms consistent with all these standards (while not assured of success) will at least not be crippled from the start.

The five basic lessons (or guidelines) about rural education reform are below.

1. *The primacy of local circumstance must be respected.* Rural America may well represent the single most diverse and heterogeneous group of individuals and communities in our society. Thus, the notion of an

educational panacea—that is, an educational reform strategy that is applicable and effective throughout rural America—is ludicrous. Any reform strategy that seeks to circumvent local traditions, values, beliefs, and capabilities, rather than building upon them, is bound to fail.

2. *The linkages between school and community must be expanded and the bonds between them strengthened.* Schools have been (and continue to be) absolutely vital as community institutions as well as educational institutions in rural areas. Reforms which, intentionally or unwittingly, restrict the linkages or weaken the bonds between the school and the community are highly counterproductive. In rural areas, schools need the community to supplement and extend their efforts, while the community needs the school both as a source of community identity and as a reinforcement for the community's childrearing practices. This active interdependence between community and school is a key attribute of rural education. Reforms that sacrifice this relationship have a detrimental effect on all parties concerned.

3. *The balance between outside regulation and local control must be made more equitable.* Rural school systems have been, are, and doubtless will continue to be both dependent upon outside assistance and subject to outside regulation. Yet, state and federal assistance to rural schools has been notably scarce while mandates and regulations have been abundant and heavy handed. The whole meaning of local control in rural America has become trivialized as a consequence of subsistence level resources coupled with a plethora of detailed state and federal requirements. Reforms that do not redress this existing imbalance, that serve to further atrophy local control or expand outside dominance, or that treat rural districts as welfare cases rather than equal partners in the educational enterprise are of no help in the quest for rural school improvement.

4. *Structural reforms and substantive reforms must be treated as separate and distinct issues.* For too long, policymakers and rural school reformers have artificially linked needed substantive improvements with their own agendas for rural structural reform. By arguing that increased student achievement, better teachers, or an improved curriculum were entirely contingent upon school consolidation, district reorganization, or some other desired organizational alteration, these educators unnecessarily confused the relevant issues, encouraged false expectations, and, most important, diverted attention, assistance, and resources away from the continuing need to upgrade the

quality of existing rural schools. Structural issues and substantive issues are each important in their own right. Reforms that attempt to manufacture relationships between these two sets of issues or that hold one set of improvements in abeyance until the other set has been accomplished do a disservice to rural schools and schoolchildren.

5. *Reform efforts must capitalize upon the strengths, as well as correct the deficiencies, of rural schools.* Historically, reformers have either disparaged the advantages inherent in small rural community schools or have taken them for granted. As a result, these advantages have often remained undeveloped potentials rather than fully utilized components of the school program. A related problem is that the reformers' analyses of rural schools have been so harsh and disapproving that they have triggered a self-fulfilling negative prophecy in many rural communities. Trying to make rural people feel defensive and demoralized about their schools has not proved a very productive strategy for inducing beneficent educational changes. Thus, reforms that do not explicitly acknowledge both the potential for and the fact of excellence in existing rural schools (in addition to seeking remedies to current problems) will serve only to alienate and discourage the community and, thereby, reduce their own chances for success.

Structural Reforms

Decisions about pedagogical practices, faculty selection, educational philosophy, curriculum design, and most other *substantive* educational issues have been the traditional province of local jurisdictions. Accordingly, state and federal education agencies have opted to assume major responsibilities for the formulation and implementation of policies about *structural* issues in education.

While it is true that local authorities help determine the success of any strategy regarding school organization and finance, it is equally true that these strategies have been (and continue to be) developed, debated, and directed outside the local community. This pattern has been particularly evident in rural education. None of the major structural reforms (such as consolidation) that have had profound impact upon rural education were initiated, championed, or, often, even desired by local rural educators, rural school board members, or other concerned rural citizens.

Congress and the U.S. Office of Education created national policies and programs while state legislatures, state boards, and state departments of education formulated statewide equivalents. The rural implications of these broad efforts were rarely accorded serious attention, not only because of the relative lack of organized rural political strength, but also because of the urban orientation of most state and federal educational policymakers. Even in states where organized rural interests did wield a significant measure of power and influence, it tended to be negative. In other words, in some states the rural lobby could occasionally kill a specific program, policy, or piece of legislation it found unacceptable, but normally it was neither willing to function as a constructive force in the formulation of alternative policies nor able to secure sufficient support for proposals that were acceptable.

Given this history, it is hardly surprising that rural communities have been adversely affected by past structural reforms. Similarly, the fact that a variety of unresolved (or more precisely, unsatisfactorily resolved) structural problems continue to plague rural education is a predictable consequence of an inadequate and inappropriate policymaking process.

Thus, any serious attempt to rectify the organizational and financial difficulties facing rural education today must directly address not only the need for new, more appropriate policies and structural changes, but also the need to initiate new policymaking procedures that incorporate detailed planning, policy analysis, and local participation components.

In considering the whole topic of rural structural reform, attention will first be accorded to those activities that can (and should) be undertaken given current knowledge and information. Subsequently, the focus will shift to a discussion of the research that still needs to be initiated.

Action Agenda

Structural reform basically has two components: changes in educational finance and changes in school and district organization. The purpose of this section is not to provide an exhaustive laundry list of possible reforms in each area, but rather to identify those reforms having the greatest potential for fostering improvement in rural education. In other words, the intention is to present those efforts and activities that should be accorded the highest priority in seeking rural structural reform.

Finance

Among financial issues, highest priority must be given to the continuation and expansion of state-level school finance reform. Since local revenue sources have proved insufficient, and a dramatic increase in federal contributions to education is not politically feasible (at least in the near future), the responsibility for ensuring an adequate level of school funds must increasingly be accepted by state legislatures and state governments. Thus far, state-level school finance reforms and expanded state aid programs have significantly benefited rural school districts. Yet, as of 1976, more than twenty states have done virtually nothing to correct existing deficiencies in their state aid programs, nor have they made any special provisions to assist financially troubled rural school districts. This situation must be remedied as soon as possible.

In seeking state-level school finance reform, rural advocates should strive for the following five goals:

1. an overall increase in state support for public education equal to at least 70 percent of the operating costs of the public schools
2. full state assumption of public school transportation and construction costs
3. a set of taxation and state aid distribution formulas which, at a minimum, do not discriminate against rural citizens and rural school districts
4. a guarantee that rural school districts receive their fair share of federal education funds that are controlled by the state
5. a decrease in the utilization of regressive taxes (such as the property tax) to raise school revenues and an increase in the utilization of more progressive taxes (such as a graduated income tax)

The second priority area in reforming rural school finance involves changes in the federal contribution to education. Federal assistance to rural districts, though desperately needed, has remained disproportionately low. For example, HEW testimony before the Senate Subcommittee on Rural Development revealed that, even though nearly one-third of the nation's schoolchildren and one-half of the nation's poor families live in nonmetropolitan areas, only 11 percent of library and materials funds, 13 percent of basic vocational aid, 14 percent of guaranteed student loan monies, 8 percent of migrant education aid, 13 percent of dropout prevention funds, and 20 percent of bilingual education monies went to nonmetropolitan areas.[1]

Equity demands that this continuing bias by the federal government against rural schools and schoolchildren be halted at once. If anything, federal assistance (which is primarily designed to assist disadvantaged students) should be highest in rural areas because rural populations have the nation's highest incidence of poverty, a marked absence of institutions and programs outside the public schools to meet the needs of disadvantaged children, and higher per pupil costs in such areas as special education because of sparse student populations.

The third, and final, priority involves the use of noninstructional education funds. Tremendous amounts of both governmental and philanthropic resources are expended each year on educational research, teacher (and other professional) training, curriculum development, innovative programs, educational media, and other supportive services. Yet, only the tiniest portion of these funds are spent either in rural school districts or on rural problems, concerns, and opportunities. Issues of how these funds should be spent are discussed later in this chapter. The point is simply that current allocation and utilization patterns for these types of education funds are highly discriminatory against rural areas. In fact, tokenism toward rural education would be a significant improvement.

Organization

Current rural school reformers must contend not only with the difficulties inherent in implementing needed organizational improvements, but also with alleviating the legacy of problems and ill will engendered by past initiatives in this area. As a consequence, rural reformers would be wise to resist the tendency to make fundamental organizational changes a central feature of their proposed reform strategy. De-emphasizing organizational alterations in favor of other equally important, but less politically sensitive, issues will significantly increase the reformer's likelihood of eventual success.

Despite this caveat, there are three key organizational reforms that can and should be undertaken with vigor. All three of these suggestions support and improve existing rural school and district organizational patterns, rather than trying to supplant them.

Highest priority in this area must be given to the eradication of all forced consolidation and reorganization. This can be accomplished through the following measures:

1. the repeal of laws and regulations that give state boards or state agencies final control over school and district organization
2. the elimination of all direct state subsidies and financial rewards for consolidating or reorganizing (such as increasing state aid to districts that consolidate)
3. the discontinuance of all indirect state subsidies and financial inducements to consolidate (such as paying a higher percentage of construction costs for large schools or districts)
4. the cessation of attempts to use minimum state standards as a way of achieving consolidation or reorganization (for example, by requiring a certain number of students or a minimum tax base for accreditation or by requiring each school or district to have a certain number of specialized school personnel)

The second priority must be the creation of state and federal programs to assist small, rural schools and districts. If long-term educational improvement in rural areas is the goal, stopping harassment of small schools and districts and ending attempts to bribe rural communities into accepting consolidation are not sufficient. Rural districts face a variety of unique organizational problems, ranging from very rapidly rising enrollments in some rural communities to the need for new strategies for integrating community residents and resources into the schools. Providing needed technical and financial assistance in solving these problems is a plausible and appropriate role for both state and federal education agencies. This process of rejuvenation must begin with a new sense of state and federal commitment to the improvement of small rural schools and districts.

The third, and final, area of rural organizational reform involves the continued experimentation and development of multidistrict educational service agencies. As of 1976, approximately half of the states have either established statewide networks of these multi-district service agencies or are in the process of doing so. Although their programs and track record are still largely embryonic (only New York State has employed a version of this model for more than a decade), these regional units clearly have enormous potential both as alternatives to consolidation and as mechanisms for providing services and fostering improvements rarely found in rural school systems. What these agencies can (and should) actually do and how to make them more accountable to their constituencies remain as unresolved issues. However, properly conceived and well-executed regional service agencies are likely to have a very bright future in advancing rural education.

Research Agenda

If enacted, these structural reforms would go a long way toward rectifying current ills and promoting vital improvements in rural education. However, they do not represent a complete action agenda. In part, the ability to fully articulate that which needs to be done is hampered by a lack of sufficient knowledge and evidence to substantiate recommendations in several policy areas. The sad fact is that evidence, in the form of careful, valid research, is sorely lacking in nearly all phases of rural education.

Thus, to complement and extend these proposed structural reforms, it is important to identify a few rural research topics that have both short-term payoffs and long-range value.

In the area of rural school finance, the two key research needs are: (1) a state-by-state analysis of the impacts of current state aid distribution formulas on rural schools and districts; and (2) the development and testing of new distribution formulas, valuation procedures, tax policies, and allocation patterns for rural school systems.

In addition to these main research thrusts, there are a variety of special topics for research that would expand existing knowledge and significantly contribute to the development of constructive school finance reforms. A broad range of research methodologies (for example, case studies, policy analyses, demonstration projects) could be utilized in undertaking work in these areas. The suggested topics are:

1. the utilization and effects of federal education funds in rural schools and districts

2. the creation of new revenue sources for rural education
3. an examination of current educational expenditure patterns in rural communities
4. strategies for increasing efficiency in rural educational institutions
5. the financial implications of major enrollment shifts in sparsely settled areas
6. alternative strategies for financing capital expenditures in rural areas
7. the development of self-help financing strategies for rural schools
8. an examination of intradistrict inequalities in rural school systems
9. the politics of school finance in rural communities

In rural school and district organization, the three key research needs are:

1. a series of methodologically sound, nonpropagandist analyses of the economic, educational, and social effects of class, school, and district size in rural communities
2. the development and testing of new delivery system models for basic, special, and vocational education in sparsely settled areas
3. a series of analyses and evaluations of key local, state, and federal policies and legislation regarding rural school and district organization

Once again, there are special research topics that can be of invaluable assistance in determining optimal (or, at least, greatly improved) organizational patterns for rural schools and districts. These topics are:

1. an evaluation of the regional (multidistrict) educational service agency model in both theory and practice
2. the organizational implications of major enrollment shifts in sparsely settled areas
3. strategies for increasing community involvement in consolidated rural schools and school districts
4. an evaluation of nonformal education programs in rural areas
5. strategies for increasing the effectiveness of rural schools as a

mechanism for rural development

6. the utilization and effects of advanced educational technologies in rural districts
7. the politics of school and district organization in rural America
8. the impacts and effects of major rural school improvement projects
9. an examination of talent banks, traveling resource centers, and "high schools without walls" as strategies for expanding educational options and overcoming the effects of sparsity in rural communities

Substantive Reforms

For reasons discussed in earlier chapters, rural school reformers focused nearly all of their energy and attention on achieving massive structural reforms. Unfortunately, this inordinate emphasis on how rural school systems should be financed and organized precluded serious consideration of what could be done to improve the overall quality of rural education.

The great debates over consolidation and reorganization raged on throughout rural America for decades. In some rural communities, the consolidation advocates eventually won, while in others, the anticonsolidation forces prevailed. Unfortunately, in most rural communities, no matter who won the fight over consolidation, it was the students who ended up losing. All too often, the net effect of rural structural reform was that some students attended deplorable small schools near their homes while others were bused long distances to equally deplorable big schools.

Clearly, the time has come for big- and small-school proponents alike to put aside their quibbling about the potential advantages of various school sizes and organizational configurations and, instead, begin to concentrate their attention and energies on realizing whatever potentials may exist in America's rural schools. Form can no longer take precedence over substance if lasting rural school improvement is the desired outcome. Therefore, rural school reform efforts that do not accord a position of prominence to the design and implementation of needed substantive changes cannot be expected to produce significant benefits for rural schoolchildren.

In formulating a research and action agenda for substantive

improvement, it is imperative that the five fundamental guidelines for all rural school reform stated earlier be heeded. In particular, the primacy of local circumstance must be remembered because successful substantive reform is inherently more idiosyncratic, culturally oriented, and locality bound than structural reform.

For example, a structural innovation such as the multidistrict educational service agency has applicability throughout rural America. Yet, in substantive terms, the services delivered by a regional unit in the South having a predominantly black, low-income constituency will (or, at least, should) be quite different than the services provided by similar units serving Appalachian coal mining communities, wealthy midwestern farming areas, Alaskan native populations, or Hispanic migrant children. Because of the remarkable diversity of cultural heritages, social and educational histories, environmental characteristics, and economic conditions which together compose rural America, it is counterproductive to either ignore these differences or pretend that they are unimportant in the development of valid substantive reforms.

Thus, the research and action agenda outlined here is meant to be suggestive rather than definitive. Although substantive reforms can encompass a wide range of concerns, the present discussion is limited to the two most critical components: curriculum and faculty.

Curriculum

Curriculum design has traditionally been a haphazard affair in rural schools. Few observers of rural education would contest that outdated texts and irrelevant curricula have become the norm in America's rural schools. Indeed, many rural districts still rely heavily upon curricular materials originally designed for urban and suburban populations back in the 1950s and early 1960s.

Newer, more appropriate curricula remain scarce for three primary reasons: (1) commercial publishers have not found it profitable to cater to the diverse populations and educational needs found in rural schools; (2) neither government agencies nor philanthropic organizations have filled this commercial void by subsidizing the development of rural-oriented curricula; and (3) the preponderance of rural districts lack the funds, expertise, and time to develop their own curricular materials.

In addition, the movement to urbanize rural schools and emulate urban and suburban educational models greatly dampened any latent desire to create a uniquely rural curriculum in most districts. Predictably, the effort to imitate what metropolitan schools used to do did not result in rural educational excellence. As a consequence, the need to develop uniquely rural curricula is as acute today as it was decades ago.

Among the needs in this area, highest priority must be given to the development of competently designed curricula that are appropriate to the communities in which they will be utilized. Nearly everyone agrees that rural schools need a better curriculum and better curricular materials. But, "better" has too often meant "more like metropolitan schools" instead of "better" in meeting the educational needs of rural children. This fundamental alteration of attitudes and orientation toward the task of rural curriculum design is a necessary precondition for all other reforms in this area.

The second priority is to build a curriculum that reflects and enhances the natural advantages of rural communities. This notion can by operationalized by

1. returning to the rural traditions of individualized instruction and cross-age teaching
2. Making extensive use of the local community as a learning resource for rural children (for example, by helping in community projects, starting community service programs, doing oral histories with local residents, and by using the local community as the subject of a variety of historical, sociological, economic, and scientific investigations by students)
3. taking advantage of the fact that most rural communities are endowed with natural environments which could be the basis of curricular materials in outdoor education, science, survival skills, physical education, and other related fields

The third priority is to design a curriculum that gives rural children a sense of options for their adult lives. Though this topic is of particular importance in rural vocational and career education, it has general applicability as well. All too often, rural schools, by virtue of the socialization they provide and the skills and aspirations they impart, discourage rural children from remaining in their own (or other) rural communities. The best curriculum for rural children is one that not only equips them with skills relevant to both rural and urban life, but also gives them sufficient unbiased information to make a judgment as to the kind of community in which they would like to live and work. Simply encouraging rural students to migrate to the cities is no longer a helpful strategy.

The fourth priority is to incorporate firm but fair performance standards into the overall rural curriculum. In many rural communities, social promotions are a longstanding practice. Yet, social promotions do a disservice to all rural children, both by devaluing the work of students earning their promotions and by guaranteeing the continuing failure of those socially promoted in higher grade levels. New rural curricula must contain both reasonable performance standards and agreed upon methods for measuring student performance. The particular standards and measurement systems employed will doubtless have a marked influence on the school's curriculum. However, if the standards and evaluation procedures are themselves reasonable, this influence is likely to be largely beneficent.

The fifth, and last, priority item in this area is the establishment of a network of individuals, agencies, and organizations committed to the improvement of rural curricula and curricular materials. It would be highly desirable for each rural teacher, or each rural school, or even each rural school district to be able to develop the kinds of curricular offerings described above using only their own funds, information, creativity, and expertise. Realistically, however, the prospects of such self-sufficiency are extremely dim. Thus, it is clear that outside assistance of some kind will be required to actually implement needed curricular reforms. While local circumstance must dictate the exact level and kinds of assistance necessary, it is a virtual certainty that everyone involved in the educational enterprise (that is, students, parents, school board members, teachers, administrators, state officials, university faculties, multidistrict agency personnel, foundation officers, federal officials, and other "experts") can and should contribute something to this effort. At a minimum, there is a need both to develop more effective information systems so that rural communities can share their ideas and experiences with each other and to conduct research that is supportive of the efforts outlined above.

Faculty

Just as rural reformers sought "better" curricula, so too have they clamored for "better" teachers. Once again, though, the definition of "better" is of considerable importance. Usually, by "better," these reformers meant "more credentialed," "more highly specialized," and "urban trained."

Yet, while there is little doubt that rural schools could benefit from the presence of better teachers, it is not at all clear that the traditional meaning of "better" is appropriate or helpful in the rural context. In fact, a very persuasive case can be made that higher academic credentials, in and of themselves, have minimal validity as a measure of actual teaching competence; that rural schools require competent generalists far more than a variety of specialists; and that teachers trained to understand and work with the unique strengths and weaknesses of rural schools are much more desirable than urban-trained and urban-oriented teachers from even the most prestigious universities.

Perhaps an example from the health field can shed some light on this point. In the past few years, there has been a significant shift in the medical profession away from training large numbers of highly sophisticated specialists and toward training family doctors (that is, general practitioners). This trend is a particular asset to rural areas in which a neurosurgeon in town is not needed nearly as much as a general practitioner who can call upon the services of a neurosurgeon when necessary.

Similarly, rural schools need teachers who are (contradictory as it may sound) specially trained to be generalists. The best rural teachers are the ones who are able to cope with sparsity, utilize community resources, invent curricular materials, and, above all else, are oriented toward teaching children rather than subjects. When a corps of specialists is available to these rural teachers (for example, through a multidistrict educational service agency), the range of human resources available to aid rural schoolchildren can be quite extensive and impressive.

Thus, the highest priority in this area is to create training programs in colleges and graduate schools of education across the country which will explicitly prepare teachers for service in rural schools. At present, there are no more than a handful of teacher-training programs in the entire nation which directly assist students interested in rural education careers. Teachers are still the backbone of any school system, and the fact that rural schools must accept teachers without specialized rural training puts them at a disadvantage they can ill afford.

#3 The second priority is to dramatically expand in-service training (and other professional development activities) for rural teachers and administrators. In most rural communities, the professional growth and development of school personnel are impeded, first, because rural districts rarely provide continuing in-service programs and, second, because the kinds of external opportunities for professional development available in urban areas (for example, teacher centers and universities) are notably absent in rural areas. It is unreasonable to expect teachers and administrators, already burdened by the heavy workloads characteristics of rural schools, to do everything on their own time and of their own initiative. Teachers need time to share ideas and problems with their counterparts, both within their own, and other, school systems. They also need the time and resources to develop curricular materials, take needed courses, and keep up with recent advances in their fields.

State and federal officials often lament the teacher quality found in rural schools. Yet, far more would be accomplished by their sponsorship of rural in-service training programs than by simply decrying the competence of rural educators. Once again, where local colleges are either inaccessible or unresponsive to this need, multidistrict educational service agencies are a potential source of assistance.

#3 The third priority is to increase the voluntary sharing of teachers, both among schools in the same district and between neighboring rural districts. Since most rural schools neither need nor can afford full-time teachers in every subject area, there is great utility in the notion of sharing teachers (for example, a music/art teacher at the elementary level and an advanced math/physics teacher at the secondary level) among rural schools and districts. Some rural districts already employ this strategy extensively, but most still haven't tried it or use it only sparingly. Done properly, sharing teachers can be a valuable way to overcome the problem of scarce human resources in sparsely settled areas.

The fourth and last priority is to create a "community faculty" to complement and extend the regular educational program in rural schools. Nearly every rural community has individuals with special talents or a knowledge of subjects not found among the regular faculty. For example, in coal mining regions, community residents could (either as volunteers or as paid part-time employees) teach labor history to local students. In black, Native American, or

Hispanic communities, local citizens could be used to develop a whole cultural heritage program in the schools. Under this program, a local cabinet maker, mechanic, agricultural extension agent, or other skilled resident could share his or her expertise with local students. In addition, retired members of the community and other older citizens often are an invaluable reservoir of untapped information and human resources which could be harnessed to advance the education of young people in rural areas.

By inaugurating such a community faculty program, extensive educational and social benefits can accrue to all rural community members. The students will have learning experiences not otherwise available to them. The school personnel will receive an infusion of needed moral and programmatic support. And the community will have the chance both to become an integral part of their children's school experience and to feel needed and wanted by people and institutions about which they care deeply. Indeed, the small-scale life style and close-knit character of most rural communities makes a community faculty both a feasible idea and a unique opportunity.

Conclusion

Having spent incalculable amounts of time and money on bribing, bullying, and coercing rural communities into accepting reforms they never sought or desired—only to discover that the long-range benefits of their efforts were marginal—leading educators and policymakers essentially wrote off rural school reform as a bad investment. In other words, after trying and failing at rural school reform, these leaders were content to ignore rural education and allow it to become a skeleton in the closet of the education profession.

It was a most unfortunate mistake because, in reality, the cause of rural school reform is anything but hopeless. The prevailing sense of hopelessness was primarily a side effect of state and federal efforts to externally impose reform upon rural districts. By trying to make rural communities the recipients, rather than the instigators, of reform, state officials and national policymakers inadvertently undermined their chances of success.

This book contends that the great majority of rural citizens are not the apathetic, reactionary, anti-education group they are often portrayed to be. There is a genuine interest in and commitment to rural school improvement among students, parents, and local educators throughout rural America. Yet, it is also clear that the reforms that engender the most support and, not coincidentally, seem to produce the most positive, significant, and lasting effects are those which are locally initiated, locally developed, and locally controlled.

Nearly everyone recognizes the need for outside resources and assistance in bringing the rural school improvement process to successful fruition. But this outside assistance must be marshalled in support of local initiatives rather than for externally mandated change.

Most rural schools have the capacity to become excellent and effective community institutions. Realizing this potential is by no means an impossible endeavor. This chapter has pointed out a variety of realistic improvements which build upon the strengths already indigenous to rural communities. The following chapter is devoted to a detailed exploration of one possible rural school reform which is based upon both a re-examination of conventional wisdom and the guidelines and lessons elucidated in this book.

Successful and beneficent rural school reforms can be achieved. Doing so requires only the combination of local initiative, external assistance, a measure of creativity, and the will to provide rural children with the best education possible. For too long we, as a society, have avoided this task. We cannot afford the human and economic costs any longer.

8 School-based
Community Development Corporations:
A New Strategy for Education and
Development in Rural America

Jonathan P. Sher

Editor's Prologue

So far, we have examined the central assumptions, policies, and reforms that have come to dominate rural education in America. Of necessity, this reassessment of conventional wisdom has focused primarily on rural education as it exists today rather than as it could, or should, exist in the future.

Nevertheless, our willingness at times to be sharply critical of current policies and practices carries with it an implicit responsibility to identify some possible remedies and promising alternatives for rural school improvement. Several of the preceding chapters included useful suggestions for future policymakers. Chapter 7 addressed the task of formulating a research and action agenda for rural education in the future.

In part, Chapter 7 argued that the development of diverse "good ideas" for implementation in rural schools should be a top priority of any rural rejuvenation effort. In keeping with this recommendation, Chapter 8 will focus on the presentation and discussion of one such "good idea": the school-based community development corporation.

Hopefully, some rural individuals will find this new strategy intriguing enough to warrant a further consideration of its merits as a way of improving the quality of life and education in their own communities. In the final analysis, though, its purpose is to illustrate new approaches to old rural problems.

The school-based community development corporation is one alternative for rural education. Other, equally reasonable alternatives can, and should, be articulated and then given every chance to succeed. Our rural schools and rural schoolchildren deserve nothing less.

Section One: Trends in Rural America: Identifying the Problems

Rural America has long been plagued by major problems in economic development and in vocational education. Although these two sets of problems are in fact intimately interrelated, they have rarely been so treated in practice. As a consequence, most economic development thrusts and vocational education reforms have remained remarkably isolated from one another, to their mutual detriment.

This chapter has two purposes. The first is to critically review the major economic development and vocational education efforts of the past two decades. The second is to propose a new mechanism, the school-based community development corporation, as a model that makes the relationships between education and development both theoretically explicit and operationally feasible.

The underlying assumption is that the kinds of additional human and financial resources that development professionals and vocational educators continually seek will not, in and of themselves, solve existing problems. New resources are important and perhaps even critical to alleviate the cycle of rural deprivation, but only in conjunction with the creation of new and substantially different strategies for change. Rural communities do not need "more of the same" in either economic development or vocational education. Rather, the pressing need is for new means to reach desired ends.

To establish a theoretical and historical context for the school-based community development corporation model, several broad trends and problems in rural America are discussed. Yet, the reform mechanism ultimately proposed, the school-based CDC, is considerably more modest in intent, design, and likely impact than the issues it addresses. In effect, this model is a "micro"-level response to several "macro"-level problems. The experiences of the past decade make clear the futility and simplemindedness of believing that any single macro-level strategy is either appropriate or feasible for all communities (or for all individuals within a single community). Macro-level solutions tend to be strong in intellectual or emotional appeal, but desperately weak in pragmatic applicability.

This chapter proposes incremental changes, rather than sweeping visionary transformations. The school-based CDC mechanism is proposed with the knowledge that, even if it is widely and properly implemented, it will not singlehandedly eliminate America's rural problems. Rather, the hope is that complementary economic and educational initiatives (local, state, and national) will also emerge and be adopted. Together, these efforts could combine into a large, multifaceted movement capable of rejuvenating rural America. However, the value and utility of the school-based CDC model is not contingent upon the emergence and acceptance of any other rural reform effort. Complementary developments would serve to heighten and expand this model's influence, but the school-based CDC is intended as a free-standing, self-contained reform strategy.

Demographic Overview

For decades, rural youth (more than 4.5 million fourteen- to eighteen-year-olds in the 14,000 small towns and countryside communities that compose rural America) have been trapped between the proverbial rock and hard place.[1] The choice for most rural young people has been both simple and disheartening: stay in the rural community and face a dearth of employment (and other economic) opportunities or migrate to a metropolitan community and become part of a large, low-echelon, surplus labor pool.

The adverse effects of this dilemma have spared neither urban nor rural communities. Rural migrants have swelled the ranks of the urban ghetto population and, thus, have increased the difficulties faced by all reformist attempts to eradicate poverty and improve opportunities in American cities.

Still, the detrimental effects on rural communities have been even more profound. Post-high school outmigration of the brightest and most capable rural youth, the very population best equipped to lead a rural renaissance, has become a well-established pattern throughout rural America.[2] Paradoxically, this mass outmigration has also been both a major cause and a predictable consequence of the continuing deprivation of most contemporary rural communities.[3]

The complexity and diversity of migration in the United States has produced widespread and persistent misconceptions. Perhaps the most pervasive myth is that rural America has experienced such an enormous long-term population depletion because of migration that today's rural community is inconsequentially small, both absolutely and relatively. The facts are substantially different.

In absolute terms, rural America experienced robust growth during the period from 1790, the first census year, through 1910, when the rural population grew from 3.7 million to 50.2 million (a more than tenfold increase); moderate growth from 1910 to 1950 when the rural population expanded from 50.2 million to 61.2 million (a 22 percent increase); and final stabilization (after a more restrictive Census Bureau redefinition of "rural" was initiated) to a 1970 total of 53.9 million rural residents.[4]

The rural component of American society is still substantial, even in relative terms. From 1790, when 95 percent of the U.S. population was labeled rural, to 1970, when 26.5 percent was so designated, rural America's own large absolute growth became overshadowed by the phenomenal growth rate for the U.S. as a whole.[5] Yet, 54 million people—more than 25 percent of the total U.S. population—live in rural America today. Even these not inconsequential sums may underestimate the actual proportion of the population that could accurately be called rural. These data used are based on the Census Bureau's definition of rural (that is, farms, open countryside, and places of 2,500 or fewer residents). Depending on the criteria for defining "rural," the rural population ranges anywhere from the most stringently conservative estimate of 37.5 million people (18.5 percent of the total U.S. population) to 65.1 million people (32.0 percent of the total U.S. population), when the most liberal guidelines are used.[6]

The rural outmigration has not resulted in the elimination of a substantial rural sector within the United States; has not so depleted the existent rural population and resource base that realistic prospects for rejuvenation have become negligible; and has not reduced rural citizens to a minority group so small and unimportant as to be undeserving of major attention and assistance.

Involuntary Rural Outmigration

There is, however, one critical characteristic that distinguishes this recent rural outmigration from other U.S. population redistributions: this outmigration has been both involuntary and employment-related. The uniqueness lies in the combination rather than in the specific components. History is filled with involuntary migrations, such as those caused by wars, famines, plagues, and other natural disasters. Nor are employment and related economic factors a new impetus for migratory behavior.

Classical migration theory is predicated upon the interplay of various economic "pushes" and "pulls." This theory assumes a range of viable options for the prospective migrant. However, implicit in the classicist's notion of an individual responding to economic "pushes" and "pulls" is the countervailing notion of an individual's ability to not respond to these same economic forces if he so chooses.[7] Such was simply not true in rural America during the post-World War II era. Thus, classical migration theory has only the most marginal explanatory power for this phenomenon.[8]

That the outmigration of American rural youth has been both involuntary and employment-related is beyond serious dispute. As Robert Coles states about the northern migration of Appalachians:

> In recent decades many mountaineers have *had to* leave the [rural] life for Ohio or Illinois or Michigan—but they still yearn for, pine for, dream about, think about, talk about the hills, the great and lovely hills. In a sense, then, Appalachian life lives on . . . in the minds and most especially the hearts of people who have gone to the cities for work, but who would, if they could, choose without a moment's hesitation to return to the Appalchian hills and mountains.[9]

Or, as Sundquist perceptively argues:

> The movement of people from smaller to larger places is to a large extent (though no one knows the exact proportions) involuntary, forced migration. Young people going freely to the cities in search of adventure and opportunity make

up part of the migrant flow, but only part; among the rest are millions of uprooted, displaced families who have little desire, and less preparation, for life in large cities and whose destination is often inevitably the city slums. These displaced families are simply forced into the migration stream by economic forces they cannot control.[10]

Perhaps the best indicator of the involuntary nature of this rural outmigration is that the trend continued unabated until about 1970, more than a decade beyond when recipient urban communities could productively absorb this influx. Rural people continued to head for the cities even when the reality, if not the hope, of opportunity there had long since faded. These individuals, at least for a short time, shared the belief that the unknown opportunities of the cities were preferable to the known absence of opportunities in rural America. For some, success in this new urban environment validated the wisdom of their migratory decisions. However, for most migrants it represented only a shifting of old deprivations to a new locale.

The rural citizenry of today is a remarkably diverse group. "Rural" and "farmer" are no longer synonymous. The massive displacement of family farmers and farm workers caused by the rise of agribusiness and the shift from labor to capital-intensive farming has had two critical consequences for contemporary rural communities.

First, statistically, the rural farm population is no longer dominant or even of major importance. In 1970, only 6.8 million (11.8 percent) of 54 million rural residents lived on operating farms.[11] Since 1940, more than 3 million farms have folded, and farms continue to fold at a rate of 2,000 a week.[12] During the 1960s, the proportion of farm people over fifty-five years of age rose by one-third, while the proportion of those under fourteen years of age declined by one-half.[13] Finally, "more than half of the farms in the country have sales of less than $5,000 a year; together, this majority of farmers accounted for only 7.8 percent of farm sales."[14] Clearly, the rural problem is far more than simply a farm problem. Consequently, the scope of rural development strategies must encompass far more than activities aimed at strengthening agricultural production.

Second, the depressed rural income profile and outright rural poverty have remained virtually intact despite a variety of reform efforts. Under current definitions, approximately 13 million rural people (nearly one in four) are living below the poverty line, while millions more hover just above it.[15] The implications seem evident. Rural development efforts that treat poverty as an isolated, individualistic phenomenon rather than as a systemic disorder are unlikely to succeed. Rural development strategies that avoid a primary focus on the creation of jobs and other income-producing opportunities for all sectors of rural society have little chance of achieving long-range positive benefits.

Various components of the so-called "vicious cycle of rural poverty"—such as lack of employment, lack of income, mechanization, and outmigration—have been identified and discussed. Over the past two decades, a number of reform activities, development thrusts, and anti-poverty programs aimed at breaking this cycle have been designed and implemented—with little evident success. Figure 8.1 presents a schema that provides a more explicit (albeit simplified) representation of this vicious cycle of rural poverty and underdevelopment.

Rural Economic Development

To destroy this cycle of rural poverty and underdevelopment, or at least to dissipate its most negative effects, governmental and philanthropic interventions have concentrated on a set of disparate activities falling under the rubric of economic development. The rationale for this emphasis stems from the particular analysis of the vicious cycle made by these agencies.

Normally, their analysis starts at the top of the cycle, with the twin problems of "lack of adequate employment opportunities" and "high unemployment and underemployment."[16] The analysis then moves backwards (counterclockwise) on the cycle, because to move forward necessitates a direct confrontation with the specter of income poverty and its politically difficult remedy—direct income redistribution. This is an area where even U.S. development angels have traditionally feared to tread. Therefore, their analysis looks backwards toward such problems as new business development and manpower training, which seem more amenable to solution within the constraints of a nonsocialist nation.

Even among those concerned about U.S. rural development, there has been (and still remains) a discernible split between individuals

FIGURE 8.1
THE CYCLE OF RURAL POVERTY AND UNDERDEVELOPMENT

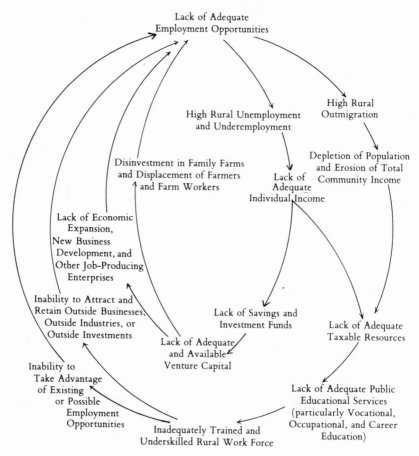

favoring "soft" development strategies (manpower training, human resource development, new careers, and other activities that stress individual attainment and rely upon an agglomeration of social, cultural, psychological, and pedagogical theories), and individuals favoring "hard" development strategies (agricultural production, industrial development, highway construction, public works, and other activities that stress the expansion of material resources within a community and rely upon various business and economic theories).

No matter which faction prevailed in a given rural area, the central fact is that decades of economic development efforts have yielded few tangible benefits for the majority of America's rural citizens. The poor are still poor. Farm closings continue unabated, causing small farmers, small businessmen, and farm workers alike to be deprived of their means of livelihood.[17] Rural America still has the nation's highest rates of poverty, illiteracy, malnutrition, infant mortality, underemployment, and substandard housing.[18] And thus, rural Americans may still accurately be characterized as the "people left behind."[19]

Why have rural areas been so impervious to even the most well-intentioned development efforts? In part, the answer lies in the inherent nature of the problem. Genuine development is rarely accomplished quickly or easily because it involves continuing individual and community commitments to change and requires major investments of time and energy.

Insufficient public and private funding has also been an effective obstacle to development. For example, the Rural Development Act of 1972 was a useful piece of legislation until it was undercut in the appropriation and allocation processes. Today, several programs of this act are funded well below the level of authorization, and some other authorized programs (such as small farm assistance) have not been funded at all. In addition, it is at least arguable that given the magnitude of America's rural development problem the act's impact would be minor even with full programmatic funding. Not only were original authorization levels set artificially low, but the act places heavy emphasis on "hard" development projects, such as water and sewer systems, to the virtual exclusion of "soft" development activities.[20]

External Control, Economic Exploitation, and Piecemeal Reforms

Inherent difficulties and inadequate funds are, however, only partial explanations for the lack of impact of rural economic development efforts. Three additional characteristics common to U.S. rural development strategies ("hard" and "soft" alike) provide some additional insights into the reasons for their failure.

First, the locus of control and decision making about both administrative and technical matters has remained with parties external to the rural communities in which development activities were implemented.[21]

Community-based control has been as potent and volatile an issue in development as it has been in education, and, as with education, the eventual outcome has been largely the same: the professionals and the existing power structure triumphed—the developers still control the "developees."[22]

"So what?" one might ask. What genuine difference does it make who controls the development process in rural areas? The difference, in fact, is significant. As Parlow perceptively notes, "The issue of 'who controls' lies at the very heart of 'who benefits.' "[23]

In community after community, state after state, region after region, the story is depressingly similar. Rural development that has not been controlled by its alleged intended beneficiaries has not resulted in a substantial alteration or improvement of the recipients' social or economic conditions. Community-based control of development by no means ensures its eventual success. However, it does at least ensure that development priorities are aligned with the perceived interests of those individuals most directly affected by them.[24]

The second characteristic of rural development efforts in the U.S. is an incorrect analysis of the rural economy which stresses rural isolation and the need to integrate rural America into the metropolitan economy.

Bringing supposedly economically isolated rural areas into the "mainstream" of the metropolitan economy has been advocated, implicitly and explicitly, by nearly every agency involved in rural development: the U.S. Department of Agriculture, the Economic Development Administration, the Tennessee Valley Authority, the Advisory Commission on Intergovernmental Relations, the Appalachian Regional Commission, and a host of Congressional committees.[25]

In fact, however, this analysis is enormously deceiving, if not blatantly incorrect. The basic error is the assumption that because most rural *individuals* are isolated from mainstream economic activity, the rural *economy,* as a whole, therefore must lack effective integration with the larger U.S. economy. In other words, if so many rural people are excluded, then the rural economy must also be excluded.[26] Nothing could be further from the truth. Ironically, a more careful analysis reveals that much of the deprivation and underdevelopment in rural America is a direct consequence of the almost complete integration of the rural economy into the metropolitan economy.

In strictly economic terms, rural America functionally resembles a colony to a much greater extent than it resembles a full and equal part of the U.S. economy. This quasi-colonial relationship explains why rural America has both the richest endowment of recoverable natural resources and, at the same time, the highest level of income poverty and material deprivation in the nation. The conclusion of a 1938 report on economic conditions in the South is applicable today to all of rural America:

> The paradox of the South is that while it is blessed by Nature with immense wealth, its people as a whole are the poorest in the country. Lacking industries, the South has been forced to trade the richness of its soil, its minerals and forests, and the labor of its people for goods manufactured elsewhere.[27]

Or, as one community activist in Kentucky more bluntly put it, "We folks in Appalachia are setting on a gold mine and starving to death."[28] Parlow notes, "Most of the region's natural resources of coal, gas, and timberland are owned by huge, multinational corporations based in the nation's urban centers. And, just as most of the coal is shipped out of the region, so too most of the profits flow quickly and directly out of the region."[29] The same pattern of tight economic integration and resource exploitation exists throughout the nation.

The real problem in rural America isn't lack of mainstream economic integration, but rather the level at which that integration occurs. The very same corporate entities that direct the mainstream U.S. economy also control, profit from, and, for all intents and purposes, own rural America. Rural America needs less, not more, integration (or, at minimum, a very different level and type of integration).

The development-related implications of using such a faulty assumption have been immense. In their headlong attempt to bring the rural and metropolitan economies closer together, U.S. development agencies have served mainly to exponentially increase metropolitan control over rural economic institutions and resources.

In the past twenty years, a major goal of rural development efforts has been to induce outside (that is, urban) industries to relocate in rural areas. To a significant degree, this strategy has "worked." Rural communities built industrial parks, improved necessary public works, and offered tremendous tax breaks to urban corporations willing to relocate in their area. Many urban enterprises took advantage of these generous offers.

Unfortunately, this strategy tends mainly to attract marginal, exploitative, "runaway" industries, which do more harm than good in rural areas. Even when a rural community was fortunate enough to attract a branch of a solid, nationally known major corporation, it rarely helped local citizens or local communities. Such corporations generally imported all managerial, professional, and skilled personnel from urban areas (hiring only local clerical and maintenance workers), did not buy raw materials or supplies locally, and did not reinvest profits locally.

Tourism and recreation have, in recent years, been designated as "targets of opportunity" for rural economic development efforts. Indeed, in a number of predominantly rural states such as Vermont, Colorado, and North Carolina, tourism has become a leading industry.

Unfortunately, largely because rural communities have lacked the capital and expertise necessary to create and sustain large-scale resorts, ski areas, and other recreational outlets, the ownership and control of such places have fallen into the hands of urban-based corporations and individual speculators. Thereafter, the economic cycle becomes depressingly familiar. The urban-based developers do not raise investment funds locally; they do not patronize local suppliers and small businessmen; they hire only low-wage, seasonal, service personnel locally; and they do not reinvest profits locally. In return for these "blessings," local residents are expected to subsidize physical improvements (for example, roads and sewers) needed by the developers, to foot the bill for an expansion of newly required social services (for example, health facilities and police protection), and to endure higher property taxes caused by the presence of the resort area or second-home community.

Rise of agribusiness. Yet, it is in agriculture that the integration of rural and metropolitan (and often even international) economies reaches its purest form. Contrary to popular belief, agriculture is no longer the domain of small, independent, family farmers. Today's agriculture is controlled by such urban corporate empires as Tenneco, Boeing, Del Monte, Ling-Temco-Vought, General Foods, and Cargill.[30] As Harris accurately notes, "A few corporate directors have more to say about agriculture than do the millions of people who live and work on the farms."[31]

Juxtaposing the following five facts clarifies some of the inherent paradoxes of modern agribusiness:

1. Consumers spent $118 billion for food in 1971. This made agriculture the largest industry in the nation—far surpassing the automobile, defense, and electronics industries.[32]
2. Hired farm workers in 1970 averaged an annual income of only $1,083. Those who also did some nonfarm work averaged an annual income of $2,461 in the same year.[33]
3. In 1970, 47.1 percent of the farm families in this country had annual incomes below $3,000.[34]
4. In 1969, 1.9 percent of all farms accounted for over 33 percent of total U.S. farm sales. And 24 food processors (out of 32,000) handled 57 percent of all U.S. food sales.[35]
5. The two most profitable sectors in agriculture are food inputs (for example, seeds, machinery, pesticides) and food distribution (for example, processing, marketing, retail sales). Both these sectors are controlled almost exclusively by huge, urban corporations.[36]

The fundamental conclusion from these facts is that agriculture is an enormously profitable sector, the benefits of which are not being reaped by the vast majority of America's rural farm population.

Two additional conclusions may be drawn. First, America's economy is so tightly meshed with that of urban America that it is almost indistinguishable as an independent entity. Many rural development problems stem directly from the fact that the rural economy has integrated itself into submission to a set of larger and more powerful urban economic forces. Second, economic exploitation is more than simply different from economic development—it is, in fact, wholly antithetic to genuine development.

The third, and final, characteristic common to U.S. rural development efforts is that such efforts have traditionally been piecemeal attempts working in relative isolation from other actual or potential development allies.

Development projects have tended to be highly sectoral. Thus, for example, manpower programs rarely paid attention to such issues as capital investment or business development activities. Similarly, "hard" development advocates rarely addressed the need to alleviate educational deprivation or institute public health measures. Unfortunately, by sticking so close to their own turf, these development efforts doomed themselves. Even if a particular development activity was carried out perfectly, its overall impact was substantially reduced, if not erased altogether, by the overwhelming force of related development problems left unaddressed.

In sum, it is evident that rural development in the United States has been plagued by more than its share of major difficulties. These problems have, to a great extent, kept development efforts from having significant, positive outcomes for rural citizens and rural communities. The five critical problems have been

1. the inherent difficulties of development
2. inadequate financing (public and private)
3. the lack of community-based control in development activities
4. the quasi-colonial integration of rural and metropolitan economies, resulting in an urban, corporate dominance of rural affairs
5. the piecemeal, isolated nature of rural development efforts

Rural Community Development Corporations

A new mechanism has evolved that has considerable potential for increasing the effectiveness of development, and thereby diminishing the cycle of rural deprivation: the community development corporation (CDC). The CDC first appeared during the late 1960s, growing out of a recognition of the inadequacy of conventional development strategies and out of the national movement toward self-determination by minority communities.[37]

What is a community development corporation? The term itself has caused some confusion. Because CDCs are both recent inventions and are designed to conform with local circumstances in the implementing community, precise definitions tend to be transitory and elusive. A CDC in Chicago may bear little obvious resemblance to a CDC in Greenville, Mississippi.[38] The existing literature[39] and the author's exposure to operating CDCs over the past three years[40] suggest the following as characteristic of the CDC model.

1. A community development corporation is a legally incorporated organization, having both for-profit and nonprofit components, which operates in minority or other economically depressed communities and which is primarily controlled (legally, politically, financially, and administratively) and primarily staffed by members

of the same (locally defined) community which is the intended beneficiary of the organization's efforts.

2. The purpose of a community development corporation is to actively promote developmental efforts of an economic, social, or political nature, which will result in a substantial improvement of the social and economic status of community residents, a strengthening of the community's bargaining position with government agencies, existing economic institutions, and all other external entities impacting the community, and, finally, a dissolution of the prevailing cycle of deprivation.

3. To accomplish these purposes, a community development corporation may undertake any, or all, of the following activities: (a) act as a prime sponsor of large-scale physical or economic development efforts, manpower and job-placement programs, or community organizing and public education campaigns; (b) act as a catalyst to secure nonexploitative outside resources such as venture capital, short- and long-term loans, government grants and contracts, or technical assistance for the community; (c) own and operate new businesses, services, or productive enterprises, or acquire existing firms in the community; (d) make the majority of shares in all CDC-owned enterprises readily available to CDC employees, members and other interested parties within the community, while the remaining (minority) shares are made available to outside investors; (e) reinvest all profits made either in an expansion of CDC-owned operations or in other community resources (physical, economic, or human), which are deemed necessary by the organization's membership.

To understand the special status accorded community development corporations within the development/antipoverty world requires some familiarity with the model's social and political origins. Unlike any conventional economic development strategy, the conception and genesis of the CDC have been guided by the assumptions, attitudes, and agendas of America's poor and minority communities. Thus, its uniqueness lies in the fact that it has largely been created by rather than for its intended beneficiaries.

As with any new movement, the rationales and motivations for creating CDCs were as varied and complex as the individuals and communities embracing them. To some, a CDC represented a chance to attack old problems from a new angle, while to others it was little more than a new angle for funding old programs. Some saw the CDC primarily as a way to use economic muscle to advance political agendas, while others seized it as a political mechanism useful in furthering economic goals. Finally, some were drawn to a CDC because of the opportunity it afforded them to constructively contribute their time, skills, and energy to their own community, while others coveted it as a way of using the community to further private ambitions. For many, the motivation to promote and implement CDCs was a subtle combination of all these ingredients and more. However, whatever personal factors were involved, poor minority communities did actively and, often, enthusiastically, embrace the CDC as a model.

Two specific circumstances played powerful catalytic roles in the creation and development of CDCs. The first was the realization that existing social programs and "soft" development activities were incapable of dispelling the fundamental causes of deprivation. The second was the desire of minority and other antipoverty activists to operationalize the twin principles of black (or brown or poor) power and community self-determination. These activists knew that making self-determination more than mere rhetoric was an effort requiring strong proactive strategies and mechanisms. As Green and Faux emphasize:

> Inasmuch as "independence" is so often equated with "financial independence" in our society, it is quite natural that the recent experience should generate an interest in controlling resources through ownership of business.[41]

In theory, at least, the CDC model was the best available answer to a set of development problems which had thus far proved intractable. In addition, the advent of this model meshed well with both the public and private agendas of numerous concerned parties.

The CDC concept gathered momentum with the emergence of major funding sources, notably the National Affairs Division of the Ford Foundation[42] and OEO's Special Impact Program.[43] Maximum public visibility and debate for the CDC movement came with the furor surrounding the Community Self-Determination Act, which was introduced in and then subsequently defeated in Congress at the end of the 1960s.[44] In subsequent years, however, the community development corporations have not only remained, but often persevered as viable mechanisms for development, while other antipoverty programs (such as the ill-fated CAP or Model Cities) have all but vanished.

A unique quality of the CDC model is its ability to combine social and economic development programs in mutually complementary ways. Where applied successfully, the leverage capabilities of this strategy far exceed the CDC's internal capacity to directly produce economic growth.

For a variety of reasons discussed below, a significant proportion of rural CDCs have either been unable to reach their full potential or have failed altogether.[45] While the little evidence that exists on CDCs indicates that their venture-success ratio is significantly higher than that of conventional new business development efforts, CDCs, by themselves, have still proved incapable of reversing a given rural community's depressed economic condition.[46]

CDC-owned and operated enterprises are a critically important component, but they are not the sole concern of an effective CDC's economic development plan. The equally important task for CDCs, through the economic and political power they can generate, is to not only induce outside investments into the community, but also to alter the terms under which such investments are made. CDCs must attract outside resources, but they must also provide safeguards to ensure that these outside interventions do not exploit the community.

All in all, it seems fair to state that, in practice, community development corporations have thus far proved to be valuable assets in the rural rejuvenation process. However, they are not now, and will never be, the whole and complete answer to rural deprivation. CDCs have brought a measure of community-based control (both in theory and practice) to the rural development process, and concomitantly, have improved the bargaining position of poor communities while decreasing the dominance of exploitative outside economic forces. However, although CDCs made significant strides in these two areas, their impact on two other longstanding problems has been marginal, at best.

Problems of inadequate financing have not subsided simply because a given rural community chose the CDC strategy. Venture capital, seed money, and sustained investments have been exceedingly difficult to acquire and maintain. Consequently, most CDC ventures either have been undercapitalized or have lacked the resources necessary to sustain businesses through the start-up years, or both. In addition, this lack of adequate capital has resulted in

CDCs being chronically either understaffed or staffed by underqualified individuals. For the CDC strategy to have a real opportunity to prove its worth, a relatively large, stable source of funds must be discovered or created.

The inherent problems of development have affected CDC-style activities as much as any other kind. Establishing successful economic ventures in depressed communities has always been a monumental task, no matter what the identity or motivation of the developer. These problems are only exacerbated when ventures are launched in markets which are already fully competitive or when the funded enterprises have only a minimal profit margin (such as retail food outlets).

As a generalization, one can say that CDCs have solved two development problems, but have left two others unsolved. What about the fifth longstanding development problem identified above—the piecemeal, sectoral, isolated nature of most development efforts?

The results to date are mixed. Clearly, CDC rhetoric has recognized and pledged itself to eradicating this problem. Yet, it is also clear that, in practice, such eradication has not come easily (and often, not at all). Advocacy activities aimed at redressing a variety of political, educational, and social service problems have met with varying results. Given the severely constrained human and financial resources controlled by most CDCs, it has been difficult to run both successful economic ventures and successful political advocacy programs.[47]

In conclusion, the community development corporation model appears to have enormous promise for remedying some of the ills that have long beset rural community development programs. However, at this stage of their implementation, CDCs still need to overcome the previously described obstacles.

Vocational Education in Rural America

Not everyone trying to eliminate the cycle of rural deprivation has adopted a direct economic development approach, of either the conventional or CDC variety. Indirect development strategies have been employed in rural communities at least as long as direct ones. Most of these indirect efforts share three fundamental assumptions.

1. Poverty and underdevelopment are as much psychological and cultural phenomena as they are economic.[48] Advocates of this position assert that development cannot occur simply by raising income, increasing job and training opportunities, or otherwise eliminating the outward manifestations of deprivation. Rather, it is necessary to alter the thinking, habits, and behavior of poor people. It is just as important to transform the victims of poverty as it is to eliminate the conditions that constitute poverty. As Lewis asserts:

> Once the culture of poverty has come into existence, it tends to perpetuate itself. By the time slum children are six or seven they have usually absorbed the basic attitudes and values of their subculture. *Thereafter, they are psychologically unready to take full advantage of changing conditions or improving opportunities that may develop in their lifetime.*[49] [Emphasis added.]

2. Development can best be achieved through activities focused on specific individuals rather than on the community as a whole. Depending on who is making the argument, the rationale is either that communities are no more than collections of individuals, so if one wants to change communities, one begins by changing individuals; or that because many rural communities are decaying and the young people continue to migrate to the cities, it makes more sense to equip individuals with the skills they need for success in an urban area than it does to worry about the deteriorating situation back home.

3. Public educational institutions are the best equipped and most appropriate agencies available to aid rural people to ameliorate the "culture of poverty" and to implement individually oriented development programs. Schools have come to be perceived as powerful agents of upward mobility for rural as well as urban youth. The depth of this faith in the schools was evidenced in the hostile reaction accorded the work of Jencks et al. for concluding that education was an inefficient and unreliable route to economic success.[50]

In recent years all three of these assumptions have been subjected to rigorous scrutiny, and some very serious reservations (shared by this author) have arisen about their validity and utility.[51]

At first glance, it appears that these three assumptions are radically different from those underlying the community economic development approach. There are, indeed, some fundamental points of contention between the approaches. Sadly, these differences have all too often led members of both factions to believe that the two approaches must be mutually exclusive. Such an either/or conclusion is, in the long run, both incorrect and self-defeating. The two sets of assumptions may be divergent, but that in no way implies that they are necessarily irreconcilable. One can legitimately believe that genuine development entails both individual and community readjustments, both economic and cultural/educational progress, and the active involvement of both public schools and private development agencies.

Of all the strategies launched to date, rural manpower programs have come the closest to bridging this gap. Such efforts usually made explicit the linkages between education and economics, and between training and employment. Unfortunately, most rural manpower efforts have been so closely allied and integrated with the conventional economic development approach that their overall impact has been marginal.[52]

In theory, the CDC strategy also provides a comprehensive development framework. Yet, in practice, the enmity and mutual suspicion between the poor and minority communities (who controlled the CDCs) and the nonpoor, nonminority "establishment" (who controlled the schools and other public agencies) resulted either in stringently limited cooperation between the two parties or, more often, no overt contact or cooperation at all. Instead of all parties working together to overcome the total community's problems, splinter groups were mobilized, each with a different development agenda, a different constituency, and a marked tendency to work at cross purposes. Not surprisingly, they all shared equally an inability to bring their efforts to fully successful fruition.

Whether the three assumptions described are correct or not, they have been the underpinnings of virtually all indirect rural development efforts. Whereas public education at all levels was intended to address the problem of eradicating "cultural deprivation," the operational responsibility for the solution of every other indirect development problem rested squarely with the vocational/occupational/career education components of rural public high schools.[53] Therefore, analyzing the current status and development-related performance of vocational education in rural America is important.

The need for vocational training, nationally, is unquestionable. In 1974, only 40 percent of all high school graduates went on directly to college.[54] when one remembers to include both high school dropouts and eventual college dropouts, it becomes apparent that approximately 75 percent of American youths currently of high school graduate age will not be completing college. Former U.S. Commissioner of Education Marland notes:

> roughly 2.5 million of our young people each year, for a variety of reasons, are voting with their feet, to say that schools and colleges are not meeting their needs. These young people do not possess the conventional credentials from their institutions; moreover, they are not equipped to enter our economic system with salable skills.[55]

The situation is even worse in rural America because many rural communities have more high school dropouts, more general diploma graduates, higher college dropout rates, and a lower percentage of graduates going on to college than the nation as a whole. The prospect facing the vast majority of these young people is obvious: work.[56]

Before considering how well rural high schools are preparing students for this eventuality, it is important to know how available rural vocational education programs are.

Though not always true in the past, today most rural high school students have access to some type of vocational education experience. Two basic delivery systems are common. Students in large, consolidated, comprehensive rural high schools generally receive vocational instruction right in these institutions. Students in smaller schools seeking vocational training commute full- or part-time either to a comprehensive high school or, more often, to a specifically designated regional vocational education facility.

Access remains a problem. In very remote or isolated rural areas, there are children who want to and could profit from vocational education, for whom programs are not available. In communities fortunate enough to have excellent vocational programs and facilities, sexual, racial, and class discrimination in admissions are by no means unknown. Ironically, at the other end of the spectrum, rural communities with substandard vocational programs and facilities tend to enroll disproportionately high numbers of poor or minority group students in the vocational track. Students in outlying areas who depend on regional vocational schools often are inhibited by the sheer time and energy needed to get to and from a distant school.

Thus, the first problem of rural vocational education is a lack of ready and equal access to vocational programs.

Even when access is not a problem, the question remains: How well are vocational education programs performing? If the findings of the National Commission on the Reform of Secondary Education are correct, the answer must be that they are doing an inefficient job. This commission asserts:

> In the American system of secondary education, "work" is a four-letter word. Far too many teachers and principals are not even sure it has redeeming social value outside the academic professions. Though the announced national commitment to vocational education goes back to the early part of the century, most programs are inconsequential. In comprehensive high schools, the vocational "track" is often worse than inconsequential.[57]

The Commission cites several reasons for this failure, but singles out one for special attention. Quoting from a report of the National Advisory Council on Vocational Education, they concur:

> At the very heart of our problem is a national attitude that says vocational education is designed for somebody else's children. This attitude is shared by businessmen, labor leaders, administrators, teachers, parents, and students. We are all guilty. We have promoted the idea that the only good education is an education capped by four years of college. This idea, transmitted by our values, our aspirations, and our silent support, is snobbish, undemocratic, and a revelation of why schools fail so many students.[58]

A review of the literature suggests that the overall poor quality of rural vocational education is directly attributable to the following four characteristics: outdated and indirect programming, migration orientation, job-specific programs, and lack of work experience opportunities.[59] Each is described below.

Outdated and irrelevant programming. This is the most pervasive problem in rural vocational education today. In the past quarter-century, rural America has been subjected to a rash of major changes, including the rise of agribusiness (which substituted capital for labor in farming enterprises); the mass exodus of rural people, particularly rural youth, to the cities; and the closing of millions of small farms. These changes have radically altered both the structure of the rural labor force and, consequently, the operative demands for rural manpower.[60] For example, Carpenter and Rodgers indicate:

> For the nation, the total farm work force is expected to *decline by 35.9 percent* from 5.6 million in 1965 to 3.6 million in 1980. Thus, a total outmigration of 2 million farm workers has been projected to take place between 1965 and 1980.[61]

Even when confronted with these fundamental changes and their obvious implications for rural vocational education, the status quo remained impervious. As Densley notes, "Though the need for farmers declines, vocational agriculture persists in being the primary vocational education offering in rural areas."[62] As far back as 1964, Venn was able to describe this problem with great precision:

> The difficulty now is that farming opportunities are non-existent for many rural youths to the extent that only a third of the 70 thousand yearly graduates of the vocational agriculture program remain in farming. With farm jobs vanishing at the rate of 250,000 a year, it is estimated that only one out of every ten youths now living on farms can look forward to employment on commercially profitable farms in 1970. Yet, in the great majority of high schools in rural America, vocational agriculture is the only pre-employment course offered.[63]

Thirteen years have passed since Venn's statement, but its relevance remains alarmingly intact.

Migration orientation. To try to rectify this obvious shortcoming in the rural vocational education strategy, some "progressive" educators proposed, and ultimately implemented, vocational programs aimed at equipping students with skills relevant to the urban labor market. The underlying assumption was that since rural youth are going to migrate anyway, schools should aid students in acquiring the skills necessary for success in an urban setting. Once again, Densley is instructive:

The majority of the rural students will ultimately seek urban jobs, therefore, curricular offerings must be broad enough to prepare rural youth for urban employment and urban life. . . . Rural conditions are improving, but placement of rural youth in urban occupations has been and continues to be a necessity.[64]

This strategy was adopted with particular zeal by the regional vocational schools that emerged in the past decade. State education officials in Georgia, for example, proudly described a regional vocational high school in the middle of rural Georgia which focuses on training programmers and other computer personnel.[65] There is nothing wrong per se with training computer technicians.[66] Rather, the problem with this strategy is twofold.

First, it is defeatist in its attitude about the plight of rural youth and rural communities. It takes outmigration, rural decay, and inadequate employment opportunities not only as current "givens," but also as long-term inevitabilities.[67] Having accepted this analysis, rural vocational educators feel justified in promoting a strategy which, by equipping youth with skills salable only in an urban job market, serves mainly to exacerbate all the current problems. The situation is reminiscent of the policies of former Agriculture Secretary Earl Butz, who predicted that small-farm decline and the loss of a million farmers by 1980 were "inevitable" and then proceeded to implement policies guaranteed to produce these results. As Hightower properly notes, "This is known as the 'inevitability' of a stacked deck."[68]

Second, for all its face validity, this strategy is not, in fact, pragmatic. Youthful rural migrants (no matter what skills they may possess) at present constitute little more than a pool of surplus labor in an already overburdened urban labor market. Unemployment rates for urban adults (skilled and unskilled) are enormous, yet they seem small when compared to the astronomical unemployment rates among urban youth.[69] Williamson's description is insightful:

Youth problems in the labor market represent yet another major theme of public and professional concern over secondary schooling. Unfortunately, the most serious of these problems do not appear to be so much a reflection of the current economic downturn as manifestations of an apparent long-term deterioration in the relative position of youth in the national employment experience. *In the past several years the youth unemployment rate has averaged between four and five times the adult rate.* In 1930, unemployment of adolescents 14 to 19 years old was approximately one and a half times the national adult rate. In 1940, it was over two and a half times the national rate. By 1960, youth's position had slipped to over three times the adult average and, by 1967, there was a further deterioration to over four and a half times that rate. . . .

The chronic problems of youth in the labor market are not confined to a deteriorating employment experience. In recent years, the nation has learned the rude fact that it is indeed possible to satiate the economy's demand for educated workers. The prospect in the years ahead of massive youth underemployment (working at less than one's full production capacity) is most discouraging.[70]

A vocational education strategy geared toward producing rural migrants is not only bad policy, but also a cruel deception. Passing the buck to urban America is a far cry from solving the problem of unemployment among rural youth.

Job-specific programs. Those rural communities uncommitted to either outdated or migration-oriented programs have often embraced the notion of providing job-specific vocational education. The idea is simple. Analyze the relevant local or area labor market, determine anticipated manpower needs, consult with area employers, and then design vocational programs that will meet anticipated needs. While this in many respects is a perfectly reasonable strategy, its overall effectiveness is greatly hampered by two unpleasant realities:

1. The relevant area labor market is often already saturated, and consequently, the openings for new competitors (young or old, specially trained or not) are marginal at best.

2. Available job openings tend to be in the low-wage, dead end, exploitative enterprises attracted by conventional rural development

programs. If one subscribes to the belief that half a loaf is better than none, this situation may be quite acceptable. Yet, for those who believe that half a loaf is not sufficient, or who are concerned about the implications of transforming America's rural population into a "servant class" catering to the needs of urban tourists, resident professionals, and second-home owners, this strategy is plainly unsatisfactory.[71]

Even leaving pragmatic, economic judgments aside, there is ample ground for suspicion of this strategy on the grounds of undesirable social and psychological impacts. As Grubb and Lazerson insightfully conclude:

> Career education is not directed at resolving social problems, developing avenues of upward mobility, or making school and work more satisfying experiences. *It is aimed instead at reducing expectations, limiting aspirations, and increasing commitments to the existing social structure.* The replacement of hazy educational goals with "realistic" vocational goals, while appearing benevolent, actually strengthens the "cooling-out" function of schooling. College graduates are less satisfied, less controllable, and less productive in menial jobs than workers without higher education, and there are few non-menial jobs. Career education attempts to attenuate this dysfunction by bringing aspirations in line with the availability of high-skill jobs, by replacing high aspirations with lower ones, and by preparing students in ways that make continuation to higher education more difficult.[72]

Job-specific vocational education may make some sense in communities having first-rate employment opportunities, or at the very least, enough jobs to warrant being specific. Such is normally not the case in rural America today. Thus, this strategy's utility in the rural context is highly limited.

Lack of work experience opportunities. Work experience is an area that deserves far greater attention in the development of improved rural vocational education programs. A 1975 report by the U.S. comptroller general indicates:

it is generally acknowledged that inclusion of actual work experience in vocational education curriculum provides students with valuable real life exposure to work requirements and helps assure they receive training appropriate to employer needs. Such experience often can better prepare students for subsequent placement in jobs related to their training. The Congress has recognized this need and, in part G, VEA specifically encouraged cooperative arrangements between schools and employers.[73]

Advocacy of the value of work experience is hardly new. Thoreau, for instance, argued:

Students should not play life, or study it merely, while the community supports them at this expensive game, but earnestly live it from beginning to end. How could youths better learn to live than by at once trying the experiment of living.[74]

Today, endorsement of the work experience concept is commonplace. For example, Marland asserts, "Neither students nor their teachers can learn what they need to know about the world of work only through a textbook."[75] The National Commission on the Reform of Secondary Education strongly recommends granting credit for work experience.[76] The new Coleman report on youth not only sanctions this concept, but urges an expansion of its application.[77] Even the U.S. Chamber of Commerce urges that a work experience component be a part of every high school student's program.[78]

However, in vocational education, endorsement and implementation are two very different and often unrelated matters. Despite all the laudatory rhetoric, painfully little use has actually been made of the work experience model in on-going vocational education programs, especially rural programs. As the comptroller general points out:

U.S. Office of Education statistics for fiscal year 1973 show that about 508,000 students—*4 percent of the total enrollment in*

vocational education—were enrolled in cooperative programs.[79] [Emphasis added.]

Williamson's comment on the implications of this lack of real
world integration is instructive:

> From the sociological point of view the schools have not
> only isolated youth from the experiences of adult society,
> but have also served to segregate youth into strict age
> cohorts. Authority and influence is coming increasingly to
> rest with an adolescent's peer group, and social relation-
> ships for youth are now rigidly age stratified. Furthermore,
> even though society in general is becoming increasingly
> rich and sophisticated in information, it is becoming poorer
> in the opportunities for meaningful educative opportuni-
> ties for action. Consequently, youth are shielded from
> responsibility and made dependent.[80]

The absence of significant work-experience opportunities for
rural vocational students (as well as regular or college-bound
students) is partly attributable to the lack of available recipient
organizations. In many rural areas, there are simply not enough
businesses, industries, or government agencies in the community able
to provide suitable work experiences for rural high school students.
This, however, is only a partial explanation of a longstanding rural
deficiency.

In the final analysis, outdated, migration-oriented, job-specific
programs and the lack of meaningful work experience opportunities
are only symptomatic of a more fundamental ill endemic to rural
vocational education. Their failure is not simply the result of poor
planning, poor program design, or poor implementation (though
there has been a substantial amount of each). Rather, their failure can
accurately be attributed to a pervasive unwillingness, or inability, to
confront the necessity of directly creating jobs as well as job
applicants. By steadfastly remaining aloof from the business of rural
economic development, vocational educators have sown the seeds of
their own destruction.

The unfortunate fact remains that there are not enough good jobs
available in urban areas, and not enough good rural nonfarm jobs
available to accommodate rural vocational education graduates.

Until rural vocational educators evidence an active involvement in on-going projects aimed at creating new jobs and rejuvenating the rural community, their efforts will continue to be inconsequential.

Section Two: The School-based CDC: An Alternative for the Future

The three major rural development strategies employed in the United States (conventional, CDC, and indirect/human resource) have achieved varying degrees of success over the years; yet all of them have been found deficient in theory, practice, or (most often) both. The evidence suggests that their deficiencies have been of a sufficient magnitude to consistently mitigate many of their potential benefits.

Thus, the oft-heard assertion of vocational educators and development specialists that simply acquiring new resources to do "more of the same" will produce better results is highly suspect. For example, if building roads is an ineffective economic development plan, then receiving more money to build more roads does nothing to increase the plan's merits. If attracting low-wage, "runaway" industries serves only to exacerbate the structural problems of rural economies, then receiving more funds to accelerate this pattern can only be counterproductive. If persistent racial or political problems impair the ability to employ available resources efficiently and effectively, then simply supplying more resources cannot solve the problem. If vocational training does not equip individuals with skills appropriate to existing or anticipated labor markets, then just allocating more resources to vocational schools will not result in increased programmatic relevance or propriety.

Securing new and expanded resources may be an important, perhaps even critical, element in making rural education and development programs succeed. However, securing these additional resources to expand deficient and ineffective efforts is likely to increase rather than alleviate existing problems.

Based on the preceding evidence and analysis, it seems reasonable and appropriate to infer: (1) that rural America has long been plagued by major problems in the areas of economic development and vocational education; (2) that even though these two sets of problems are intimately interrelated, they have rarely been treated as such in practice; (3) that, as a consequence, most economic development thrusts and vocational education programs have been remarkably isolated from one another, to their mutual detriment; (4) that as long as these efforts retain their traditional patterns of isolationism and sectoralism, they will be unable to significantly reduce their high incidence of failure; and (5) that the solution lies in an infusion of new financial and human resources coupled with the introduction of new, well-integrated strategies, programs, and institutional capacities for rural education and development.

Acceptance of the above assertions requires proposing a viable alternative. The task is to formulate and evaluate potential strategies, programs, and institutions which can integrate education and development more completely, maximize the strengths and minimize the weaknesses of current efforts, and thereby begin to obviate the cycle of rural deprivation. The remainder of this chapter is addressed to this critical task.

Rejuvenating rural America will be a long-term and formidable process, including such diverse components as an improvement of access to quality health care, a physical rehabilitation of rural communities, and a dramatic expansion of employment (and other economic) opportunities. Numerous efforts on a wide variety of fronts will be required. The problems besetting rural America are simply too personalistic, variable, and heavily determined by local circumstance to be amenable to solution by any single reform strategy. It is futile to assume the existence of any "quick fix" or "panacea" that (even if applied across the board) will be able to eliminate the aftereffects of decades of decline and deprivation.

To use an analogy to the military, it appears likely that rural problems can best be eradicated not by the big bomb approach, nor by the shotgun approach, but rather by the utilization of several well-placed bullets. "Bullets" refers to a small set of key reforms focused enough to be effective, powerful enough to make a difference, and yet, modest enough to be realizable in the foreseeable future.

Rather than explicitly identifying and describing the full range of promising "bullets" appropriate for rural America (if such a task were even possible), this chapter proposes one such "bullet": the school-based community development corporation.

What Is A School-Based CDC?

The notion of the school-based CDC is an original invention of the author of this chapter; it has neither been implemented anywhere in the United States nor been the subject of any known discussions, debates, or analyses. Therefore, it is unlikely to be considered as a possible rural reform strategy without a detailed presentation.

At least in theory, the school-based CDC "bullet" is a potential mechanism for the coordinated adoption and implementation of other essential "bullets." A particular strength of the school-based CDC is its ability to function as both catalyst and implementing agency for a broad and diverse range of needed reforms in rural education and development. This relatively unique quality provides another justification for an extended focus on the school-based CDC.

The basic concept of a school-based community development corporation is simple. Under the auspices of the school board responsible for the local public high school, a new affiliate organization (the CDC) is legally incorporated. Broadly stated, the purposes of this new organization are: (1) to function as a full-fledged CDC working for the economic and social welfare of the community as a whole; and (2) to complement or eventually supplant existing public vocational education programs and institutions, while concomitantly becoming an integral part of the educational experience of most rural high school students.

With initial financing coming from a combination of grants, loans, and special bond issues, the school-based CDC will own and operate businesses, services, and other productive enterprises in the local community. Primarily using student labor under the supervision of regular faculty members and a special community faculty, the school-based CDC will perform the functions of *an economic development program* (by generating or attracting income-producing opportunities for the local community); *a community planning agency* (by serving as the focal point and coordinating unit for all local development thrusts); *a manpower development project* (by training groups of young workers equipped with marketable skills, by encouraging the development of managerial and entrepreneurial abilities in students and other community residents, and by upgrading the skills of involved faculty members); *a career education program* (by integrating a student's work experience and classroom components in educationally relevant ways); *a community services agency* (by acting as an advocate for the community in securing needed outside social services and by delivering selected local social and recreational services); and finally, *a nonpartisan political institution* (by sponsoring discussions, seminars, and workshops on critical community problems and by serving as a continuing forum for the exploration and debate of local, state, and national issues).

It is anticipated that the school-based CDC's economic ventures will be financially self-supporting once they emerge from the early start-up period. Hopefully, they will also produce profits, which can be reinvested in CDC-owned enterprises or used to subsidize the CDC's nonprofit activities.

The objectives, organization, governance, financing, and programmatic components (economic, educational, and others) of school-based CDCs are elaborated below. The suggestions offered are simply suggestions. Every aspect of this model can, should, and undoubtedly will be altered to some degree during actual implementation. The tendency toward conformity with local needs, local interests, and local circumstances is both desirable and, more or less, inevitable. The lessons garnered from the "Great Society" experience all indicate that a given reform's success is highly contingent upon the degree to which it is both accepted by and appropriate to the local implementing community. Thus, the model presented here should not be regarded as an unalterable fait accompli, but rather as a systematic strategy for rural education and development which can either be adopted, as is, or adapted as necessary.

Objectives

In conventional rural development and vocational education programs, the basic objectives are usually very simple, straightforward, and noncontroversial. The prevailing pattern is to have one general overall objective (for example, "to stimulate economic growth in Countryside County" or "to provide vocational training for the students of Countryside High School") as well as a set of more specific, complementary subobjectives (for example, "to attract outside industries and investments" or "to equip vocational students with marketable skills"). Occasionally, arguments arise about these objectives. However, they almost always turn out to be an expression of dissatisfaction with how an objective has been operationalized, rather than an inherent dissatisfaction with the objective itself.

In contrast, community development corporations have had a tumultuous relationship with this whole issue. Theoretically, CDCs accord equal emphasis to three major sets of objectives: economic, social, and political. The tripartite nature of these objectives is a constant theme of the relevant literature.

Not surprisingly, the need to reconcile, balance, and coordinate three such seemingly disparate objectives has proved a major, and continuing, source of conflict. The crux of the problem is that attempting to combine this range of social, political, and economic agendas (particularly in an egalitarian manner) forces CDCs into the position of having to pursue objectives which are, at best, extremely difficult to achieve given present constraints, or, at worst, mutually exclusive.

Fortunately, the available evidence on currently operating CDCs offers a substantially more sanguine picture of how this issue has actually been resolved. Far from each objective undermining the others, most CDCs have found all these objectives both essential and mutually reinforcing. In fact, the least successful CDCs tend to be those which devote an inordinate amount of attention or a disproportionately high level of resources toward the accomplishment of any single objective.[81]

The focus now shifts from an exploration of the general objectives of any community development corporation to a more specific consideration of the objectives of the school-based model. Once again, the school-based CDC's objectives are twofold: (1) to function as a full-fledged CDC working for the economic and social welfare of the community as a whole; and (2) to complement or eventually supplant existing public vocational education programs and institutions, while concomitantly becoming an integral part of the educational experience of most rural high school students.

From the outset, some distinctive features of the school-based CDC model become apparent. By adding education to its repertoire of primary objectives, the school-based CDC significantly changes the programmatic content, institutional framework, and potential constituency characteristic of "regular" CDCs. Similarly, the inclusion of social, political, and economic objectives dramatically alters the traditional orientations of rural vocational education programs.

The most pronounced effect of these changes will probably be found in how these objectives are interpreted and operationalized. Because the school-based CDC is a public (or quasi-public) institution rather than a private one, and because it serves the whole community rather than any single age, income, or racial group, its objectives may be quite different from those of other kinds of CDCs.

The most obvious example lies in the area of political objectives. "Regular" CDCs were intended to strengthen the political power and advance the political agendas of their own distinct constituencies (that is, poor and/or minority community residents) within the local community. In other words, the fundamental political objective of "regular" CDCs was to alter the political balance within the local community so that it became more favorable to the CDC's constituents.

However, within the context of the school-based CDC, political objectives assume a wholly different meaning and purpose. The primary mission in this area will no longer be the redistribution of power *within* the community, but rather the pursuit of increased political influence for the community in dealing with outside corporations, institutions, and government agencies. Because it represents the entire local community, the school-based CDC will focus on an elevation of that community's status and control in relation to outside forces and interests.

As a result of these redefined objectives, social programs will have to be redesigned, economic programs will have to be able to utilize new kinds of human and financial resources, and educational programs will have to be geared to the needs of a broader and more heterogeneous segment of the community. The exact nature and dimension of these changes will vary enormously depending on local circumstance.

Yet, the creation of new interpretations for old objectives is not the only area that is likely to be marked by controversy. Some fundamental disagreements can be expected over the specific mix of educational, economic, social, and political goals which are integral to the school-based CDC concept.

The failings of rural economic development (conventional and CDC) and rural vocational education are attributable not only to operational deficiencies, but also to the isolation existing between such efforts. Thus, the creation of an institution such as the school-based CDC, which is explicitly designed to integrate education and development, appears to be both desirable and long overdue.

As noted above, "regular" CDCs have often been able to integrate seemingly divergent goals in a mutually beneficial and mutually reinforcing manner. This harmonious balance has usually been the result of a flexible, nondoctrinaire approach to the issue of equality among objectives. By rotating emphasis and resources, as appropriate, the successful CDCs have been able to tolerate short-term dominance and subservience among objectives without having to forego long-term equality. There is no inherent reason to believe that this same pattern cannot be effectively replicated in school-based CDCs.

Organization, Governance, and Financing

Objectives, especially unusual or complex objectives, are singularly important in the formulation of rural education and development strategies, but that does not require they be treated with piety or regarded as sacrosanct. Goals that prove to be both appropriate and achievable are, of course, preferable to those without such qualities. Yet, history is replete with examples of policies, programs, and institutions that have succeeded despite, rather than because of, their objectives. Conversely, equally often a particular strategy has failed, even though it was graced with impeccable objectives.

The reason is simple. Objectives are only a partial determinant of success. When compared with many structural and operational factors, the internal validity of one's goals has proved a poor predictor, and an even worse explanation, of success. Therefore, our focus will now shift to the examination of one variable which is of critical importance to the successful fruition of the school-based CDC strategy: how the school-based community development corporation is organized.

To design a theoretically sound and operationally feasible organizational framework, primary consideration must be given to two issues: *legal status* and *institutional autonomy*. In most cases, a specific legal status implies rather than dictates the form and content of the resolution of organizational issues.

Legal Status

Before examining in detail possible legal and organizational alternatives for school-based community development corporations, we must answer the central underlying question about their legal status: Under what legal authority may such institutions exist at all?

To date, most rural community development corporations have been a composite of two legally distinct organizations. The ownership of business and other economic enterprises has normally been handled through the chartering of a private, for-profit corporation. On the other hand, the CDC's social and community action components (research, community organizing, and the like) have been managed through the incorporation of a private, nonprofit entity. This nonprofit component is often referred to as a 501(c)(3) organization, because of the kind of tax-exempt status accorded it by the Internal Revenue Service.

Adding a set of educational activities (or even a whole private, nonprofit school) to these existing CDCs would be perfectly legal and would serve mainly to reinforce the legitimacy of their tax exemption. Thus, there are no known legal barriers to a private, nonprofit CDC possessing educational objectives or engaging in educational pursuits.

However, the notion of establishing a public CDC through a local school district is an idea of indeterminate legality, subject to the interpretation of state law. Each state is guided by its own set of education laws, but some relevant general patterns do exist.

The school-based CDC is an original and unique invention, never before proposed for adoption in this country, so there are no direct legal precedents on which to base a judgment about its propriety as a public sector institution. There is no state that specifically forbids the creation and operation of such a unit. It makes good sense to resolve all legal problems prior to implementation, so that the CDC will not later need to be diverted from its primary missions to handle avoidable legal battles and complications.

Another fundamental question is whether school districts can legally operate the kinds of businesses and other revenue-producing enterprises that characterize community development corporations. There is no definitive answer available. It becomes, once again, a matter of interpreting (or changing) state law. However, there is every reason to be optimistic if the school-based CDC is clearly defined and carefully presented.

Even if the CDC's basic legality is accepted as a given, there is still a profound need to determine the particular type of legal status that is most appropriate and advantageous. To accomplish its stated objectives (including the educational goals), is it wisest to promote the development of public, quasi-public, or private CDCs?

An appropriate legal status cannot be determined solely theoretically and without reference to the needs, constraints, and characteristics of the implementing community. There is no single magic organizational pattern which makes sense, or which is even possible, for all rural communities. Diversity is the hallmark of rural America, so such new rural institutions as the school-based CDC must be flexible enough to reflect this diversity. Three basic organizational models for the school-based CDC (public, quasi-public, and private) are possible.

Public Model

The public school-based CDC will most likely be the standard model, both in frequency of utilization and in the broad range of communities for which it is relevant. (This model is therefore the reference point for the general discussions and assertions about school-based CDCs in this chapter.)

The basic concept is simple. Under the auspices of the school board responsible for the operations of the local public high school, a community development corporation is incorporated as a wholly owned and operated venture of the local public school district. Its legal status would be that of a special purpose public educational institution, not unlike existing vocational schools, special education facilities, and adult education centers. Its staff would be public employees; its buildings would be public facilities; its programs would serve the public; and its practices would be a matter of public policy. It is, in short, intended to be a public institution in every usual and legal sense of the term.

This legal status will prevent the public model from having the kind of institutional autonomy normally enjoyed by private sector enterprises. However, even within the framework of the local school district, institutional autonomy (as a problem of organization) is still a valid issue. The nature of the relationship existing between the CDC and the school board, as well as between the CDC and other school components, can significantly influence both the dimensions and quality of the CDC's operations. Basically, there are three available options.

Free-standing CDC. The first option would be to create a free-standing CDC. Under this preferred plan, the CDC would be an independent institution within the school district, as illustrated in Figure 8.2. The intent of this option is to install the CDC as an entity which, in hierarchical terms. is equivalent to the other major operational units of the school district. This equivalency and the fact that the CDC would be separate and immediately recognizable distinguish this alternative.

The advantages are substantial. The CDC's special purposes and relative autonomy will afford it the opportunity to create internal policies and practices that are uniquely suited to its needs and objectives. In addition, because it would neither be part of, nor bound to accept the precedents of any existing school units, the CDC's operational flexibility and programmatic control will be greatly enhanced. Finally, the CDC's independence from, yet comparable status to, existing school units increases its ability to attract an excellent staff and a higher level of outside resources.

Yet, there are potential disadvantages in using this approach. The possibility of the free-standing CDC being perceived as a threatening, rival institution by existing school units is far from remote. Such a perception would, in turn, probably lead to outright hostility and an unwillingness to assist (or even cooperate with) the CDC. The resultant isolation, harassment, and political retributions would, of course, be damaging (if not fatal) to the free-standing CDC's overall performance.

Vocational school-based CDC. The second option is to create a vocational school-based CDC. Figure 8.3 displays the basic organization pattern. A CDC operating within this framework will find itself in a position of relative security because it will not have to create everything from scratch. Because the CDC is part of the vocational high school, it will be able to take advantage of existing facilities and equipment, current students, faculty and administrative personnel, on-going programs and outside affiliations, and established policies and practices, as well as the measure of political protection that automatically accrues to new efforts of an old, stable institution.

Unfortunately, with rare exceptions, the freedom and security available through the vocational school-based CDC option exacts an

FIGURE 8.2

<u>FREE-STANDING CDC</u>

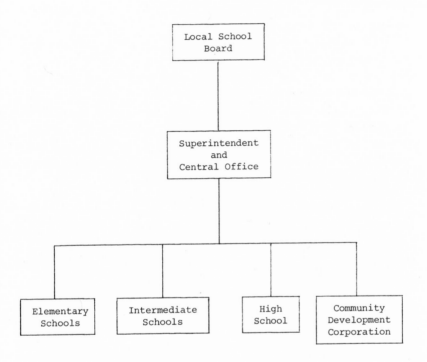

unreasonable and debilitating price because the heritage of rural vocational schools constitutes a nearly perfect antithesis to the whole concept of school-based CDCs. In the best of all possible worlds, the vocational school-based CDC idea might have genuine merit because of the firm and secure institutional framework it provides for the CDC. However, the deficiencies of current rural vocational schools are so pronounced that implementing this alternative would serve primarily to undermine the value and utility of the CDC strategy.

High school-based CDC. Most rural school districts do not operate

FIGURE 8.3

VOCATIONAL SCHOOL-BASED CDC

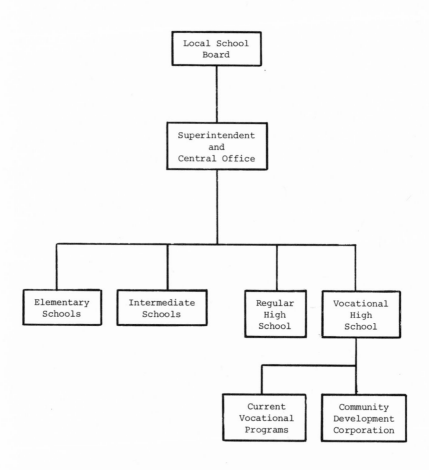

their own vocational schools. Rather, they "tuition out" students to larger neighboring districts with vocational facilities, join in the formation of a regional vocational school, or offer a limited vocational curriculum as part of the regular high school program. Public school districts of this kind have available a third option: to create a high school-based CDC. Figure 8.4 presents a basic organizational chart for this alternative.

The distinctive strengths of this model can be summed up in one

FIGURE 8.4

HIGH SCHOOL-BASED CDC

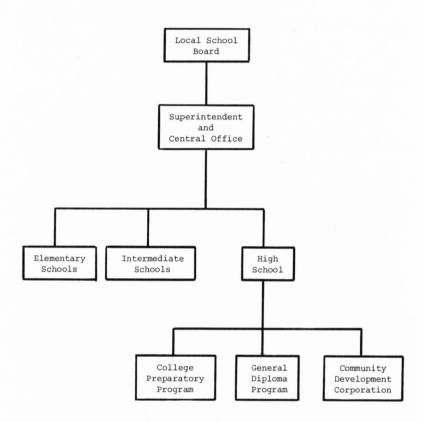

word: integration. By diminishing the risks of isolation inherent in the free-standing model while concomitantly making the full organizational capabilities of the high school available, this option can almost guarantee that the CDC will not be crippled by dissent, divisive politics, or deteriorating cooperation within the local school district. In addition, the community development corporation as an educational program serving the needs of all high school students has a better chance of attaining its full potential in this option than in either of the others.

Yet, the high school-based CDC concept is not devoid of drawbacks. The most obvious problem is that rural school districts, as a group, do not tend to be progressive, activist organizations. Without such characteristics, however, the high school-based CDC's operations will probably be hampered by the school's attempts to make it conform to the standard policies and practices of the school's other components. In such a situation, the blending of programs and resources ceases to be an instance of integration and cooperation and instead becomes simply a muddled example of co-optation.

Free-standing, vocational school-based, and high school-based community development corporations are the three basic organizational alternatives available within the public sector. Each is endowed with unique benefits and burdened by peculiar problems. Each is a potentially viable option for the implementation of a CDC, and yet there are situations in which each option loses its viability. Sensitivity to local circumstance will not, indeed cannot, guarantee eventual success for any CDC venture. However, it will at least ensure that the CDC does not needlessly defeat itself by failing to take seriously enough of the context of its implementation.

Rural communities will usually choose the public CDC model because it is the only one that automatically confers control of the CDC to the local community as a whole. The desire for local control of education and of development is a powerful and deeply rooted force in rural America. Thus, rural communities interested in having a CDC at all probably will prefer and more readily accept a CDC that they can directly control, rather than one that they just patronize.

Nevertheless, there will occasionally be rural communities for which the public school-based CDC model in any form is unacceptable. For such communities, there are two alternatives that will permit the development of a viable school-based CDC: the quasi-public model and the private model.

Quasi-Public Model

The quasi-public school-based CDC model will probably be employed most frequently in rural communities in states controlled by an unusually conservative legislature or state bureaucracy. Where opposition to the public model is championed by forces and authorities external to the local community interested in having a school-based CDC, the quasi-public model may well be the best option.

The basic concept is simple. Under the auspices of a broad cross section of community leaders (usually including most, if not all, school board members) a community development corporation is incorporated as a quasi-public, nonprofit, free-standing institution. As part of its mission, the quasi-public CDC will design and operate a vocational education program open to any and all local public high school students and other interested community residents. Though the ownership and control of the CDC and its programs would legally remain in private hands (the CDC's founders), all of its activities would be directed toward public purposes. For example, instead of using the profits of CDC economic ventures to pay dividends to CDC stockholders (as is the case now in existing private CDCs), the quasi-public model would channel all profits back into the educational program and other needed nonprofit ventures. By renting the CDC's facility for educational purposes, as well as by "tuitioning out" students to it, the local community will be able to play a direct and vital role in the sustenance of this CDC.

The major substantive advantage of the quasi-public model is its enormous flexibility. For example, state certification requirements for public school staffs are often so formal and rigid that it would be very difficult to hire some of the skilled community residents the CDC may want or need to employ (such as a local carpenter to teach building skills). In a quasi-public CDC, however, it would be quite easy to hire such individuals. These quasi-public institutions would also face substantially less severe political battles over the selection of appropriate economic ventures than would their public counterparts.

Still, there are disadvantages in the quasi-public strategy. Foremost is that a CDC having this legal status would be ineligible for some critically important revenue (for example, state aid and general obligation bonds) and technical assistance sources available only to public institutions. In addition, since public ownership and control of the CDC and its ventures are not possible, the quasi-public model is likely to attract far less active community support and assistance. Finally, if the state feels genuinely threatened by these quasi-public CDCs, there are doubtless some measures that could be enforced by the state to halt or hamper these CDCs.

Private Model

The private school-based CDC model will be adopted primarily by those rural communities that are either divided by irreconcilable local opposition to the CDC or that have an ongoing private CDC already in existence. Once again, the basic concept is simple. Under the auspices of some definable faction within the local community (for example, blacks, poor people, liberals), two corporations are created. One is a private, for-profit economic development group and the other is a private, nonprofit 501(c)(3) organization. This nonprofit organization can establish either a private, tuition charging, proprietary vocational school, or, through a contract with the local school district, a work experience/training program for a small select group of public high school students.

There is a precedent for such an organization. The Lummi Indian Tribe founded, and currently operates, a private vocational school that is directly tied to its CDC's activities. The Lummi CDC's prime economic venture is the Aquaculture Project, so, not surprisingly, their school is focused on training skilled workers in this field.[82]

The advantages of this strategy are similar to those of the quasi-public model. However, the disadvantages are much more serious because the private CDC-based school

1. will be able to gain access to only marginal levels of new public resources
2. will only offer a very limited education and training program
3. will attract less skilled and qualified staff members
4. will serve only a limited, homogeneous constituency
5. will only superficially integrate education and development initiatives in the community

Therefore, while this private model will be suitable and beneficial for some rural communities, it is the least desirable organizational model in theory and the one least likely to achieve widespread implementation.

Governance

Because of the burgeoning awareness throughout society that "who controls" a given program or institution is intimately interrelated with "who benefits" from its activities, governance issues have acquired importance and controversiality rare in the past. This general trend toward heightened emphasis on governance has been particularly prevalent in education and economic development.

Until quite recently, the governance of public educational programs and institutions was a nonissue. Day-to-day administration and management have long been the prerogative of the superintendent and other professional school administrators, while overall policy and decision-making powers have been the exclusive province of the local school board. However, the participation guidelines of federal programs, the increase in state-level policymaking, and advent of community control/citizen participation movements, and the increasing assertiveness of teachers' unions have all combined in the past decade to erode traditional governance patterns and procedures in education.

The traditional laissez-faire approach to rural economic development has also come under increasing scrutiny and attack. Though more sporadic and low key, the movement to inaugurate citizen controls over rural development has gained strength in recent years. Some states (such as Vermont) have passed laws to regulate the nature and extent of development; other states (such as Montana) have outlawed major agribusiness initiatives; and, in nearly every state, local community organizing around development issues has emerged. The most concerted effort has been in the creation and implementation of community development corporations.

Citizen participation and community-based control remain cardinal and inviolable principles of the CDC strategy. Past attempts to circumvent these twin principles have resulted either in outright organizational collapse, or, at best, the evolution of a group that is a CDC in name only.[83] Thus, while the governance mechanisms employed by CDCs vary considerably in accordance with local circumstances and preferences, they all share a practical, operational commitment to extensive citizen involvement in and direction of the CDC.

What happens to governance in a school-based CDC? In the private model, governance is relatively simple. Control of this type of CDC is vested in and determined by the special constituency to be served by the organization; for example, blacks or low-income individuals. Normally, the most fundamental CDC policies and practices are established by all interested constituents at annual or semiannual meetings and revised by this same group as necessary. To handle ongoing oversight, policy, and decision-making responsibilities, an executive committee or board of directors is created. This group is usually elected by the CDC's membership at the aforementioned meetings. The board, in turn, appoints a chief administrative officer (the director) to manage the organization and to hire all other needed staff members. Committees are often established by recruiting interested CDC members to advise the board, membership, and staff on policy and programs in areas of substantive concern, such as health, housing, and economic development. Adding an education component to this kind of CDC would probably not significantly alter the organization's governance structure. An education director and staff would be hired, and a CDC Committee on Education would be created.

Though endowed with considerable discretion in governance, the quasi-public CDCs still must adhere to a few more rules than their private counterparts. Because this type of CDC is, by definition, intended to pursue exclusively public purposes, it must be perceived as being at least roughly representative of the community it serves. For example, a quasi-public CDC located in a very low-income, 85 percent black, farming community which has an exclusively white, middle-class, mercantile board of directors is unlikely to be viewed as a credible community institution.

In practice, the nucleus of community leaders necessary in the CDC's planning and incorporation processes will probably bestow effective control of the CDC upon themselves. The principal mechanism available to ensure this is the nonelected, self-appointing, self-perpetuating board of directors. If the quasi-public CDC's founders genuinely represent the whole community, and are perceived as including a broad cross section of community leaders, then this strategy may have merit as a long-term governance plan. Its advantage lies in the relative unanimity of purpose, harmony, and lack of political in-fighting such a mechanism is likely to encourage. If, however, the original group starting the quasi-public CDC is perceived as clearly imbalanced, or weighted toward one particular community subgroup and set of interests, then this strategy will be unable to retain any semblance of legitimacy in the long run.

It is the public school-based CDC that is the most likely to be widely adopted. This, coupled with the need of any public institution to be accountable, makes a sensible governance structure imperative.

In the public vocational school-based and high school-based CDCs, it must be decided whether or not governance will be handled through existing channels. Because these two public options are both designed to function as new programs within pre-existing institutions, the tendency would normally be to make the CDC subject to the governance mechanisms and procedures guiding its host institution. Realistically speaking, this would mean that, in most cases, the CDC would operate under the auspices of the existing building principal, the district superintendent, and the local school board.

While this approach may be fine for other new and innovative programs, like career or bilingual education, it is not optimal for a program such as the CDC, which is intended to serve constituencies and conduct activities far beyond the traditional school boundaries. Perhaps the best remedy is to have the existing school board designate a seven-member CDC advisory board composed of one assigned school board member, one faculty representative elected by his/her colleagues, one student representative elected by the other students, one minority group representative recommended by the CDC director and approved by the school board, one low-income representative recommended by the CDC director and approved by the school board, and two members elected at large by the community. The district superintendent, CDC directors, and building principal should also serve as nonvoting, ex-officio members of this committee. However, this advisory group is worthless unless the school board is willing to delegate (either legally or by agreement) the bulk of its programmatic policy and decision-making powers to the CDC advisory board.

The free-standing CDC is different from the other two public models only in degree. Because the free-standing CDC is designed to be an autonomous institution, rather than simply a new program, the kind of special advisory board arrangement described earlier is more readily understandable and justifiable. In the vocational school-based and high school-based CDCs, the existence of a strong, independent advisory board is greatly preferable to the regular educational governance system. In the free-standing CDC, however, the creation of such a board is essential. The autonomy and flexibility that are supposed to characterize this free-standing model are likely to become undermined and rendered inoperative in the absence of such an advisory board.

Financing

One of the foremost determinants of any strategy's ultimate success is the ability to attract and secure needed resources. With ample resources, sensible innovations can become a significant and effective force for improvement. However, without these requisite resources, innovations tend to remain just good ideas.

This general principle applies to the school-based community development corporation. It is imperative to analyze the resource base that can be marshalled to support the school-based CDC strategy. In doing so, however, it becomes abundantly clear that presently utilized resource supplies are incapable of either initiating or sustaining a school-based CDC. Historically, both rural education programs and rural economic development efforts have been enormously hampered by insufficient funding.

"Regular" rural CDCs have, for the most part, limped along financially because of their traditional dependence on two inconsistent and unstable funding sources: the U.S. Office of Economic Opportunity (an agency beset by financial and political woes of its own) and a few private philanthropic agencies (most notably the Ford Foundation). Occasionally, other public and private bodies have supported a particular CDC's activities through investments, grants, loans, or contracts, but such assistance has tended to be both sporadic and relatively small-scale.

The primary result of this adverse financial situation has been the undercapitalization that characterizes existing rural CDCs. The lack of sufficient venture capital to purchase the land, facilities, equipment, materials and supplies needed to launch economic enterprises having reasonable hopes for success is not only detrimental in its own right, but also serves to trigger a devastating downward spiral within the CDC. Figure 8.5 delineates the progression of this downward spiral.

Inadequate financing has also been a consistent trait of rural school systems. In addition to the excessive reliance on local property taxes shared by school districts throughout the United States, rural schools have historically received a disproportionately low percentage of available state, federal, and philanthropic resources for education.[84] This has meant that rural schools having the inclination to expand their programs or experiment with new innovations have rarely been able to generate the resources these new thrusts demand. The

FIGURE 8.5

THE DOWNWARD SPIRAL CAUSED BY UNDERCAPITALIZATION OF A CDC

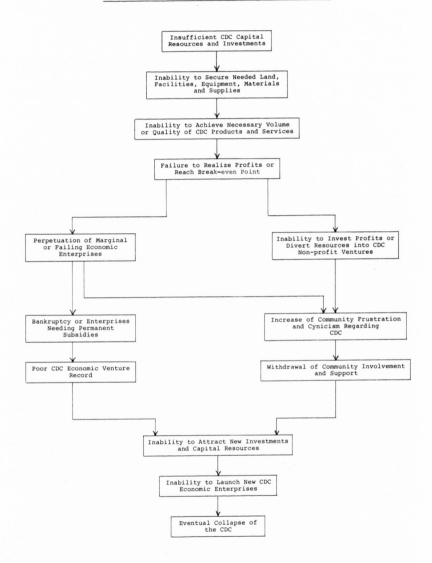

realistic prospects for financing a school-based CDC solely out of current school revenues are virtually nonexistent.

The question becomes: Worthy as it may be, does an innovation of the CDC's scope and magnitude have a reasonable chance to secure the financing required for success? Conceptually, the answer is unreservedly affirmative. One of the school-based CDC's main attributes as a rural education and development strategy is its potential for tapping hitherto unavailable combinations and sources of revenue. Once again, however, this statement's applicability is contingent upon the specific type of school-based CDC being considered.

Financially, the private model is the least advantageous. The major sources of funding would continue to be the same inadequate ones employed by current rural CDCs. While adding an education component to the CDC may moderately increase overall revenues (through outside grants to the CDC, tuitions paid by the local school district, or some combination of these two alternatives), these new revenues will do little more than meet the new expenditure requirements stemming from actually running the education program. In other words, no real net financial advantage is likely to accrue to the CDC as a result of pursuing educational objectives.

Most important, however, the private school-based CDC model will have no discernible effect on the problem of undercapitalization, and thus will remain largely irrelevant to the solution of the major fiscal difficulty confronting rural community development corporations.

By contrast, the quasi-public model does address itself directly to the resolution of CDC undercapitalization. Quasi-public CDCs have ready access to a source of revenue that is beyond the reach of their private counterparts. The comparative advantage here lies in the quasi-public CDC's ability to generate capital through the issuance of bonds.

The potential economic implications of possessing this bonding capacity are enormous. For the first time, a CDC will have open access to a long-term, stable, well-endowed funding source which can provide the CDC with most, if not all, of its capital requirements. This, in turn, will ensure three other critically important results: (1) it will remove the primary trigger of the downward economic spiral that has plagued rural CDCs; (2) it will dramatically improve the CDC's economic venture record by providing CDC enterprises with the resources necessary to facilitate the development of products and services of sufficient volume and quality to be competitive and economically viable; and (3) it will enable the CDC to consider a variety of profitable business, resource development, and industrial opportunities previously rejected by CDC planners on the grounds of insufficient capital. In the final analysis, the difference between having and not having this bonding capacity is much like the difference between manufacturing shoestrings and having to live on one.

For the quasi-public CDC, rental revenue bonds are the simplest, most secure, and therefore the best, option. The basic idea is that the quasi-public CDC would develop a total bond package (for example, $250,000 for land acquisition; $4,000,000 in building and renovation costs; and $750,000 in equipment purchases—a $5 million capital expenditure program), the repayment of which would be guaranteed by a formal agreement from the local school district that they would rent all CDC facilities for the duration of the bond term. Once the bond is completely repaid, the standard practice has been to relinquish ownership of these facilities to the school district.

The other possibility in rental revenue agreements is for the quasi-public CDC to undertake a construction program which is large and flexible enough to allow joint ownership or tenancy of the proposed facilities. This is a particularly exciting possibility in rural areas because it could, for example, mean that for the first time a comprehensive community center would be brought into existence. The community center could be built with the intent of housing the CDC, local government offices, social service programs, a library, a health clinic, recreation facilities, and other community-oriented efforts.

Another alternative is to use the revenues generated by the quasi-public CDC's productive enterprises as security for the repayment of bond obligations. Just as in any other business, the CDC could expend a certain percentage of its gross income on debt retirement. Assuming adequate CDC income over time, this could become a stable and dependable source of repayment revenues. However, bond raters, agents, and buyers are not known for their liberal assumptions about repayment sources. Without an established and distinguished venture success record, it is doubtful that this last type of CDC bond would sell at all.

The financial foundations of the quasi-public school-based CDC appear to be both respectable and reasonably secure. Quasi-public CDCs will have access to all the institutions and programs aiding private CDCs (that is, federal contracts, philanthropic grants, and private sector loans and investments), yet they will also have the opportunity to issue revenue bonds. Thus, while (as will be discussed shortly) the quasi-public model cannot approach the assets of the public model, it does at least possess a potential resource base that is far in excess of that available to its private counterparts.

Public model's advantages. It is in the public model that the financial advantage inherent to the school-based CDC strategy achieves full fruition. The potential range and level of resources that can be marshalled in support of public school-based CDCs is nothing short of amazing.

Like current rural vocational education programs, the public school-based CDC would be eligible for a portion of the local school district's operating budget, as well as being able to share in the district's other human, material, financial, and political resources. This kind of CDC is a legitimate recipient for the resources flowing from state and federal initiatives in the areas of vocational and career education. It would also have access to a wide variety of state and federal programs established for the purchase, renovation, or construction of public school facilities.[85] If this CDC were located in an area served by a regional educational service agency, it would be able to utilize the regional unit's technical assistance expertise and any other relevant regional programs. Finally, like any other public education agency, the school-based CDC could vie for existent philanthropic (and other private sector) grants designed to help improve our nation's schools.

Like conventional rural economic development programs, the public school-based CDC would be eligible for an array of existing state and federal rural development programs, assistance, and funding. For example, this CDC could benefit from Economic Development Administration grants, Small Business Administration loans, Labor Department initiatives (such as those sanctioned under the Comprehensive Employment and Training Act [CETA]), Agriculture Department programs, and various regional development funds and activities such as those generated by the Appalachian Regional Commission. In addition, there are numerous private sector sources of assistance (financial and otherwise) that could be deployed in support of the public CDC.

Like private community development corporations, the public school-based CDC would be eligible to receive funds from the OEO (now called the Community Services Administration) Title VII program. And, of course, philanthropic sources, which have strongly backed the CDC concept, would be likely supporters of this new

CDC model.

Finally, like quasi-public community development corporations, the public school-based CDC would also have the authority to issue revenue bonds.

Beyond this plethora of potential revenue sources, the public school-based CDC will probably be able to secure needed additional funds from three additional sources. The first would be the revenues generated by the CDC's own economic ventures. All profits, if and when they are secured, can immediately be reinvested in an expansion of ongoing CDC enterprises, the creation of new CDC businesses, the development of related nonprofit services, or any other legitimate public purpose. The second includes the funds available through three recent public programs: General Revenue Sharing, the Rural Development Act, and Community Development Block Grants. Though legally, the public CDC cannot be a direct recipient of these funds (only "general purpose" governments can qualify), it is likely that rural communities would be willing to allocate a sizeable portion of funds received here toward necessary new CDC thrusts.

Finally, additional funds can be generated through the issuance of a "full faith and credit" bond. As a public institution, the CDC can (through the local school district) issue these bonds in addition to any revenue bonds. The basic idea is that the local community pledges its "full faith and credit" as a guarantee of bond repayment.

The "bottom line" is clearly that public school-based community development corporations are able to tap a unique and unprecedented combination of revenue sources to further their own purposes and programs. In financial terms, the public CDC model is unquestionably the most advantageous.

Anatomy of a School-based CDC

The CDC model is more than just a set of structural arrangements or financing possibilities or legal underpinnings. Knowledge about these kinds of options is important, but equally important is a sense of the CDC as an integral entity, as a coherent and viable mechanism for effectively intervening in the serious educational and social problems of rural America. If the school-based CDC model is still just a gleam in the eye of this inventor, it is a gleam that has unified purposes and goals. By attempting to specify some guidelines for school-based CDC economic and vocational programs, some meat will be put on the skeletal structures outlined in the preceding sections. Hopefully, thereby, the reader will get some sense of how a real live school-based CDC might operate and function.

Delineating school-based CDC programs is problematic because the range of possibilities is enormous and the potential permutations within that range are virtually endless. In fact, the likelihood of any two rural communities adopting the exact same set of activities is infinitesimal. Additionally, differences in the particular CDC model employed, the level of resources captured, and circumstantial variables in the local implementing community preclude the development of definitive, universally applicable program plans. Consequently, the presentations made below are illustrative rather than conclusive.

Still, formulating some preliminary guidelines can be useful. Therefore, the school-based CDC as an economic development strategy and as a vocational education program will be discussed briefly in the context of the public CDC model. (With appropriate modifications, the points are relevant to all the CDC models.)

Economic Program

During the initial stages of implementation, efforts directed toward ensuring the economic viability of the school-based CDC must take precedence over all other concerns. In part, this refers to the CDC's ability to attract necessary outside resources and funding for all its programs. Mainly, however, it is meant to establish the primacy of creating successful, income-producing economic ventures.

Determining the appropriate productive enterprise, or enterprises, is the single most important decision the school-based CDC must confront during the early planning and implementation processes. Though there are a myriad of factors that must be weighed, the following six guidelines should be observed.

1. Avoid businesses (such as retail food outlets) that have low profit margins and need high-volume sales.
2. Avoid businesses that cater strictly to the local market.
3. Avoid businesses requiring very large capital investments in equipment and machinery.
4. Avoid businesses that involve very sophisticated technologies

and that require a highly skilled and technically proficient work force.

5. Avoid businesses in which there is any direct conflict or competition with existing locally owned establishments.
6. Build upon the talents, interests, and resource bases that exist within the local community.

Education Program

Though economic viability must be the first priority of the school-based CDC, the tendency to subordinate educational objectives to the pursuit of pecuniary goals should be resisted. Ignoring education or making it only a tangential concern of the CDC will ultimately prove self-defeating. One of the primary characteristics of this model is the interdependence existing between education and economic development. In fact, an optimal CDC would be one in which the economic and educational functions are virtually indistinguishable; that is, one in which work activities were designed to be educational and educational activities were designed to further the CDC's work. Of course, optimal situations like this are often elusive. However, even in less than perfect circumstances, education and economic development must be more than just related—they must also be mutually reinforcing.

How can the principle of interdependence be operationalized within the context of a rural school-based community development corporation? Once again, there can be no circumvention of the primacy of local circumstance. There are, however, some general guidelines that have broad applicability and that should help resolve programmatic conflicts.

Vocational education programs

1. should derive their curriculum from the ongoing economic efforts of the CDC
2. must maintain a high level of academic integrity
3. should develop both a stable core curriculum and a flexible program of elective courses
4. must be open to all members of the local community
5. should incorporate a job-rotation plan for all students

By utilizing the school-based CDC strategy, rural vocational education could, for the first time, make a lasting and significant contribution to the lives of America's rural students and to the rejuvenation of America's rural communities.

Notes

Introduction

1. For exact statistics and further information on this topic, see Vera J. Banks, *Farm Population Estimates, 1975* (Washington, D.C.: U.S. Department of Agriculture, Economic Research Service, October 1976).
2. See Chapter 8, note 6.
3. See Chapter 8, note 6; also see "Trends in Rural America," Chapter 8.
4. Calvin L. Beale, *The Revival of Population Growth in Nonmetropolitan America* (Washington, D.C.: U.S. Department of Agriculture, Economic Research Service, June 1975), p. 3. Beale goes on to state:

    As might be expected [counties adjacent to metropolitan areas] have had the highest population growth since 1970 (4.7 percent) and have acquired about five-eighths of the total net in-movement into all nonmetro counties. However, the more significant point is that nonadjacent counties have also increased more rapidly than metro counties (3.7 percent vs. 2.9 percent). Thus, the decentralization trend is not confined to metro sprawl. It affects nonmetro counties well removed from metro influence. Indeed, the trend can be said especially to affect them (pp. 6-7).

5. U.S. Bureau of the Census, *General Social and Economic Statistics*, Census of the Population, 1970; Final Report PC(1)-C1 (Washington, D.C.: U.S. Government Printing Office, 1972), Table 88, p. 386.
6. U.S. Bureau of the Census, *Population Characteristics* (Washington, D.C.: U.S. Government Printing Office, March 1974).
7. Marian Wright Edelman, Marylee Allen, Cindy Brown, Ann Rosewater et al., *Children Out of School in America* (Cambridge, Mass.: Children's Defense Fund, 1974), p. 37.
8. Ibid.

9. Ibid. The 1970 census revealed that absenteeism, permanent or chronic, varies with the income, education, and occupation of the parents, as well as their race and residence. Children's enrollment varies inversely with the income and education level of the parents. Nonwhites are less likely to enroll than whites. The percentage of children not enrolled is greatest for children of farmworkers (7 percent), a figure even higher than that for children of the unemployed. Additionally, the nonenrollment rate is greater for children of farmers than for those in most occupations.

10. See, for example: James S. Coleman et al., *Equality of Educational Opportunity* (Washington, D.C.: U.S. Department of Health, Education and Welfare, U.S. Office of Education, OE-38001, 1966); W. Vance Grant and C. George Und, *Digest of Educational Statistics: 1974 Edition* (Washington, D.C.: National Center for Educational Statistics, U.S. Department of Health, Education and Welfare, 1975); Lewis R. Tamblyn, *Inequality: A Portrait of Rural America* (Washington, D.C.: Rural Education Association, 1973).

11. National Assessment of Educational Progress, *General Information Yearbook* (Washington, D.C.: U.S. Government Printing Office, December 1974). See also George Henderson, *National Assessment and Rural Education* (Las Cruces, New Mexico: ERIC Clearinghouse on Rural Education and Small Schools, December 1973). Note: NAEP invented its own definition called "extreme rural." This denotes nonmetropolitan communities with a population under 8,000 and a work force that is primarily agricultural rather than professional or industrial.

12. See Chapter 3 for a detailed discussion of this point. See also Roger G. Barker and Paul V. Gump, *Big School, Small School* (Stanford, Calif.: Stanford University Press, 1964); and Ivan D. Muse, Robert J. Parsons, and Edward M. Hoppe, "A Study of Rural Teachers and Rural Schools as Perceived by School Administrators, Teachers, Parents, and Students" (Salt Lake City, Utah: Brigham Young University, 1975).

13. Two facts should be remembered in reading these two tables. First, since "nonmetropolitan" includes places up to a population of 50,000, the size differences between city schools and districts and very rural ones are significantly underestimated. Second, because of a lack of available data, these tables do not distinguish between elementary and secondary school size. A more sophisticated presentation of the data would probably show high school size to be

somewhat larger and elementary school size somewhat smaller than the averages appearing in these tables.

Chapter 1

1. *Fourth Annual Report of the Massachusetts Board of Education* (Boston, Mass.: Dutton and Wentworth, 1841), p. 22.

2. Rush Welter, *Popular Education and Democratic Thought in America* (New York: Columbia University Press, 1962), p. 73.

3. *The Common Journal*, vol. 2, no. 15 (Boston, Mass., August 1, 1840).

4. David M. Ludlum, *Social Ferment in Vermont 1791-1860* (New York: AMS Press, 1966), p. 229.

5. Ibid., p. 232.

6. Donald R. Warren, *To Enforce Education* (Detroit, Mich.: Wayne State University Press, 1974).

7. Robert H. Wiebe, *The Search for Order* (New York: Hill and Wang, 1967).

8. Samuel Bowles and Herbert Gintis, *Schooling in Capitalist America* (New York: Basic Books, 1976).

9. Richard Hofstadter, *The Age of Reform* (New York: Vintage Books, 1955), p. 46.

10. *Thirteenth Annual Report of the Massachusetts Board of Education* (Boston, Mass.: Dutton and Wentworth, 1853), p. 49.

11. *Twenty-Fourth Annual Report of the Massachusetts Board of Education* (Boston, Mass.: Dutton and Wentworth, 1860), p. 75.

12. Ibid, p. 76.

13. Edward DeAntonio, "Coming of Age in the Industrialist State: The Ideology and Implementation of Rural School Reform 1893-1925" (Ph.D. dissertation, Cornell University, 1971), p. 3.

14. National Education Association, *Report of the Committee of Twelve on Rural Schools* (Chicago, Ill.: University of Chicago Press, 1897).

15. Louis W. Rapeer, *The Consolidated Rural School* (New York: Charles Scribner & Sons, 1920), p. 4.

16. Julius Boraas and George Selke, *Rural School Administration and Supervision* (New York: Heath and Co., 1926), p. 8.

17. Ellwood Cubberley, *Rural Life and Education* (Cambridge, Mass.: Riverside Press, 1914).

18. David B. Tyack, *The One Best System* (Cambridge, Mass.:

Harvard University Press, 1974), p. 14.

19. Raymond E. Callahan, *Education and the Cult of Efficiency* (Chicago, Ill.: University of Chicago Press, 1962), p. 8.

20. Ibid., pp. 1-2.

21. *Thirty-Fourth Vermont School Report, 1896* (Montpelier, Vt.: Watchman Publications, 1896), p. 99.

22. *Biennial Report of the State Superintendent of the State of Wisconsin* (Madison, Wis.: Democratic Printing Co., 1901), p. 32.

23. *Biennial Report for the State of Arkansas, 1893-94* (Morrilton, Ark.: Pilot Printing, 1894), p. 19.

24. *Thirty-Sixth Vermont School Report, 1900* (Montpelier, Vt.: Watchman Publications, 1900).

25. Una Bedicheck and George Baskett, *The Consolidation of Rural Schools With and Without Transportation*, Bulletin of the University of Texas, no. 43 (October 1, 1904), p. 6.

26. Cubberley, *Rural Life and Education*, pp. 69-71.

27. *Thirty-Third Vermont School Report, 1894* (Montpelier, Vt.: Watchman Publications, 1894), p. 62.

28. Julius B. Arp, *Rural Education and the Consolidated School* (Yonkers-on-Hudson, N.Y.: World Book Co., 1918).

29. J. W. Faulk, *Consolidation of Schools and Transportation of Pupils in Lafayette Parish, La.*, U.S. Bureau of Education Rural School Leaflet No. 19 (Washington, D.C.: Government Printing Office, 1923).

30. Ibid.

31. Edward A. Bateman, *Development of the County-Unit School District in Utah* (New York: Teachers College Contributions to Education No. 790, 1940), p. 37.

32. A. Montoya, *The Consolidated Schools of Bernalillo County, New Mexico*, U.S. Bureau of Education Rural School Leaflet No. 22 (Washington, D.C.: Government Printing Office, 1924).

33. Ibid.

34. Ibid.

35. Frank Jones, *The Rural Schools*, pages from the Biennial Report of the State Superintendent of Public Instruction of Indiana (Indianapolis, Ind.: William Burford, 1900).

36. O. H. Greist, *Consolidation of Schools in Randolph County, Indiana*, U.S. Bureau of Education. Rural School Leaflet No. 12 (Washington, D.C.: Government Printing Office, 1923).

37. Charles H. Judd, *Rural School Survey of New York State* (Philadelphia, Pa.: William Fell Co., 1923), p. 119.

38.   Ibid.
39.   Carl Griffey, *The History of Local School Control in the State of New York* (New York: Teachers College, 1936), p. 67.
40.   Bowles and Gintis, *Schooling in Capitalist America*, p. 199.
41.   Guy M. Whipple, ed., *The Thirtieth Yearbook of the National Society for the Society of Education, Part I* (Bloomington, Ill.: Public School Publishing Co., 1931), p. 1.
42.   Harold W. Foght, *Rural Education*, U.S. Bureau of Education, Bulletin No. 7 (Washington, D.C.: Government Printing Office, 1919), p. 4.
43.   *Schools in Small Communities*, Seventeenth Yearbook of the American Association of School Administrators (Washington, D.C.: National Education Association, 1939), p. 29.
44.   Floyd W. Reeves, ed., *Education for Rural America* (Chicago, Ill.: University of Chicago Press, 1945), p. 35.
45.   Edgar Morphet, Roe Johns, and Theodore Reller, *Educational Administration: Concepts, Practices, and Issues* (Englewood Cliffs, N.J.: Prentice-Hall, 1959), p. 226.
46.   Suzanne K. Stemnock, *Summary of Research on Size of Schools and School Districts* (Washington, D.C.: Educational Research Service, 1974).

Chapter 2

1.   According to the U.S. Office of Education figures, the number of traditional high schools declined from 16,460 in 1930 to 6,618 in 1970. Yet, in 1930, the average secondary school had 234 pupils, while in 1950 the figure had risen to 457 pupils, and, as of 1972, the average secondary enrollment was 710 pupils.
2.   The most frequently cited problems were inadequate financing, inefficient and uneconomic operations, low achievement, inadequate staffing, and lack of programmatic quality and diversity.
3.   David B. Tyack, *The One Best System* (Cambridge, Mass.: Harvard University Press, 1974), p. 25. Note: Tyack cites the following references: Robert R. Alford, "School District Reorganization and Community Integration," *Harvard Educational Review* 30 (Fall 1960): 350-71; Joint Committee on Rural Schools, G. A. Works, Chairman, *Rural School Survey of New York State* (New York: William F. Fell, 1922).

4. It is possible to connect the issues raised here about rural consolidation with the current debate over school district reorganization to achieve desegregation in metropolitan areas. This chapter does not, however, have anything to contribute to the determination of constitutionally appropriate desegregation strategies. It would be absolutely incorrect to imply that the arguments found in this chapter somehow support the continuation of segregated neighborhood schools in urban America.

5. Some definitions are in order. First, our definition of a small school is: (1) any elementary school that supports no more than one classroom per grade level (thus, for example, a K-8 school having an average of 20 pupils in each grade; that is, a total attendance of 180 pupils, fits our definition of smallness); and (2) any high school with a graduating class of less than 100 pupils (Conant's definition). Second, our definition of "rural" is the open countryside and all nonmetropolitan places having a total population of less than ten thousand residents.

6. In recent years, serious doubts have been raised about the validity of the scale economies presumed to exist in the private sector. Examples of this literature include E. F. Schumacher, *Small is Beautiful* (New York: Harper & Row, 1973); John M. Blair, *Economic Concentration: Structure, Behavior, and Public Policy* (New York: Harcourt, Brace, Jovanovich, 1974); Barry A. Stein, *Size, Efficiency, and Community Enterprise* (Cambridge, Mass.: Center for Community Economic Development, 1974); Jim Hightower, Susan DeMarco, Susan Sechler, *Corporate Giantism in the Food Economy* (Washington, D.C.: Agribusiness Accountability Project, 1974).

7. Fred White and Luther Tweeten, "Optimal School District Size Emphasizing Rural Areas," *American Journal of Agricultural Economics* (February 1973), p. 51.

8. Ibid.

9. Ibid., p. 52.

10. Manuel Zymelman, *Financing and Efficiency in Education* (Boston, Mass.: Nimrod Press, 1973), p. 274.

11. Interview with Mr. Charles Johnson, superintendent of the Northeast Washington County (Vermont) Supervisory Union, July 1975.

12. William P. McLure, "School Finance in District Reorganization," *Phi Delta Kappan* 32 (March 1953): 321-26.

13. Calvin Greider, "Relation of School District Reorganization to

Finance in Business Administration," *Review of Educational Research* 17 (April 1947): 167-77.

14. Suzanne K. Stemnock, *Summary of Research on Size of Schools and School Districts* (Washington, D.C.: Educational Research Service, 1974).

15. Sam M. Lambert et al., *One Teacher Schools Today* (Washington, D.C.: National Education Association, 1960).

16. This NEA report states that in 1950, average enrollment in one-teacher schools, nationally, was twenty. And, even in 1960, the pupil-teacher ratio was 17:1.

17. To make matters worse, consolidation advocates often used urban data or examples to convince rural communities of the necessity of rural consolidation. Thus, the consolidation literature is sprinkled with references to research indicating that optimal district size is ten to twenty thousand or more. However, careful examination of these citations almost invariably shows that they are referring to research done in Los Angeles, metropolitan St. Louis, or other urban centers.

18. Three studies support this. Willard A. Wright and Wilfred H. Pine, *Costs of Rural High Schools in Central Kansas, 1956-57*, Bulletin 429, Agricultural Experiment Station (Manhattan, Kans.: Kansas State University, 1961); Elchannan Cohn, "Economies of Scale in Iowa High School Operations," *Journal of Human Resources* (Fall 1968), pp. 422-34; John Riew, "Economies of Scale in High School Operations," *Review of Economics and Statistics* (August 1966), pp. 280-87.

19. Cohn, "Economies of Scale in Iowa High School Operations."

20. Examples of this research include: P. L. Rajpal, "A Study of Relationships Between Expenditure and Quality Characteristics of Education in Iowa Public Schools" (Ph.D. dissertation, University of Iowa, 1967); Harold D. Patterson, "Relationships Between Size of Secondary Schools and Selected Teacher Characteristics" (Ph.D. dissertation, George Peabody College for Teachers, 1964); K. C. DeGood, "Profile of the Small High School," *Educational Leadership* 18 (December 1960): 180-82; Jack B. Collingsworth, "An Analysis of the Relationship of Size of Arkansas High Schools to Selected Qualifications of High School Teaching Personnel" (Ph.D. dissertation, University of Arkansas, 1961); Harold J. Morris, "Relationship of School Size to Per Pupil Expenditure in Secondary Schools in Nine Southern States" (Ph.D. dissertation, George Peabody College for Teachers, 1964).

21.   Had pupil-teacher ratios remained at 17:1 instead of 20:1 in this example, a minimum of $24,000 in additional salary funds would be required. Similarly, adding an assistant principal or a full-time librarian or full-time athletic coach or a new specialist would further increase the consolidation deficit.

22.   Samples of this literature are: *Planning for School District Organization*, Great Plains School District Organization Project, 1968, which presents several volumes of position papers supporting reorganization; Donald T. Donley, *Organizing for a Child's Learning Experience: A Report on a Study of School District Organization in Massachusetts* (Boston, Mass.: Massachusetts Advisory Council on Education, 1971); and Edward J. Fabian, *Vermont School District Organization Report* (Montpelier, Vt.: Vermont Department of Education, May 1975).

23.   Testimony of Robert Isenberg, associate executive secretary, American Association of School Administrators, before the Senate Select Committee on Equal Educational Opportunity (Washington, D.C., September 1, 1971), p. 6334.

24.   The six studies reviewed were: Henry J. Schmandt and G. Ross Stephens, "Measuring Municipal Output," *National Tax Journal* 3 (December 1960): 369-75; Werner Hirsch, "Determinants of Public Education Expenditures," *National Tax Journal* 8 (March 1960): 29-40; W. Hirsch, "Expenditure Implications of Metropolitan Growth and Consolidation," *Review of Economics and Statistics* 41 (August 1959): 232-41; H. Thomas James, James A. Kelly, and Walter Garms, *Determinants of Educational Expenditures in Large Cities of the U.S.* (Stanford, Calif.: Stanford University Press, 1966); N. Harrison, "Economy of Scale as a Cost Factor in Financing Public Schools," *National Tax Journal* 17 (March 1964): 92-95; and Herbert J. Kiesling, "Measuring a Local Government Service: A Study of Efficiency of School Districts in New York" (Dissertation, Harvard University, 1965).

25.   Werner Hirsch, "Determinants of Public Education Expenditures," *National Tax Journal* 13 (March 1960): 39.

26.   G. Kahn and W. Hughes, *Statistics for Local Public School District Reorganization to State Aid Distribution Systems*, Special Study Eleven, National Education Finance Project, Part II, 1970, pp. 126-34.

27.   Zymelman, *Financing and Efficiency in Education*, p. 180.

28.   Based on the equation 300 (pupils) x $1000 (per pupil expenditure) x .088 (the average budget percentage allocated for administration in districts up to 300 pupils).

29. Based on the equation 3000 (pupils) x $1000 (per pupil expenditure) x .052 (the average budget percentage allocated for administration in districts having 3000 pupils).

30. Fabian, *Vermont School District Organization Report*, pp. 38-39.

31. Clifford Hooker and Van D. Mueller, *The Relationship of School District Reorganization to State Aid Distribution Systems*, Special Study Eleven, National Education Finance Project, Part II, 1970, pp. 126-34.

32. Recent court decisions in New Jersey, California, and Texas have raised the issue. The Supreme Court in *Rodriguez vs. San Antonio Independent School District* has said that the state has no constitutional obligation to equalize wealth per pupil. See John E. Coons et al., *Private Wealth and Public Expenditure* (Cambridge, Mass.: Harvard University Press, 1970) for a detailed analysis of the inequalities in wealth and recommendations for removing them.

33. Unified districts are generally considered to be the most equalizing type of organization. Table 2.3 does not include elementary districts, secondary districts, or any other type which, if included, would further increase the variation.

34. Hooker and Mueller, *The Relationship of School District Reorganization*, pp. 178-79.

35. Fabian, *Vermont School District Organization Report*, pp. 38-39.

36. Hooker and Mueller, *The Relationship of School District Reorganization*, pp. 178-79.

37. North Dakota Statewide Study of Education, *Educational Development for North Dakota, 1967-75*, "*The Overview*" (Grand Forks, N.D.: University of North Dakota, 1967), pp. 15-17.

38. Burton Krietlow, *Long Term Study of Educational Effectiveness of Newly Formed Centralized School Districts in Rural Areas*, Reports 1, 2, and 3 (Madison, Wis.: University of Wisconsin, 1962, 1966, 1971).

39. James Bryant Conant, *The American High School Today*, Carnegie Series in American Education (New York: McGraw-Hill, 1959).

40. Ibid.

41. Ibid.

42. Raymond Callahan, *Education and the Cult of Efficiency* (Chicago, Ill.: University of Chicago Press, 1962).

43. Ibid.

44. Conant, *The American High School Today*, p. 40.

45. Ibid., p. 15.

46. Ibid., p. 14.

47. Ibid., pp. 24-25.

48. One of the study's ironies is that schools O and P are described as rural consolidated schools.
49. Ibid., p. 29.
50. Ibid., pp. 114-17.
51. Ibid., p. 37.
52. According to the 1970 U.S. Census.
53. To ensure comparability with Conant's study, no controls for IQ or family socio-economic status are used in the presentation of the Vermont data. As evidence presented later in this chapter indicates, using such controls tends only to further the comparative advantage of small schools.
54. Enrollment and performance data used are from "A Study of Vermont High School Graduates: Class of 1974" (Montpelier, Vt.: Statistics and Information Division, Vermont State Department of Education, January 1975).
55. For more detailed information on Vermont high schools see Chapter 7.
56. All cost data are from "A Comparison of Tuition Rates and Per Pupil Costs for Tuition Purposes, 1973-74" (Montpelier, Vt.: Statistics and Information Division, Vermont State Department of Education, January 1975).
57. The key resources most often identified include high per pupil expenditures, advanced curricular offerings, faculty salaries, experience and credentials, new equipment and facilities, and the number of books in the school library.
58. James Coleman et al., *Equality of Educational Opportunity* (Washington, D.C.: U.S. Government Printing Office, 1966); Frederick Mosteller and Daniel P. Moynihan, eds., *On Equality of Educational Opportunity* (New York: Random House, 1972); Christopher Jencks et al., *Inequality* (New York: Basic Books, 1972).
59. See particularly Jencks et al., *Inequality*; and Donald M. Levine and Mary Jo Bane, *The Inequality Controversy* (New York: Basic Books, 1975).
60. See, for example, Charles E. Silberman, *Crisis in the Classroom* (New York: Random House, 1970); Neil Postman and Charles Weingartner, *The School Book* (New York: Delacorte Press, 1973); and Harvey A. Averich et al., *How Effective is Schooling? A Critical Review of Research* (Santa Monica, Calif.: The Rand Corporation, 1972).
61. See Rachel Bussard (Tompkins), "Qualifying Paper," Graduate

School of Education (Boston, Mass.: Harvard University, 1972), pp. 54-55, for a summary table of fourteen different studies. The most frequently cited of these studies are William H. Drier, "Differential Achievement of Rural Graded and Ungraded School Pupils," *Journal of Educational Research, Basic Skills as Related to Size of School and Type of Organization*, Monograph (Iowa City, Ia.: State University of Iowa, School of Education, 1949); and Krietlow, *Long Term Study of Educational Effectiveness of Newly Formed Centralized School Districts in Rural Areas*. Much of the research presented in this chapter originally appeared in Dr. Tompkins' "Qualifying Paper," cited above.

62. Only four of the fourteen took IQ and social class into account in some way.

63. See Bussard (Tompkins), "Qualifying Paper," pp. 54-55.

64. Leonard S. Feldt, "Relationship Between Pupil Achievement and High School Size" (University of Iowa, 1960), p. 8.

65. Timothy Weaver, "The Case Against the Preston County Comprehensive Facilities Plan for Consolidating the Schools" (Boston University, unpublished paper, 1975).

66. Coleman, *Equality of Educational Opportunity*.

67. Ibid.

68. A. Summers and B. Wolfe, "Which School Resources Help Learning?" *Business Review* (February 1975).

69. M. Alkins, *Economy of Scale in the Production of Selected Educational Outcomes* (Washington, D.C.: AERA, 1968).

70. Thrasher and Turner, *School Size Does Make a Difference* (San Diego, Calif.: Institute for Educational Management, 1970), as reported by Ian Templeton, "School Size," *Educational Management Review Series*, ED 072 505 (December 1972).

71. Herbert J. Kiesling, *High School Size and Cost Factors*, Report of U.S. DHEW Project No. 6-1590, March 1968.

72. Ibid., p. 77.

73. Richard Raymond, "Determinants of Primary and Secondary Education in West Virginia," *Journal of Human Resources*, vol. 3, no. 4 (Fall 1968), pp. 450-70.

74. Raymond's study population were those graduates from West Virginia's fifty-five county school systems enrolling at West Virginia University during the early and mid-1960s.

75. Ibid., p. 467.

76. Krietlow, *Long Term Study of Educational Effectiveness of Newly Formed Centralized School Districts in Rural Areas*.

77.   Ibid.

78.   Ibid.

79.   Ibid.

80.   Ibid.

81.   Ibid.

82.   Ibid.

83.   Thrasher and Turner, *School Size Does Make a Difference*; Charles W. Bernhardt, "The Effect of Per Pupil Expenditure and High School Size Upon Academic Success in College" (Ph.D. dissertation, Ball State University, 1968); J. R. Bertrand, "Relation Between Enrollment of High School from which Students Graduated and Academic Achievement of Agriculture Students at Texas A&M," *Journal of Experimental Education*, vol. 25, pp. 59-69; F. A. Burger, *Cultural Forces and Academic Success in College Freshmen*, Bulletin of the Bureau of School Services (Lexington, Ky.: University of Kentucky, 1960), vol. 33, no. 1 (September); D. P. Hoyt, "Size of High School and College Grades," *Personnel and Guidance Journal*, vol. 37, pp. 569-73; I. I. Lathrop, "Scholastic Achievement at Iowa State College Associated with High School Size and Course Pattern," *Journal of Experimental Education*, vol. 29, pp. 37-48.

84.   J. C. Bledore, "An Analysis of the Relationship of Size of High School to Marks Received by Graduates in the First Year of College," *Journal of Educational Sociology*, vol. 26, pp. 414-18; L. H. Thomberg, "College Scholarships and Size of High School," *School and Society*, vol. 20, pp. 189-92.

85.   P. S. Droyer, "Some Suggestions Concerning the Relationship Existing Between Size of High School Attended and Success in College," *Journal of Education Research*, vol. 32, pp. 271-80.

86.   H. F. Garratt, "A Review and Interpretation of Investigations of Factors Related to Scholastic Success in Colleges of Agriculture and Science and Teachers' Colleges," *Journal of Experimental Education*, vol. 18, pp. 91-138.

87.   Krietlow, *Long Term Study of Educational Effectiveness of Newly Formed Centralized School Districts in Rural Areas*.

88.   William H. Sewell and Arthur O. Haller, "Educational and Occupational Perspectives of Farm and Rural Youth," in *Rural Youth in Crisis: Facts, Myths and Social Change*, Lee Burchinal, ed. (Washington, D.C.: Government Printing Office, 1964), pp. 149-72.

89.   Ibid.

90.   Roger G. Barker and Paul V. Gump, *Big School, Small School*

(Stanford, Calif.: Stanford University Press, 1964).
91. Ibid., p. 196.
92. Ibid., p. 196.
93. Ibid., p. 197.
94. Ibid., p. 152.
95. Weaver, "The Case Against the Preston County Comprehensive Facilities Plan for Consolidating the Schools."
96. Coleman, *Equality of Educational Opportunity.*
97. Ibid.
98. Barker and Gump, *Big School, Small School.*
99. Ibid., p. 169.
100. Ibid., p. 157.
101. Weaver, "The Case Against the Preston County Comprehensive Facilities Plan for Consolidating the Schools."
102. Gerald J. Kluempke, "The Emerging Role of the Regional Service Center in Rural Areas," *Proceedings of the Second National Conference of NFIRE* (Las Cruces, N.M.: ERIC/CRESS, 1974), p. 9.
103. Callahan, *Education and the Cult of Efficiency.*
104. Quoted in Elinor Ostrom, "On Righteousness, Evidence and Reform: The Police Story," *Urban Affairs Quarterly*, vol. 4, no. 4 (June 1975), p. 466.
105. Callahan, *Education and the Cult of Efficiency.*
106. Tyack, *The System.* The quotation Tyack uses here is from Ellwood P. Cubberley, *Rural Life and Education: A Study of the Rural School Problem as a Phase of the Rural Life Problem* (Boston, Mass.: Houghton Mifflin, 1916).
107. Ostrom, "On Righteousness, Evidence and Reform: The Police Story," p. 467.
108. Barker and Gump, *Big School, Small School.*
109. Ibid.
110. David Cohen and Michael Garet, "Reforming Educational Policy with Applied Research," *Harvard Educational Review*, vol. 45, no. 1 (February 1975), pp. 17-43. See particularly pp. 40-43.

Chapter 3

1. Dennis Farney, "As a Tiny Rural School Nears End of Line, Feelings are Mixed," *Wall Street Journal*, May 8, 1970.
2. Great Plains School District Organization Project, *Report Card,*

Great Plains Study, State of Nebraska (1968).

3. *New Land Review* (Summer 1975), p. 10.

4. Ibid., p. 11.

5. Ibid., p. 11.

6. Ibid., p. 11.

7. Julia Weber Gordon, *My Country School Diary* (New York: Dell Publishing Co., 1946), p. xiv.

8. Sher and Tompkins present the conflicting evidence in Chapter 2 of this book.

9. Massachusetts State Department of Education, *Research and Development Bulletin*, 1973.

10. Joel Spring, *The Sorting Machine* (New York: McKay, 1976); see also Martin Carnoy, ed., *Schooling in a Corporate Society* (New York: McKay, 1972).

11. George Herbert Betts, *New Ideals in Rural Schools* (Boston, Mass.: Houghton Mifflin, 1913), pp. 5-6.

12. Jim Hightower, Susan DeMarco, et al., *Hard Tomatoes, Hard Times* (Cambridge, Mass.: Schenkman, 1974).

13. Nels Ackerson, "Rural Youth in a Changing World," speech presented to the National Outlook Conference on Rural Youth, October 1967, Washington, D.C.

14. Ellwood P. Cubberley, *Rural Life and Education* (Boston, Mass.: Houghton Mifflin, 1914), pp. 84-85.

15. Homer Seerley, *The Country School* (New York: Charles Scribner's Sons, 1913), p. 11.

16. See, for example, the work of David Tyack, George Betts, or Clifton Johnson.

17. Clifton Johnson, *The Country School* (New York: Thomas Y. Crowell & Co., 1907), p. 93.

18. Ibid., pp. 143-45.

19. Seerley, *The Country School*, p. 35.

20. *Thirteenth Annual Vermont School Report*, 1869.

21. Charles D. Lewis, *The Rural Community and its Schools* (New York: American Book Company, 1937), p. 281.

22. Betts, *New Ideals*, p. 98.

23. Johnson, *The Country School*, p. 51.

24. Betts, *New Ideals*, pp. 25-26.

25. Lewis, *The Rural Community*, pp. 57-58.

26. David Tyack, *The One Best System* (Cambridge, Mass.: Harvard University Press, 1974).

27. Lewis, *The Rural Community*, pp. 26-27.

28. For an account of this process, see Tyack, *The One Best System*, p. 185ff.

29. National School Boards Association Research Report, *The People Look at their School Boards*, no. 1, 1975, p. 33.

30. Ibid., p. 34.

31. Ivan D. Muse, Robert J. Parsons, and Edward M. Hoppe, "A Study of Rural Teachers and the Rural Schools as Perceived by School Administrators, Teachers, Parents, and Students" (Salt Lake City, Utah: Brigham Young University, 1975), p. 31.

32. Ibid., p. 16.

33. National Education Association, *The County Superintendent of Schools in the United States, 1950* (1950), p. 149.

34. Muse et al., "A Study of Rural Teachers," p. 34.

35. Ibid., p. 16.

36. Gertrude McPherson, *Small Town Teacher* (Cambridge, Mass.: Harvard University Press, 1972), pp. 130-131.

37. Muse et al., "A Study of Rural Teachers," pp. 22-23.

38. Jonathan Sher, "The Current Status of Rural Education," an overview prepared for the Office of the Assistant Secretary of Education, HEW (1976), pp. 1-2.

39. For a characteristic example of this type of research, see Paul Ford, "Small High Schools: Myth, Reality, Potential," *The Bulletin of the National Association of Secondary School Principals*, vol. 51, no. 317 (March 1967), pp. 89-95. This article is discussed in part in this chapter.

40. J. A. Coleman et al., *Youth: Transition to Adulthood*, Report of the Panel on Youth of the President's Science Advisory Committee (Chicago, Ill.: University of Chicago Press, 1974); see also B. F. Brown et al., *The Reform of Secondary Education: A Report to the Public and the Profession*, National Commission on the Reform of Secondary Education (New York: McGraw-Hill, 1973).

41. Susan Abramowitz, "The Effects of Mini-School Size on the Organization and Management of Instruction," paper presented at the Annual Meeting of the American Educational Research Association, San Francisco, Calif., April 19-23, 1976, p. 24.

42. D. Katz, "Morale and Motivation in Industry," in W. Dennis, ed., *Current Trends in Industrial Psychology* (Pittsburgh, Pa.: University of Pittsburgh Press, 1949), pp. 145-71.

43. D. Betz, "The Effect of Organization Size Upon Normative

Diversity," *Social Science Quarterly* 53 (1972): 984-90.
44. R. G. Barker and L. S. Barker, "Behavior Units for the Comparative Study of Culture," in B. Kaplan, ed., *Studying Personality Cross-Culturally* (New York: Harper & Row, 1961), pp. 457-76; Kelley and Thibaut, "Experimental Studies of Group Problem Solving and Process," in G. Lindzey, ed., *Handbook of Social Psychology* (Cambridge, Mass.: Addison-Wesley, 1954), pp. 735-85; R. F. Bales and E. F. Borgatta, "Size of Group as a Factor in the Interaction Profile," in A. Hare, E. Borgatta, and R. Bales, eds., *Small Groups: Studies in Social Interaction* (New York: Knopf, 1955), pp. 396-413.
45. Suzanne K. Stemnock, *Summary of Research on Size of Schools and School Districts* (Washington, D.C.: Educational Research Service, Inc., 1974), p. 7.
46. Ibid., p. 6.
47. R. G. Barker and P. Gump, *Big School, Small School* (Stanford, Calif.: Stanford University Press, 1964).
48. Leonard Baird, "Big School, Small School: A Critical Examination of the Hypothesis," *Journal of Educational Psychology*, vol. 60, no. 4, pt. I, p. 259.
49. Farney, "As a Tiny Rural School Nears End of Line."
50. Stemnock, *Summary of Research on Size*, p. 9.
51. E. Rogers and L. Svenning, "The Dilemma of Small Schools" (mimeographed), 1972, pp. 2-3.
52. McPherson, *Small Town Teacher*, p. 89.
53. R. Rosenthal and L. Jackson, *Pygmalion in the Classroom* (New York: Holt, Rinehart and Winston, 1968).
54. Muse et al., "A Study of Rural Teachers," p. 30.
55. Rogers and Svenning, "The Dilemma of Small Schools," pp. 1-9.
56. Ford, "Small High Schools," p. 91.
57. Muse et al., "A Study of Rural Teachers," p. 27.
58. Ford, "Small High Schools," p. 93.
59. For evidence of this trend, see Rogers and Svenning, "The Dilemma of Small Schools."
60. Muse et al., "A Study of Rural Teachers," p. 3.
61. Rogers and Svenning, "The Dilemma of Small Schools," pp. 3-9.
62. Muse et al., "A Study of Rural Teachers," p. 25.
63. Tyack, *The One Best System*, p. 20.
64. Ford, "Small High Schools," p. 91.

65. Farney, "As a Tiny Rural School Nears End of Line."

66. Ford, "Small High Schools," pp. 90-91.

67. For evidence that this is the case, see Lewis Tamblyn, "What is Happening in Rural Education Today: A Status Report," and "The Future of the Rural and Small School," papers presented at the Rural Education Conference, Southern Illinois University, April 24-25, 1975.

68. Muse et al., "A Study of Rural Teachers," app. p. 4.

69. Ford, "Small High Schools," p. 93.

70. Roscoe Buckland, ed., *Rural School Improvement Project Report* (Lexington, Ky.: Transylvania Printing Co., 1958). Evidence that this is happening is derived from the most recent U.S. Census statistics. It was also the subject of a recent *Time Magazine* cover story.

71. Roscoe Buckland, ed., *Rural School Improvement Project Report*, p. i.

72. Ibid., p. 109.

73. Ibid., p. 96.

74. Stephen Fitzsimmons et al., *Rural America: A Social and Educational History of Ten Communities (Vol. I)* (Cambridge, Mass.: Abt Associates, 1975), p. 79.

75. *Promising Practices in Small High Schools* (Portland, Ore.: Northwest Regional Educational Laboratory, 1971).

76. Experimental Schools Project Report, pp. 602-625.

77. "The Old Open Classroom: Claire Oglesby's 'Magic' Works," *The Common*, vol. 1, no. 2 (March 1973).

78. Cubberley, *Rural Life and Education*, p. 113.

79. Muse et al., "A Study of Rural Teachers," p. 9.

80. Buckland, *Rural School Improvement Project Report*, p. 79.

81. *Promising Practices in Small High Schools*, p. 26.

82. Ibid., p. 28.

83. Ibid., pp. 11-13.

84. For examples in preschool education, see *Promising Practices in Early Childhood Education* or *The Annual Reports of the Appalachian Educational Laboratory, 1971-73* (Charleston, W. Va.: Appalachian Regional Educational Laboratory).

85. Peter Schrag, *Voices in the Classroom* (Boston, Mass.: Beacon Press, 1965), p. 140.

86. Stanton Leggett, Arthur Shapiro, Aaron Cohodes, and C. W. Brubaker, "The Case for a Small High School," *Nation's Schools*, vol. 86, no. 3 (September 1970), p. 45.

87. *Promising Practices in Small High Schools*, p. 13.

88.   Robert Rotberg, "Education," *New York Times*, June 3, 1976.
89.   Schrag, *Voices in the Classroom*, p. 46.

Chapter 4

1.   See David Tyack, *The One Best System* (Cambridge, Mass.: Harvard University Press, 1974), and John E. Coons et al., *Private Wealth and Public Education* (Cambridge, Mass.: Harvard University Press, 1970) for summary discussions of early history. The best historical source on rural finance policy in this period is Ellwood P. Cubberley, *School Funds and Their Apportionment* (New York: Columbia Teachers College, 1905).
2.   Cubberley again is the best source of information on early state grant programs. He, in fact, argued for equalization through state funding.
3.   George D. Strayer and R. M. Haig, *Financing of Education in the State of New York* (New York: Macmillan Co., 1923). This particular foundation concept has been called the Strayer-Haig Plan.
4.   C. S. Benson, *The Economics of Public Education* (Boston, Mass.: Houghton Mifflin, 1961).
5.   C. S. Benson, *The Cheerful Prospect: A Statement on the Future of Public Education* (Boston, Mass.: Houghton Mifflin, 1965); see also Coons et al., *Private Wealth*.
6.   Coons et al., *Private Wealth*.
7.   For example, *Serrano vs. Priest*, 5 Cal. 3d 584 (1971); *Van Dusartz vs. Hatfield*, Oct. 1971; and *San Antonio Independent School District et al. vs. Rodriguez et al.*, 1973.
8.   *San Antonio vs. Rodriguez*, ibid.
9.   Ibid.
10.   Urban Institute, *Public School Finance: Present Disparities and Fiscal Alternatives*, vol. 1, a report prepared for the President's Commission on School Finance, chapter 5, pp. 245-70.
11.   Ibid.
12.   Clifford I. Hooker and Van D. Mueller, *The Relationship of School District Reorganization to State Aid Distribution Systems*, National Education Finance Project Special Study Eleven (Minneapolis, Minn.: Educational Research and Development Council of the Twin Cities Metropolitan Area, Inc., 1970).
13.   Ibid.

14. "Financing Connecticut Schools," Final Report of the Commission to Study School Finance and Equal Educational Opportunity (January 1975).
15. John J. Callahan and William H. Wilken, eds., *School Finance Reform: A Legislator's Handbook* (Washington, D.C.: National Conference of State Legislatures, 1976), chapter 1.
16. The whole procedure of school finance reform has really been a leveling up of poorer districts. Rich districts have been maintained at existing levels of support so that they did not lose money.
17. Callahan and Wilken, *School Finance Reform.*
18. Ibid. States were able to lower property taxes without increasing state taxes because of budget surpluses from an expanding income and sales tax base during inflationary years and federal revenue sharing.
19. See *Ohio's New Plan of State Aid: Will it Meet the Challenge?* (Cleveland, Ohio: Citizens Council for Ohio Schools, 1975). The plan was enacted in Am. Sub. SB 170, Ohio General Assembly.
20. Robert O. Bothwell et al., "Geographic Adjustments to School Aid Formulae," in Callahan and Wilken, eds., *School Finance Reform.*
21. Ibid., pp. 29-42.
22. Bruce Gensemer, "Personal Income Variations Among Ohio School Districts and Their Implications for the Guaranteed-Yield Formula," Preliminary Report to the Education Review Committee, Ohio General Assembly, June 25, 1976. (Permission has been granted by the author to quote from this article.)
23. Ibid., p. 2.
24. Bothwell, "Geographic Adjustments to School Aid Formulae," p. 35.
25. John Callahan, William H. Wilken, and M. Tracy Sallerman, *Urban Schools and School Finance Reform: Promise and Reality* (Washington, D.C.: The National Urban Coalition, 1973). This is a good summary view of urban costs and the effect of state aid systems on them.
26. Roe J. Johns, "The Cost of Delivering Equivalent Educational Services," in K. Forbes Jordan and Kern Alexander, eds., *Future in School Finance: Working Toward a Common Goal* (Gainesville, Fla.: National Educational Finance Project, 1975), pp. 86-100.
27. Ibid., pp. 94-95.
28. Ibid., pp. 92-93.
29. See W. Norton Grubb, "Cost of Education Indices: Issues and

Methods," *School Finance Reform: A Legislator's Handbook*, pp. 87-93, for a good discussion of the considerations necessary in developing a formula.

30.   U.S. Bureau of the Census, *General Social and Economic Statistics*, Census of the Population, 1970; Final Report PC(1)-C1; U.S. Summary (Washington, D.C.: U.S. Government Printing Office, 1972), Table 88, p. 386.

31.   Ibid. See also J. Alan Thomas, *Financing Rural Education* (Austin, Texas: National Educational Laboratory Publishers, 1974).

32.   Joel S. Berke, *Answers to Inequity* (Berkeley, Calif.: McCutchan Publishing Corp., 1974), p. 95.

33.   Ibid., p. 95.

34.   U.S. Bureau of the Census, 1972, pp. 398-401.

35.   National Center for Education Statistics, *Bond Sales for Public School Purposes, 1973-74* (Washington, D.C.: U.S. Department of Health, Education, and Welfare).

36.   Roe J. Johns and Kern Alexander, *Alternative Programs for Financing Education* (Gainesville, Fla.: National Educational Finance Project, 1971), p. 149.

37.   Lawrence C. Pierce et al., *State School Finance Alternatives* (Eugene, Ore.: Center for Educational Policy and Management, University of Oregon, May 1975), p. 89.

38.   Ibid., p. 87.

39.   Ibid., p. 89.

40.   Ibid.

41.   Edward Fabian et al., *School District Organization Report* (Montpelier, Vt.: State Department of Education, 1975).

42.   Callahan and Wilken, *School Finance Reform*.

43.   Ibid.

44.   Gilbert Steiner, in a forthcoming Brookings publication on national policy for children, espouses this view and uses the phrase "unlucky children."

45.   See U.S. Congress (Senate) Committee on Agriculture and Forestry, Subcommittee on Rural Development, *HEW Programs for Rural America* (Washington, D.C.: U.S. Government Printing Office, 1975), pp. 39-61. Nonmetro areas serve one-third of the nation's schoolchildren and yet receive 11 percent of library and materials funds, 13 percent of basic vocational aid, and 13 percent of dropout prevention funds.

46.   Three sources are useful in understanding capital costs. For

traditional analysis of capital costs, see Roe L. Johns and Edgar L. Morphet, *The Economics and Financing of Education*, 2d ed. (Englewood Cliffs, N.J.: Prentice-Hall, 1969), pp. 376–406, and W. Monfort Barr, *Financing Public Elementary and Secondary School Facilities in the US*, Study No. 7 (Gainesville, Fla.: National Educational Finance Project, 1971). For current analysis in a particular state, see Lawrence Pierce et al., *State School Finance Alternatives* (Eugene, Ore.: University of Oregon, Center for Educational Policy and Management, 1975).

Chapter 5

1. James West, *Plainville, U.S.A.* (New York: Columbia University Press, 1945), p. 115.

2. Arthur J. Vidich and Joseph Bensman, *Small Town in Mass Society: Class, Power, and Religion in a Rural Community* (Princeton, N.J.: Princeton University Press, 1958), p. 40.

3. David B. Tyack, *The One Best System: A History of American Urban Education* (Cambridge, Mass.: Harvard University Press, 1974); also see Chapter 1.

4. See Chapter 2.

5. Work on this study began in May 1975. The analysis has been in progress since then. Dr. Weaver was invited into the Preston County case in Spring 1975 as a voluntary advisor to a group of citizens who were concerned about the school board's plan to consolidate. His role in assisting the citizens group, known as Equality for All Prestonians (EAP), has been to help organize data, link EAP to outside resources, and act as a technical consultant and on occasion as spokesman at school board meetings. Dr. Weaver wishes to stress the research contained herein is not simply the result of his own work. Volunteers from EAP have worked long hours to gather and organize materials. The school board and superintendent have also cooperated in providing materials when requested. Thus, whatever the merits of this work, Dr. Weaver wishes to credit the people of Preston County, West Virginia.

6. Population figures are taken from the *Comprehensive Facilities Plan* (Kingwood, W. Va.: Preston County Board of Education, 1975). Telephone listings are taken from the 1975-76 directories published by the five telephone companies serving Preston County. Listings include businesses (small and large retail, wholesale, insurance,

finance, manufacturing, distributors, etc.), governmental (federal, state, and local, schools, fire departments, police departments, water and sewerage, etc.); professional (physicians, lawyers, accountants, social workers, and ministers) and other nonresidential; e.g., churches, fraternal orders. The count of listings was made strictly by location. That is, if an insurance business was located at a Kingwood address, but included in the Tunnelton directory, it was counted once for Kingwood but not for Tunnelton. The same applies to professional listings; a place of business was counted once. It turns out that all doctors and lawyers whose businesses are located in a community (mostly Kingwood) also live in that community. The same cannot, however, automatically be said for other professional employees such as teachers and nurses. Although the County Courthouse obviously adds to the listing in Kingwood, the bulk of the 283 listings are business and professional, far exceeding any other community in the county.

7.   *Comprehensive Facilities Plan*, p. B-17.

8.   Howard B. Allen and Robert D. Baldwin, "Preston County's Secondary Schools: Problems, Prospects, and Program for Progress," a report to the Preston County Board of Education, Kingwood, W. Va., 1965.

9.   Masters Enterprises, *Project DAVE*, a report to the Preston County Board of Education, Kingwood, W. Va., 1968.

10.   M. J. Conrad, George Fisher, and Don Partridge, "A Plan to Equalize Educational Opportunity and Improve Educational Facilities: A Report to the Preston County Board of Education" (Columbus, Ohio: Ohio State University, 1971).

11.   The state superintendent and state board of education, in the case of Preston County, approved the county's plan on June 13, 1975, although Preston County was unable to pass a bond issue in three attempts. Evidently, the state's chief school officer and state board members interpreted the intent of the law broadly with regard to matching funds. The state board approved funds for Preston County contingent upon the county's stated plan to present another bond in the future.

12.   Cases in point are Etam, Horse Shoe Run, and Eglon, all of which were adversely affected by all three bond issues, and all of which opposed it. Albright is also instructive. The September 18, 1973, bond proposal would have placed the nearest high school, which was at Kingwood, several miles further away by relocating it

in the Valley District. The Albright vote was 20 percent for the September 18, 1973, bond. When the switch back to Kingwood High was proposed in the October 8, 1974, bond, the Albright vote for the bond rose to 47.62 percent. The same thing is found in the Pleasant District vote, whose residents were also adversely affected in the plan to relocate Kingwood High School in Valley District. Residents of Pleasant District attended Kingwood High School and would have had to travel further to attend once the school was relocated in Valley District. A further example occurred, this time at the elementary level. When the Tunnelton, Newburg, and Fellowsville elementary was shifted from near Tunnelton to a location in or near Fellowsville, the Fellowsville precinct vote rose from 41.54 percent to 57.32 percent. The Evansville precinct, nearby, also rose for the same reason from 54.72 percent to 68.63 percent (that is, children in Evansville would be closer to the new elementary school).

13. The group is represented by counsel, has filed a petition with the West Virginia State Department of Education, and has been represented at a special West Virginia Department of Education hearing on the Preston County matter. The effects of the group on voting results is evident between October 8, 1974, and November 23, 1974. The results of organized opposition are particularly evident in Union and Reno Districts voting patterns.

14. The combined space eliminated by the plan in Phase I is approximately 60,350 square feet. The plan calls for approximately 83,500 square feet of new construction or a net gain of 23,150 square feet. Most of the net gain is found in the Terra Alta gymnasium and vo-ag building, which at present contains 4,800 square feet (according to Masters Enterprises), but will be replaced with 31,694 square feet of new construction. The plan overall replaces 35,500 square feet of elementary space with 51,806 square feet of new construction most of which is found in one building, the new Kingwood elementary.

15. *Comprehensive Facilities Plan.*

16. Ibid.

17. Ibid.

18. Ibid.

19. Ibid.

20. Allen and Baldwin, "Preston County's Secondary Schools."

21. Yao-Chi Tu and Luther Tweeten, "The Impact of Busing on Student Achievement," in *Growth and Change*, vol. 4, no. 4 (October 1973).

22.   Ibid.
23.   Summers and Wolfe, "Which School Resources Help Learning?" (Philadelphia, Pa.: Federal Reserve Bank, 1975), p. 8.
24.   *Comprehensive Facilities Plan.*
25.   *Directions for Educational Development in Appalachia: Report of an Educational Needs and Feasibility Study Involving the Appalachian Areas of Six States* (Charleston, W. Va.: Appalachian Educational Laboratory, November 1971). See page 54.
26.   *Update on Education: A Digest of the National Assessment of Educational Progress* (Denver, Colo.: Education Commission of the States, 1975).
27.   Masters Enterprises, *Project DAVE.*
28.   *Directions for Educational Development in Appalachia.*
29.   This quote is from Justice Powell's Opinion in *San Antonio School District et al., Appellants, vs. Demetrio P. Rodriguez et al., On Appeal from the United States District Court for the Western District of Texas, March 21, 1973.*
30.   In Preston County, the rule of thumb turned out to be that a reduction of eight high schools with 1,941 students to three schools with the same number of students yielded a net gain of approximately five teachers while providing no advantages in course offerings. However, because of the state aid formula in West Virginia, staffing costs are not significantly different between the two plans. Estimates were that each new teacher hired under this plan would cost the local district only about $850 per year.
31.   The studies are too numerous to list here but especially important are Summers and Wolfe, "Which School Resources Help Learning?" and James S. Coleman et al., "Equality of Educational Opportunity" (Health, Education, and Welfare, Office of Education, 38001, 1966). (Coleman found size of 12th grade to be negatively correlated with verbal achievement; each 200 students associated with a decline of one-fifth grade level in achievement. Summers and Wolfe found that each increase of 300 students in school size decreased minority achievement by 3.5 months.) More recently Christopher Jencks and Marsha Brown examined the effects of school inputs on cognitive growth and found them to be small. See Jencks and Brown, "Effects of High Schools on their Students," *Harvard Education Review,* vol. 45, no. 3 (August 1975). Especially important to this study is Richard Raymond's research, discussed in detail in this section, which shows negative relationships between

school size and college achievement.

32. See Chapter 2.
33. *San Antonio vs. Rodriguez.*
34. Roger G. Barker and Paul V. Gump, *Big School, Small School* (Stanford, Calif.: Stanford University Press, 1964).
35. *Bartlett vs. White Pine School District.*
36. Ibid.
37. Ibid.
38. Richard Raymond, "Determinants of Primary and Secondary Education in West Virginia," *Journal of Human Resources*, vol. 3, no. 4 (Fall 1968), pp. 450-70.
39. Ibid.
40. Ibid.
41. Ibid.
42. Tyack, *The One Best System.*
43. *Preston County News*, Editorial, May 4, 1976.
44. *Preston County News*, March 18, 1976.
45. *Preston County News*, April 20, 1976.
46. *Preston County News*, March 18, 1976.
47. Tyack, *The One Best System.*
48. Among other things the achievement ideology stresses the importance of doing well academically, taking subjects, scoring well on tests; that is, things that are recognized as legitimate by the educational profession. The mere fact that some cannot, or choose not to, do well in this sense serves to strengthen and perpetuate the importance of big schools. These are values that are important to the middle class because they serve to distinguish those who possess them from others. Since the middle class cannot ever hope to penetrate the highest class structure (whose criteria for membership is inherited wealth), its establishment of identity in this manner is crucial, and it must depend, in a sense, on the existence of a lower class.
49. The drive is for a system *efficiently* operated by professionals who know best. The "moneysworth" argument was often used in Preston County, and in many respects was (at least overtly) the most important one. However, it is clear from the evidence that those making this argument were economically uninformed. The economic argument was simply not a relevant argument in Preston County for several reasons. First, no one, except outside consultants, ever seriously believed the one high school concept was feasible due to the geography of the area. Thus, most of the consolidation plans would

not have enlarged school size enough to have effected any major gains in economic efficiency or administrative efficiency. Any gains that were obvious were more than offset by much higher transportation costs. For instance, our analysis showed that reducing eight high schools to three, as compared to a reduction of eight to seven, produced a net savings of only five teaching positions. Furthermore, the board's own estimate of total net savings in administrative and maintenance costs almost exactly equaled its estimate of increased transportation costs. Another factor is the state's school aid formula which entitles Preston County to at least twenty-one additional "incentive" teachers—teachers fully supported by the state rather than local funds. Given these factors, the economic consideration was minimal, yet a spokesman for consolidation argued at a state meeting: "The five high school plan offers *major* economic advantages." (*Preston County News*, April 8, 1975) Although major economic advantages were attributed to the board's plan, careful scrutiny did not reveal any.

Chapter 6

1.   See Edward Fabian et al., *Vermont School District Organization Report* (Montpelier, Vt.: State Department of Education, May 1975).

2.   Leonard Tashman, Chairman, *The Report of the Governor's Panel on State Aid to Education* (Montpelier, Vt.: State of Vermont, January 1975).

3.   L. L. Ecker-Racz, *Alternatives to Strengthen Vermont's Schools*, a Joint Project of the National Education Association and the Vermont Education Association, September 1973.

4.   Temporary Advisory Commission, *Report to the 1968 General Assembly of the State of Vermont* (Montpelier, Vt.: State of Vermont, December 31, 1967).

5.   Arthur D. Little, Inc., *A Study of the State Department of Education*, a report to the Commissioner of the State Board of Education, C-68305, April 1967.

6.   Tri-partite Committee on School District Reorganization, *Task Force Report*, jointly sponsored by Vermont Education Association and the Vermont Superintendents Association (Montpelier, Vt.: State of Vermont, 1964).

7.   Educational Task Force, *Report to the Governor* (Montpelier, Vt.:

State of Vermont, October 1963).

8. Carnegie Commission Report, *Report of the Commission to Investigate the Educational System and Conditions of Vermont* (Brattleboro, Vt.: Vermont Printing Co., 1914).

9. Ibid., p. 39.

10. Mason Stone, *History of Education: State of Vermont* (Montpelier, Vt.: Capital City Press, 1935), p. 340.

11. Vermont Commission on Country Life, *Rural Vermont: A Program for the Future* (Burlington, Vt.: Free Press Printing Co., 1931).

12. Vermont State Education Commission, *Vermont's System of Education* (Brattleboro, Vt.: Vermont Printing Co., 1934), p. 23.

13. Ibid., p. 26.

14. *Eighteenth Vermont Biennial Report, 1950* (Montpelier, Vt.: State of Vermont, December 1, 1947), p. 58.

15. *Report of the Commission to Study Supervision of Schools* (Montpelier, Vt.: State of Vermont, 1954).

16. Edgar Flinton, "Adequacy of the Socio-Economic Community as the Local School District in Vermont" (Ph.D. dissertation, Harvard University, 1952).

17. Educational Task Force, *Report to the Governor*, 1963, Appendix 1.

18. Tashman, *Report of the Governor's Panel on State Aid to Education*, p. 65.

19. *Montpelier Times-Argus*, August 1, 1974.

20. Ibid.

21. Ibid., May 1, 1974.

22. Fabian et al., *Vermont School District Reorganization Report*, p. 18.

23. Jonathan P. Sher and Rachel B. Tompkins, "Economy, Efficiency, and Equality: The Myths of Rural School and District Consolidation" (Washington, D.C.: National Institute of Education, July 1976), p. 29.

24. Burton Krietlow, *Long Term Study of Educational Effectiveness of Newly Formed Centralized School Districts in Rural Areas*, Reports 1, 2, 3 (Madison, Wis.: University of Wisconsin, 1962, 1966, 1971).

25. Margaret E. Goertz, *Evaluating Vermont's System of Education and a Plan for Equalizing State and Local Education Finance Programs* (Washington, D.C.: Education Policy Research Institute, December 1976), p. 2.

26. Fabian, *Vermont School District Reorganization Report*, pp. 34-35.

27. *White River Valley Herald* (Randolph, Vt.), December 1975.

28. The interviews for this chapter were taped during 1975-76. The

participants were: *Ethan Allen—Supervisory Union #10:* superintendent, principal, head guidance counselor, five senior high teachers, three students, chairman of Union School Board, business manager; *Maple Union—Supervisory Union #20:* superintendent, principal, guidance counselor, one teacher, three students, member of Union School Board; *Dewey Union—Supervisory Union #30:* superintendent, principal of high school, principal of one elementary school, business manager, guidance counselor, member of Union School Board, social psychology class, one teacher; *Village High School—Supervisory Union #40:* superintendent, guidance counselor, five teachers, four students, principal (not taped); *State personnel and other educators:* two members of State Board of Education, commissioner of education, retired commissioner of education, member of Senate Education Committee, director of Vermont Education Association (VEA), associate director of VEA, director of Vermont State School Directors Association, director of state administrative services, superintendent's liaison to state, state director of elementary and secondary education, two superintendents of other districts, principal of small high school (nonunion), former school directors of Supervisory Union #30, shared resource teacher, former superintendent of Supervisory Union #30 (not taped).

29. Fabian et al., *Vermont School District Reorganization Report*, p. 32.
30. Ibid., p. 33.
31. Clifford Hooker and Van D. Mueller, *The Relationship of School District Reorganization to State Aid Distribution Systems*, Special Study Eleven, National Education Finance Project, Part III, 1970, pp. 126-34.
32. Roger G. Barker and Paul V. Gump, *Big School, Small School* (Stanford, Calif.: Stanford University Press, 1964).
33. Ted Bradshaw, Charlotte Hanna, and Steven Hochschlid, *Post-Secondary Education Access Study* (Montpelier, Vt.: September 1974).
34. Ibid., p. 19.
35. Ibid., p. 21.

Chapter 7

1. See U.S. Congress (Senate) Committee on Agriculture and Forestry, Subcommittee on Rural Development, *HEW Programs for*

Rural America (Washington, D.C.: U.S. Government Printing Office, 1975), pp. 39-61.

Chapter 8

1. The definition of "rural" used here encompasses all individuals living outside of established Standard Metropolitan Statistical Areas (SMSAs) on farms, in the open countryside, or in places with less than 10,000 residents. Census figures reveal that this included 13,836 places and 49,411,743 people in 1970. Other definitions of "rural" (discussed in note 6) significantly alter both the magnitude and composition of this population. Though all such definitions are imprecise and suggestive rather than universal and absolute, the one delineated above is the reference point for the discussions about "rural" or "nonmetropolitan" problems in this chapter. [Source: U.S. Census Bureau, *Characteristics of the Population* (Washington, D.C.: U.S. Government Printing Office, 1970), vol. 1.]

    Nationally, the 14-18-year-old cohort (inclusive) composed 9.25 percent of the total U.S. population. If this approximation is applied to the rural population under discussion here (49,411,743), the figure 4,570,586 becomes a reasonable estimate for the total number of rural youth (14-18). [Source: U.S. Census Bureau, *Characteristics of the Population*, vol. 1, tables 4, 5, 17.]

2. Historically, voluntary rural-to-urban migrants (both in the U.S. and internationally) have tended to be more intelligent and more flexible than the norm for the population in their communities of origin. Recent evidence about U.S. rural outmigration indicates conformity to this pattern. For instance, in discussing selectivity in the migration process, Rieger states:

> Still, the gist of much of the literature is that migrants tend to be superior to non-migrants in those characteristics associated with occupational success: for example, they may be somewhat more intelligent and better educated, come from higher socio-economic backgrounds, and exhibit greater achievement orientation than the non-migrants.

The literature on this topic includes: Jon H. Rieger, "Geographic Mobility and the Occupational Attainment of Rural Youth: A

Longitudinal Evaluation," *Rural Sociology,* vol. 37 (June 1972); Harry Schwarzweller and J. Brown, "Social Class Origins, Rural-Urban Migration, and Life Chances," *Rural Sociology,* vol. 32 (March 1967); Parker W. Maulden, "Selective Migration from Small Towns," *American Sociological Review,* vol. 5 (October 1940); Noel P. Gist and C. D. Clark, "Intelligence as a Selective Factor in Rural-Urban Migrations," *American Journal of Sociology,* vol. 44 (July 1938); Peter M. Blau and Otis Dudley Duncan, *The American Occupational Structure* (New York: John Wiley & Sons, 1967).

3.   For further information on causes, consequences, and patterns of recent rural outmigration, see: James S. Brown and George A. Hillery, "The Great Migration, 1940-1960," in *The Southern Appalachian Region: A Survey,* Thomas Ford, ed. (Lexington, Ky.: University of Kentucky Press, 1962); N. M. Hansen, *Rural Poverty and the Urban Crisis: A Strategy for Rural Development* (Bloomington, Ind.: Indiana University Press, 1971); President's National Advisory Commission on Rural Poverty, *The People Left Behind* (Washington, D.C.: U.S. Government Printing Office, 1967); Okon Uya, "Black Migrations: A Bibliographical Essay," *Current Bibliography on African Affairs,* vol. 5 (1972); U.S. Congress, Senate, Committee on Agriculture and Forestry, *Characteristics of U.S. Rural Areas with Noncommuting Population* (Washington, D.C.: U.S. Government Printing Office, 1972); Lloyd Bacon, "Poverty Among Interregional Rural-to-Urban Migrants," *Rural Sociology,* vol. 36 (June 1971); Calvin Goldscheider, *Population, Modernization, and Social Structure* (Boston, Mass.: Little, Brown and Co., 1971); Jon H. Rieger, "Geographic Mobility and the Occupational Attainment of Rural Youth: A Longitudinal Evaluation," *Rural Sociology,* vol. 37 (June 1972); Calvin L. Beale, "Rural-Urban Migration of Blacks: Past and Future," American Agriculture Economics Association Meeting, December 1970; Gladys K. Bowles, "A Profile of the Incidence of Poverty Among Rural-Urban Migrants and Comparative Populations," Rural Sociological Society Meeting, August 1970.

4.   U.S. Census Bureau, *Characteristics of the Population,* vol. 1, pt. 1: "Number of Inhabitants—United States Summary" (Washington, D.C.: U.S. Government Printing Office, 1973).

5.   The figures for the growth of the United States as a whole (see ibid.) are given in Table N1.

TABLE N1

GROWTH OF THE UNITED STATES,
1790-1970

Year	Millions	% Growth	Year	Millions	% Growth
1790	3.9	--	1890	63.0	25.5
1800	5.3	35.1	1900	76.2	21.0
1810	7.2	36.4	1910	92.2	21.0
1820	9.6	33.1	1920	106.0	15.0
1830	12.9	33.5	1930	123.2	16.2
1840	17.1	32.7	1940	132.2	7.3
1850	23.2	35.9	1950	151.3	14.5
1860	31.4	35.6	1960	179.3	18.5
1870	38.6	22.6	1970	203.2	13.3
1880	50.2	30.2			

6. There are five basic population-based (as opposed to spatial or occupational) definitions of "rural": (a) Rural Nonmetropolitan—"All farms, open countryside and places of less than 2,500 residents outside SMSAs." This is the most restrictive definition. (b) Expanded Rural Nonmetropolitan—"All farms, open countryside and places of less than 10,000 residents outside SMSAs." This definition is used occasionally in Congressional legislation and is also used in this chapter. (c) Census Rural—"All farms, open countryside and places of less than 2,500 residents, both within and outside of SMSAs." This, in simplified terms, is the U.S. Census Bureau's definition. (d) Nonmetropolitan— "All farms, open countryside and places of less than 50,000 residents outside SMSAs." This distinction (rather than urban-rural) is increasingly used for analytic purposes. (e) Combination Rural—"Census rural definition plus all nonmetropolitan places between 2,500 and 10,000." Though rarely used now, this definition is both the most permissive and in many respects the most reasonable.

Table N2 shows the results of using each of the five rural definitions. The point is not that any single definition is clearly correct while the others are clearly invalid. Each has both a measure of validity and specific limitations. It is important to be aware of the potential range of this rural constituency and the dramatic differ-

TABLE N2

TOTAL RURAL POPULATION
USING ALTERNATIVE DEFINITIONS

Definition	In (Millions)	1970 % of Total U.S. Population
A	37.5	18.5
B	49.4	24.9
C	53.9	26.5
D	63.8	31.4
E	65.1	32.0

ences resulting from seemingly innocuous alterations in the definitions used.

7. "Responding" and "choosing" both imply that at least a modicum of free will had to be possessed by the prospective migrants for them to fall within the parameters of classical migration theory. This assumption of free will was the rationale behind excluding migrations caused by war, famine, or natural disaster from consideration in constructing a theory about migration.

8. The validity of classical migration theory can be challenged on a number of grounds. For example, its great reliance on economic factors has grossly underestimated the importance of noneconomic forces and variables in the migration process. Two American examples illustrate how economic motives for migration are by no means always the sole critical factor. Alexis de Tocqueville, in *Democracy in America*, G. Lawrence, trans. (New York: Harper & Row, 1966), referring to the early migrants settling America, asserted:

> What most distinguished them from all others was the very aim of their enterprise. No necessity forced them to leave their country; they gave up a desirable social position and assured means of livelihood; nor was their object in going to the New World to better their position or accumulate wealth; they tore themselves away from home comforts in obedience to a purely intellectual craving; in facing the inevitable sufferings of exile they hoped for the triumph of an idea.

Similarly, Harry Caudill, in *Night Comes to the Cumberlands* (Boston, Mass.: Little, Brown and Co., 1962), when discussing the westward movement of Appalachians, noted:

> The lure of free land was certainly a powerful magnet which attracted many mountaineers deeper into the hinterland of the range, and a few of them farther westward into the "open country." But it must not be supposed that the enticement of land ownership was the most important cause of the new westward migration. While the population was sparse, indeed, by modern standards, these wild woodsmen had begun to yearn for escape from a land so crowded that neighbors could be found within a few miles of the cabin door. They had "gone wild" in the still solitudes of their forests, and they hungered for new expanses of virgin wilderness where their lives might be unrestricted by even the frail inhibitions imposed by the meager society that had coalesced around them. It was largely for this reason that the mountaineers began to move westward in ever-increasing numbers.

For further elaboration, see Peter Uhlenberg, "Noneconomic Determinants of Nonmigration: Sociological Considerations for Migration Theory," *Rural Sociology*, vol. 38 (Fall 1973); William Petersen, "A General Typology of Migration," *American Sociological Review*, vol. 23 (1958).

9. Robert Coles, *The South Goes North* (Boston, Mass: Little, Brown and Co., 1967), pp. 313-14.

10. James Sundquist, "Where Shall They Live?" *Public Interest* (Fall 1971), p. 90.

11. The figure of 6.8 million nonmetropolitan farm residents was culled from Table 1 (p. 50) of a monograph by E. Moe and L. Tamblyn, *Rural Schools as a Mechanism for Rural Development,* ERIC/ CRESS, 1974. The authors indicate that this tabulation was derived from 1970 Census data by the Economic Research Service of the U.S. Department of Agriculture.

12. Jim Hightower, Susan De Marco, et al., *Hard Tomatoes, Hard Times* (Cambridge, Mass.: Schenkman, 1973), pp. 2-3.

13. Ibid.

14. Ibid.

15. For data, see: Jerry J. Berman, "Rural Poverty, Welfare, and

Income Maintenance: Need and Non-Response (Washington, D.C.: Center for Community Change, 1975); L. Tamblyn, *Inequality: A Portrait of Rural America* (Washington, D.C.: Rural Education Association, 1973), pp. 8-9; Bureau of Census, *Current Population Reports*, series P. 60, no. 97: "Money Income in 1973 of Families and Persons in the United States" (January 1975), table 24, p. 46; Jean Brackett, "Urban Family Budgets Updated to Autumn, 1973," *Monthly Labor Review* (August 1974), pp. 57-62. Berman states on this point: "Based on Brackett's calculations, and factoring in inflation to date, the figure of $9,000 for a family of four in an urban area is arrived at. Typically, the rural budget is figured as 7 percent lower, which yields the figure $8,370."

16. "Adequate" is here defined both quantitatively and qualitatively. Specifically, to be considered adequate, employment opportunities must be available for a broad spectrum of the rural community and must provide considerably more than minimal benefits, incomes, and advancement possibilities.

17. The Agribusiness Accountability Project (AAP) (as well as some farm organizations) has estimated that for every six farms that shut down, one small rural business is forced to close. For example, in 1973, more than 16,000 (net) independent, small-town businesses folded. (See Hightower, De Marco, et al., *Hard Tomatoes.*)

18. See, for example: Berman, "Rural Poverty"; U.S. Congress, Senate, Committee on Government Operations, *Toward a National Growth Policy: Federal and State Developments in 1972*, Committee Print (Washington, D.C.: U.S. Government Printing Office, 1973); Tamblyn, *Inequality*; Executive Office of the President, Office of Budget and Management, *Social Indicators, 1973* (Washington, D.C.: U.S. Government Printing Office, 1974); *Working Papers of the First National Conference on Rural America* (Washington, D.C.: Rural America, 1975); Census Bureau, "Social and Economic Characteristics of the Population in Metropolitan and Non-Metropolitan Areas: 1960 and 1970," *Current Population Reports*, no. 37, 1973; U.S. Congress, Senate, Committee on Government Operations, *The Economic and Social Conditions of Rural America in the 1970's* (Washington, D.C.: Government Printing Office, 1971).

19. This statement, of course, does not apply to all rural communities and all rural residents. Rural areas include everything from prosperous farming areas, stable college towns and recreation-oriented communities to decaying company towns and wholly

depressed areas. While the adverse conditions described in this paper are to be found throughout the nation's rural areas, they are more prevalent in the South as a region, and among Blacks, Hispanics, and Native Americans. However, the preponderance of negative social, educational, and economic indices for rural America as an aggregate entity supports the characteristics employed here.

20. See the following for an elaboration of the provisions and limitations of this act: U.S. Congress, Senate, Committee on Agriculture and Forestry, *The Rural Development Act of 1972—Analysis and Explanation—Public Law 92-419*, Committee Print (Washington, D.C.: U.S. Government Printing Office, 1972); U.S. Congress, Senate, Committee on Agriculture and Forestry, *Implementation of the Rural Development Act. Part 1: Hearings Before the Subcommittee on Rural Development*, Committee Print (Washington, D.C.: U.S. Government Printing Office, 1973); U.S. Congress, Senate, Committee on Agriculture and Forestry, *Program and Plans for Implementation of the Rural Development Act of 1972*, Committee Print (Washington, D.C.: U.S. Government Printing Office, 1973); U.S. Department of Agriculture, *Rural Development Goals: First Annual Report of the Secretary of Agriculture to Congress Regarding the Rural Development Act of 1972* (Washington, D.C.: U.S. Government Printing Office, 1974).

21. The exception to this pattern is the Community Development Corporation (CDC) model, discussed in detail later in this chapter.

22. Interestingly, this has been the outcome in both governmental and philanthropic development interventions.

23. Anita Parlow et al., *The Appalachian Regional Commission: Boon or Boondoggle?* (Washington, D.C.: A.R.C. Accountability Project, 1974), p. 6.

24. This is not an unrecognized phenomenon. In 1967, the President's Commission on Rural Poverty asserted,

The Commission believes that without citizen responsibility, which includes the active involvement and participation of all, antipoverty and economic development programs will flounder. Therefore, the Commission recommends that increased attention be given to involving the poor in the affairs of the community, on both local and areawide levels.

This same basic principle was asserted by a congressional report on amendments to the Foreign Assistance Act:

Over the years, in exercising legislative oversight with

respect to the administration of the foreign assistance
program, [the House Foreign Affairs Committee] has
observed that there is a close relationship between popular
participation in the process and the eventual success
achieved [quoted in Stewart Perry, "Federal Support for
CDCs" (Cambridge, Mass.: Center for Community Economic Development, 1974)].

25.   See, for example: Advisory Commission on Intergovernmental
Relations, "Regional Decision Making: New Strategies for Substate
Districts," vol. 1: *Substate Regionalism and the Federal System* (Washing-
ton, D.C.: U.S. Government Printing Office, 1973); Rand Corpora-
tion, *Review of Federal Programs to Alleviate Rural Deprivation* (Washing-
ton, D.C., 1974); U.S. Congress, Senate, Committee on Government
Operations, *Toward a National Growth and Development Policy: Legislative
and Executive Action in 1970-71*, Committee Print (Washington, D.C.:
U.S. Government Printing Office, 1972); U.S. Department of
Agriculture, *Rural Development: Fifth Annual Report of the Secretary to the
Congress* (Washington, D.C.: U.S. Government Printing Office,
1974); U.S. Department of Agriculture, *National Growth: The Rural
Component* (Washington, D.C.: U.S. Government Printing Office,
1971); U.S. Department of Commerce, Economic Development
Administration, *Multi-jurisdictional Planning Areas in the United States*, 2d
ed. (Washington, D.C.: U.S. Government Printing Office, 1971);
William S. Bonner and Robert K. Middleton, *Regional Communities: A
Planning and Development Concept for Non-Metropolitan Areas* (Little
Rock, Ark.: University of Arkansas, 1971); Chamber of Commerce
of the United States, Task Force on Economic Growth and Opportunity, *Rural Poverty and Regional Progress in an Urban Society* (Washington, D.C.: U.S. Government Printing Office, 1969); U.S. Congress,
Senate, Committee on Agriculture and Forestry, *Rural Development—
1971*, Committee Print (Washington, D.C.: U.S. Government Printing Office, 1972).

26.   The contention that masses of rural people have been "left
behind" and excluded is not in question. The President's Commission
on Rural Poverty was justified in asserting:

For all practical purposes, then, most of the 14 million
people in our [rural] poverty areas are outside our market
economy. So far as they are concerned, the dramatic
economic growth of the United States might as well never

have happened. It has brought them few rewards. They are
on the outside looking in, and they need help.

27. National Emergency Council, *Report on Economic Conditions of the South* (Washington, D.C., 1938), as quoted in the lead editorial of *Southern Exposure*, vol. 2, nos. 2 and 3 (Fall 1974).

28. Statement by Joe Begley, Chairman, Citizen's League to Protect the Surface Rights in Letcher County, Kentucky, as quoted in Jim Branscome and Peggy Matthews, "Selling the Mountains," *Southern Exposure*, vol. 2, no. 2 (Fall 1974): 123.

29. Parlow, *Appalachian Regional Commission*, pp. 11-12.

30. Hightower, De Marco, et al., *Hard Tomatoes*.

31. Letter from Senator Fred R. Harris of Oklahoma to David Ramage and Phil Moore, September 22, 1972.

32. Hightower, De Marco, et al., *Hard Tomatoes*. They go on to state:

> Increasingly, agriculture production is vertically integrat-
> ed, markets are concentrated and dinner is prepackaged by
> corporate America. ITT serves up Gwaltney ham and
> Wonder Bread. The turkey comes from Greyhound Cor-
> poration's Armour Division. Dow Chemical brings the
> lettuce, while Tenneco provides fresh fruits. Count on
> Boeing for the potatoes and American Brands for Motts
> Apple Sauce. Coca Cola serves orange juice and, for
> dessert, there are strawberries from Purex [p. 4].

33. Ibid.; Berman, "Rural Poverty"; U.S. Department of Agriculture, Economic Research Service, "The Hired Farm Working Force of 1970," *Agricultural Economic Report No. 201* (Washington, D.C.: U.S. Government Printing Office, 1971).

34. Hightower, De Marco, et al., *Hard Tomatoes*.

35. Bill Finger, Cary Fowler, and Chip Hughes, "Agribusiness Gets the Dollar," *Southern Exposure*, vol. 2, no. 2 (Fall 1974): 153.

36. Jim Hightower, *Eat Your Heart Out* (New York: Crown, 1972).

37. Though the parallels are by no means perfect, it is clear that entities operating in a manner similar to CDCs were, in fact, in existence long before the 1960s. Barringer [in *Maine Manifest* (Augusta, Maine: Tower Publishing, 1974)], for example, indicates:

> The Massachusetts Bay Company of New England's first
> permanent settlers is an early example of the community
> development concept. Its original asset was a royal grant

of land between the Charles and Merrimack Rivers, extending westward indefinitely to "the South Sea." After 1629, its charter was entrusted completely to the settlers of the colony, each having one vote in its policy decisions regardless of how much he had invested in its enterprise.

In rural America, the best example of a predecessor organization was the small farmer-owned agricultural cooperative. In recent years, agricultural cooperatives have come to resemble (or, in some cases, be indistinguishable from) large agribusiness corporations, but such was not always true. Thus, the cooperative movement remains as an example of the kind of independent, voluntary, community-based, collective economic enterprise CDCs came to represent. For more information on agricultural cooperatives, see: Massey, *Southern Exposure*; Linda Kravitz, *Who's Minding the Co-Op?* (Washington, D.C.: Agribusiness Accountability Project 1974); Ray Marshall and Lamond Godwin, *Cooperatives and Rural Poverty in the South* (Baltimore, Md.: Johns Hopkins Press, 1971); Rita Kelley, *The Cooperative Approach in Rural Development* (Cambridge, Mass.: Center for Community Economic Development, 1973); Jerry Voorhis, *A New Look at the Principles and Practices of Cooperatives* (Washington, D.C.: Cooperative League of the U.S.A., 1966); U.S. Department of Agriculture, *Cooperatives in the American Private Enterprise System* (Washington, D.C.: U.S. Government Printing Office, 1968).

38. Initially, the community development corporation model was created for use in urban ghetto areas. However, it was quickly adapted for utilization in depressed rural areas as well. The original urban bias of CDCs is exemplified by Geoffrey Faux's pioneering work *CDCs: New Hope for the Inner City*, Report of the Twentieth Century Fund Task Force on Community Development Corporations (New York: Twentieth Century Fund, 1971).

39. An excellent annotated bibliography on CDCs is Florence Contant, *Community Development Corporations: An Annotated Bibliography* (Cambridge, Mass.: Center for Community Economic Development, 1974).

40. As education director at the Center for Community Change, a Washington-based nonprofit organization which (among other activities) delivers intensive comprehensive technical assistance to approximately twenty CDCs (urban and rural) nationwide.

41. Gerson Green and Geoffrey Faux, "The Social Utility of Black Enterprise," W. F. Haddad and G. D. Pugh, eds., *Black Economic*

Development (Englewood Cliffs, N.J.: Prentice-Hall, 1969).

42. M. Sviridoff, *Community Development Corporations* (New York: Ford Foundation, 1974).

43. Original CDC funding from OEO came from Title 1-D (Special Impact), which was a 1966 amendment to the authorizing legislation. Subsequent OEO funding was "legitimized" by the passage of Title VII in later OEO legislation, which specifically authorized "community economic development" activities. See Perry, *Federal Support for CDCs*. To show the level and duration of OEO's commitment to rural CDCs, Perry provides a table (Table N3 on p. 386).

44. For a review of the debate over the Community Self-Determination Act, see: U.S. Congress, House, *Congressional Record*, H7011-22 and H7037, 90th Congress, 2d sess., 1968, p. 114; U.S. Congress, Senate, *Congressional Record*, S9269-85, 90th Congress, 2d sess., 1968, p. 114; John McClaughry, "Black Ownership and National Politics," in *Black Economic Development*, W. F. Haddad and G. D. Pugh, eds. (Englewood Cliffs, N.J.: Prentice-Hall, 1969); L. O. Kelso, F. F. Piven, R. Marshall, G. Alperovitz et al., "Community Self-Determination: The Bill and the Debate" (Special Issue) *New Generation*, vol. 50 (Fall 1968); Kenneth Miller, "Community Capitalism and the Community Self-Determination Act," *Harvard Journal on Legislation*, vol. 6 (May 1969); Gar Alperovitz, Stephen Carr, John McClaughry, and Rhea Wilson, *Community Development Corporations—A New Model*, Laboratory for Environmental Studies (Cambridge, Mass.: MIT Press, 1968).

45. For an example of a trouble-ridden rural CDC, see Barry Stein, *Throw the Rascals Out: A Case Study of the Northeastern Oklahoma CDC* (Cambridge, Mass.: Center for Community Economic Development, 1973).

46. The most extensive and respected evaluation of actual CDC performance was the 1972 Abt Associates' report on CDCs funded through OEO's Special Impact Program. Abt concluded, in part:

About 50% of the ventures [started by the CDCs studied] are projected to reach a six-month breakeven by the end of the first four years of venture life. National experience for small business starts shows 80% going out of business within the first five years. [Abt Associates, Inc., *An Evaluation of the Special Impact Program, First Phase Report*, vol. 1, Summary (Cambridge, Mass.: Abt, 1972), p. 8.]

TABLE N3

ALLOCATION OF SPECIAL IMPACT PROGRAM FUNDS TO
RURAL CDCs

(Amounts in Thousands of Dollars)

	FY 69	FY 70	FY 71	FY 72	FY 73	Total
East Central Committee for Opportunity, Georgia	482	100	754	1,187	--	2,523
Home Education Livelihood Program, New Mexico	708	412	701	20	1,000	2,841
Job Start, Kentucky	368	--	1,003	17	1,200	1,588
SE Alabama CDC	270	100	570	--	200	1,140
SW Virginia Comm. Dev. Fund	548	500	800	15	1,924	3,787
New Communities, Inc., Ga.	98	30	term.	--	--	128
NE Oklahoma CDC	50	825	50	2,500	--	3,425
Las Colonias, Texas	--	97	--	term.	--	97
Westside Planning Group, Fresno, Calif.	--	100	150	1,160	500	1,910
Adela DC, Utah	--	100	--	995	--	1,095
Delta Foundation, Miss.	--	1,288	--	1,058	600	2,946
Seminole Employment & Economic Dev. Corp., Fla.	--	800	--	--	1,000	1,800
Community Enterprise DC, Alaska	--	1,187	2,650	38	2,369	6,244
Lokahi-Pacific Corp., Kihei, Hawaii	--	1,000	--	--	--	2,000
Community Investment & Dev., Inc., Ark.	--	500	792	--	1,200	2,492
Impact Seven, Inc., Wis.	--	650	--	--	1,000	1,650
Midwest Minnesota CDC	--	750	--	870	--	1,620
Standing Rock Industries, N.Dak.	--	1,100	--	150	500	1,750
Lummi Indian Tribal Enterprises, Washington	--	500	--	1,711	600	2,811
TENCO Developments, Tenn.	--	--	--	82	800	822
TOTAL	2,524	10,039	7,470	9,803	13,893	42,729

SOURCE: Adapted from Brian J. Reilly, "Distribution of SIP Funds," CCED Newsletter, February 1973.

NOTE: Table is arranged in chronological order of funding.

In discussing the achievements (or lack of same) of federal "black capitalism" programs, Tabb, "Viewing Minority Economic Development," concludes:

> It has also been pretty much of a failure in its own terms. As the Small Business Administration (SBA) loans to minority group members expanded beyond the relatively small number of potentially successful businesses, the loss rate increased dramatically—rising more than three-fold between 1966 and 1968. The Minority Enterprise Small Business Investment Companies (MESBIC) program, which succeeded the SBA minority loan program as the major Administration effort, sought to enlist the involvement of the largest corporations in the country. Initiated with the same fanfare as the special SBA program, it offered a 15:1 leverage on private funds through a complex of guarantees, matching provisions, tax benefits, and insurance schemes. The program's results to date have been extremely disappointing.
>
> While the number of black-owned businesses as a percentage of the total in inner city areas is increasing, this has largely taken place without government assistance. The marginal nature of most of them has disappointed even those who saw black capitalism as a way of amassing significant resources in black hands.

47. See, for example: Stanley Holt, "What Every Community Organization Should Know About Community Development," *Just Economics*, 1974; Michael Zweig, "The Dialectics of Black Capitalism" *Review of Black Political Economy* 2 (Spring 1972): 25-37; Frederick Sturdivant, "Community Development Corporations: The Problem of Mixed Objectives," *Law and Contemporary Problems* 36 (Winter 1971): 35-50; Rosabeth Kanter, "Some Social Issues in the Community Development Corporation Proposal," C. G. Benello and D. Roussapoulas, eds., *The Case for Participatory Democracy* (New York: Grossman, 1971).

48. This is commonly known as the "culture of poverty" theory, championed by Oscar Lewis, among others. Its adherents often characterize rural Americans as "culturally disadvantaged." The validity of this theory has been fiercely contested in recent years on grounds of racism, classism, and lack of evidence. There have also been objections that this theory tends to foster the nonsensical belief

that "the traits of the poor are the cause of the traits of the poor." See J. Roach and O. Gursslin, "An Evaluation of the Concept 'Culture of Poverty,'" in Roach, Gross, and Gursslin, *Social Stratification in the United States* (Englewood Cliffs, N.J.: Prentice-Hall, 1969). For examples of the U.S. literature on this topic (pro and con), see: William Ryan, *Blaming the Victim* (New York: Random House, 1971); Charles Valentine, *Culture and Poverty: Critique and Counter-Proposals* (Chicago, Ill.: University of Chicago Press, 1969); Oscar Lewis, *La Vida: A Puerto Rican Family in the Culture of Poverty—San Juan and New York* (New York: Random House, 1965); Lee Rainwater, "The Problem of Lower Class Culture and Poverty War Strategy," in *On Understanding Poverty*, D. Moynihan, ed. (New York: Basic Books, 1969); A. Passow, M. Goldberg, and A. Tannerbaum, eds., *Education of the Disadvantaged* (New York: Holt, Rinehart and Winston, 1967); B. Bloom, A. David, and R. Hess, *Compensatory Education for Cultural Deprivation* (New York: Holt, Rinehart and Winston, 1966).

49.   Oscar Lewis, "The Culture of Poverty," *Scientific American*, vol. 185, no. 16 (October 1966). Note that Lewis estimates that less than one-fourth of the people classified as poor in the U.S. fit this cultural pattern.

50.   Christopher Jencks, Marshall Smith, Henry Acland, Mary Jo Bane, David Cohen, Herbert Gintis, Barbara Heynes, and Stephen Michelson, *Inequality: A Reassessment of the Effect of Family and Schooling in America* (New York: Basic Books, 1972).

51.   For a brief overview of the literature on assumption number 1, see note 44. For assumption number 2, see the literature cited in this chapter. For assumption number 3, see Jencks et al., *Inequality: A Reassessment*; Donald M. Levine and Mary Jo Bane, *The Inequality Controversy: Schooling and Distributive Justice* (New York: Basic Books, 1975); Colin Greer, *The Great School Legend* (New York: Viking, 1973); David B. Tyack, *The One Best System* (Cambridge, Mass.: Harvard University Press, 1974); Ivan Berg, *Education and Jobs: The Great Training Robbery* (New York: Praeger Publications, 1970); Jacob Mincer, *Schooling, Experience, and Earnings* (Washington, D.C.: National Bureau of Economic Research, 1974); James S. Coleman et al., *Equality of Educational Opportunity* (Washington, D.C.: U.S. Government Printing Office, 1966); Michael B. Katz, *Class Bureaucracy, and Schools: The Illusion of Educational Change in America* (New York: Praeger Publications, 1971).

52.   For further information on rural manpower programs, see:

Marshall and Godwin, *Cooperatives and Rural Poverty in the South*; Parlow, *Appalachian Regional Commission*; Berg, *Education and Jobs*; Tom Karter, *Manpower Programs and Metropollyana, Conference Working Paper No. 6*, First National Conference on Rural America (Washington, D.C.: Rural Housing Alliance and Rural America, Inc., 1975); Janet Derr, *Rural Social Problems, Human Services, and Social Policies, Working Paper 4: Employment and Manpower*, Social Welfare Research Institute (Denver, Colo.: University of Denver, 1970); B. Eugene Griessman, *Planned Change in Low-Income Rural Areas: An Evaluation of Concerted Services in Training and Education*, Center for Occupational Education (Raleigh, N.C.: North Carolina State University, 1969); Center for Rural Manpower and Public Affairs, Michigan State University, *Manpower Planning for Jobs in Rural America*, Conference Proceedings, 1973; Raymond Schmitt, U.S. Congress, Senate Agriculture Committee, *Manpower Training and Employment Programs Serving Rural America*, Committee Print (Washington, D.C.: U.S. Government Printing Office, 1973).

53.   For simplicity, rural vocational/occupational/career education programs will all be referred to as "vocational" unless otherwise specified in the text. Interestingly, most rural school districts use the term "vocational education" for any school activity that is work-oriented and work-related. "Career education" has not had much of an impact on rural schools to date, perhaps because "career education" advocates have ignored rural problems. For example, Sidney Marland (former U.S. commissioner of education), in his 334-page tome on career education, devoted exactly *two paragraphs* to rural issues (and, even then, only to describe an unusual, non-school-based program).

54.   This estimate was made by the staff at the National Center for Educational Statistics during a December 1975 interview with the author.

55.   Sidney P. Marland, *Career Education: A Proposal for Reform* (New York: McGraw-Hill, 1974), p. 21. Marland used annual approximations based on aggregate 1970-73 data.

56.   This is not quite as dismal as first appears because, as career educators persistently note, the U.S. Bureau of Labor Statistics has predicted that over the next decade 80 percent of all available jobs will not require a college degree. For further information, see M.A. Farber, "U.S. Predicts 80% of Jobs Won't Require Degree," *New York Times*, June 28, 1970.

57. The National Commission on the Reform of Secondary Education, *The Reform of Secondary Education* (New York: McGraw-Hill, 1973), p. 50.

58. Ibid., p. 51, quoting the National Advisory Council on Vocational Education, *Vocational Education Amendments of 1968, P.L. 90-576, Annual Report* (Washington, D.C.: Department of Health, Education, and Welfare, July 15, 1969).

59. For a good summary of the literature, see B. E. Griessman and K. G. Densley, *Review and Synthesis of Research on Vocational Education in Rural Areas*, ERIC Clearinghouse on Rural Education and Small Schools and ERIC Clearinghouse on Vocational and Technical Education, December 1969. Other useful documents include: Laure M. Sharp, "Vocational Education for Disadvantaged Groups," in Sommers and Little, *Vocational Education: Today and Tomorrow* (Madison, Wis.: University of Wisconsin, 1971); and Earl Carpenter and John Rodgers, *Review and Synthesis of Research in Agricultural Education*, ERIC Clearinghouse on Vocational and Technical Education, 1970. For further sources, see Barry Stein, *The Biggest Little Conglomerate in the World: Community Economic Development in Kentucky* (Cambridge, Mass.: Center for Community Economic Development, 1973).

60. See, particularly, Marshall and Godwin, *Cooperatives and Rural Poverty in the South.*

61. Carpenter and Rodgers, *Review and Synthesis of Research in Agricultural Education*, p. 6. The data they cite are from Earl O. Heady et al., *Manpower Requirements and Demand in Agriculture by Regions and Nationally, with Estimation of Vocational Training and Educational Needs and Productivity* (Ames, Ia.: Iowa State University, 1966).

62. Kenneth Densley, in Griessman and Densley, *Review and Synthesis of Research*, p. 44.

63. Grant Venn, *Man, Education and Work: Post-Secondary Vocational and Technical Education*, American Council on Education (Washington, D.C.: U.S. Government Printing Office, 1964), p. 75.

64. Densley, in Griessman and Densley, *Review and Synthesis*, pp. 44, 63-64. As a reference for these statements, Densley cites the Advisory Council on Vocational Education, *Vocational Education: The Bridge Between Man and His Work* (Washington, D.C.: U.S. Government Printing Office, 1968), and Burchinal, Haller, and Taves, *Career Choices of Rural Youth in a Changing Society* (Minneapolis, Minn.: University of Minnesota, 1962).

65. Based on author's interview with Oscar Joiner, associate

commissioner of education, state of Georgia, 1971.

66. However, it must be remembered that rural youth trained in this field have no effective choice other than to migrate to the nearest big city.

67. Clay Cochran (director of the Rural Housing Alliance) labels this kind of assumption as "metropollyana," which he defines as "the belief, usually tacit, that sooner or later all of the people will move to the big city and live happily ever after." (As quoted in *Toward a Platform for Rural America, Report on the First National Conference on Rural America* (Washington, D.C.: Rural Housing Alliance and Rural America, Inc., 1975.)

68. Jim Hightower, *Food, Farmers, Corporations, Earl Butz . . . and You* (Washington, D.C.: Agribusiness Accountability Project, 1974).

69. For example, according to the latest Bureau of Labor Statistics estimates, unemployment among ghetto youth (a category in which rural migrants commonly find themselves) ranges as high as 75 percent in many metropolitan areas.

70. John N. Williamson, "The Quest for Alternative Routes to Adulthood" (unpublished paper, National Institute of Education, 1975), p. 6. Williamson cites the work of Berg, *Education and Jobs*, and Harold Goldstein, "Youth in the Labor Market: Trends in Employment and Unemployment," in *The Transition from School to Work*.

71. That this "country gentleman–servant class" split has indeed begun is attested to by Branscome and Matthews, "Selling the Mountains," as follows:

> The developers' intrusions penetrate all levels of mountain society. Mountain women become summer maids, mountain farmers become caddies, mountain politicians become lackies, and a whole style of life begins to change.

72. W. Norton Grubb and Marvin Lazerson, "Rally 'Round the Workplace: Continuities and Fallacies in Career Education," *Harvard Educational Review* 45, no. 4 (November 1975): 473.

73. Comptroller General of the United States, General Accounting Office, *What is the Role of Federal Assistance for Vocational Education? A Report to the Congress* (Washington, D.C.: U.S. Government Printing Office, 1975), p. 77.

74. Henry David Thoreau, *Walden* (New York: W. W. Norton and Co., 1941), p. 65.

75. Marland, *Career Education: A Proposal for Reform*, p. 240.

76. National Commission on the Reform of Secondary Education,

The Reform of Secondary Education, p. 60.

77. James S. Coleman, *Youth: Transition to Adulthood, Report of the Panel on Youth of the President's Science Advisory Committee* (Washington, D.C.: U.S. Government Printing Office, 1974).

78. U.S. Chamber of Commerce, *Career Education and the Business Man* (Washington, D.C.: U.S. Government Printing Office, 1973).

79. Comptroller General of the United States, *What is the Role of Federal Assistance for Vocational Education?*, p. 77.

80. Williamson, "The Quest for Alternative Routes to Adulthood," p. 28.

81. These conclusions are derived from the author's experience and contact with urban and rural CDCs over the past three years, interviews with staff members at the Center for Community Change, the analyses in such documents as the three recent case studies on rural CDCs by Barry Stein, and an excellent book by John Hall Fish entitled *Black Power/White Control: The Struggle of the Woodlawn Organization in Chicago* (Princeton, N.J.: Princeton University Press, 1973).

82. Barry Stein, *The Lummi Indians* (Cambridge, Mass.: Center for Community Economic Development, 1974), pp. 22-23.

83. Once again, see Stein, *Throw the Rascals Out,* for a detailed account of one such collapse.

84. For further information and statistics on this point, see Jonathan P. Sher, *Public Education in Rural America, Working Paper #9, First National Conference on Rural America* (Washington, D.C.: Rural America, Inc., 1975).

85. For a review of these federal and state programs, as well as an excellent overview of educational facility financing strategies in the U.S., see W. Monfort Barr and William R. Wilkerson, *Innovative Financing of Public School Facilities* (Danville, Ill.: Interstate Printers and Publishers, Inc., 1973). For more detailed information of specific facility financing practices, see the following: Clayton D. Hutchins and Elmer C. Deering, *Financing Public School Facilities*, U.S. Department of Health, Education, and Welfare (Washington, D.C.: U.S. Government Printing Office, 1959); Educational Facility Laboratories, *Guide to Alternatives for School Financing* (New York, 1971); Advisory Commission on Intergovernmental Relations, *Federal Approaches to Aid State and Local Capital Financing* (Washington, D.C.: U.S. Government Printing Office, 1970).